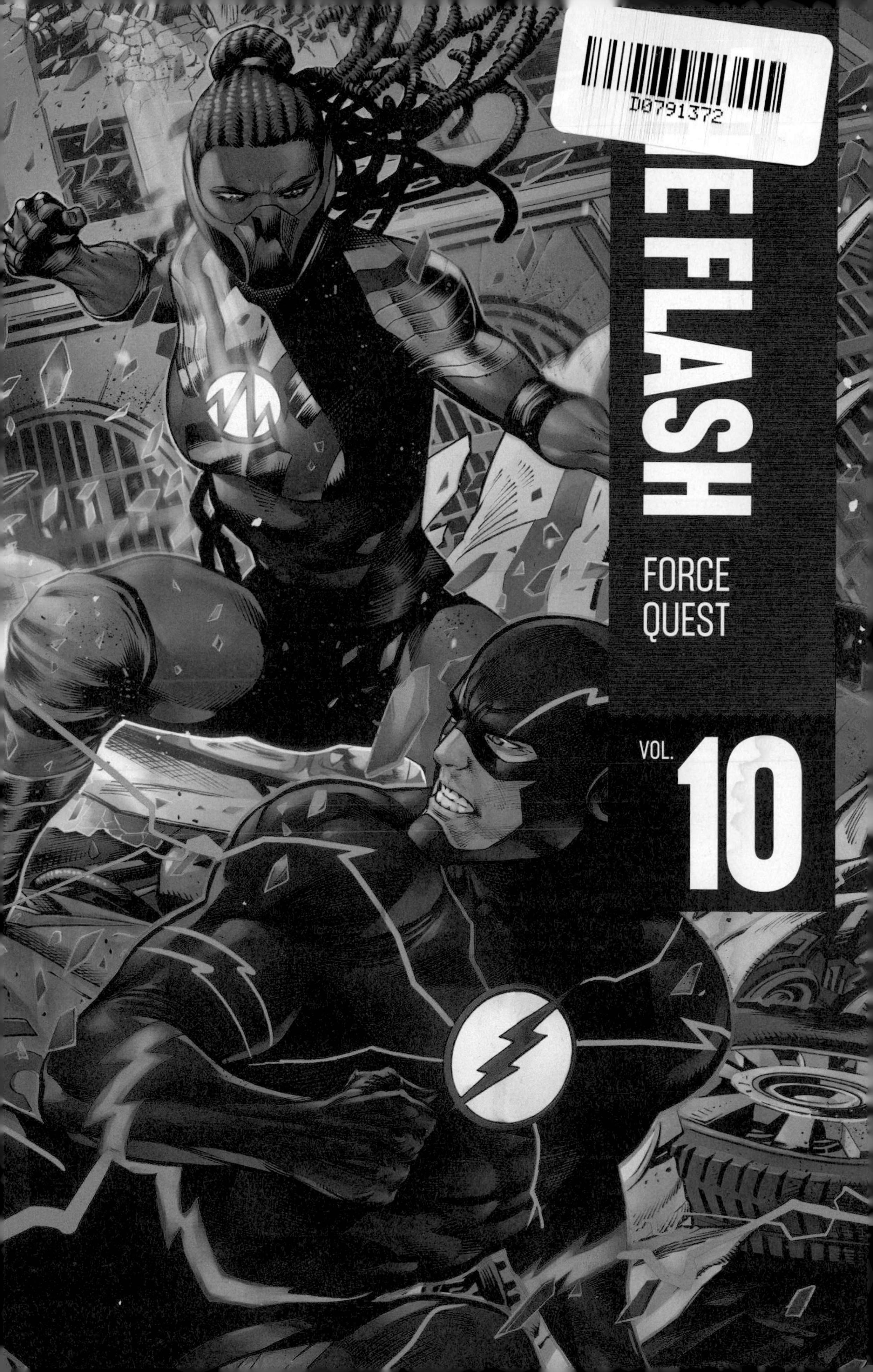
E FLASH
FORCE
QUEST
VOL.
10

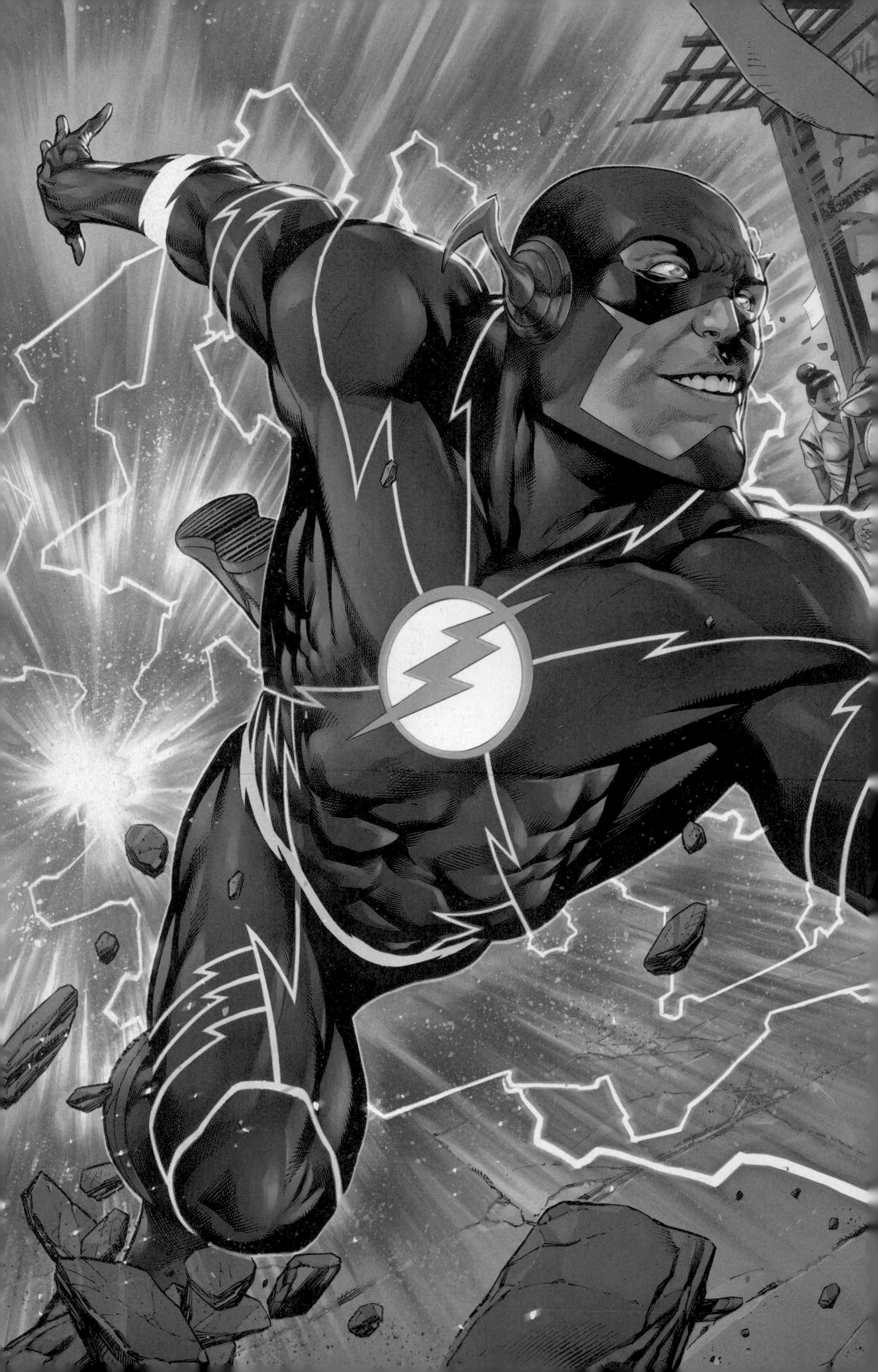

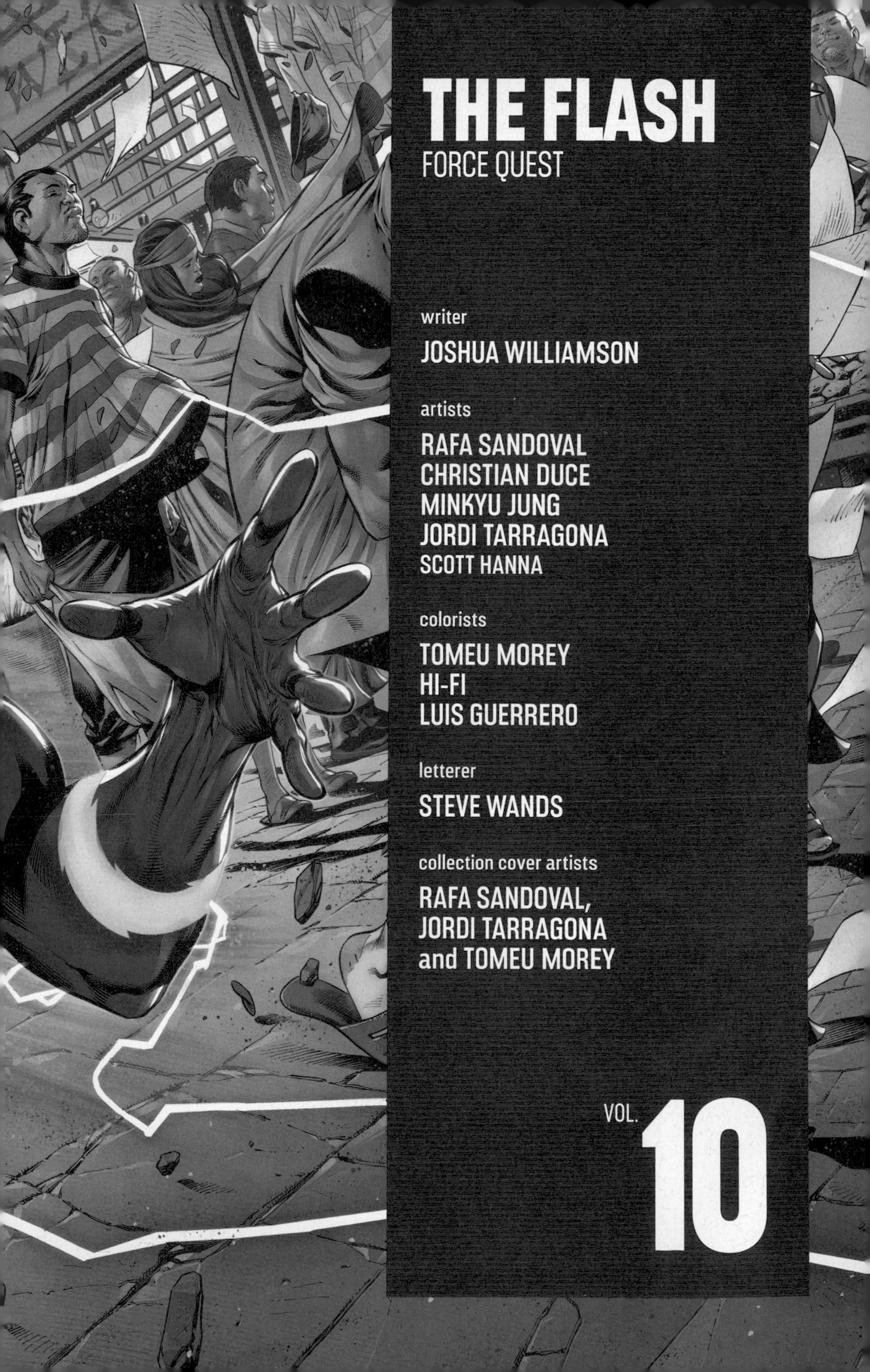

THE FLASH
FORCE QUEST

writer

JOSHUA WILLIAMSON

artists

RAFA SANDOVAL
CHRISTIAN DUCE
MINKYU JUNG
JORDI TARRAGONA
SCOTT HANNA

colorists

TOMEU MOREY
HI-FI
LUIS GUERRERO

letterer

STEVE WANDS

collection cover artists

RAFA SANDOVAL,
JORDI TARRAGONA
and TOMEU MOREY

VOL. **10**

PAUL KAMINSKI, REBECCA TAYLOR Editors – Original Series
ANDREW MARINO Assistant Editor – Original Series
JEB WOODARD Group Editor – Collected Editions
ERIKA ROTHBERG Editor – Collected Edition
STEVE COOK Design Director – Books
CURTIS KING JR. Publication Design
DANIELLE DIGRADO Publication Production

BOB HARRAS Senior VP – Editor-in-Chief, DC Comics

JIM LEE Publisher & Chief Creative Officer
BOBBIE CHASE VP – Global Publishing Initiatives & Digital Strategy
DON FALLETTI VP – Manufacturing Operations & Workflow Management
LAWRENCE GANEM VP – Talent Services
ALISON GILL Senior VP – Manufacturing & Operations
HANK KANALZ Senior VP – Publishing Strategy & Support Services
DAN MIRON VP – Publishing Operations
NICK J. NAPOLITANO VP – Manufacturing Administration & Design
NANCY SPEARS VP – Sales
JONAH WEILAND VP – Marketing & Creative Services
MICHELE R. WELLS VP & Executive Editor, Young Reader

THE FLASH VOL. 10: FORCE QUEST

Published by DC Comics. Compilation and all new material Copyright © 2019 DC Comics. All Rights Reserved.
Originally published in single magazine form in THE FLASH 58-63. Copyright 2018, 2019 DC Comics. All Rights
Reserved. All characters, their distinctive likenesses and related elements featured in this publication are
trademarks of DC Comics. The stories, characters and incidents featured in this publication are entirely fictional.
DC Comics does not read or accept unsolicited submissions of ideas, stories or artwork.
DC – a WarnerMedia Company.

DC Comics, 2900 West Alameda Ave., Burbank, CA 91505
Printed by LSC Communications, Owensville, MO, USA. 8/10/20. Second Printing.
ISBN: 978-1-77950-156-1

Library of Congress Cataloging-in-Publication Data is available.

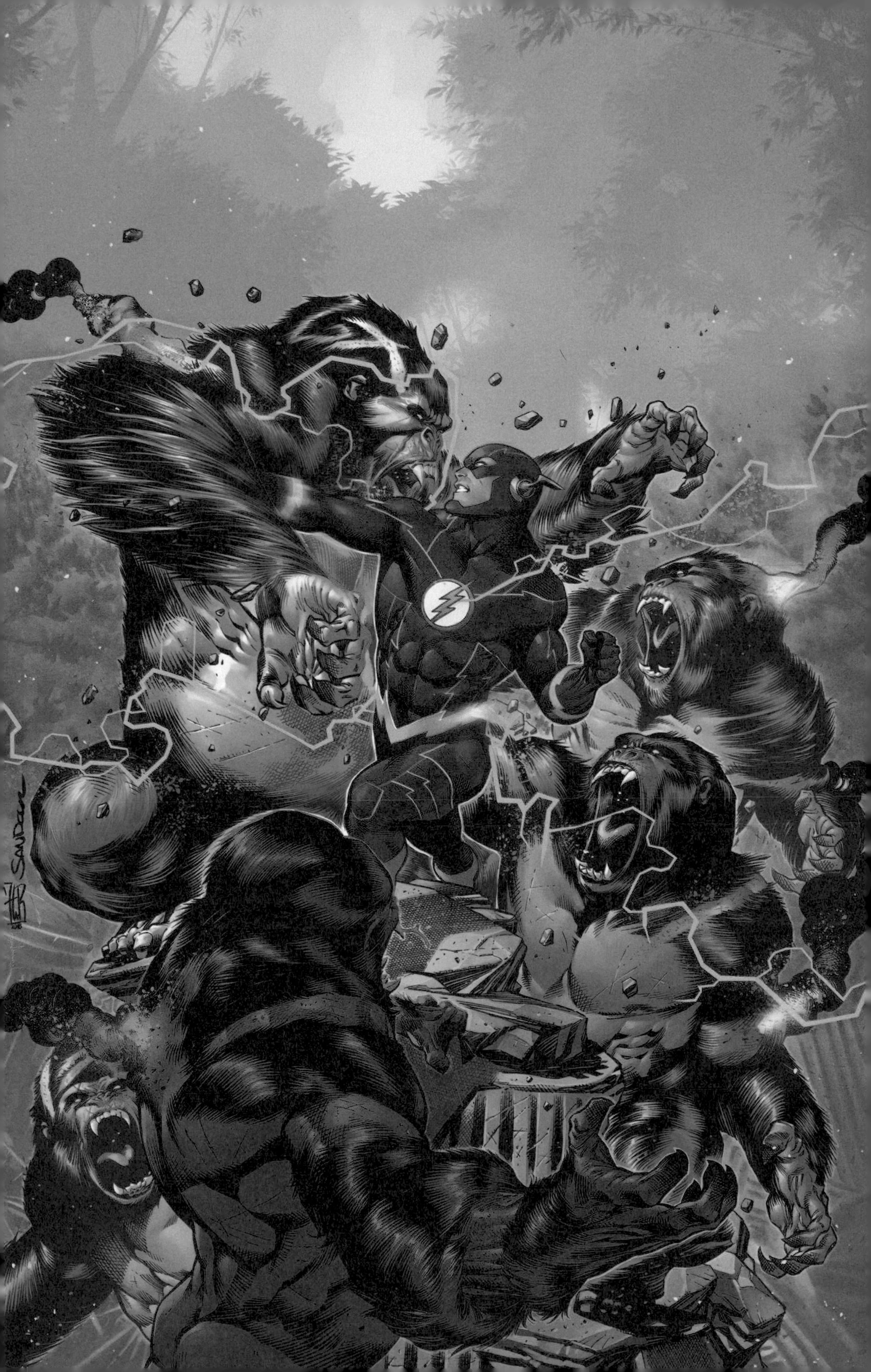

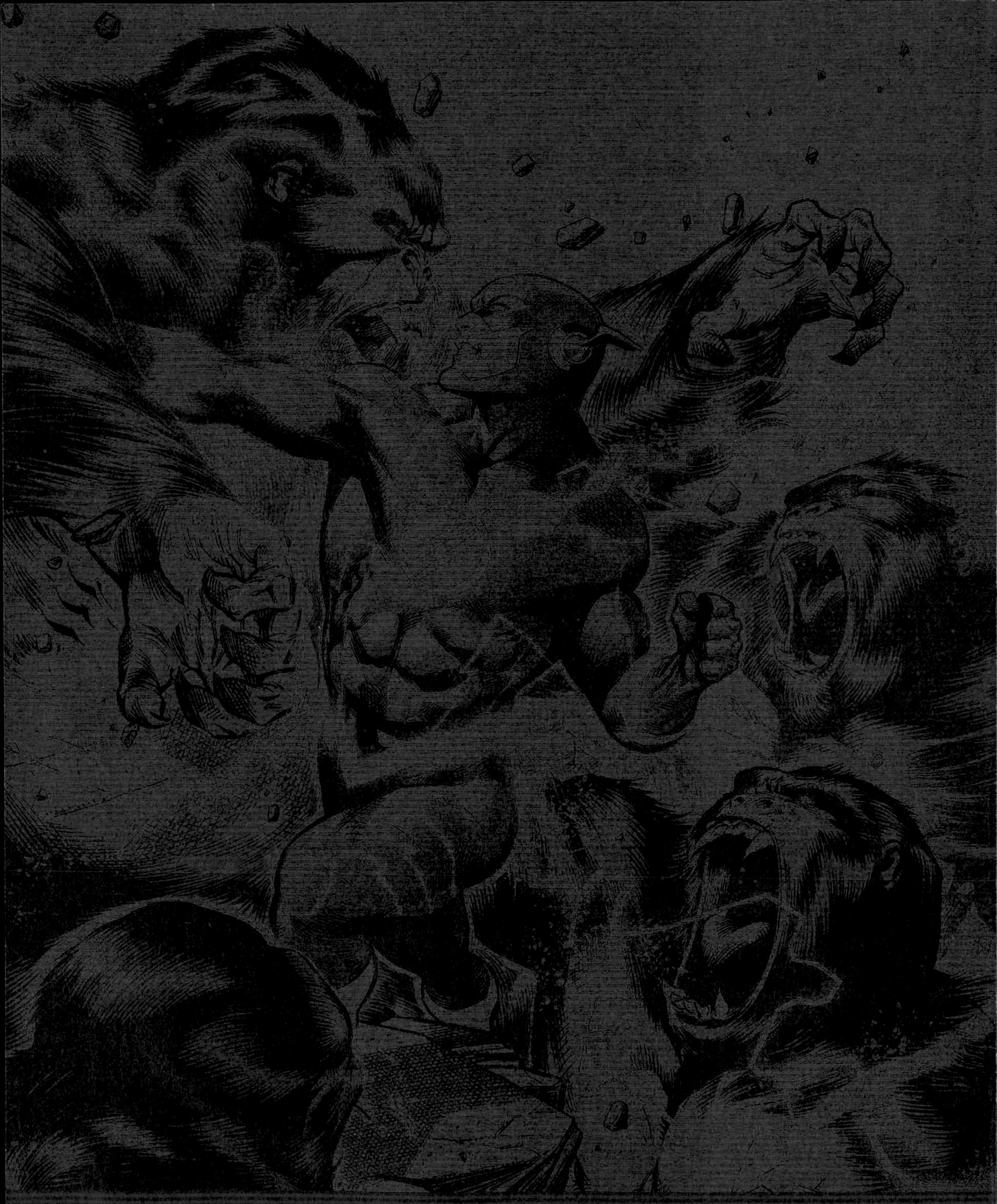

THE FLASH

#58

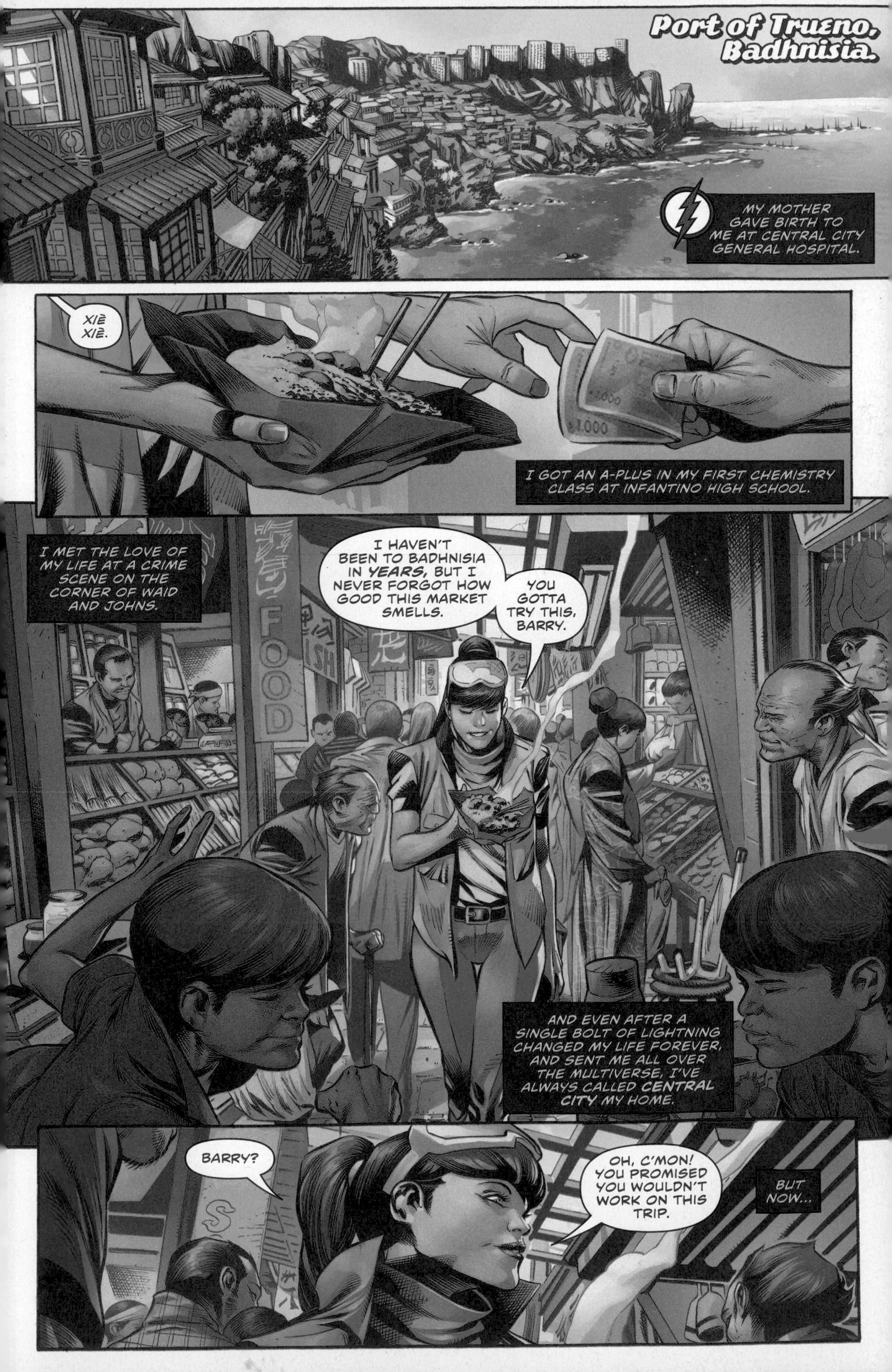
Port of Trueno, Badhnisia.
MY MOTHER GAVE BIRTH TO ME AT CENTRAL CITY GENERAL HOSPITAL.
XIÈ XIÈ.
I GOT AN A-PLUS IN MY FIRST CHEMISTRY CLASS AT INFANTINO HIGH SCHOOL.
I MET THE LOVE OF MY LIFE AT A CRIME SCENE ON THE CORNER OF WAID AND JOHNS.
I HAVEN'T BEEN TO BADHNISIA IN YEARS, BUT I NEVER FORGOT HOW GOOD THIS MARKET SMELLS.
YOU GOTTA TRY THIS, BARRY.
FOOD
FISH
AND EVEN AFTER A SINGLE BOLT OF LIGHTNING CHANGED MY LIFE FOREVER, AND SENT ME ALL OVER THE MULTIVERSE, I'VE ALWAYS CALLED CENTRAL CITY MY HOME.
BARRY?
OH, C'MON! YOU PROMISED YOU WOULDN'T WORK ON THIS TRIP.
BUT NOW...

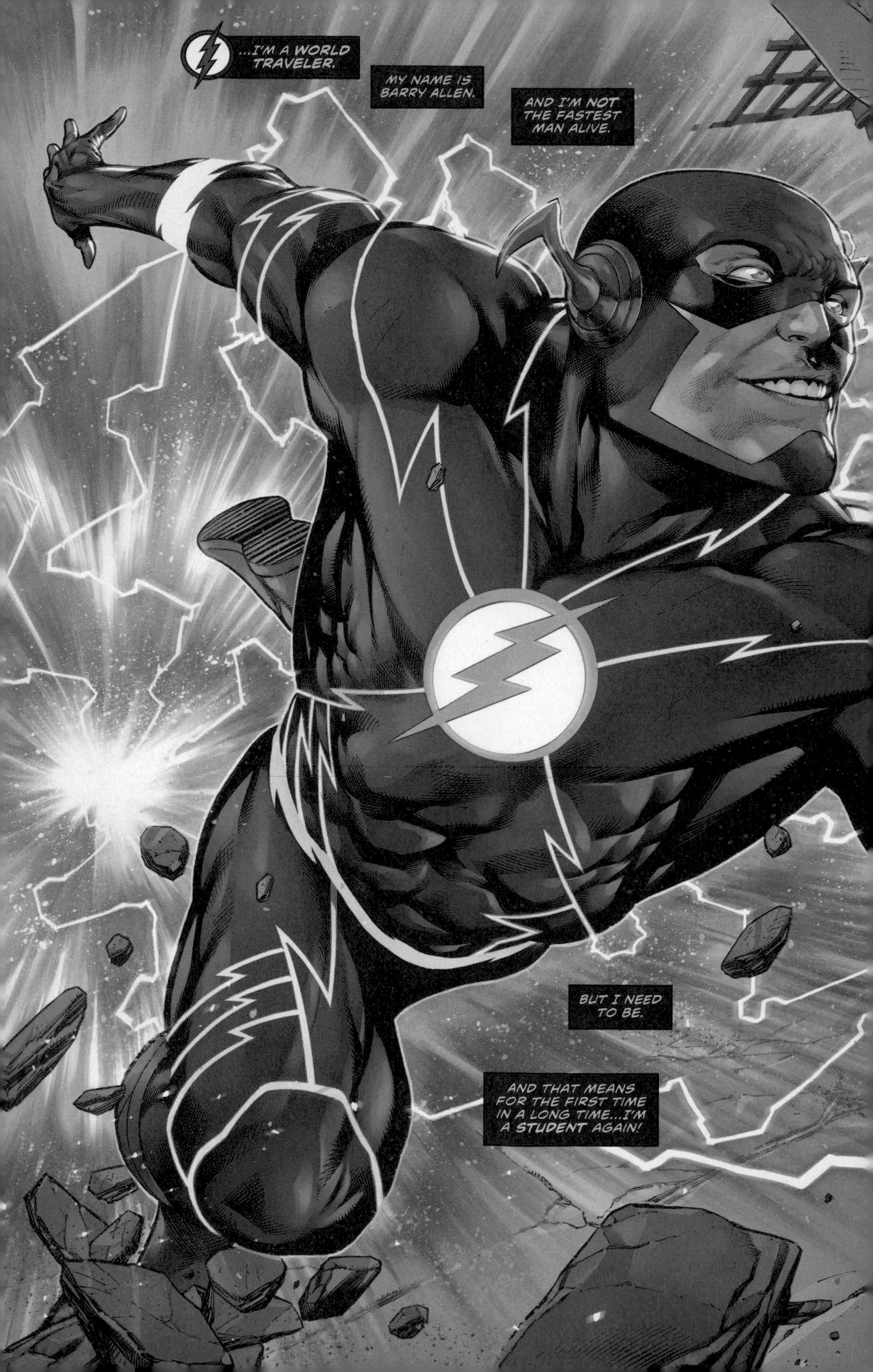
...I'M A WORLD TRAVELER.
MY NAME IS BARRY ALLEN.
AND I'M NOT THE FASTEST MAN ALIVE.
BUT I NEED TO BE.
AND THAT MEANS FOR THE FIRST TIME IN A LONG TIME...I'M A STUDENT AGAIN!

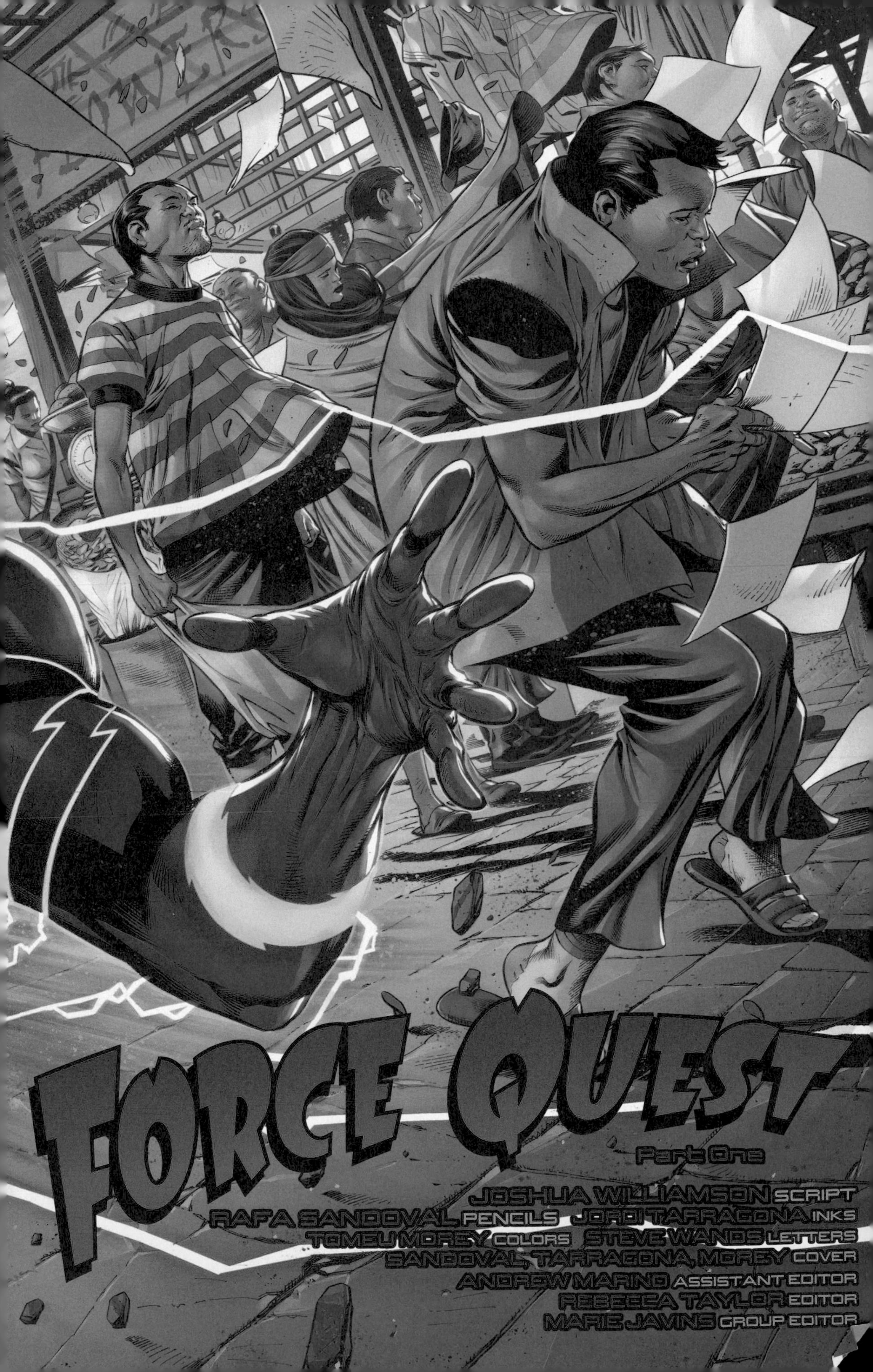
FORCE QUEST
Part One
JOSHUA WILLIAMSON SCRIPT
RAFA SANDOVAL PENCILS JORDI TARRAGONA INKS
TOMEU MOREY COLORS STEVE WANDS LETTERS
SANDOVAL, TARRAGONA, MOREY COVER
ANDREW MARINO ASSISTANT EDITOR
REBECCA TAYLOR EDITOR
MARIE JAVINS GROUP EDITOR

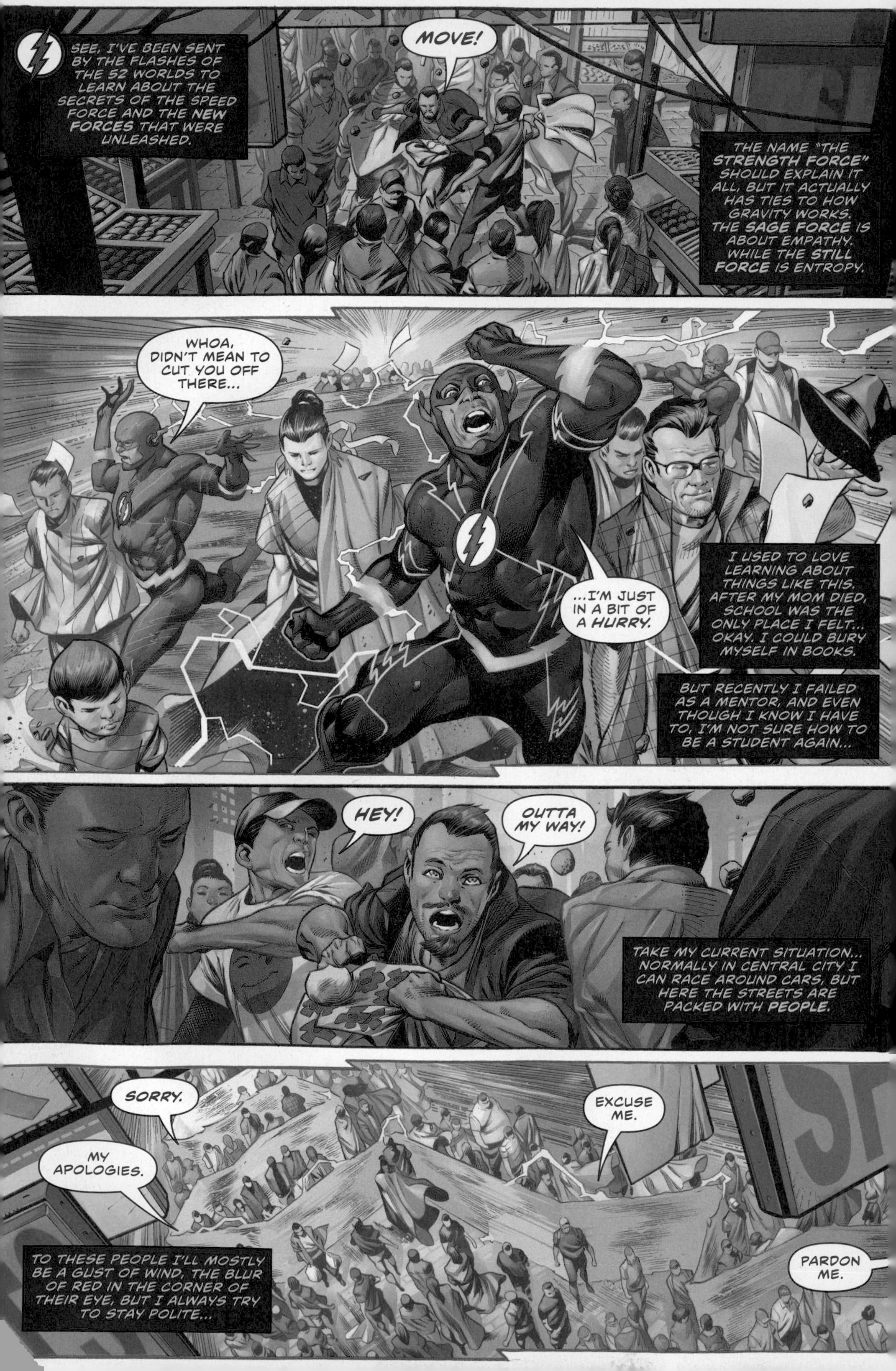
SEE, I'VE BEEN SENT BY THE FLASHES OF THE 52 WORLDS TO LEARN ABOUT THE SECRETS OF THE SPEED FORCE AND THE NEW FORCES THAT WERE UNLEASHED.
MOVE!
THE NAME "THE STRENGTH FORCE" SHOULD EXPLAIN IT ALL, BUT IT ACTUALLY HAS TIES TO HOW GRAVITY WORKS. THE SAGE FORCE IS ABOUT EMPATHY. WHILE THE STILL FORCE IS ENTROPY.
WHOA, DIDN'T MEAN TO CUT YOU OFF THERE...
...I'M JUST IN A BIT OF A HURRY.
I USED TO LOVE LEARNING ABOUT THINGS LIKE THIS. AFTER MY MOM DIED, SCHOOL WAS THE ONLY PLACE I FELT... OKAY. I COULD BURY MYSELF IN BOOKS.
BUT RECENTLY I FAILED AS A MENTOR, AND EVEN THOUGH I KNOW I HAVE TO, I'M NOT SURE HOW TO BE A STUDENT AGAIN...
HEY!
OUTTA MY WAY!
TAKE MY CURRENT SITUATION... NORMALLY IN CENTRAL CITY I CAN RACE AROUND CARS, BUT HERE THE STREETS ARE PACKED WITH PEOPLE.
SORRY.
MY APOLOGIES.
EXCUSE ME.
TO THESE PEOPLE I'LL MOSTLY BE A GUST OF WIND, THE BLUR OF RED IN THE CORNER OF THEIR EYE, BUT I ALWAYS TRY TO STAY POLITE...
PARDON ME.

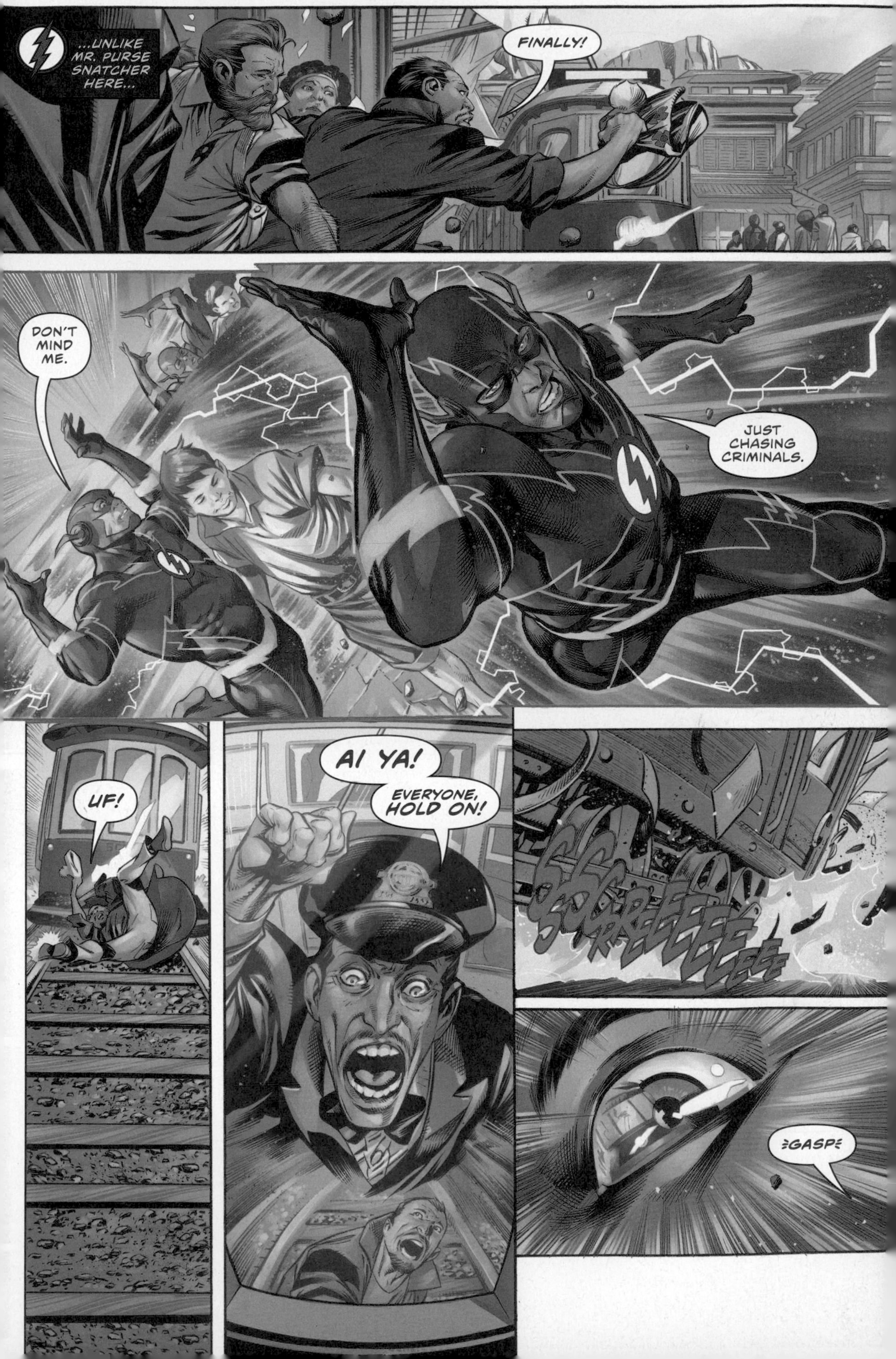
...UNLIKE MR. PURSE SNATCHER HERE...
FINALLY!
DON'T MIND ME.
JUST CHASING CRIMINALS.
UF!
AI YA!
EVERYONE, HOLD ON!
SSCREEEEEEE
GASP

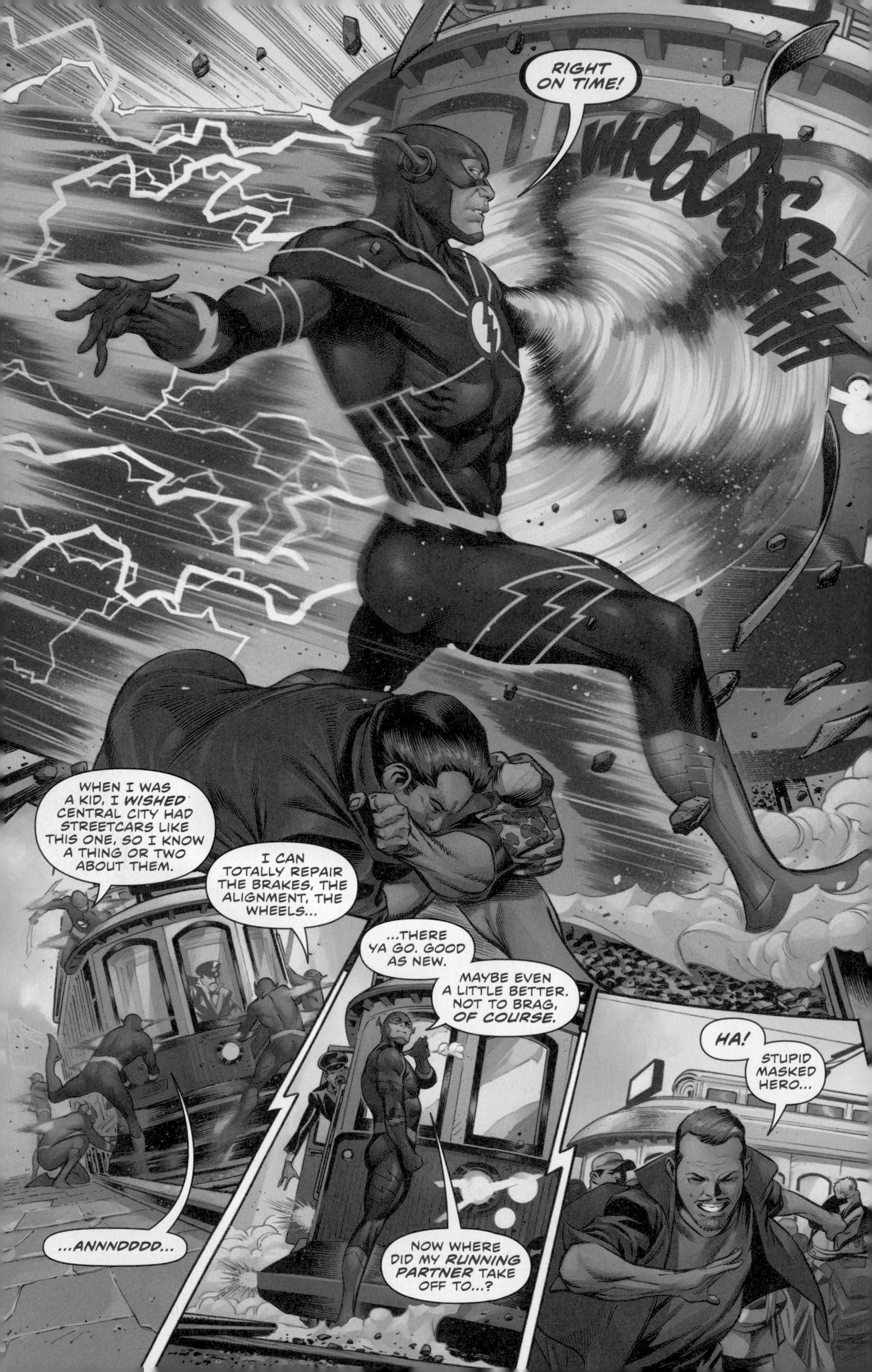

RIGHT ON TIME!
WHOOSHHH
WHEN I WAS A KID, I WISHED CENTRAL CITY HAD STREETCARS LIKE THIS ONE, SO I KNOW A THING OR TWO ABOUT THEM.
I CAN TOTALLY REPAIR THE BRAKES, THE ALIGNMENT, THE WHEELS...
...ANNNDDDD...
...THERE YA GO. GOOD AS NEW.
MAYBE EVEN A LITTLE BETTER. NOT TO BRAG, OF COURSE.
NOW WHERE DID MY RUNNING PARTNER TAKE OFF TO...?
HA!
STUPID MASKED HERO...

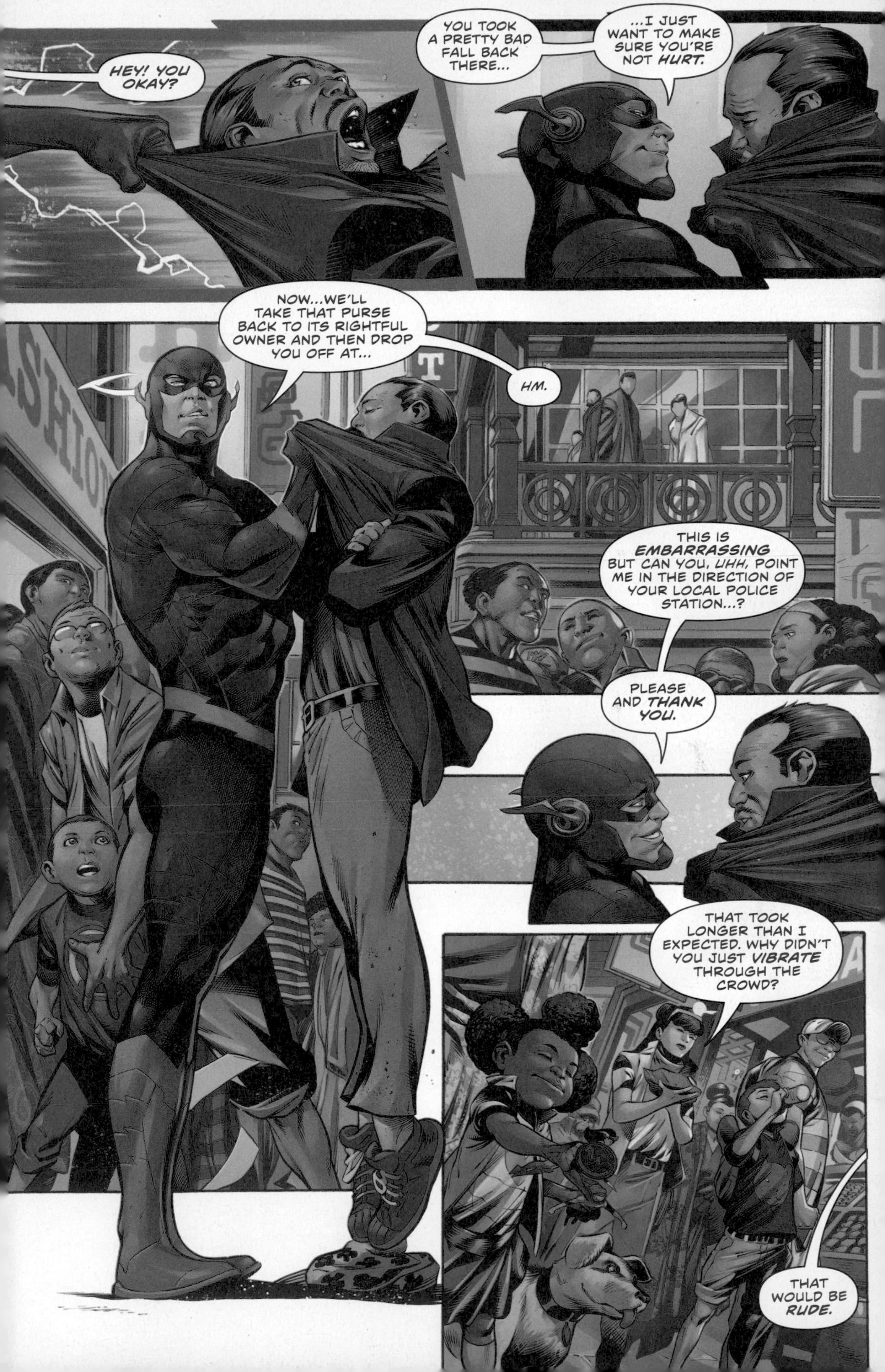
HEY! YOU OKAY?
YOU TOOK A PRETTY BAD FALL BACK THERE...
...I JUST WANT TO MAKE SURE YOU'RE NOT HURT.
NOW...WE'LL TAKE THAT PURSE BACK TO ITS RIGHTFUL OWNER AND THEN DROP YOU OFF AT...
HM.
THIS IS EMBARRASSING BUT CAN YOU, UHH, POINT ME IN THE DIRECTION OF YOUR LOCAL POLICE STATION...?
PLEASE AND THANK YOU.
THAT TOOK LONGER THAN I EXPECTED. WHY DIDN'T YOU JUST VIBRATE THROUGH THE CROWD?
THAT WOULD BE RUDE.

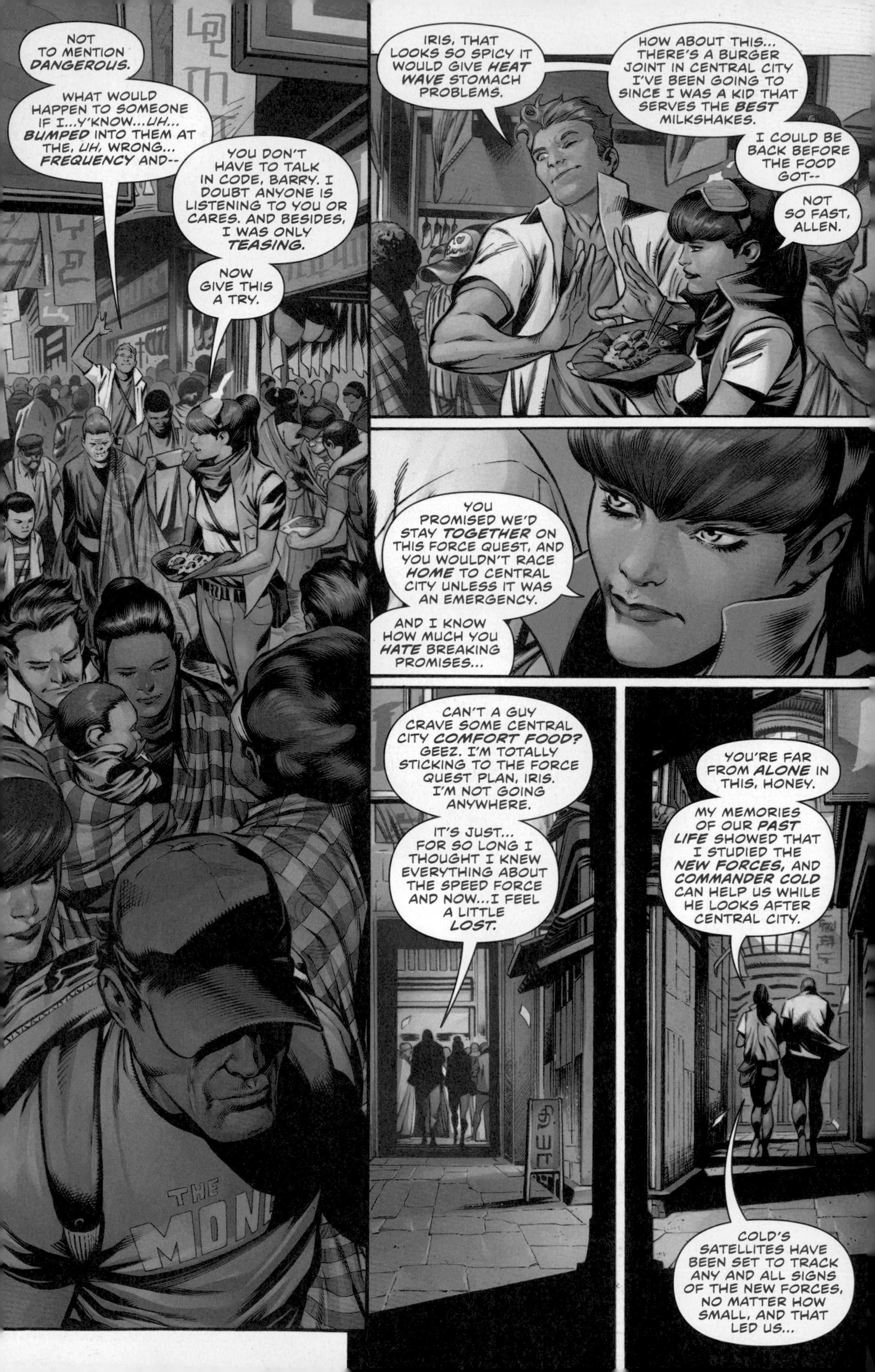

NOT TO MENTION *DANGEROUS*.
WHAT WOULD HAPPEN TO SOMEONE IF I...Y'KNOW...*UH*... *BUMPED* INTO THEM AT THE, *UH*, WRONG... *FREQUENCY* AND--
YOU DON'T HAVE TO TALK IN CODE, BARRY. I DOUBT ANYONE IS LISTENING TO YOU OR CARES. AND BESIDES, I WAS ONLY *TEASING*.
NOW GIVE THIS A TRY.
THE MON
IRIS, THAT LOOKS SO SPICY IT WOULD GIVE *HEAT WAVE* STOMACH PROBLEMS.
HOW ABOUT THIS... THERE'S A BURGER JOINT IN CENTRAL CITY I'VE BEEN GOING TO SINCE I WAS A KID THAT SERVES THE *BEST* MILKSHAKES.
I COULD BE BACK BEFORE THE FOOD GOT--
NOT SO FAST, ALLEN.
YOU PROMISED WE'D STAY *TOGETHER* ON THIS FORCE QUEST, AND YOU WOULDN'T RACE *HOME* TO CENTRAL CITY UNLESS IT WAS AN EMERGENCY.
AND I KNOW HOW MUCH YOU *HATE* BREAKING PROMISES...
CAN'T A GUY CRAVE SOME CENTRAL CITY *COMFORT FOOD?* GEEZ. I'M TOTALLY STICKING TO THE FORCE QUEST PLAN, IRIS. I'M NOT GOING ANYWHERE.
IT'S JUST... FOR SO LONG I THOUGHT I KNEW EVERYTHING ABOUT THE SPEED FORCE AND NOW...I FEEL A LITTLE *LOST*.
YOU'RE FAR FROM *ALONE* IN THIS, HONEY.
MY MEMORIES OF OUR *PAST LIFE* SHOWED THAT I STUDIED THE *NEW FORCES*, AND *COMMANDER COLD* CAN HELP US WHILE HE LOOKS AFTER CENTRAL CITY.
COLD'S SATELLITES HAVE BEEN SET TO TRACK ANY AND ALL SIGNS OF THE NEW FORCES, NO MATTER HOW SMALL, AND THAT LED US...

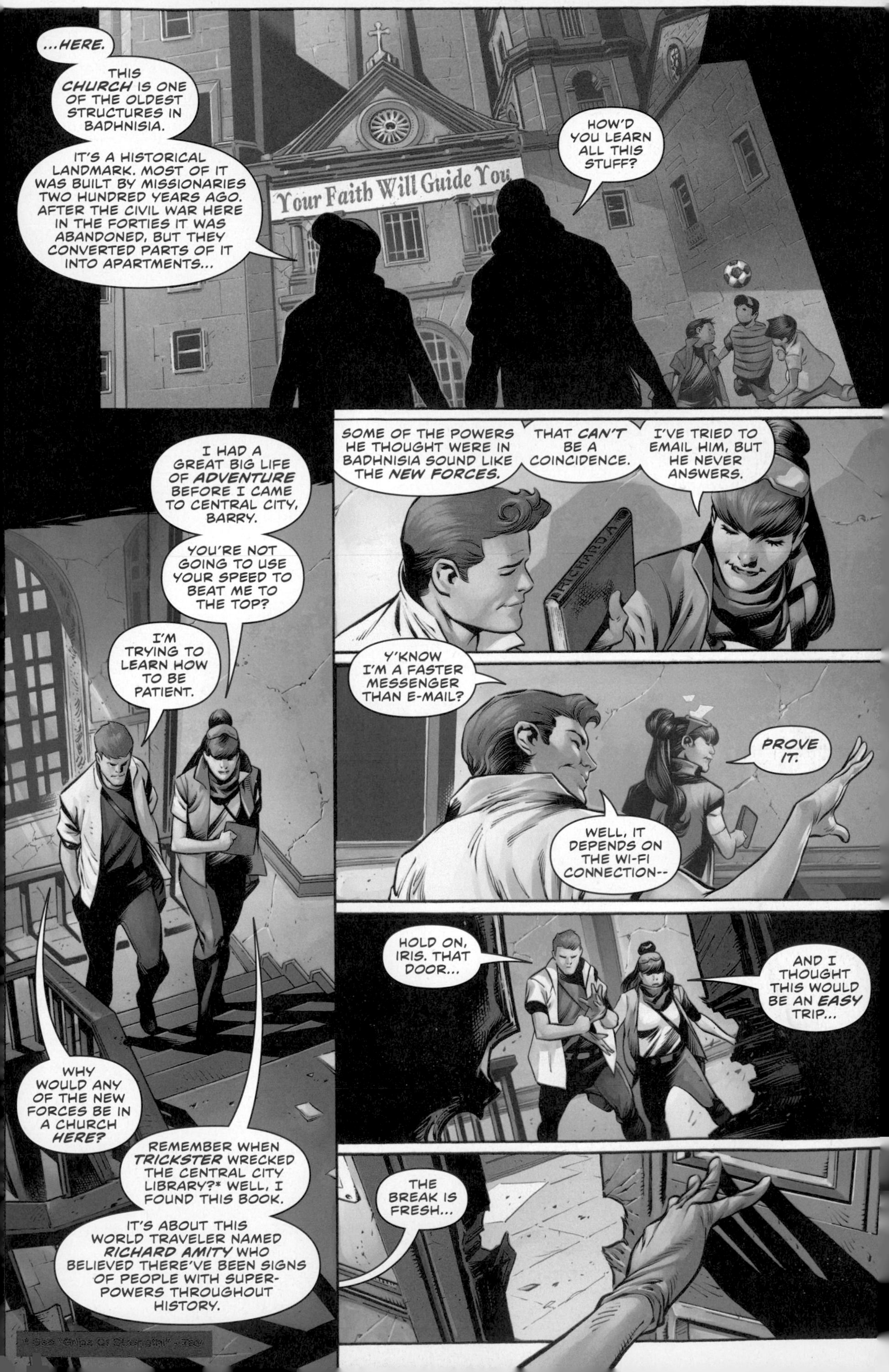
...HERE.
THIS CHURCH IS ONE OF THE OLDEST STRUCTURES IN BADHNISIA.
IT'S A HISTORICAL LANDMARK. MOST OF IT WAS BUILT BY MISSIONARIES TWO HUNDRED YEARS AGO. AFTER THE CIVIL WAR HERE IN THE FORTIES IT WAS ABANDONED, BUT THEY CONVERTED PARTS OF IT INTO APARTMENTS...
Your Faith Will Guide You
HOW'D YOU LEARN ALL THIS STUFF?
I HAD A GREAT BIG LIFE OF ADVENTURE BEFORE I CAME TO CENTRAL CITY, BARRY.
YOU'RE NOT GOING TO USE YOUR SPEED TO BEAT ME TO THE TOP?
I'M TRYING TO LEARN HOW TO BE PATIENT.
WHY WOULD ANY OF THE NEW FORCES BE IN A CHURCH HERE?
REMEMBER WHEN TRICKSTER WRECKED THE CENTRAL CITY LIBRARY?* WELL, I FOUND THIS BOOK.
IT'S ABOUT THIS WORLD TRAVELER NAMED RICHARD AMITY WHO BELIEVED THERE'VE BEEN SIGNS OF PEOPLE WITH SUPER-POWERS THROUGHOUT HISTORY.
* See "Grips Of Strength!"
SOME OF THE POWERS HE THOUGHT WERE IN BADHNISIA SOUND LIKE THE NEW FORCES.
THAT CAN'T BE A COINCIDENCE.
I'VE TRIED TO EMAIL HIM, BUT HE NEVER ANSWERS.
RICHARD A
Y'KNOW I'M A FASTER MESSENGER THAN E-MAIL?
PROVE IT.
WELL, IT DEPENDS ON THE WI-FI CONNECTION--
HOLD ON, IRIS. THAT DOOR...
AND I THOUGHT THIS WOULD BE AN EASY TRIP...
THE BREAK IS FRESH...

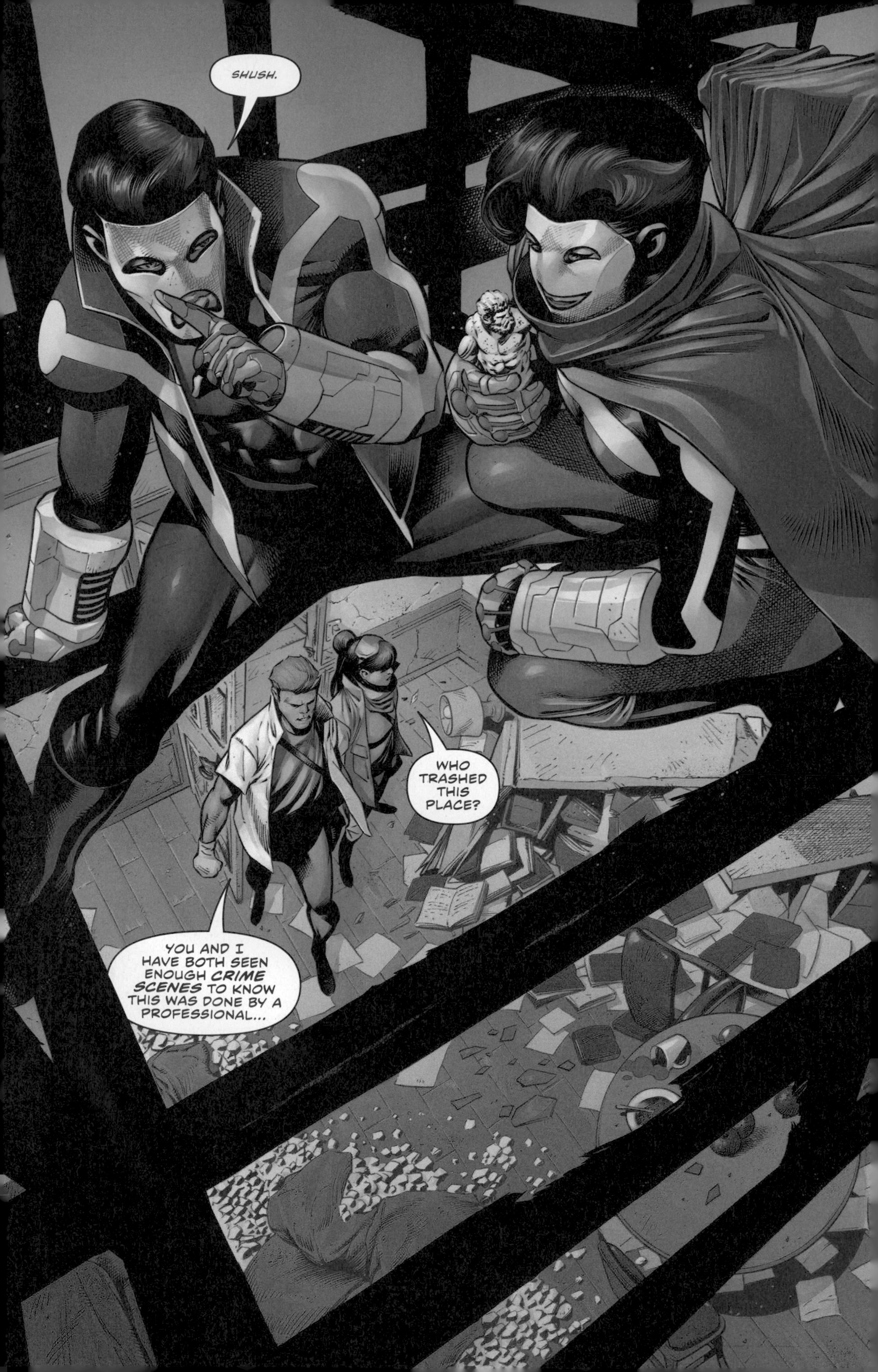
SHUSH.
WHO TRASHED THIS PLACE?
YOU AND I HAVE BOTH SEEN ENOUGH CRIME SCENES TO KNOW THIS WAS DONE BY A PROFESSIONAL...

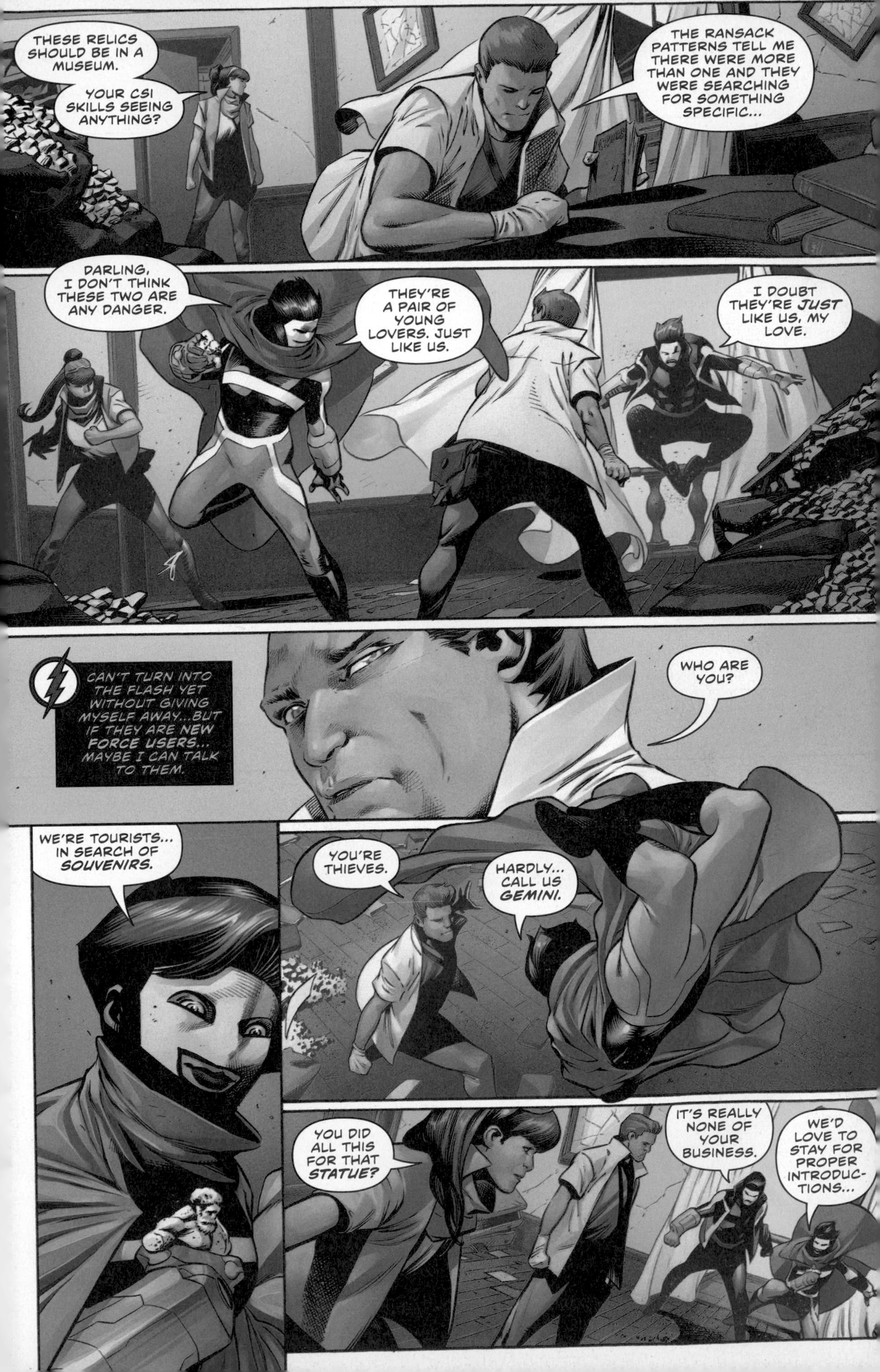
THESE RELICS SHOULD BE IN A MUSEUM.
YOUR CSI SKILLS SEEING ANYTHING?
THE RANSACK PATTERNS TELL ME THERE WERE MORE THAN ONE AND THEY WERE SEARCHING FOR SOMETHING SPECIFIC...
DARLING, I DON'T THINK THESE TWO ARE ANY DANGER.
THEY'RE A PAIR OF YOUNG LOVERS. JUST LIKE US.
I DOUBT THEY'RE JUST LIKE US, MY LOVE.
CAN'T TURN INTO THE FLASH YET WITHOUT GIVING MYSELF AWAY...BUT IF THEY ARE NEW FORCE USERS... MAYBE I CAN TALK TO THEM.
WHO ARE YOU?
WE'RE TOURISTS... IN SEARCH OF SOUVENIRS.
YOU'RE THIEVES.
HARDLY... CALL US GEMINI.
YOU DID ALL THIS FOR THAT STATUE?
IT'S REALLY NONE OF YOUR BUSINESS.
WE'D LOVE TO STAY FOR PROPER INTRODUCTIONS...

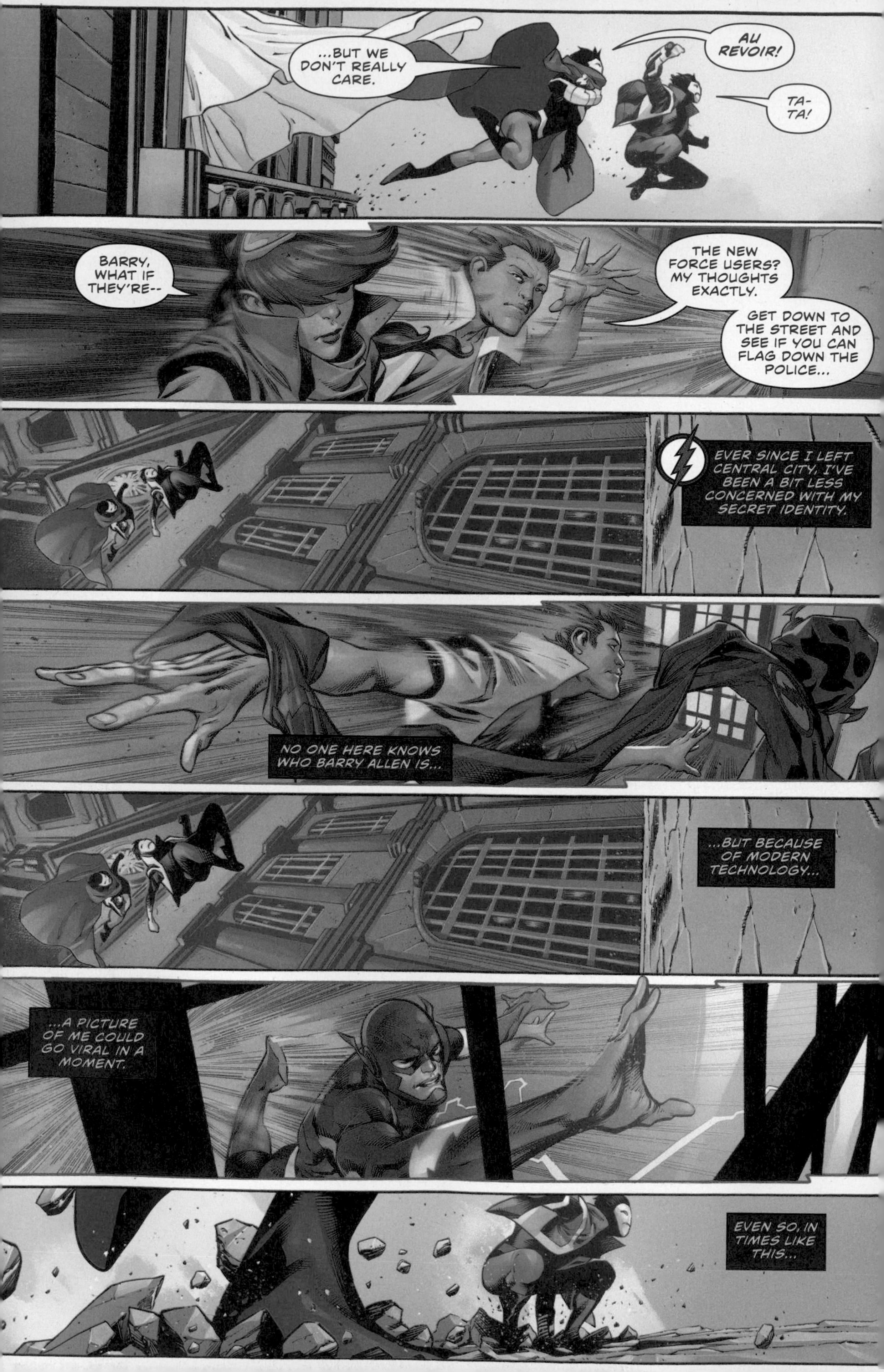
...BUT WE DON'T REALLY CARE.
AU REVOIR!
TA-TA!
BARRY, WHAT IF THEY'RE--
THE NEW FORCE USERS? MY THOUGHTS EXACTLY.
GET DOWN TO THE STREET AND SEE IF YOU CAN FLAG DOWN THE POLICE...
EVER SINCE I LEFT CENTRAL CITY, I'VE BEEN A BIT LESS CONCERNED WITH MY SECRET IDENTITY.
NO ONE HERE KNOWS WHO BARRY ALLEN IS...
...BUT BECAUSE OF MODERN TECHNOLOGY...
...A PICTURE OF ME COULD GO VIRAL IN A MOMENT.
EVEN SO, IN TIMES LIKE THIS...

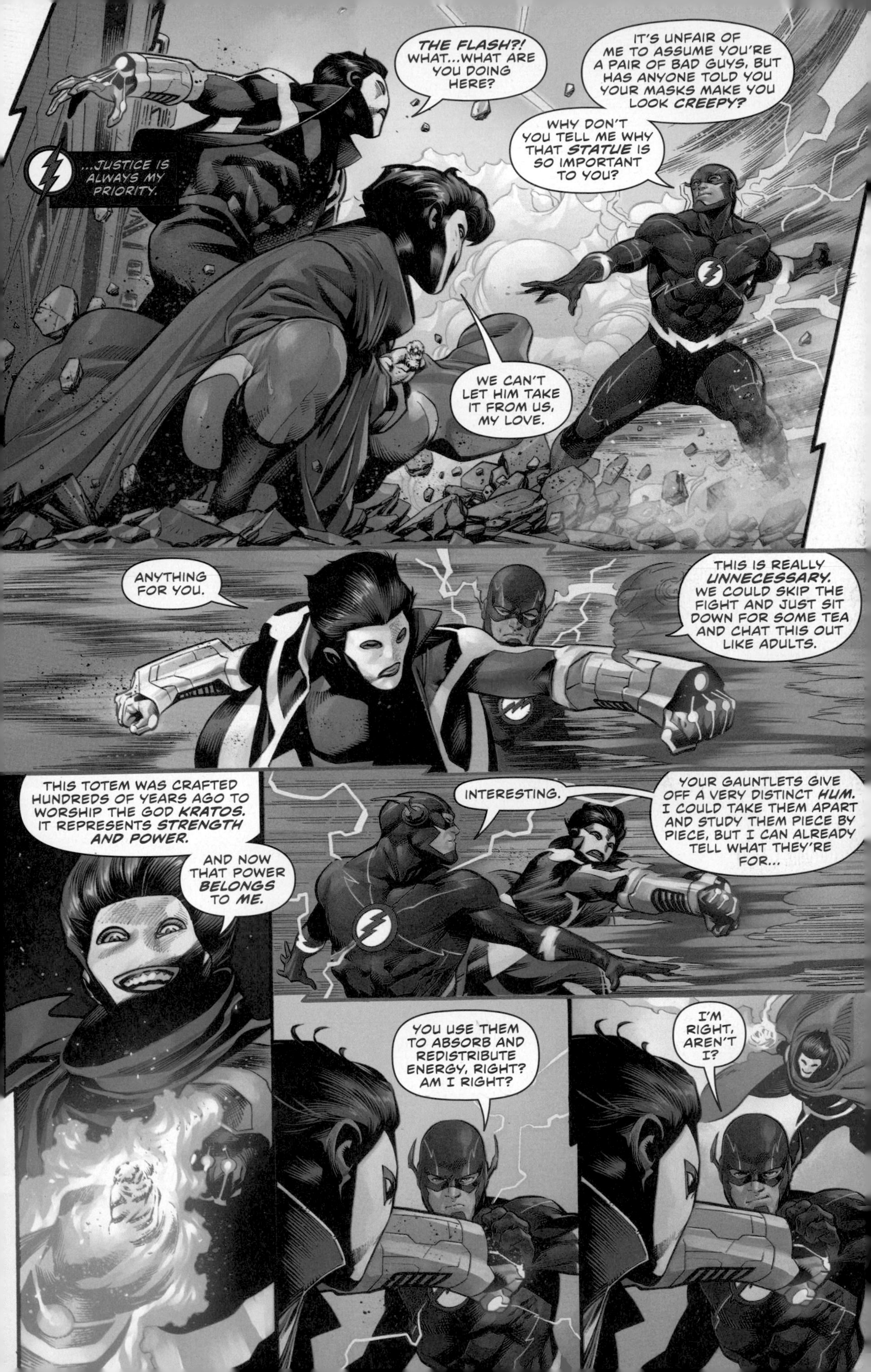
...JUSTICE IS ALWAYS MY PRIORITY.
THE FLASH?! WHAT...WHAT ARE YOU DOING HERE?
IT'S UNFAIR OF ME TO ASSUME YOU'RE A PAIR OF BAD GUYS, BUT HAS ANYONE TOLD YOU YOUR MASKS MAKE YOU LOOK CREEPY?
WHY DON'T YOU TELL ME WHY THAT STATUE IS SO IMPORTANT TO YOU?
WE CAN'T LET HIM TAKE IT FROM US, MY LOVE.
ANYTHING FOR YOU.
THIS IS REALLY UNNECESSARY. WE COULD SKIP THE FIGHT AND JUST SIT DOWN FOR SOME TEA AND CHAT THIS OUT LIKE ADULTS.
THIS TOTEM WAS CRAFTED HUNDREDS OF YEARS AGO TO WORSHIP THE GOD KRATOS. IT REPRESENTS STRENGTH AND POWER.
AND NOW THAT POWER BELONGS TO ME.
INTERESTING.
YOUR GAUNTLETS GIVE OFF A VERY DISTINCT HUM. I COULD TAKE THEM APART AND STUDY THEM PIECE BY PIECE, BUT I CAN ALREADY TELL WHAT THEY'RE FOR...
YOU USE THEM TO ABSORB AND REDISTRIBUTE ENERGY, RIGHT? AM I RIGHT?
I'M RIGHT, AREN'T I?

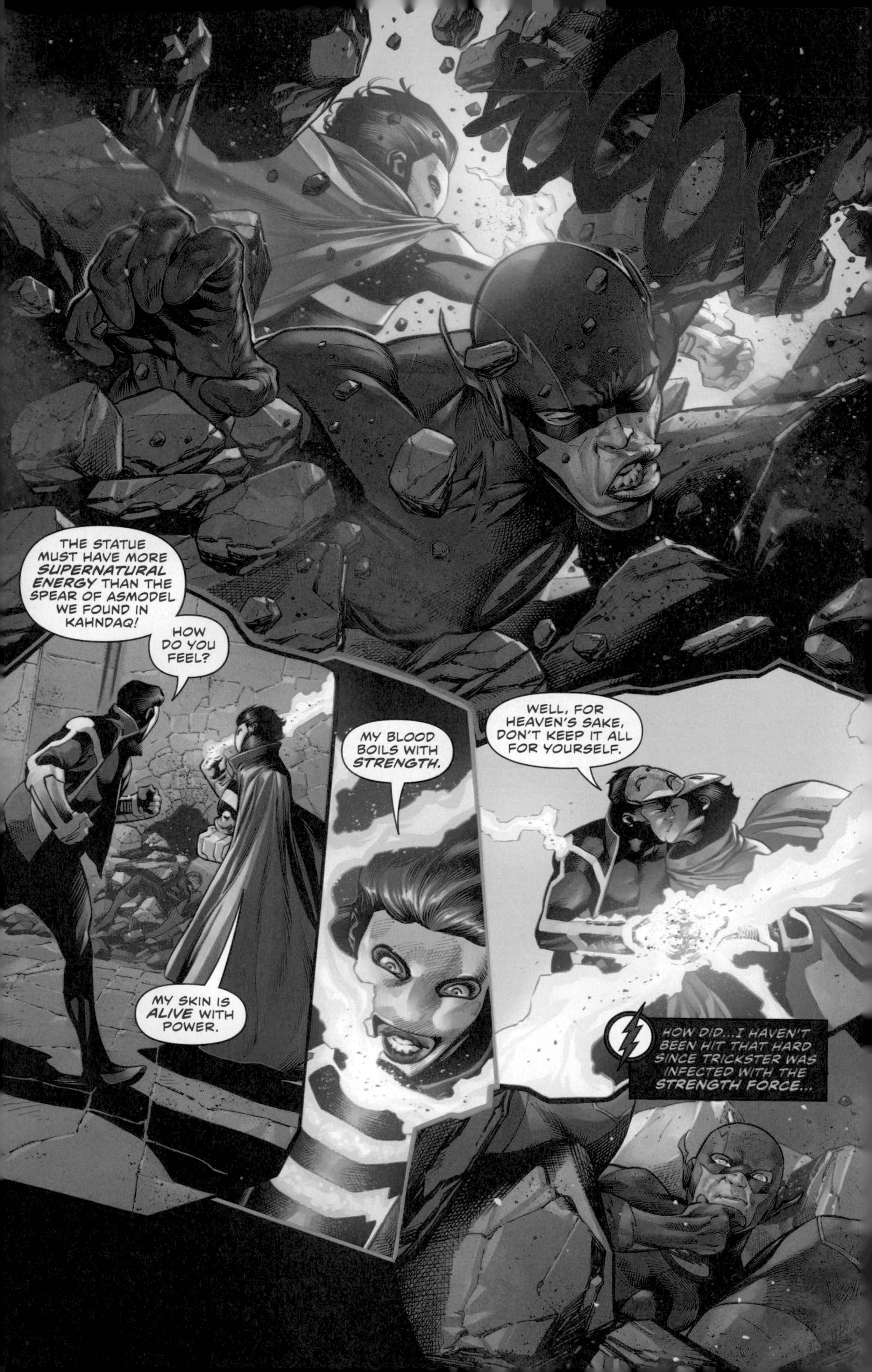
BOOOM!
THE STATUE MUST HAVE MORE SUPERNATURAL ENERGY THAN THE SPEAR OF ASMODEL WE FOUND IN KAHNDAQ!
HOW DO YOU FEEL?
MY SKIN IS ALIVE WITH POWER.
MY BLOOD BOILS WITH STRENGTH.
WELL, FOR HEAVEN'S SAKE, DON'T KEEP IT ALL FOR YOURSELF.
HOW DID...I HAVEN'T BEEN HIT THAT HARD SINCE TRICKSTER WAS INFECTED WITH THE STRENGTH FORCE...

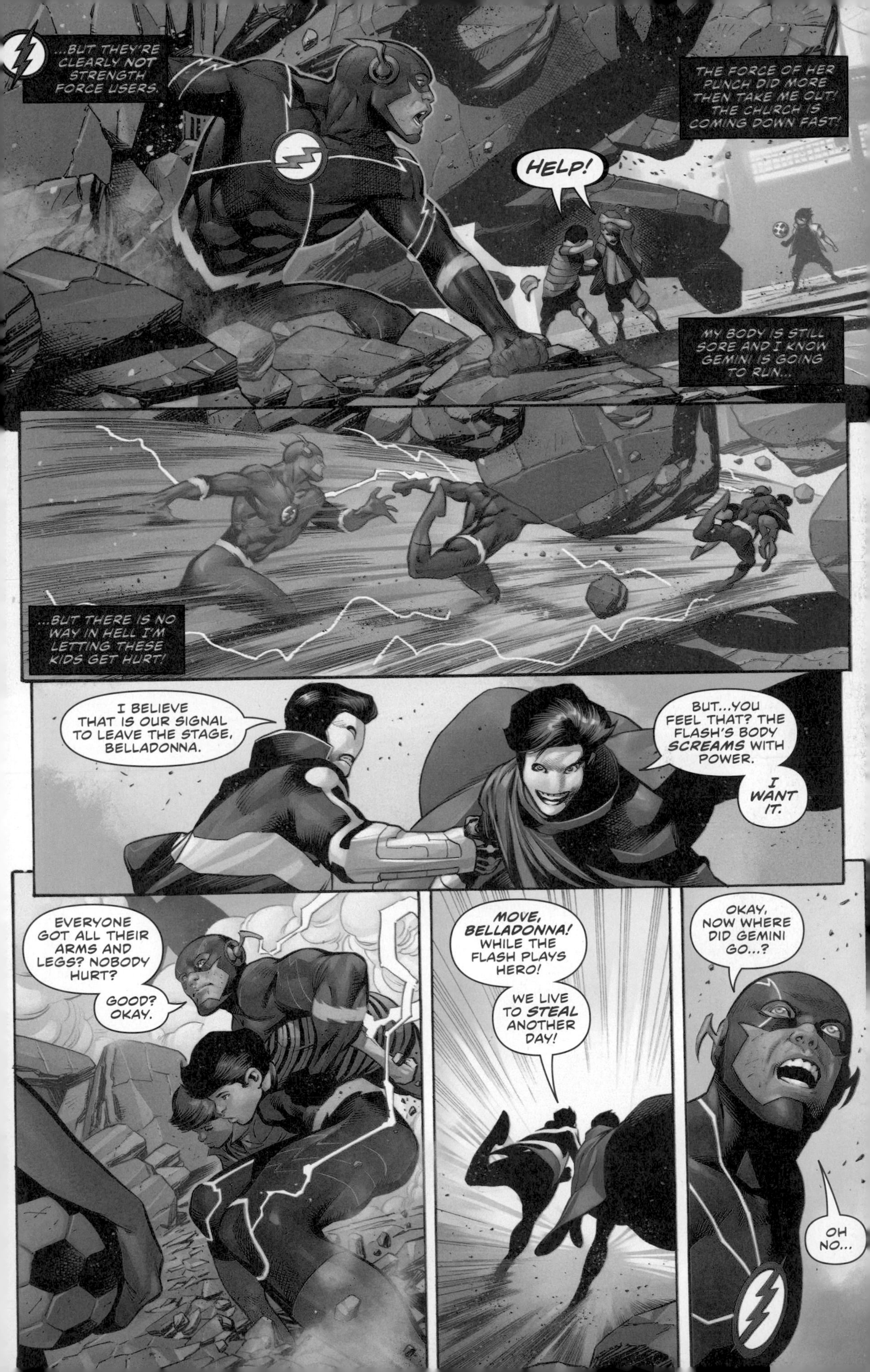
...BUT THEY'RE CLEARLY NOT STRENGTH FORCE USERS.
THE FORCE OF HER PUNCH DID MORE THEN TAKE ME OUT! THE CHURCH IS COMING DOWN FAST!
HELP!
MY BODY IS STILL SORE AND I KNOW GEMINI IS GOING TO RUN...
...BUT THERE IS NO WAY IN HELL I'M LETTING THESE KIDS GET HURT!
I BELIEVE THAT IS OUR SIGNAL TO LEAVE THE STAGE, BELLADONNA.
BUT...YOU FEEL THAT? THE FLASH'S BODY SCREAMS WITH POWER.
I WANT IT.
EVERYONE GOT ALL THEIR ARMS AND LEGS? NOBODY HURT?
GOOD? OKAY.
MOVE, BELLADONNA! WHILE THE FLASH PLAYS HERO!
WE LIVE TO STEAL ANOTHER DAY!
OKAY, NOW WHERE DID GEMINI GO...?
OH NO...

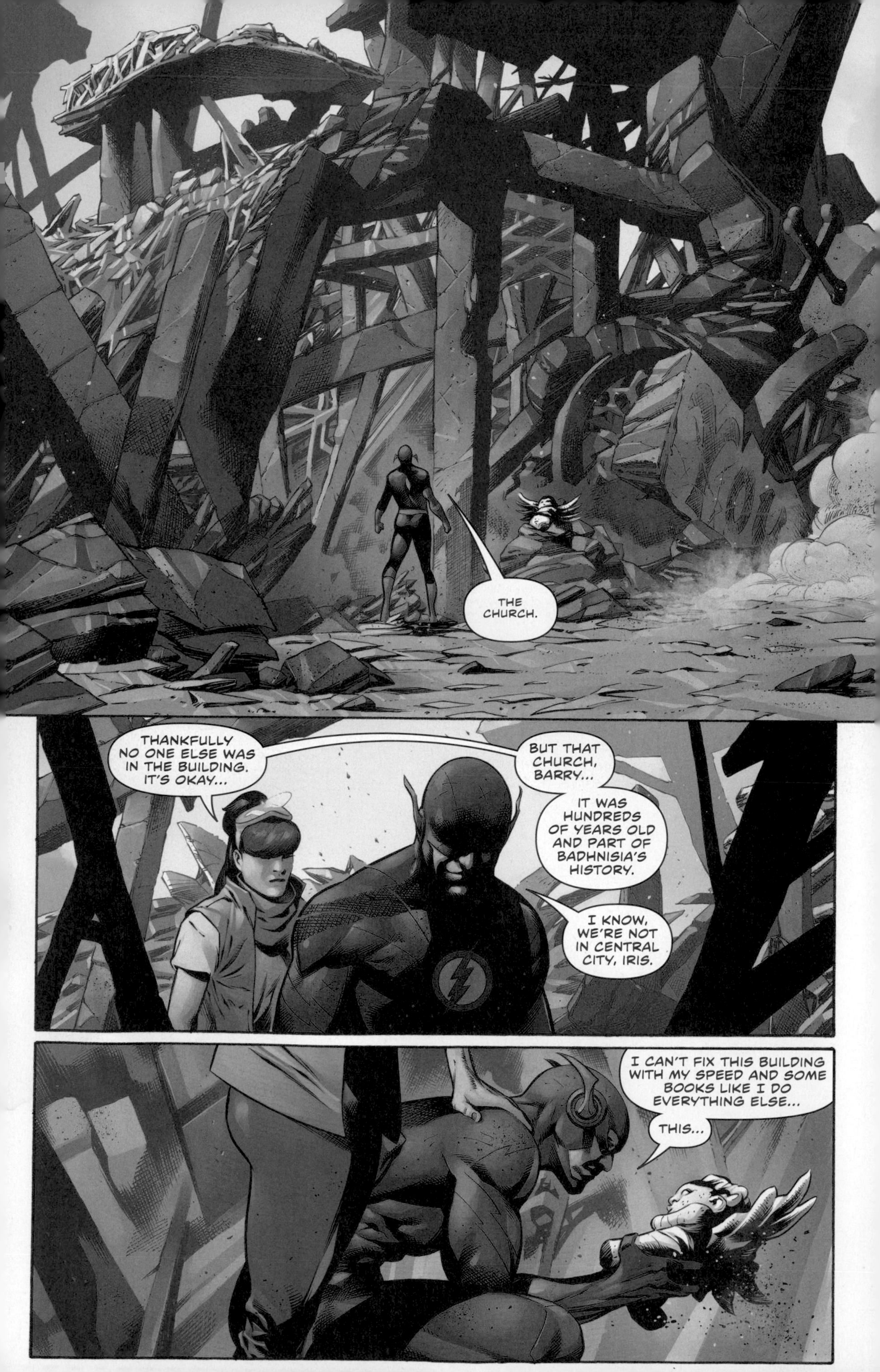
THE CHURCH.
THANKFULLY NO ONE ELSE WAS IN THE BUILDING. IT'S OKAY...
BUT THAT CHURCH, BARRY...
IT WAS HUNDREDS OF YEARS OLD AND PART OF BADHNISIA'S HISTORY.
I KNOW, WE'RE NOT IN CENTRAL CITY, IRIS.
I CAN'T FIX THIS BUILDING WITH MY SPEED AND SOME BOOKS LIKE I DO EVERYTHING ELSE...
THIS...

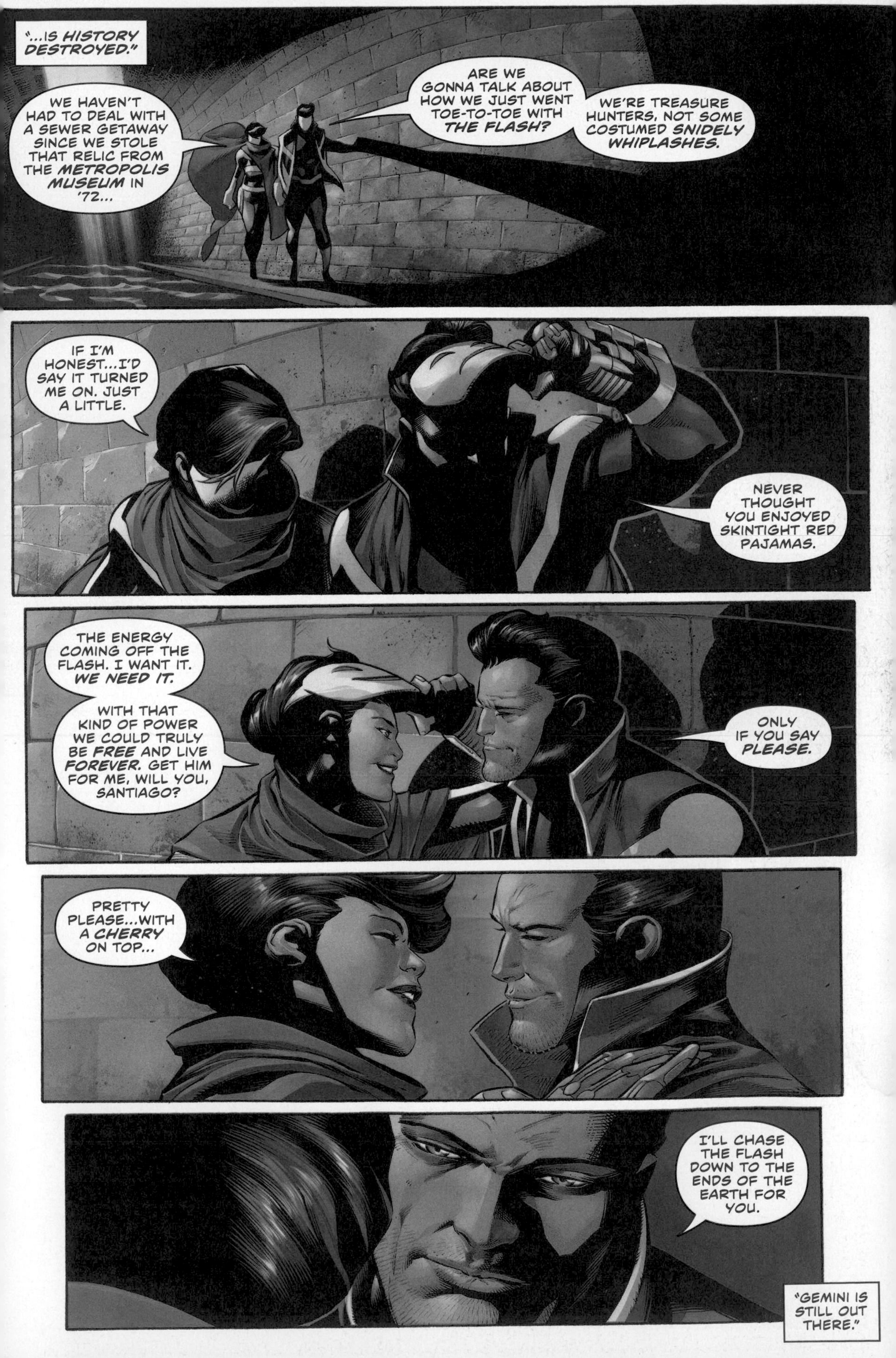
"...IS HISTORY DESTROYED."
WE HAVEN'T HAD TO DEAL WITH A SEWER GETAWAY SINCE WE STOLE THAT RELIC FROM THE METROPOLIS MUSEUM IN '72...
ARE WE GONNA TALK ABOUT HOW WE JUST WENT TOE-TO-TOE WITH THE FLASH?
WE'RE TREASURE HUNTERS, NOT SOME COSTUMED SNIDELY WHIPLASHES.
IF I'M HONEST...I'D SAY IT TURNED ME ON. JUST A LITTLE.
NEVER THOUGHT YOU ENJOYED SKINTIGHT RED PAJAMAS.
THE ENERGY COMING OFF THE FLASH. I WANT IT. WE NEED IT.
WITH THAT KIND OF POWER WE COULD TRULY BE FREE AND LIVE FOREVER. GET HIM FOR ME, WILL YOU, SANTIAGO?
ONLY IF YOU SAY PLEASE.
PRETTY PLEASE...WITH A CHERRY ON TOP...
I'LL CHASE THE FLASH DOWN TO THE ENDS OF THE EARTH FOR YOU.
"GEMINI IS STILL OUT THERE."

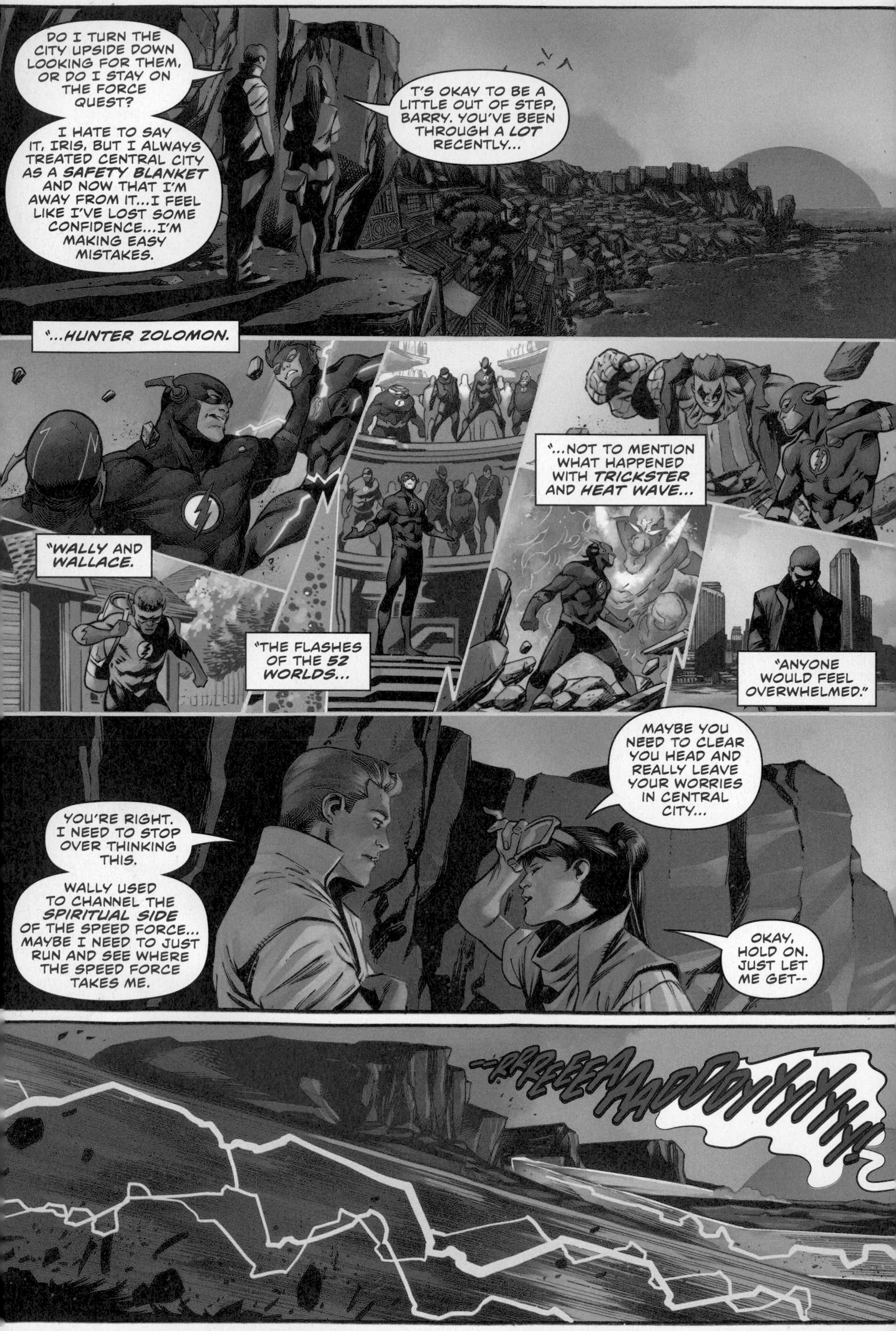
DO I TURN THE CITY UPSIDE DOWN LOOKING FOR THEM, OR DO I STAY ON THE FORCE QUEST?
I HATE TO SAY IT, IRIS, BUT I ALWAYS TREATED CENTRAL CITY AS A SAFETY BLANKET AND NOW THAT I'M AWAY FROM IT...I FEEL LIKE I'VE LOST SOME CONFIDENCE...I'M MAKING EASY MISTAKES.
T'S OKAY TO BE A LITTLE OUT OF STEP, BARRY. YOU'VE BEEN THROUGH A LOT RECENTLY...
"...HUNTER ZOLOMON.
"WALLY AND WALLACE.
"THE FLASHES OF THE 52 WORLDS...
"...NOT TO MENTION WHAT HAPPENED WITH TRICKSTER AND HEAT WAVE...
"ANYONE WOULD FEEL OVERWHELMED."
MAYBE YOU NEED TO CLEAR YOU HEAD AND REALLY LEAVE YOUR WORRIES IN CENTRAL CITY...
YOU'RE RIGHT. I NEED TO STOP OVER THINKING THIS.
WALLY USED TO CHANNEL THE SPIRITUAL SIDE OF THE SPEED FORCE... MAYBE I NEED TO JUST RUN AND SEE WHERE THE SPEED FORCE TAKES ME.
OKAY, HOLD ON. JUST LET ME GET--
--RREEEEAADDDYYYYYY!

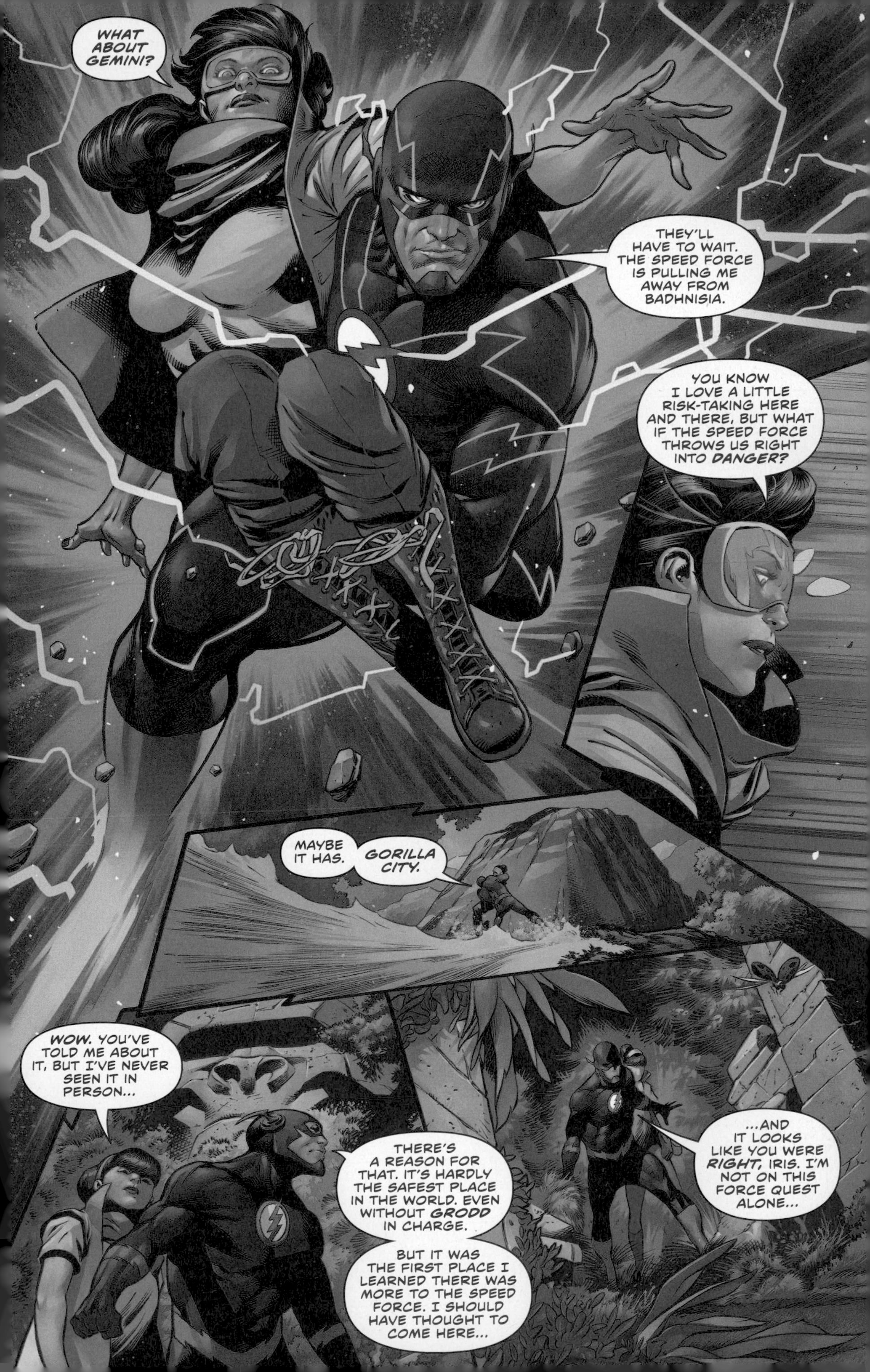
WHAT ABOUT GEMINI?
THEY'LL HAVE TO WAIT. THE SPEED FORCE IS PULLING ME AWAY FROM BADHNISIA.
YOU KNOW I LOVE A LITTLE RISK-TAKING HERE AND THERE, BUT WHAT IF THE SPEED FORCE THROWS US RIGHT INTO DANGER?
MAYBE IT HAS.
GORILLA CITY.
WOW. YOU'VE TOLD ME ABOUT IT, BUT I'VE NEVER SEEN IT IN PERSON...
THERE'S A REASON FOR THAT. IT'S HARDLY THE SAFEST PLACE IN THE WORLD. EVEN WITHOUT GRODD IN CHARGE.
BUT IT WAS THE FIRST PLACE I LEARNED THERE WAS MORE TO THE SPEED FORCE. I SHOULD HAVE THOUGHT TO COME HERE...
...AND IT LOOKS LIKE YOU WERE RIGHT, IRIS. I'M NOT ON THIS FORCE QUEST ALONE...

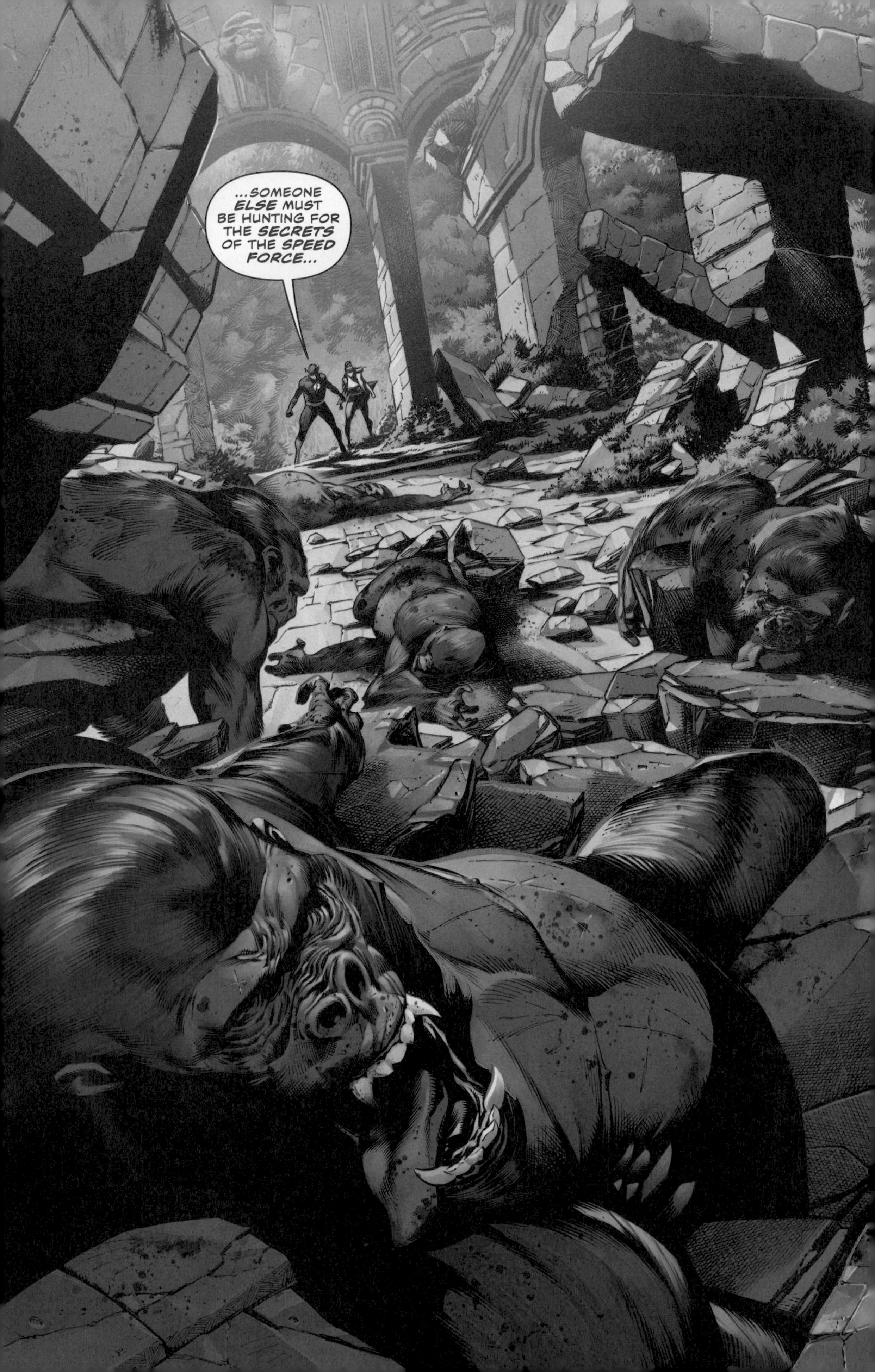
...SOMEONE ELSE MUST BE HUNTING FOR THE SECRETS OF THE SPEED FORCE...

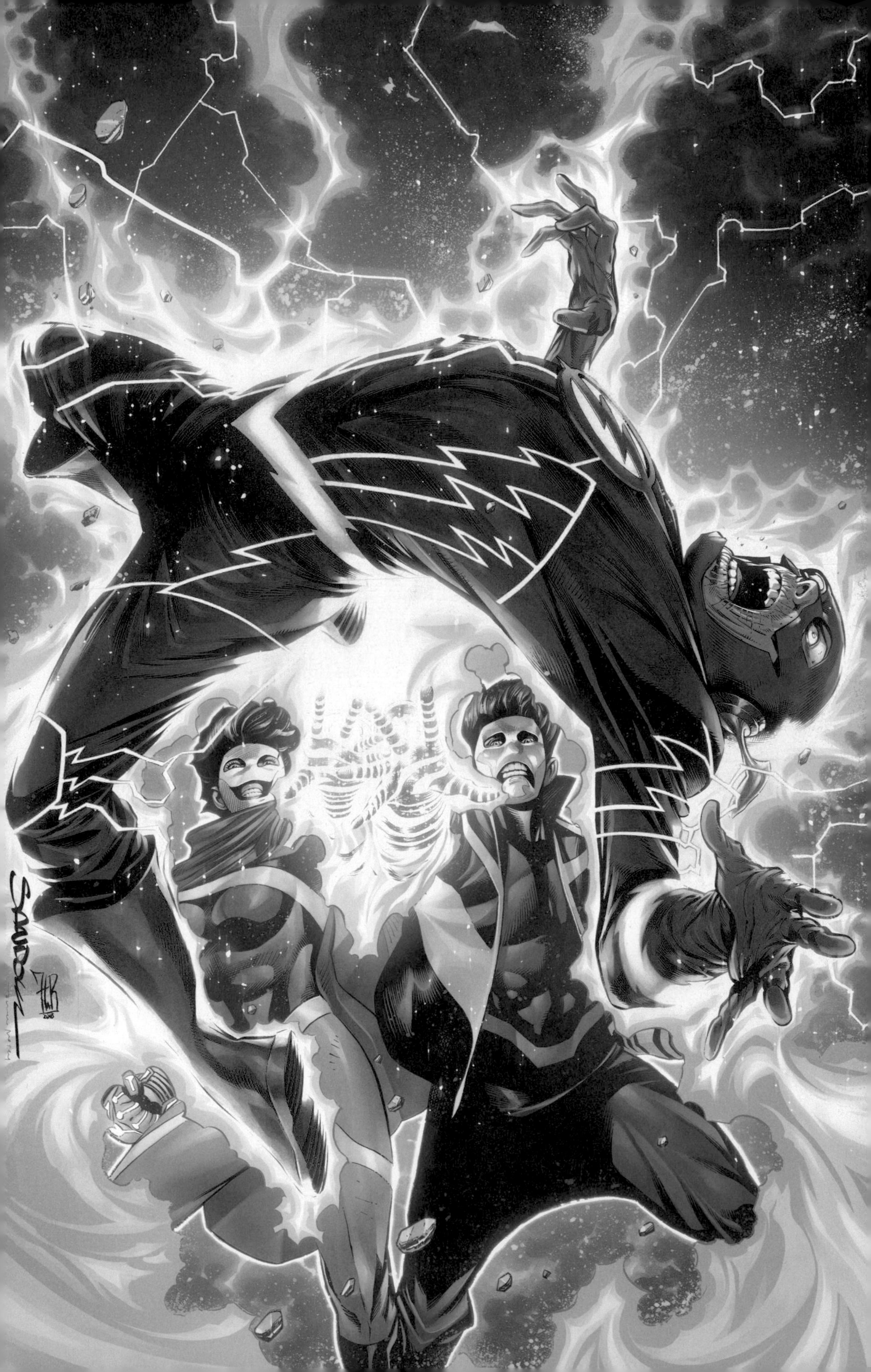

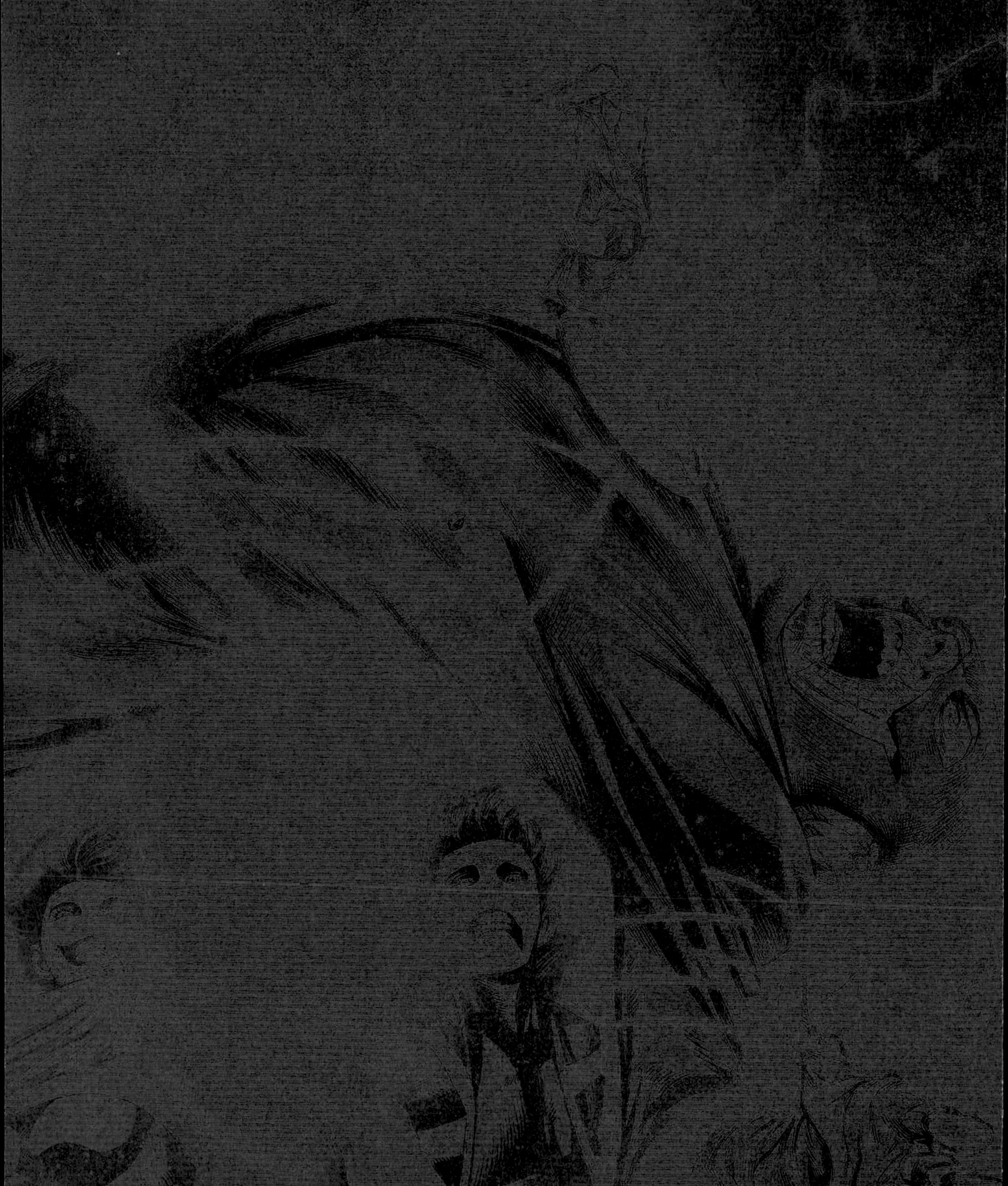

THE FLASH

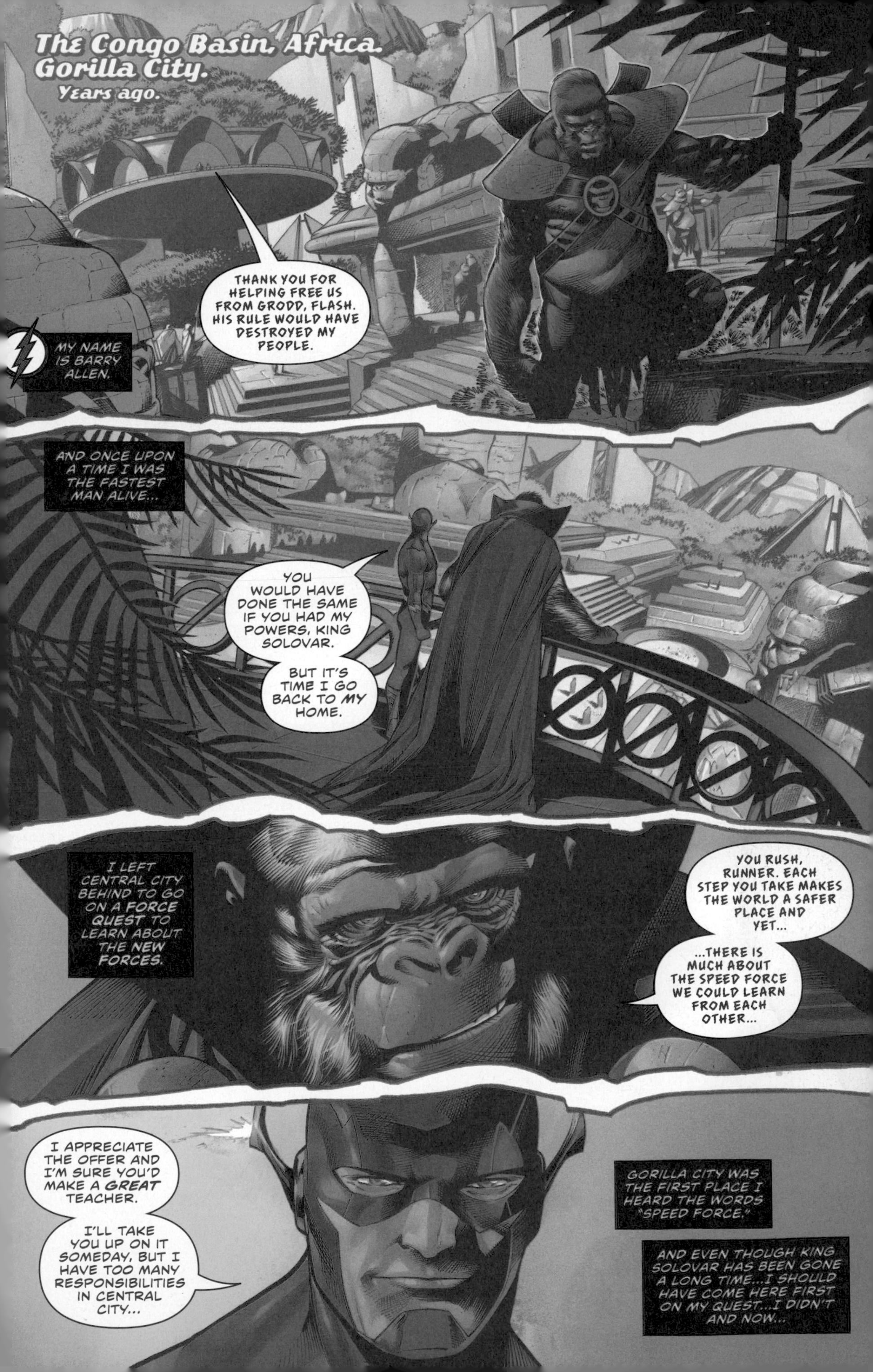
The Congo Basin, Africa.
Gorilla City.
Years ago.
THANK YOU FOR HELPING FREE US FROM GRODD, FLASH. HIS RULE WOULD HAVE DESTROYED MY PEOPLE.
MY NAME IS BARRY ALLEN.
AND ONCE UPON A TIME I WAS THE FASTEST MAN ALIVE...
YOU WOULD HAVE DONE THE SAME IF YOU HAD MY POWERS, KING SOLOVAR.
BUT IT'S TIME I GO BACK TO MY HOME.
I LEFT CENTRAL CITY BEHIND TO GO ON A FORCE QUEST TO LEARN ABOUT THE NEW FORCES.
YOU RUSH, RUNNER. EACH STEP YOU TAKE MAKES THE WORLD A SAFER PLACE AND YET...
...THERE IS MUCH ABOUT THE SPEED FORCE WE COULD LEARN FROM EACH OTHER...
I APPRECIATE THE OFFER AND I'M SURE YOU'D MAKE A GREAT TEACHER.
I'LL TAKE YOU UP ON IT SOMEDAY, BUT I HAVE TOO MANY RESPONSIBILITIES IN CENTRAL CITY...
GORILLA CITY WAS THE FIRST PLACE I HEARD THE WORDS "SPEED FORCE."
AND EVEN THOUGH KING SOLOVAR HAS BEEN GONE A LONG TIME...I SHOULD HAVE COME HERE FIRST ON MY QUEST...I DIDN'T AND NOW...

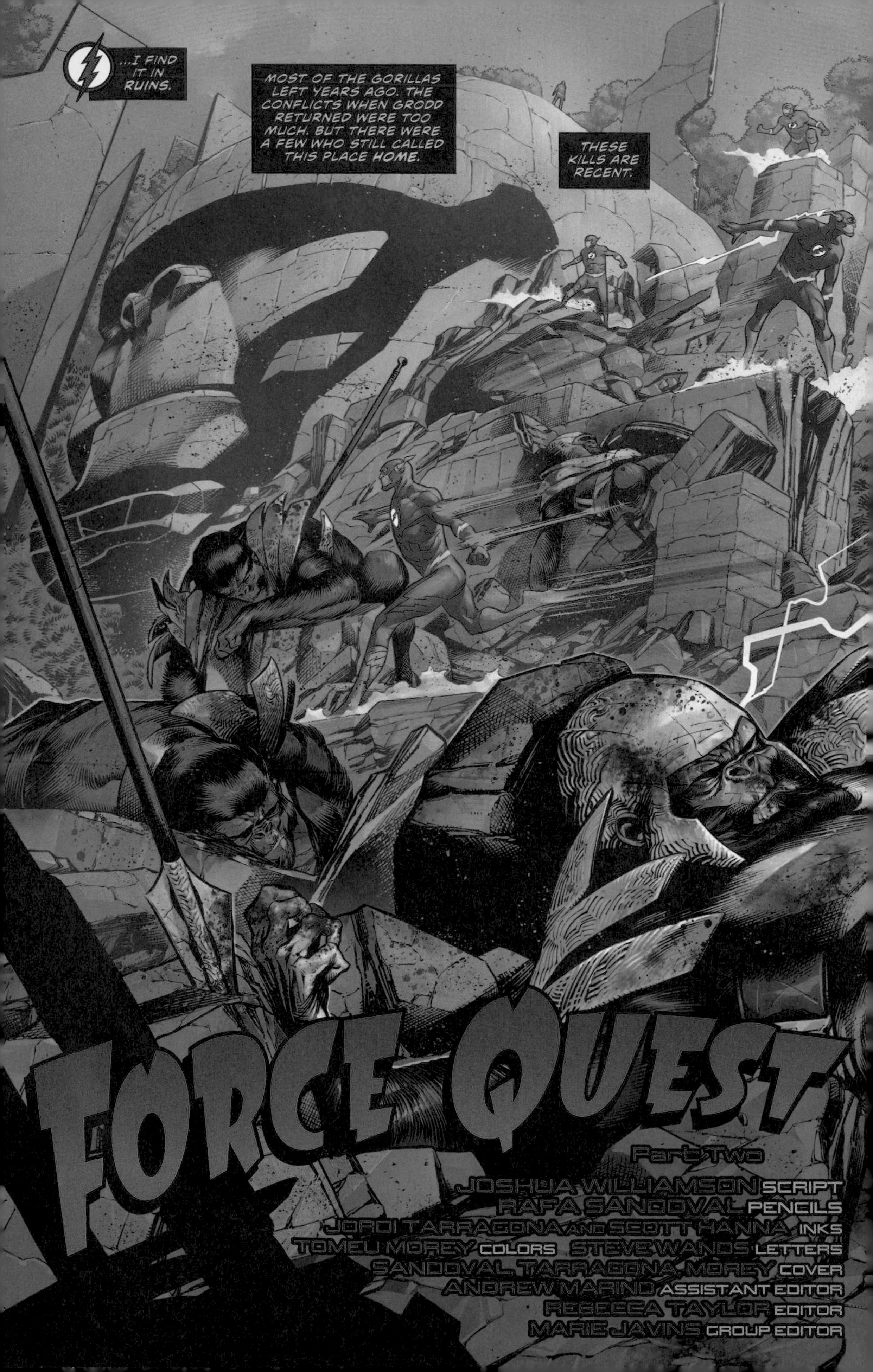

...I FIND IT IN RUINS.
MOST OF THE GORILLAS LEFT YEARS AGO. THE CONFLICTS WHEN GRODD RETURNED WERE TOO MUCH. BUT THERE WERE A FEW WHO STILL CALLED THIS PLACE HOME.
THESE KILLS ARE RECENT.
FORCE QUEST
Part Two
JOSHUA WILLIAMSON SCRIPT
RAFA SANDOVAL PENCILS
JORDI TARRAGONA AND SCOTT HANNA INKS
TOMEU MOREY COLORS STEVE WANDS LETTERS
SANDOVAL, TARRAGONA, MOREY COVER
ANDREW MARINO ASSISTANT EDITOR
REBECCA TAYLOR EDITOR
MARIE JAVINS GROUP EDITOR

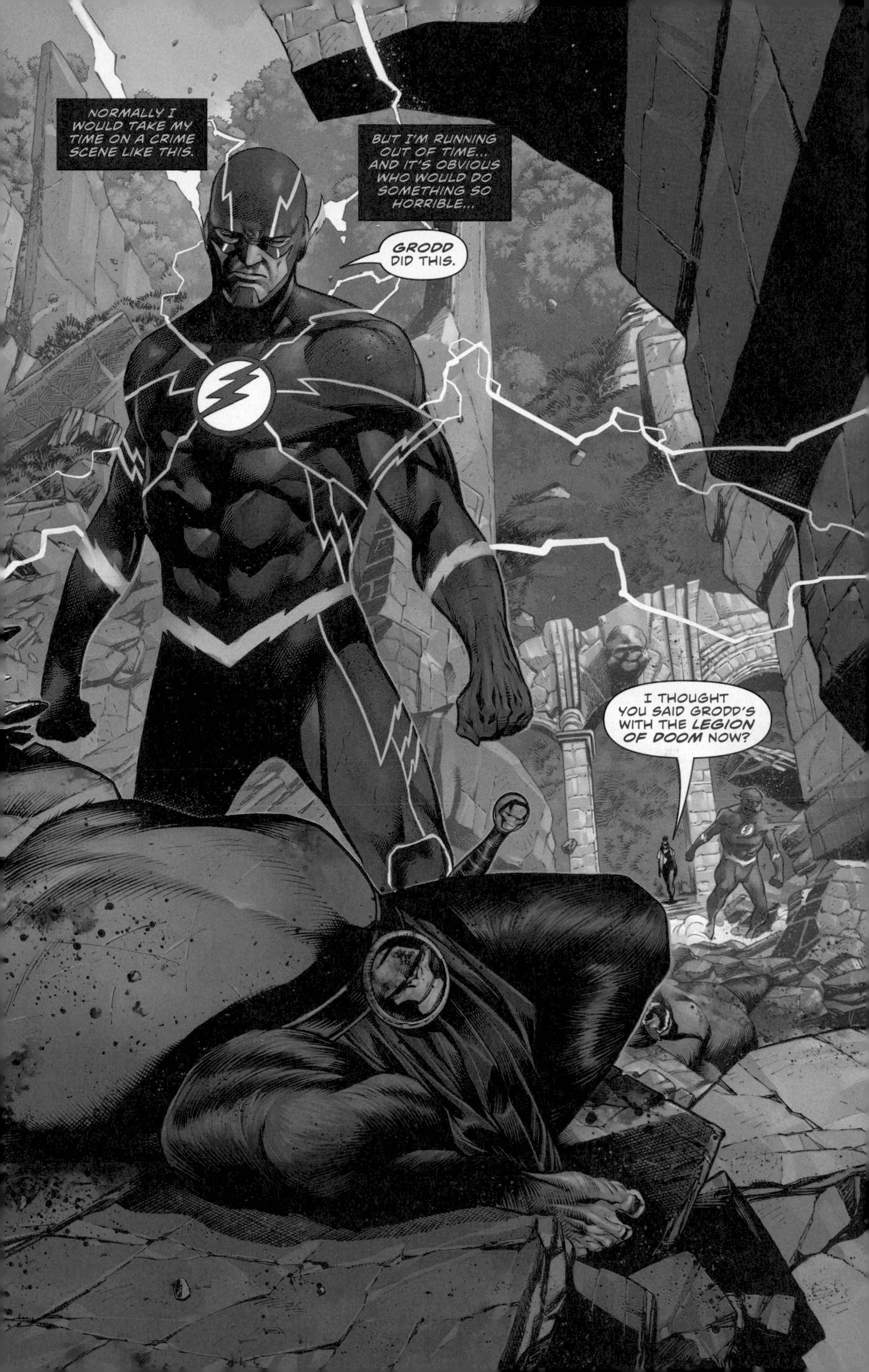
NORMALLY I WOULD TAKE MY TIME ON A CRIME SCENE LIKE THIS.
BUT I'M RUNNING OUT OF TIME... AND IT'S OBVIOUS WHO WOULD DO SOMETHING SO HORRIBLE...
GRODD DID THIS.
I THOUGHT YOU SAID GRODD'S WITH THE LEGION OF DOOM NOW?

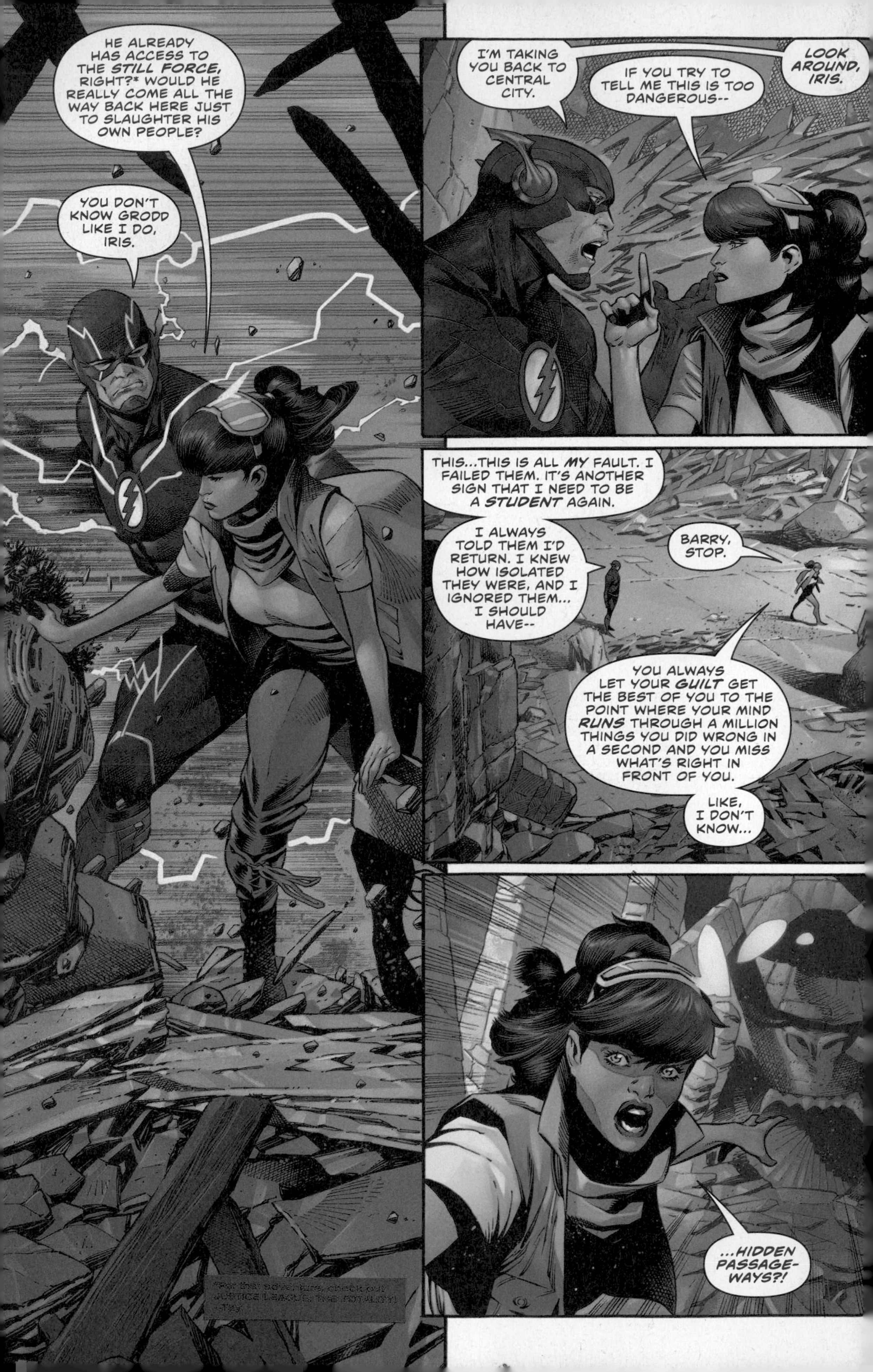
HE ALREADY HAS ACCESS TO THE STILL FORCE, RIGHT?* WOULD HE REALLY COME ALL THE WAY BACK HERE JUST TO SLAUGHTER HIS OWN PEOPLE?
YOU DON'T KNOW GRODD LIKE I DO, IRIS.
*For that adventure, check out
I'M TAKING YOU BACK TO CENTRAL CITY.
IF YOU TRY TO TELL ME THIS IS TOO DANGEROUS--
LOOK AROUND, IRIS.
THIS...THIS IS ALL MY FAULT. I FAILED THEM. IT'S ANOTHER SIGN THAT I NEED TO BE A STUDENT AGAIN.
I ALWAYS TOLD THEM I'D RETURN. I KNEW HOW ISOLATED THEY WERE, AND I IGNORED THEM... I SHOULD HAVE--
BARRY, STOP.
YOU ALWAYS LET YOUR GUILT GET THE BEST OF YOU TO THE POINT WHERE YOUR MIND RUNS THROUGH A MILLION THINGS YOU DID WRONG IN A SECOND AND YOU MISS WHAT'S RIGHT IN FRONT OF YOU.
LIKE, I DON'T KNOW...
...HIDDEN PASSAGE-WAYS?!

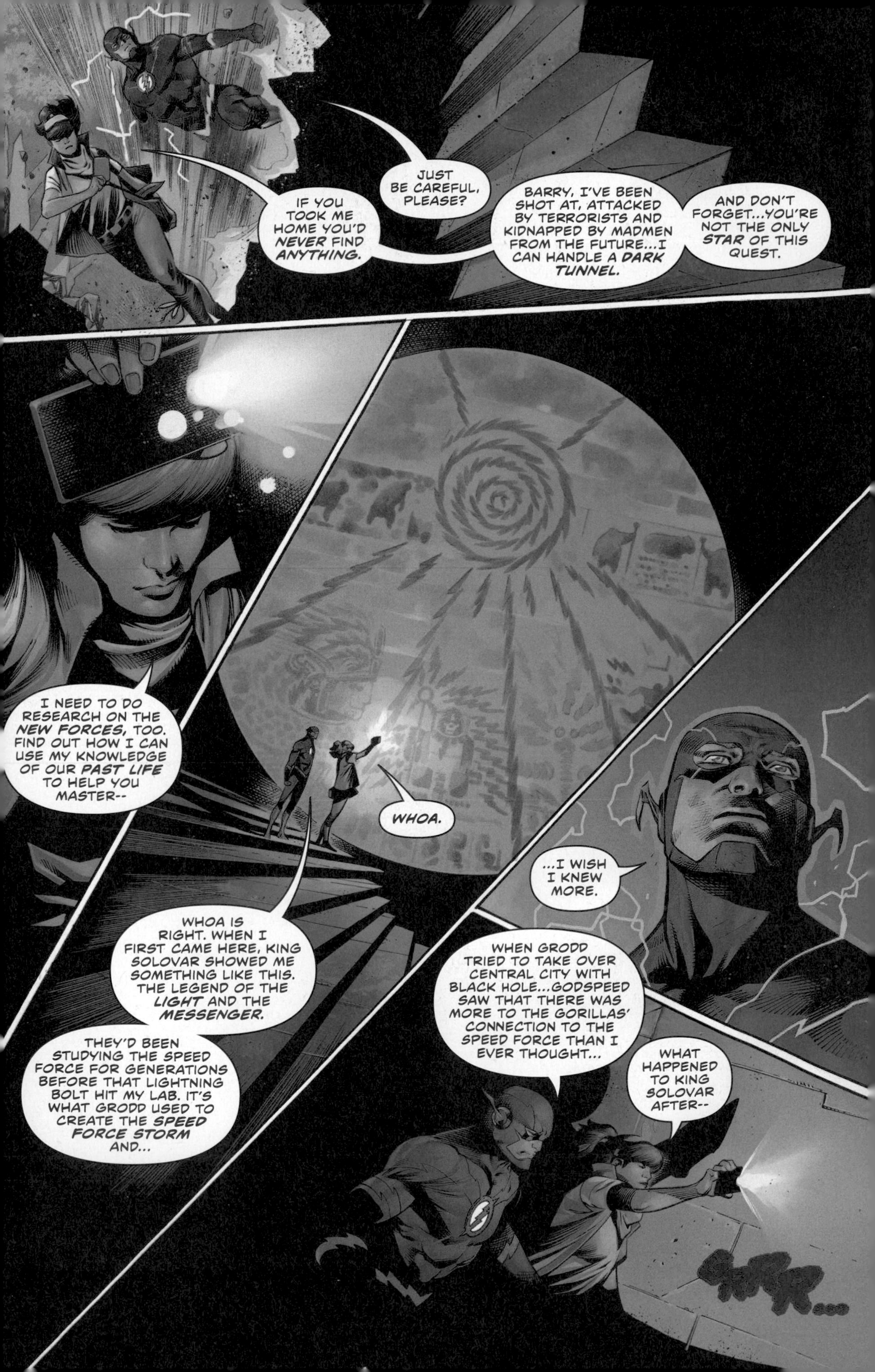
JUST BE CAREFUL, PLEASE?
IF YOU TOOK ME HOME YOU'D NEVER FIND ANYTHING.
BARRY, I'VE BEEN SHOT AT, ATTACKED BY TERRORISTS AND KIDNAPPED BY MADMEN FROM THE FUTURE...I CAN HANDLE A DARK TUNNEL.
AND DON'T FORGET...YOU'RE NOT THE ONLY STAR OF THIS QUEST.
I NEED TO DO RESEARCH ON THE NEW FORCES, TOO. FIND OUT HOW I CAN USE MY KNOWLEDGE OF OUR PAST LIFE TO HELP YOU MASTER--
WHOA.
...I WISH I KNEW MORE.
WHOA IS RIGHT. WHEN I FIRST CAME HERE, KING SOLOVAR SHOWED ME SOMETHING LIKE THIS. THE LEGEND OF THE LIGHT AND THE MESSENGER.
THEY'D BEEN STUDYING THE SPEED FORCE FOR GENERATIONS BEFORE THAT LIGHTNING BOLT HIT MY LAB. IT'S WHAT GRODD USED TO CREATE THE SPEED FORCE STORM AND...
WHEN GRODD TRIED TO TAKE OVER CENTRAL CITY WITH BLACK HOLE...GODSPEED SAW THAT THERE WAS MORE TO THE GORILLAS' CONNECTION TO THE SPEED FORCE THAN I EVER THOUGHT...
WHAT HAPPENED TO KING SOLOVAR AFTER--
SKTTK...

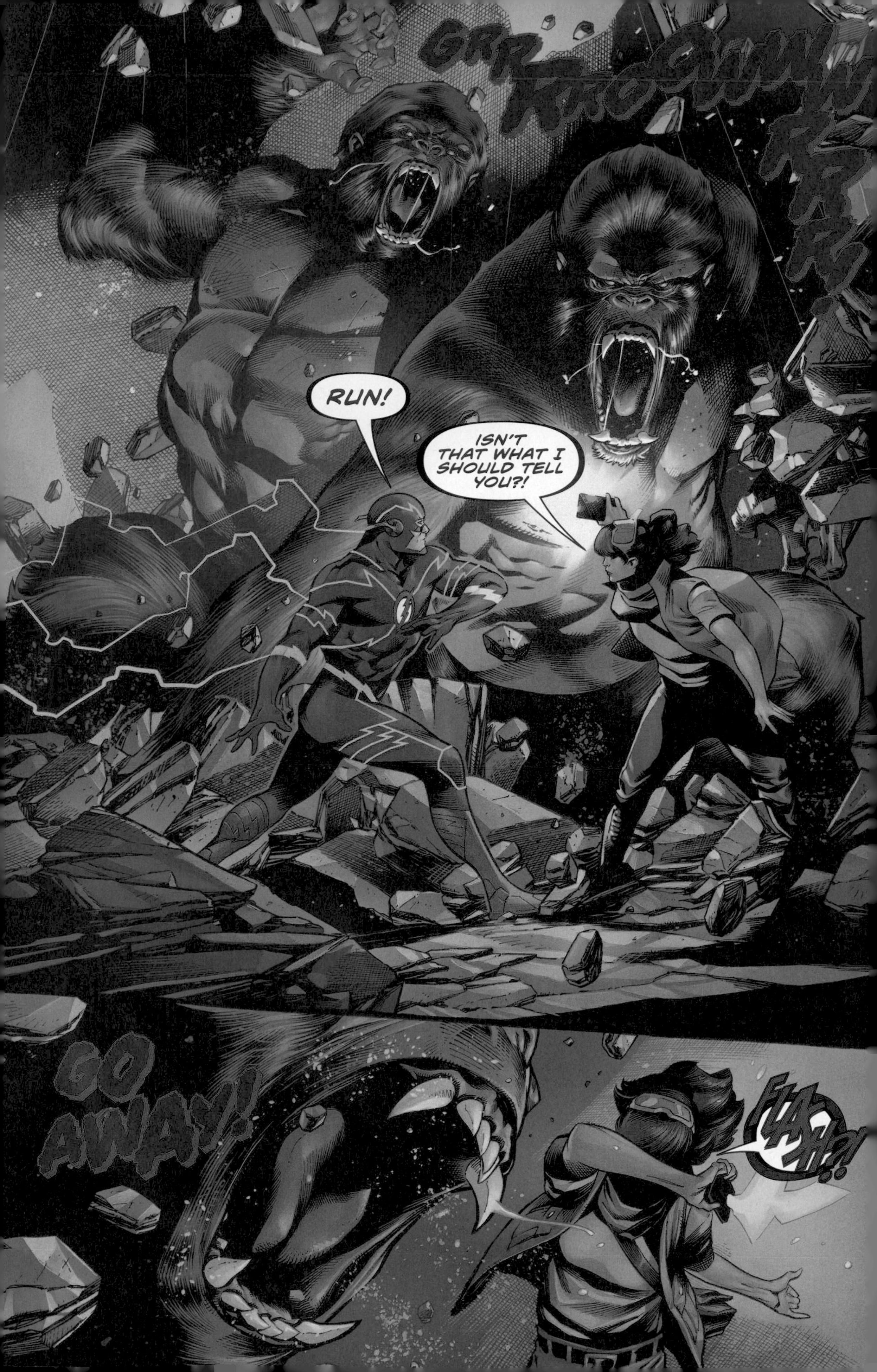
GRR
RUN!
ISN'T THAT WHAT I SHOULD TELL YOU?!
GO AWAY!
FLASH?!

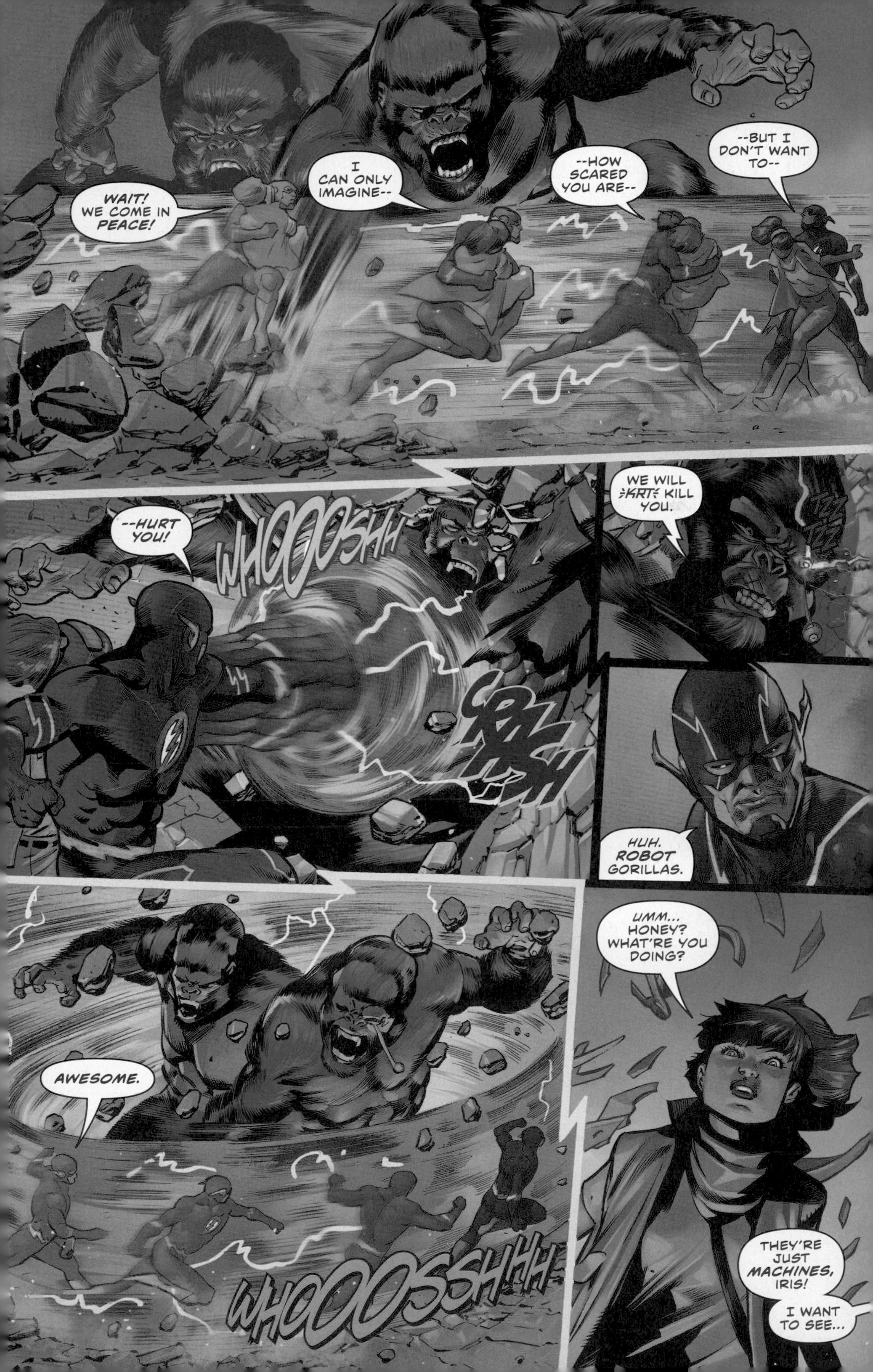
WAIT! WE COME IN PEACE!
I CAN ONLY IMAGINE--
--HOW SCARED YOU ARE--
--BUT I DON'T WANT TO--
--HURT YOU!
WHOOOSHH
CRUNCH
WE WILL KRT KILL YOU.
TZZ TZZ
HUH. ROBOT GORILLAS.
AWESOME.
WHOOOOSSHHH
UMM... HONEY? WHAT'RE YOU DOING?
THEY'RE JUST MACHINES, IRIS!
I WANT TO SEE...

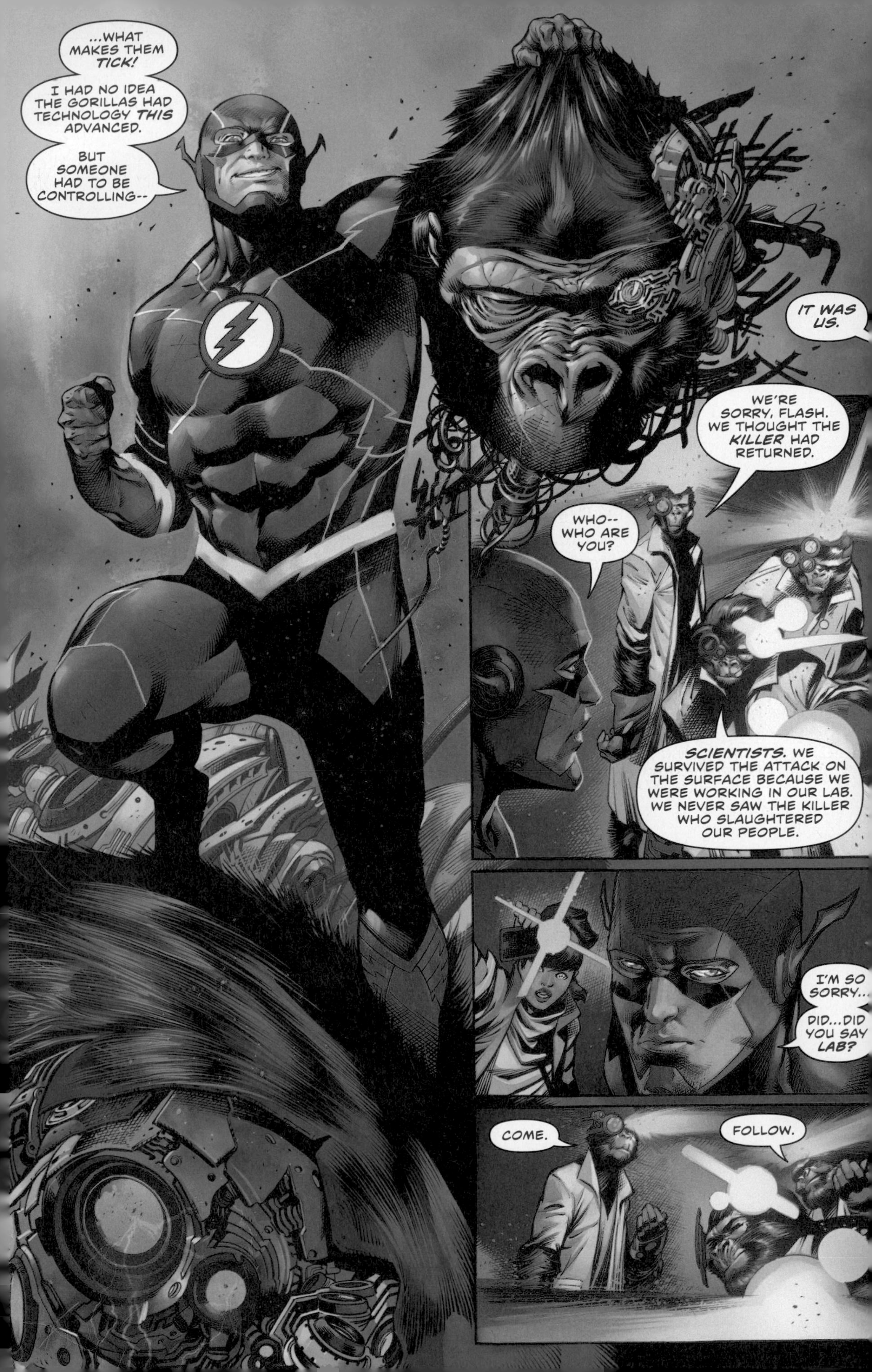
...WHAT MAKES THEM TICK!
I HAD NO IDEA THE GORILLAS HAD TECHNOLOGY THIS ADVANCED.
BUT SOMEONE HAD TO BE CONTROLLING--
IT WAS US.
WE'RE SORRY, FLASH. WE THOUGHT THE KILLER HAD RETURNED.
WHO-- WHO ARE YOU?
SCIENTISTS. WE SURVIVED THE ATTACK ON THE SURFACE BECAUSE WE WERE WORKING IN OUR LAB. WE NEVER SAW THE KILLER WHO SLAUGHTERED OUR PEOPLE.
I'M SO SORRY...
DID...DID YOU SAY LAB?
COME.
FOLLOW.

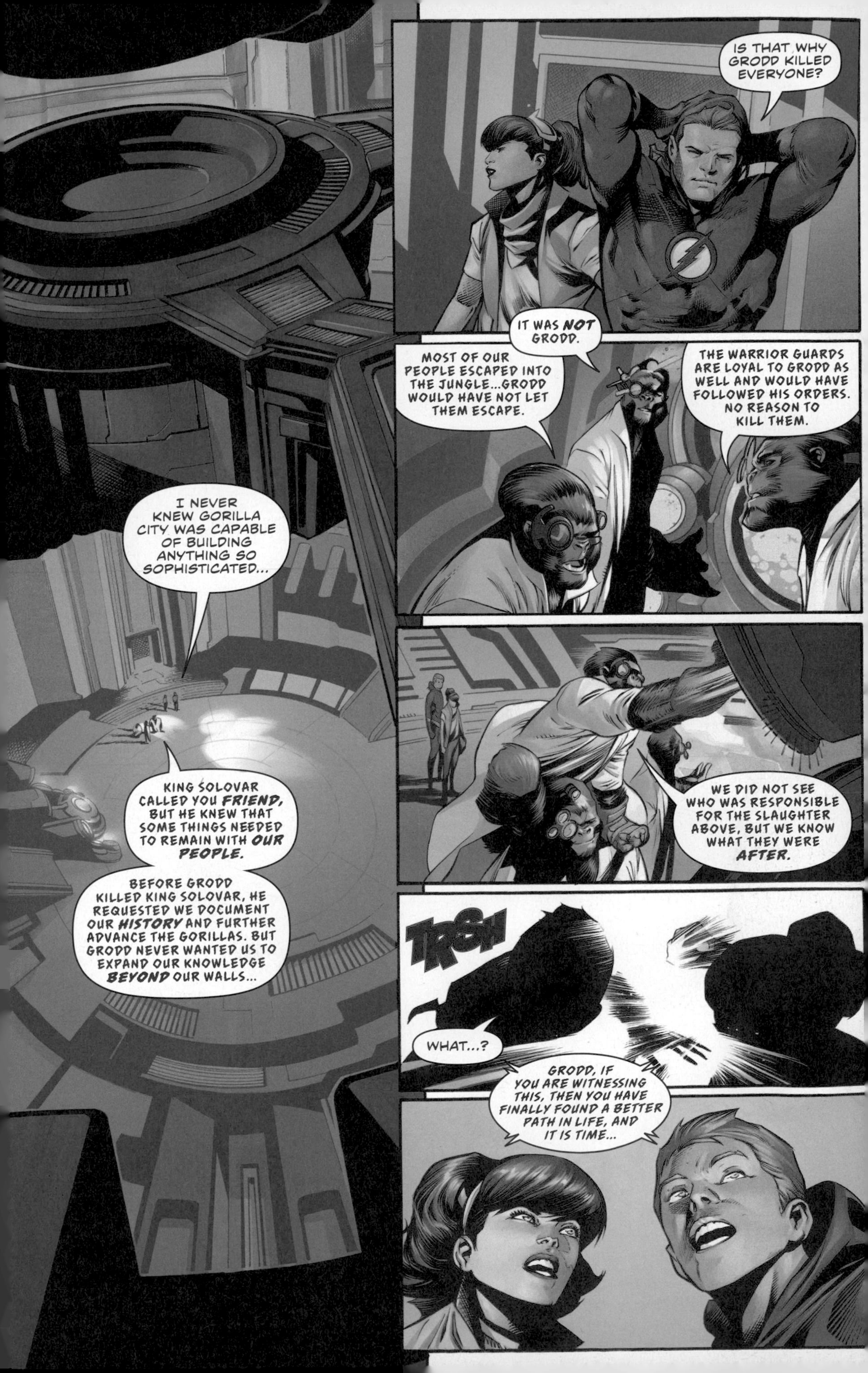
I NEVER KNEW GORILLA CITY WAS CAPABLE OF BUILDING ANYTHING SO SOPHISTICATED...
KING SOLOVAR CALLED YOU FRIEND, BUT HE KNEW THAT SOME THINGS NEEDED TO REMAIN WITH OUR PEOPLE.
BEFORE GRODD KILLED KING SOLOVAR, HE REQUESTED WE DOCUMENT OUR HISTORY AND FURTHER ADVANCE THE GORILLAS. BUT GRODD NEVER WANTED US TO EXPAND OUR KNOWLEDGE BEYOND OUR WALLS...
IS THAT WHY GRODD KILLED EVERYONE?
IT WAS NOT GRODD.
MOST OF OUR PEOPLE ESCAPED INTO THE JUNGLE...GRODD WOULD HAVE NOT LET THEM ESCAPE.
THE WARRIOR GUARDS ARE LOYAL TO GRODD AS WELL AND WOULD HAVE FOLLOWED HIS ORDERS. NO REASON TO KILL THEM.
WE DID NOT SEE WHO WAS RESPONSIBLE FOR THE SLAUGHTER ABOVE, BUT WE KNOW WHAT THEY WERE AFTER.
TRSH
WHAT...?
GRODD, IF YOU ARE WITNESSING THIS, THEN YOU HAVE FINALLY FOUND A BETTER PATH IN LIFE, AND IT IS TIME...

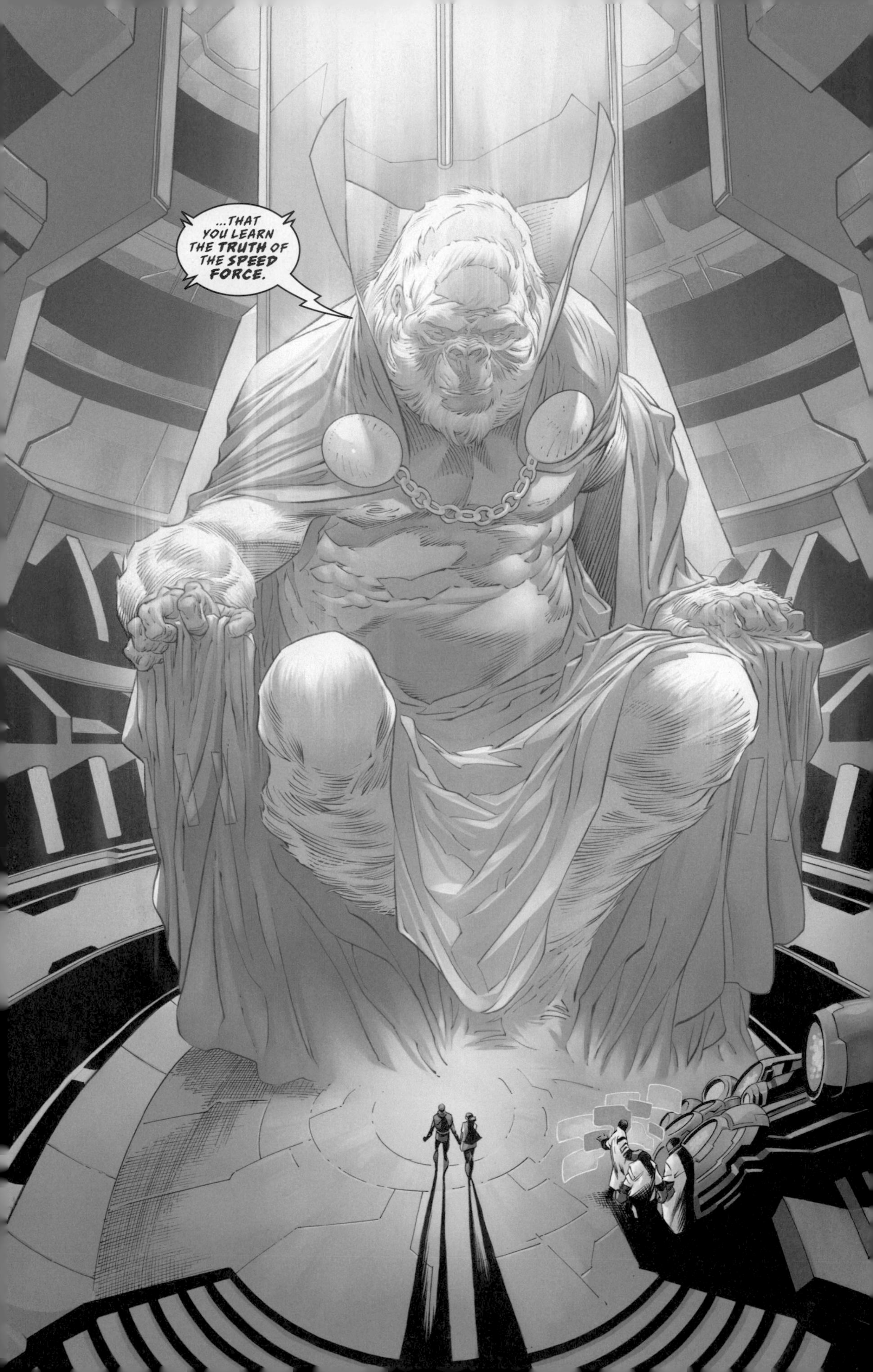
...THAT YOU LEARN THE TRUTH OF THE SPEED FORCE.

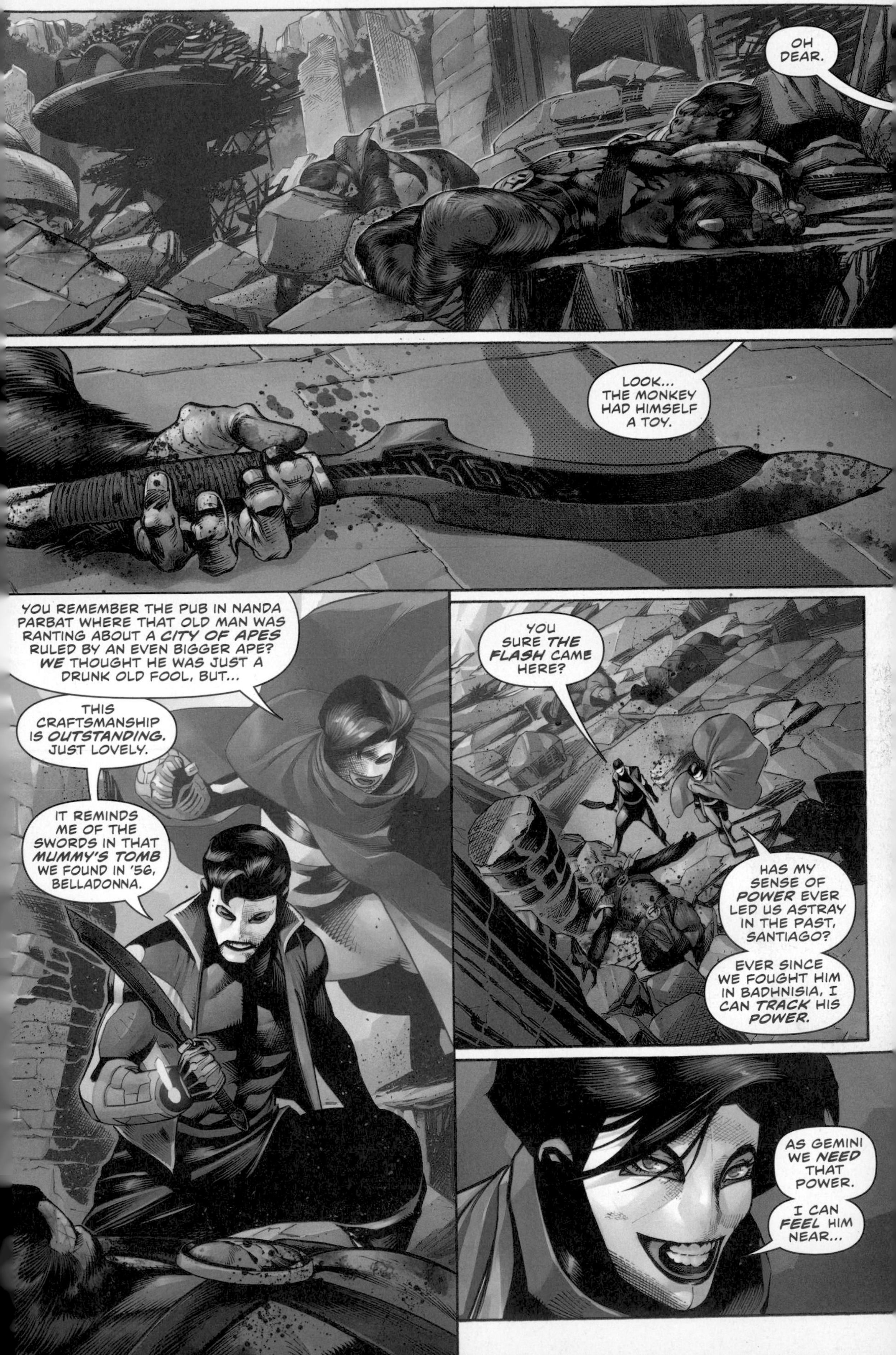
OH DEAR.
LOOK... THE MONKEY HAD HIMSELF A TOY.
YOU REMEMBER THE PUB IN NANDA PARBAT WHERE THAT OLD MAN WAS RANTING ABOUT A *CITY OF APES* RULED BY AN EVEN BIGGER APE? *WE* THOUGHT HE WAS JUST A DRUNK OLD FOOL, BUT...
THIS CRAFTSMANSHIP IS *OUTSTANDING.* JUST LOVELY.
IT REMINDS ME OF THE SWORDS IN THAT *MUMMY'S TOMB* WE FOUND IN '56, BELLADONNA.
YOU SURE *THE FLASH* CAME HERE?
HAS MY SENSE OF *POWER* EVER LED US ASTRAY IN THE PAST, SANTIAGO?
EVER SINCE WE FOUGHT HIM IN BADHNISIA, I CAN *TRACK* HIS *POWER.*
AS GEMINI WE *NEED* THAT POWER.
I CAN *FEEL* HIM NEAR...

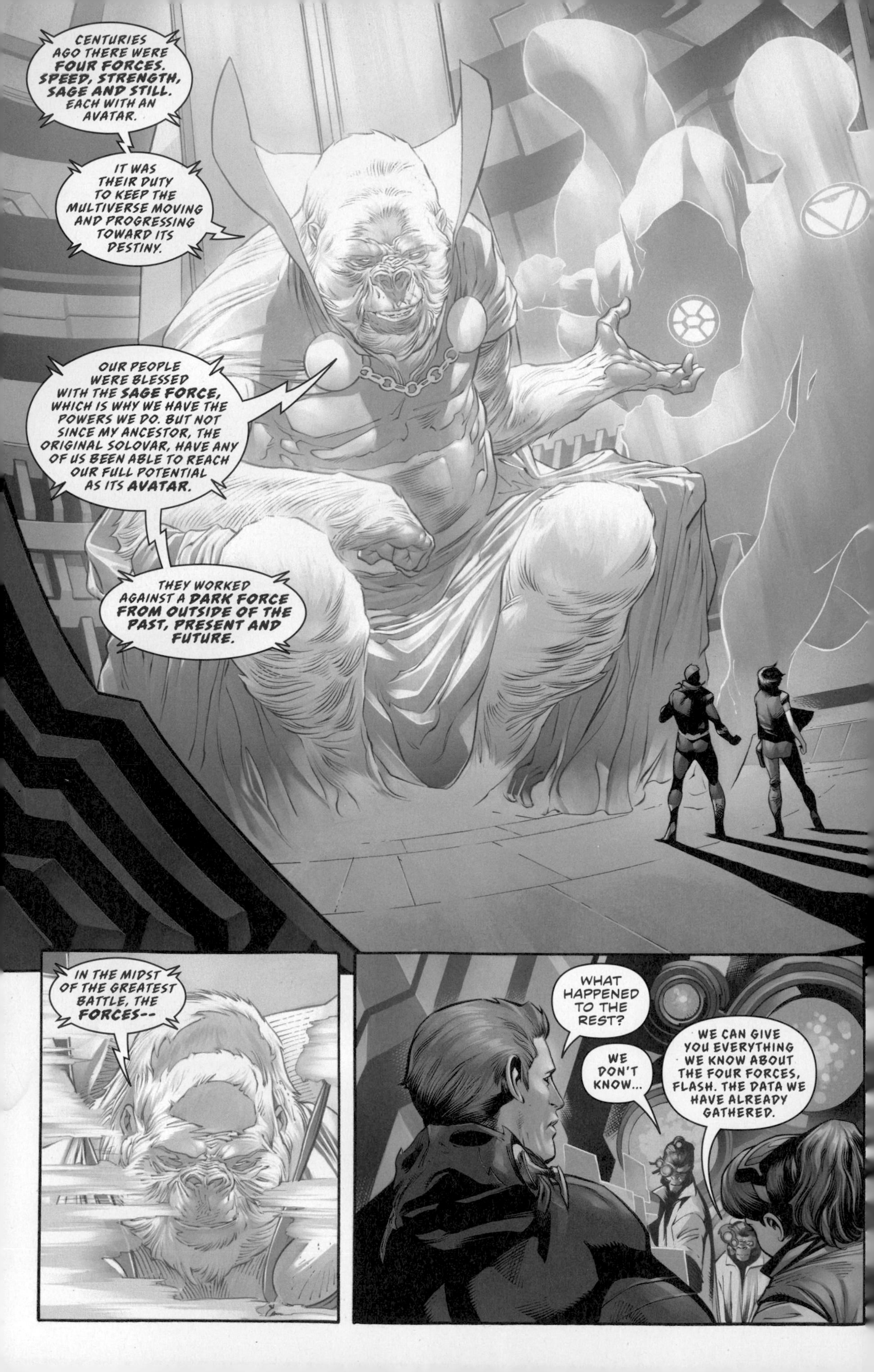

CENTURIES AGO THERE WERE FOUR FORCES. SPEED, STRENGTH, SAGE AND STILL. EACH WITH AN AVATAR.
IT WAS THEIR DUTY TO KEEP THE MULTIVERSE MOVING AND PROGRESSING TOWARD ITS DESTINY.
OUR PEOPLE WERE BLESSED WITH THE SAGE FORCE, WHICH IS WHY WE HAVE THE POWERS WE DO. BUT NOT SINCE MY ANCESTOR, THE ORIGINAL SOLOVAR, HAVE ANY OF US BEEN ABLE TO REACH OUR FULL POTENTIAL AS ITS AVATAR.
THEY WORKED AGAINST A DARK FORCE FROM OUTSIDE OF THE PAST, PRESENT AND FUTURE.
IN THE MIDST OF THE GREATEST BATTLE, THE FORCES--
WHAT HAPPENED TO THE REST?
WE DON'T KNOW...
WE CAN GIVE YOU EVERYTHING WE KNOW ABOUT THE FOUR FORCES, FLASH. THE DATA WE HAVE ALREADY GATHERED.

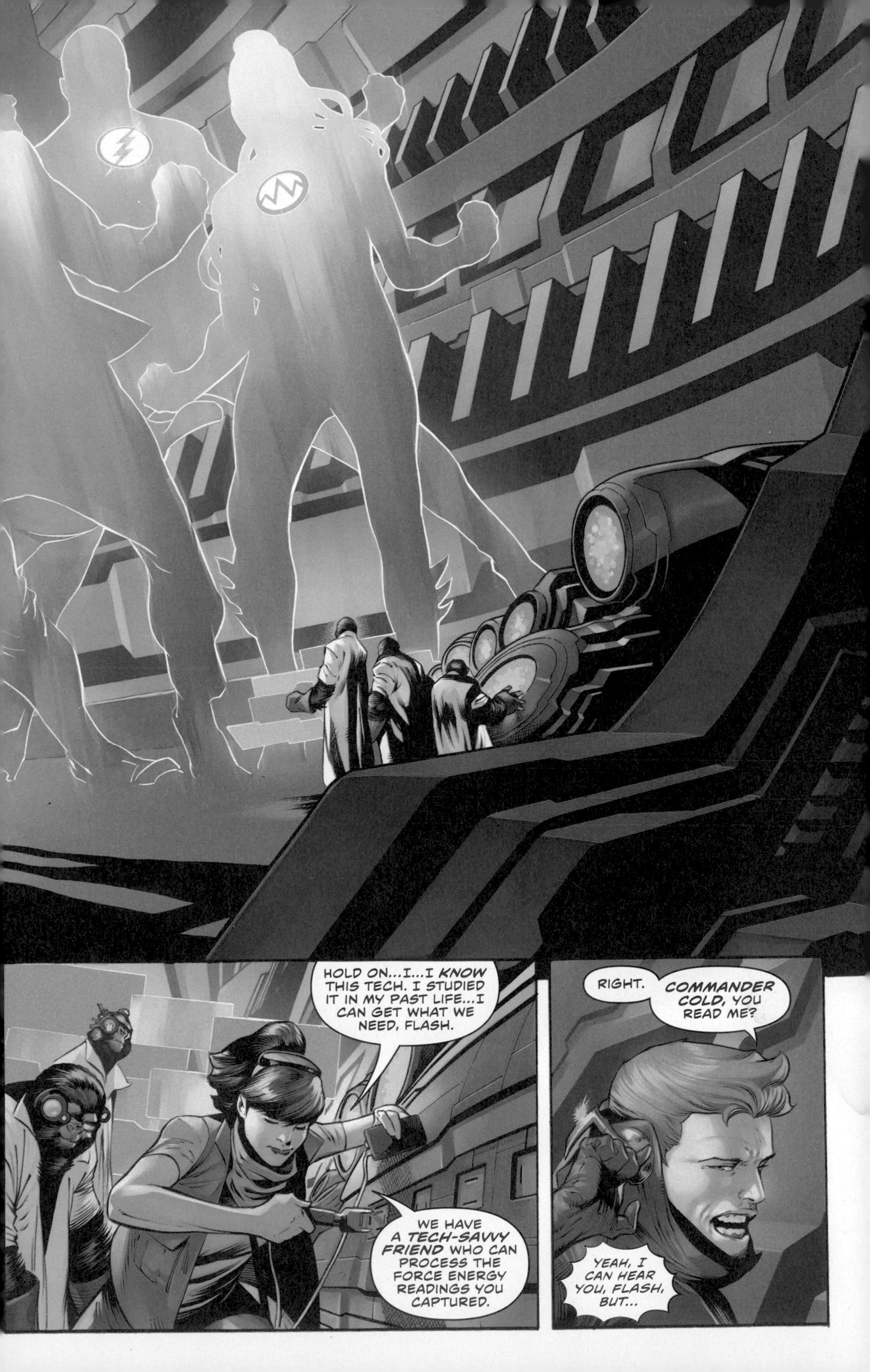
HOLD ON...I...I KNOW THIS TECH. I STUDIED IT IN MY PAST LIFE...I CAN GET WHAT WE NEED, FLASH.
WE HAVE A TECH-SAVVY FRIEND WHO CAN PROCESS THE FORCE ENERGY READINGS YOU CAPTURED.
RIGHT.
COMMANDER COLD, YOU READ ME?
YEAH, I CAN HEAR YOU, FLASH, BUT...

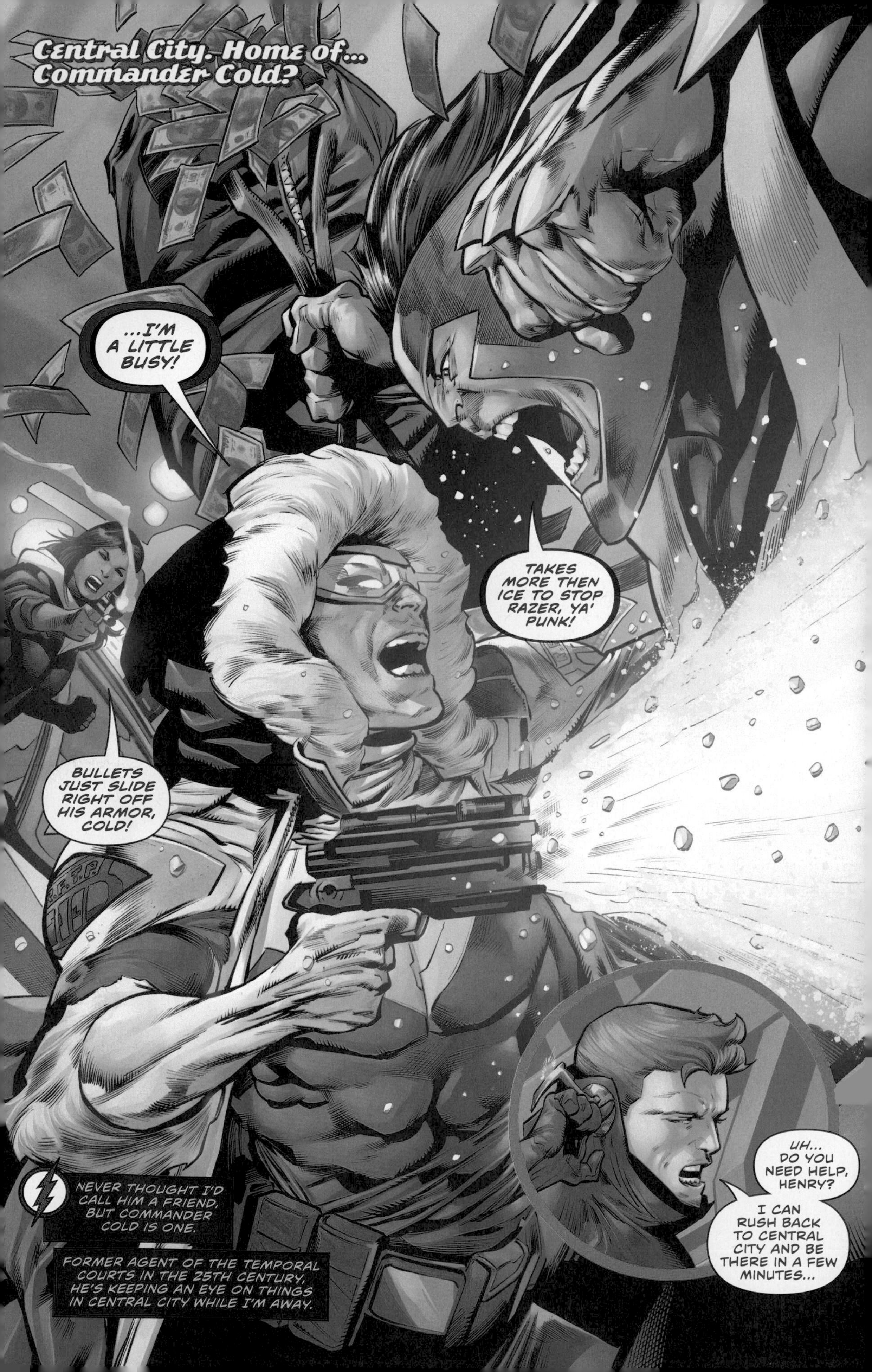
Central City. Home of... Commander Cold?
...I'M A LITTLE BUSY!
TAKES MORE THEN ICE TO STOP RAZER, YA' PUNK!
BULLETS JUST SLIDE RIGHT OFF HIS ARMOR, COLD!
NEVER THOUGHT I'D CALL HIM A FRIEND, BUT COMMANDER COLD IS ONE.
FORMER AGENT OF THE TEMPORAL COURTS IN THE 25TH CENTURY, HE'S KEEPING AN EYE ON THINGS IN CENTRAL CITY WHILE I'M AWAY.
UH... DO YOU NEED HELP, HENRY?
I CAN RUSH BACK TO CENTRAL CITY AND BE THERE IN A FEW MINUTES...

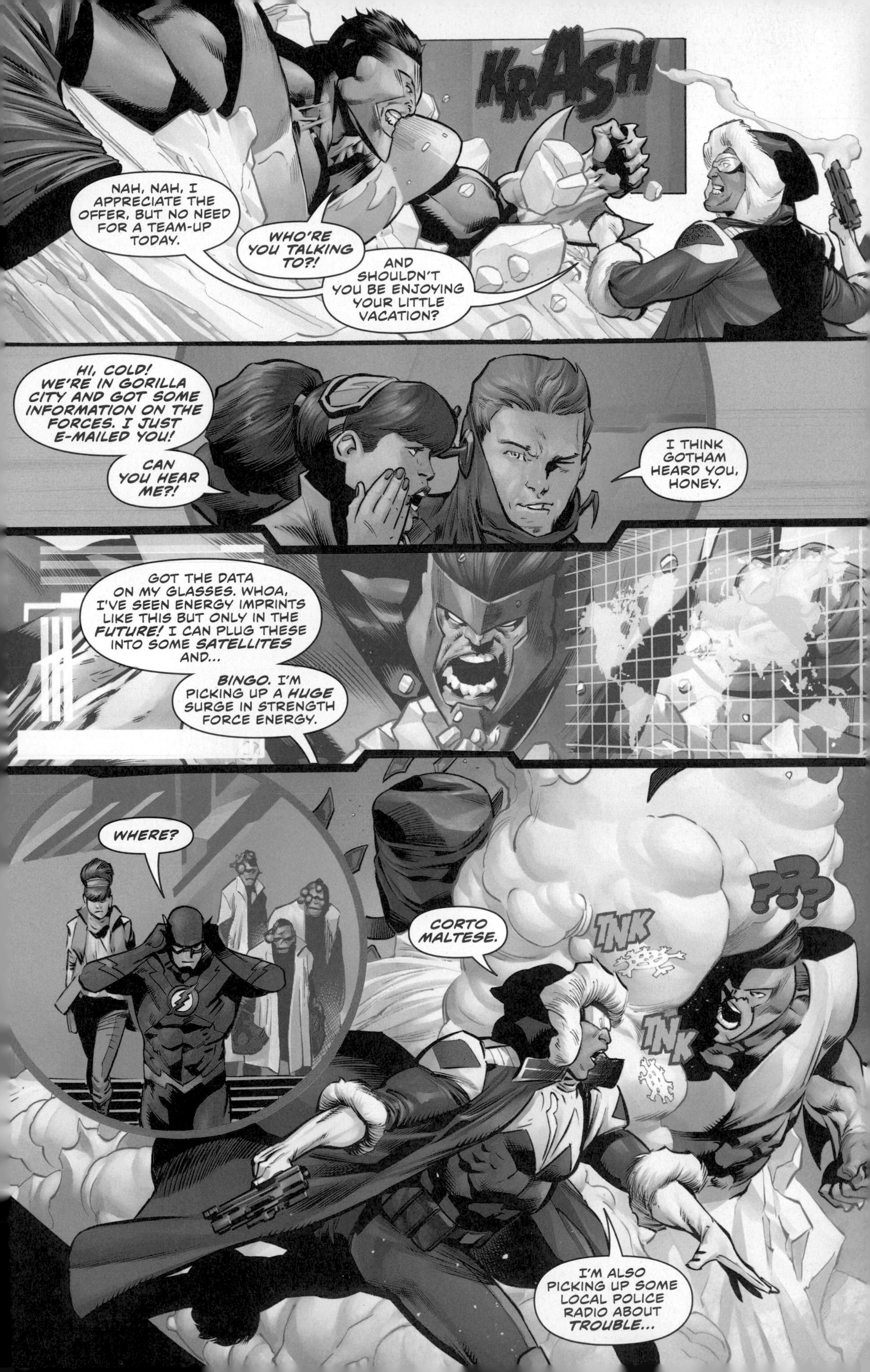
KRASH
NAH, NAH, I APPRECIATE THE OFFER, BUT NO NEED FOR A TEAM-UP TODAY.
WHO'RE YOU TALKING TO?!
AND SHOULDN'T YOU BE ENJOYING YOUR LITTLE VACATION?
HI, COLD! WE'RE IN GORILLA CITY AND GOT SOME INFORMATION ON THE FORCES. I JUST E-MAILED YOU!
CAN YOU HEAR ME?!
I THINK GOTHAM HEARD YOU, HONEY.
GOT THE DATA ON MY GLASSES. WHOA, I'VE SEEN ENERGY IMPRINTS LIKE THIS BUT ONLY IN THE FUTURE! I CAN PLUG THESE INTO SOME SATELLITES AND...
BINGO. I'M PICKING UP A HUGE SURGE IN STRENGTH FORCE ENERGY.
WHERE?
CORTO MALTESE.
TNK
TNK
???
I'M ALSO PICKING UP SOME LOCAL POLICE RADIO ABOUT TROUBLE...

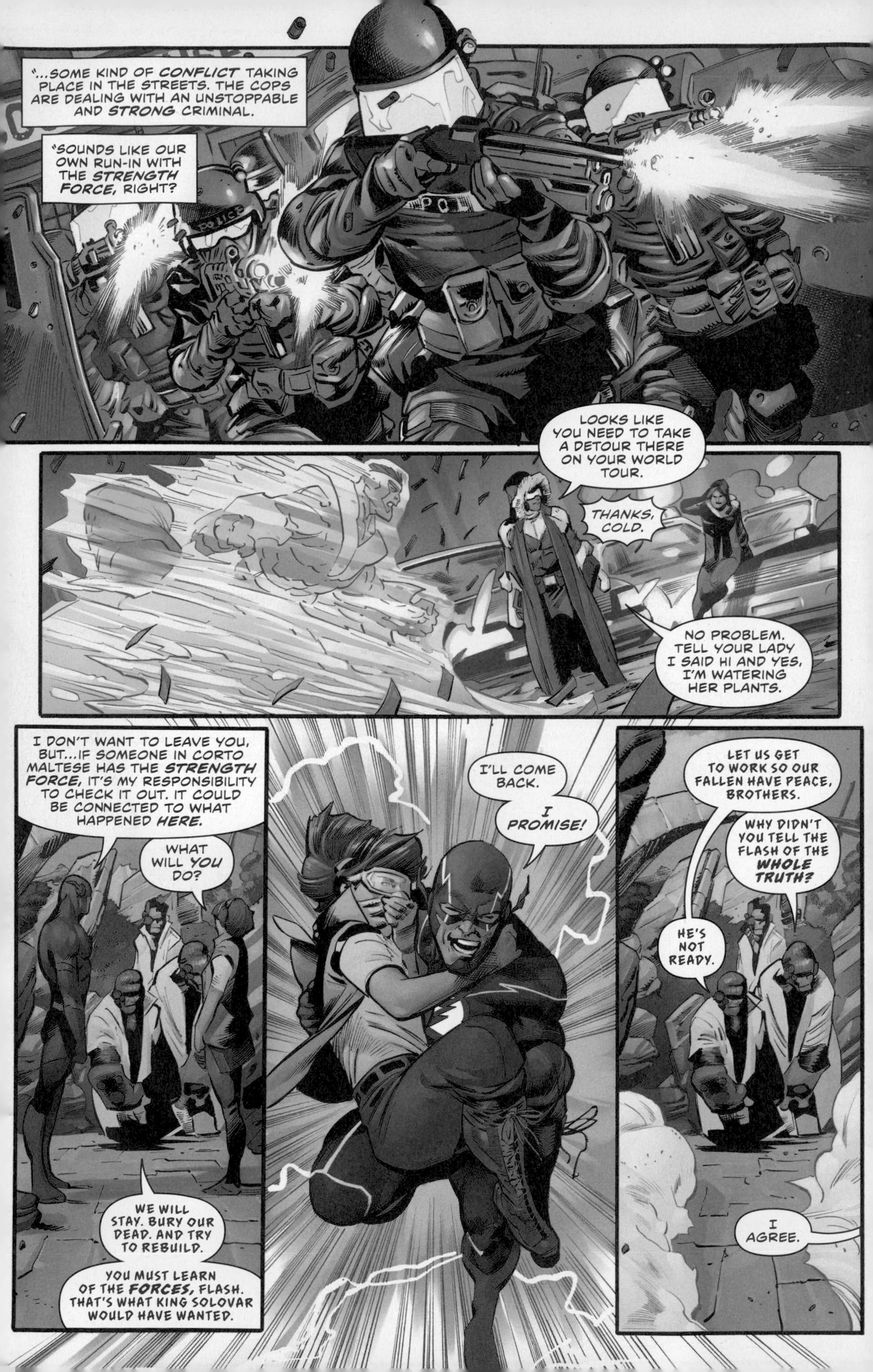
"...SOME KIND OF CONFLICT TAKING PLACE IN THE STREETS. THE COPS ARE DEALING WITH AN UNSTOPPABLE AND STRONG CRIMINAL.
"SOUNDS LIKE OUR OWN RUN-IN WITH THE STRENGTH FORCE, RIGHT?
LOOKS LIKE YOU NEED TO TAKE A DETOUR THERE ON YOUR WORLD TOUR.
THANKS, COLD.
NO PROBLEM. TELL YOUR LADY I SAID HI AND YES, I'M WATERING HER PLANTS.
I DON'T WANT TO LEAVE YOU, BUT...IF SOMEONE IN CORTO MALTESE HAS THE STRENGTH FORCE, IT'S MY RESPONSIBILITY TO CHECK IT OUT. IT COULD BE CONNECTED TO WHAT HAPPENED HERE.
WHAT WILL YOU DO?
WE WILL STAY. BURY OUR DEAD. AND TRY TO REBUILD.
YOU MUST LEARN OF THE FORCES, FLASH. THAT'S WHAT KING SOLOVAR WOULD HAVE WANTED.
I'LL COME BACK.
I PROMISE!
LET US GET TO WORK SO OUR FALLEN HAVE PEACE, BROTHERS.
WHY DIDN'T YOU TELL THE FLASH OF THE WHOLE TRUTH?
HE'S NOT READY.
I AGREE.

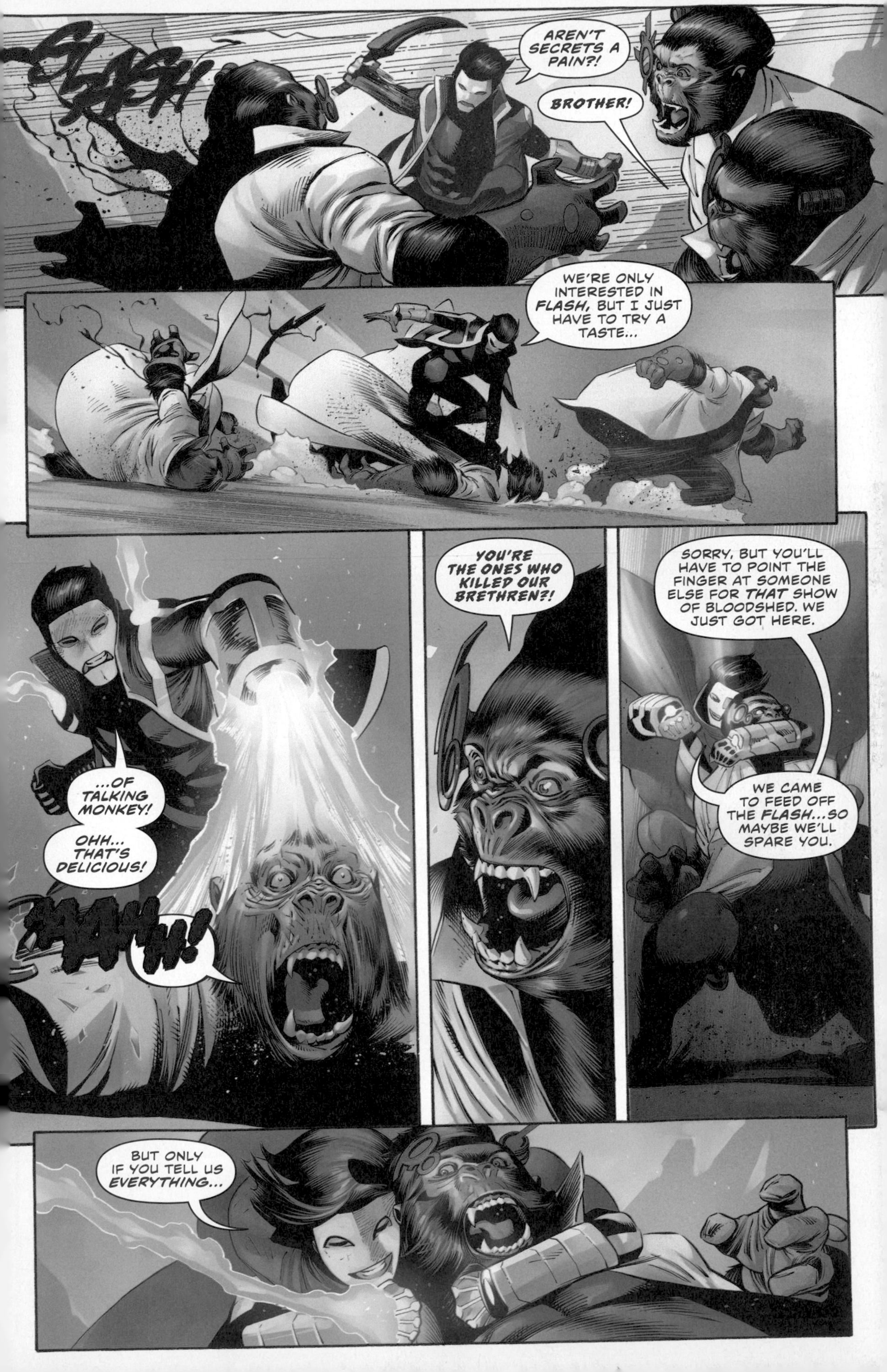
AREN'T SECRETS A PAIN?!
BROTHER!
WE'RE ONLY INTERESTED IN FLASH, BUT I JUST HAVE TO TRY A TASTE...
...OF TALKING MONKEY!
OHH... THAT'S DELICIOUS!
YOU'RE THE ONES WHO KILLED OUR BRETHREN?!
SORRY, BUT YOU'LL HAVE TO POINT THE FINGER AT SOMEONE ELSE FOR THAT SHOW OF BLOODSHED. WE JUST GOT HERE.
WE CAME TO FEED OFF THE FLASH...SO MAYBE WE'LL SPARE YOU.
BUT ONLY IF YOU TELL US EVERYTHING...

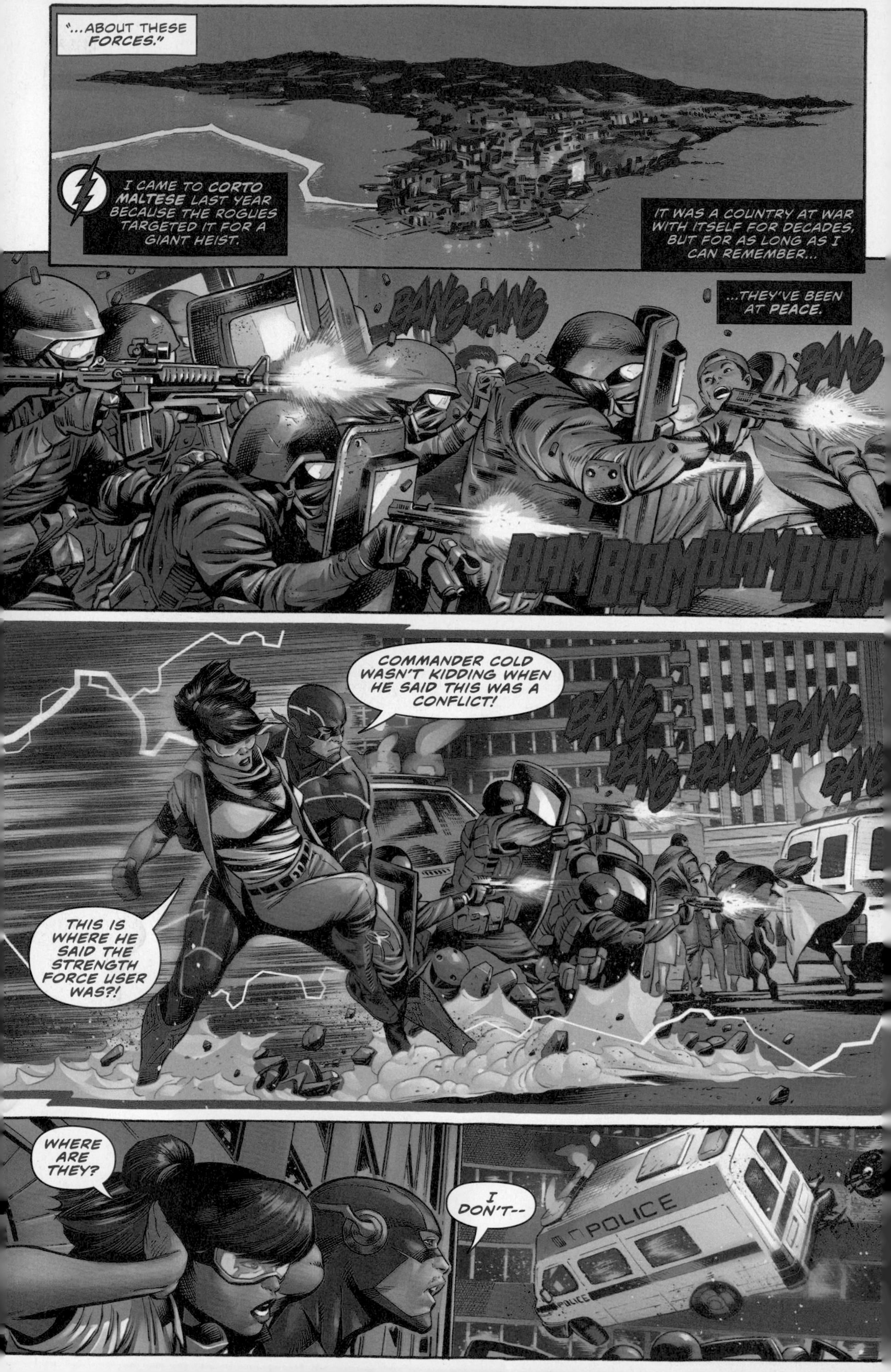
"...ABOUT THESE FORCES."
I CAME TO CORTO MALTESE LAST YEAR BECAUSE THE ROGUES TARGETED IT FOR A GIANT HEIST.
IT WAS A COUNTRY AT WAR WITH ITSELF FOR DECADES, BUT FOR AS LONG AS I CAN REMEMBER...
BANG BANG
...THEY'VE BEEN AT PEACE.
BANG
BLAM BLAM BLAM BLAM
COMMANDER COLD WASN'T KIDDING WHEN HE SAID THIS WAS A CONFLICT!
BANG BANG BANG BANG BANG
THIS IS WHERE HE SAID THE STRENGTH FORCE USER WAS?!
WHERE ARE THEY?
I DON'T--
POLICE

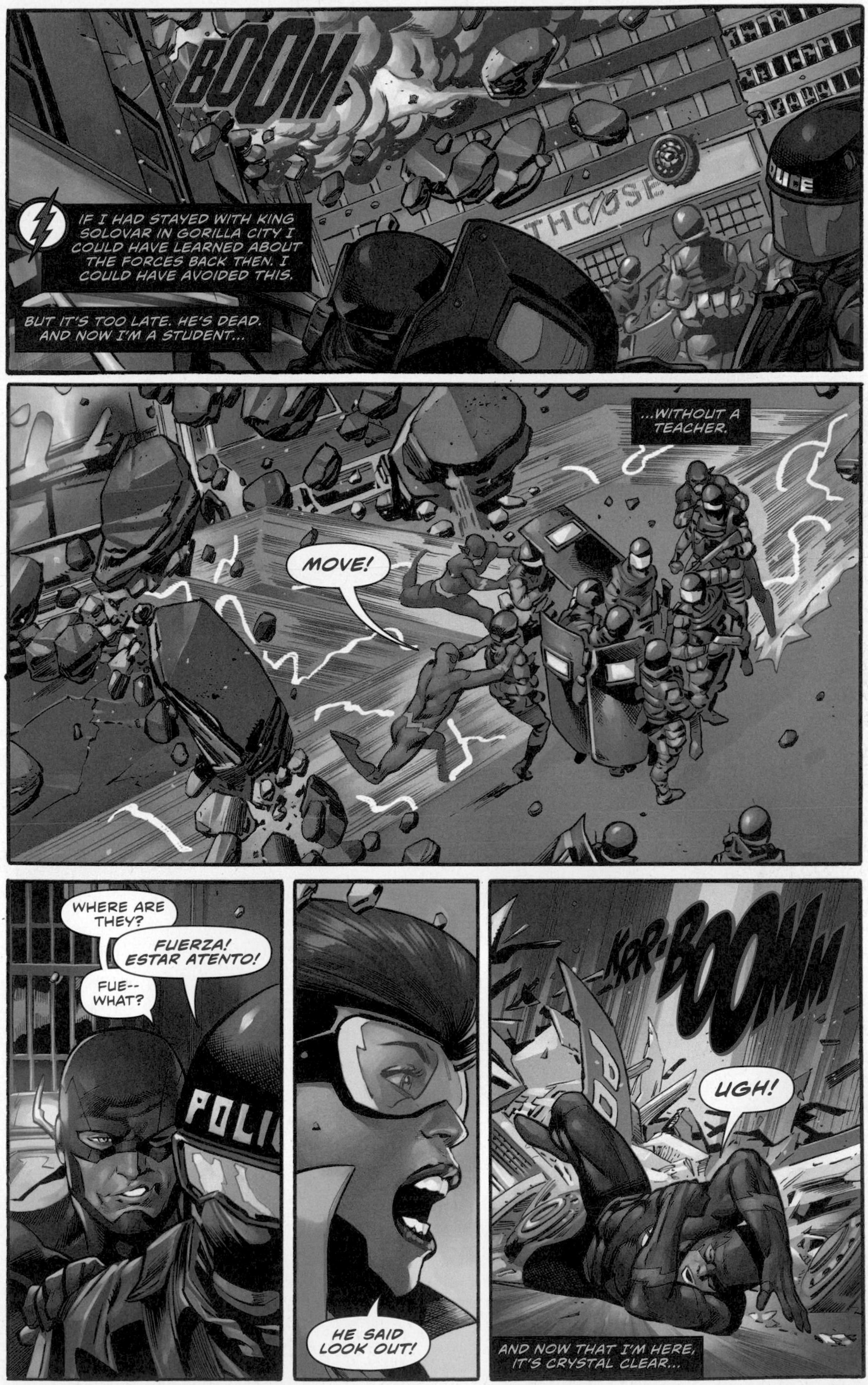
BOOM
IF I HAD STAYED WITH KING SOLOVAR IN GORILLA CITY I COULD HAVE LEARNED ABOUT THE FORCES BACK THEN. I COULD HAVE AVOIDED THIS.
BUT IT'S TOO LATE. HE'S DEAD. AND NOW I'M A STUDENT...
...WITHOUT A TEACHER.
MOVE!
WHERE ARE THEY?
FUERZA! ESTAR ATENTO!
FUE-- WHAT?
POLI
HE SAID LOOK OUT!
KRR-BOOMM
UGH!
AND NOW THAT I'M HERE, IT'S CRYSTAL CLEAR...

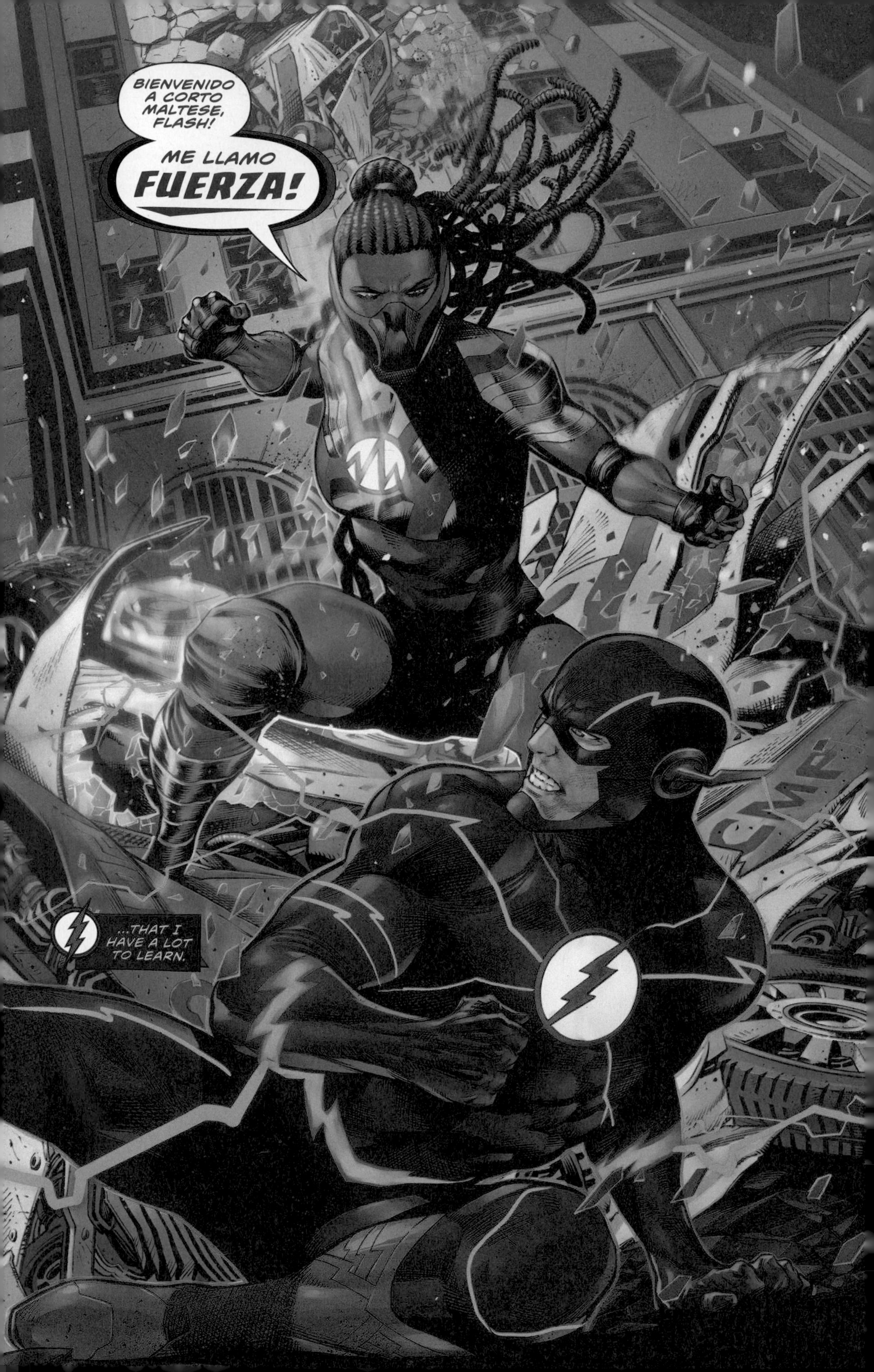
BIENVENIDO A CORTO MALTESE, FLASH!
ME LLAMO FUERZA!
...THAT I HAVE A LOT TO LEARN.

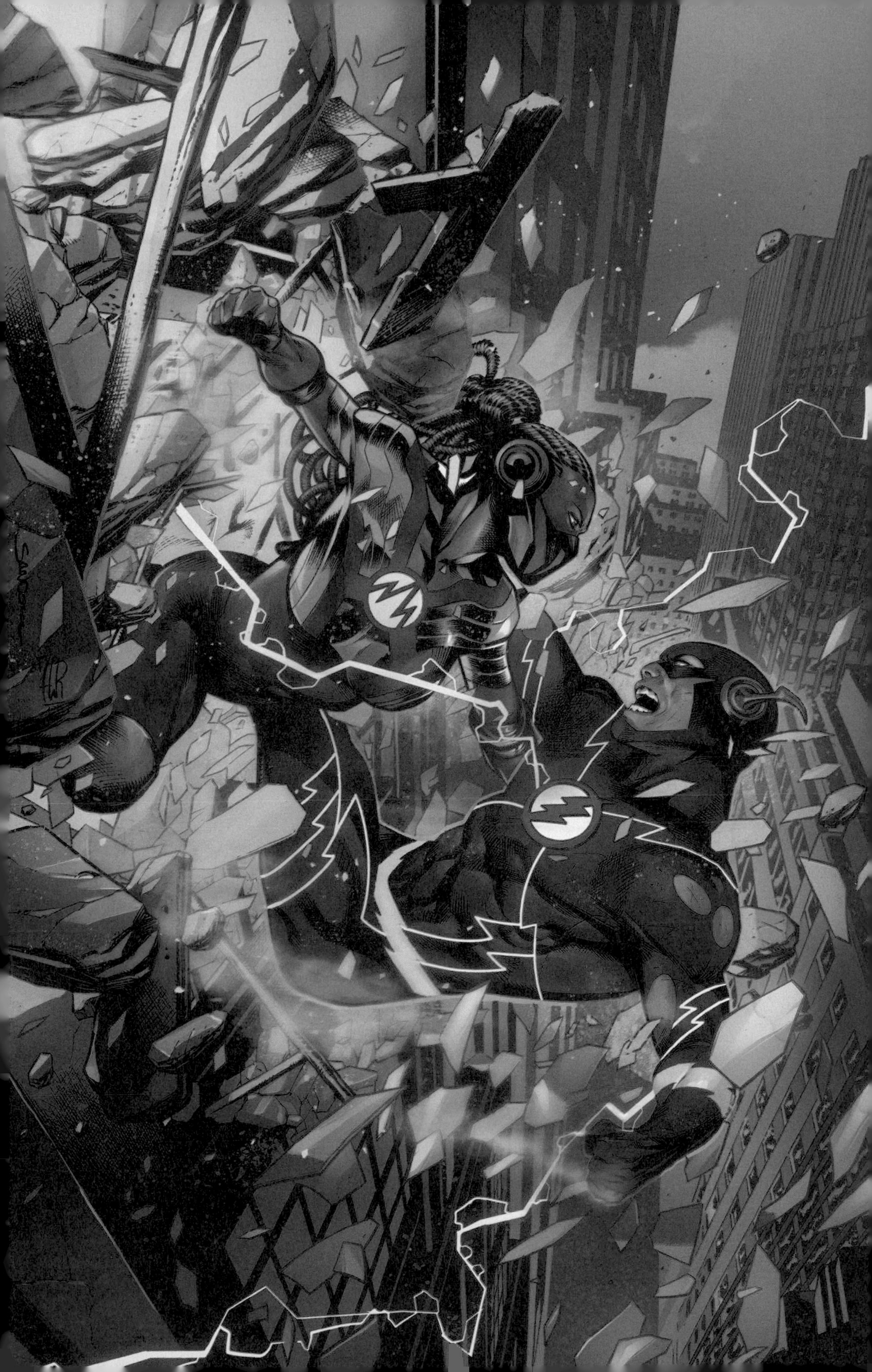

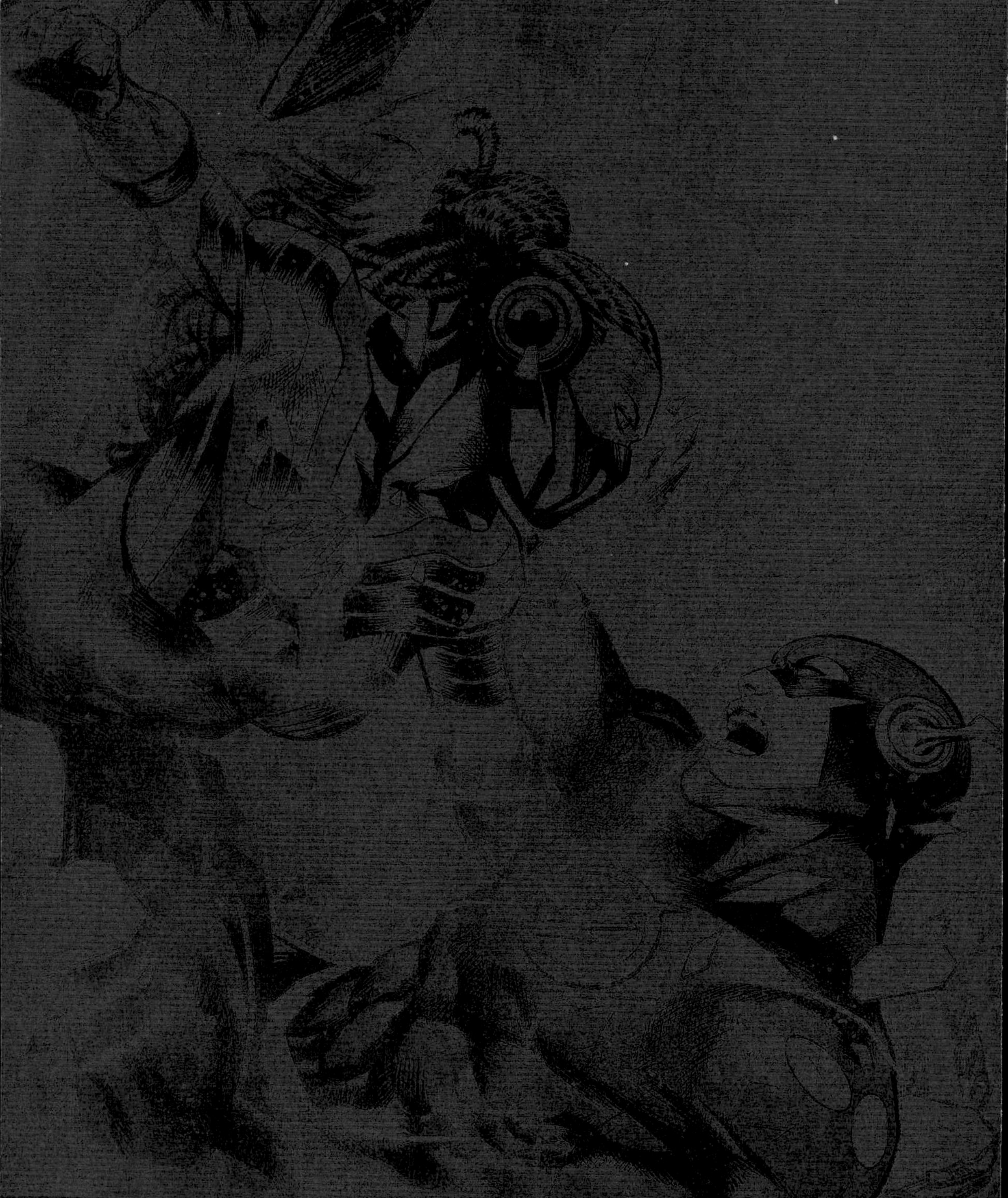

THE FLASH
#60

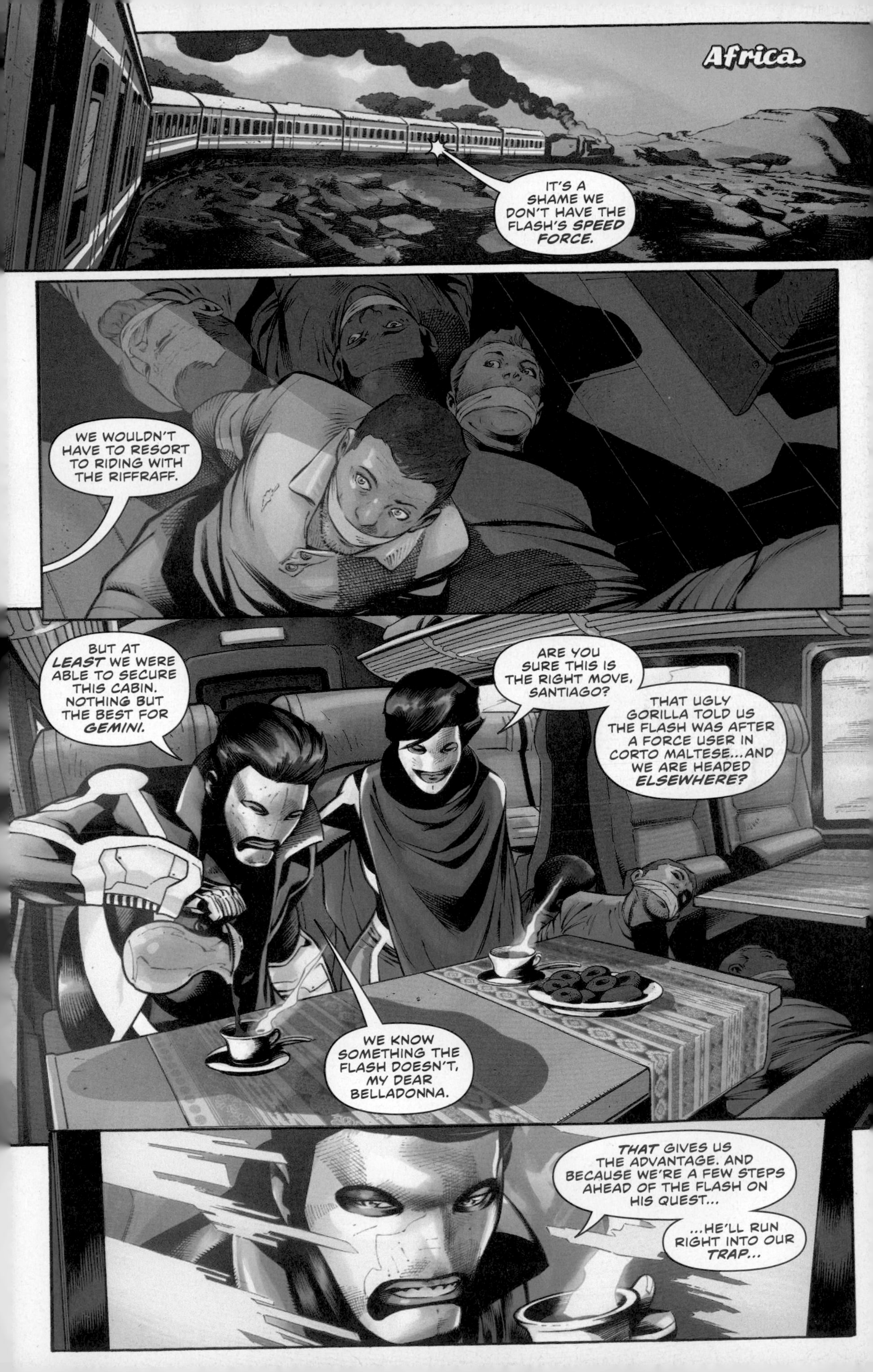
Africa.
IT'S A SHAME WE DON'T HAVE THE FLASH'S SPEED FORCE.
WE WOULDN'T HAVE TO RESORT TO RIDING WITH THE RIFFRAFF.
BUT AT LEAST WE WERE ABLE TO SECURE THIS CABIN. NOTHING BUT THE BEST FOR GEMINI.
ARE YOU SURE THIS IS THE RIGHT MOVE, SANTIAGO?
THAT UGLY GORILLA TOLD US THE FLASH WAS AFTER A FORCE USER IN CORTO MALTESE...AND WE ARE HEADED ELSEWHERE?
WE KNOW SOMETHING THE FLASH DOESN'T, MY DEAR BELLADONNA.
THAT GIVES US THE ADVANTAGE. AND BECAUSE WE'RE A FEW STEPS AHEAD OF THE FLASH ON HIS QUEST...
...HE'LL RUN RIGHT INTO OUR TRAP...

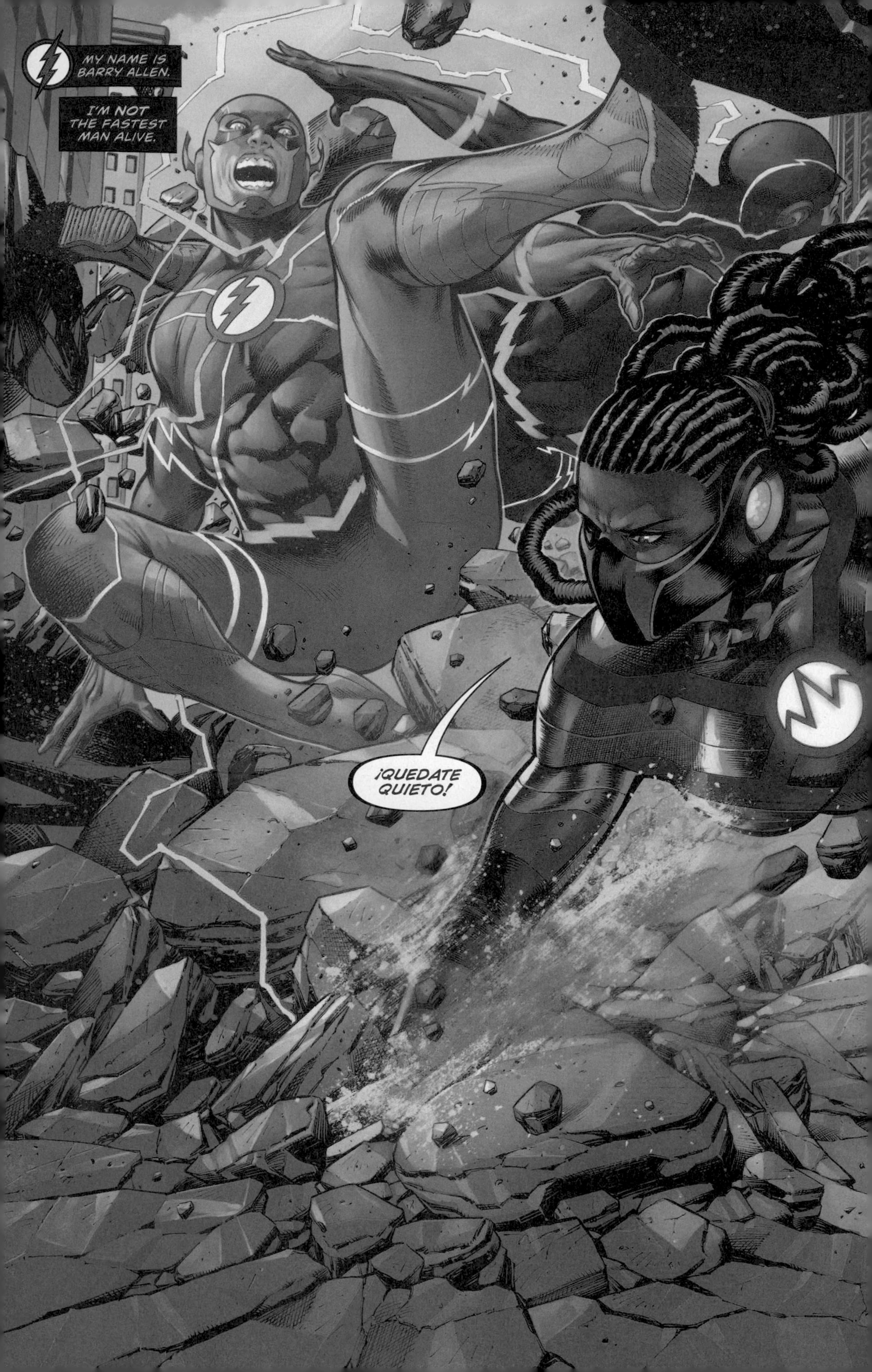
MY NAME IS BARRY ALLEN.
I'M NOT THE FASTEST MAN ALIVE.
¡QUEDATE QUIETO!

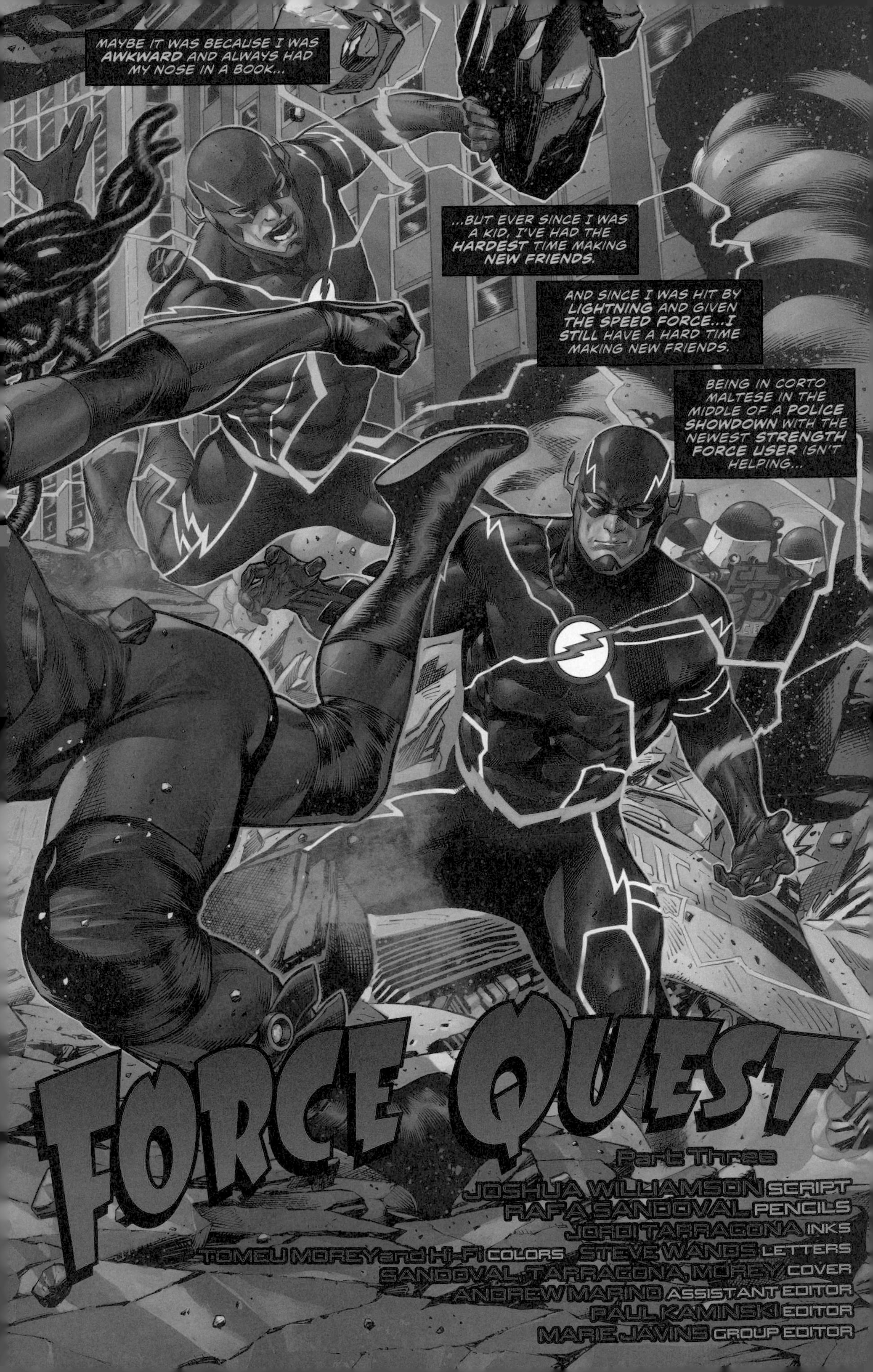
MAYBE IT WAS BECAUSE I WAS AWKWARD AND ALWAYS HAD MY NOSE IN A BOOK...
...BUT EVER SINCE I WAS A KID, I'VE HAD THE HARDEST TIME MAKING NEW FRIENDS.
AND SINCE I WAS HIT BY LIGHTNING AND GIVEN THE SPEED FORCE...I STILL HAVE A HARD TIME MAKING NEW FRIENDS.
BEING IN CORTO MALTESE IN THE MIDDLE OF A POLICE SHOWDOWN WITH THE NEWEST STRENGTH FORCE USER ISN'T HELPING...
FORCE QUEST
Part Three
JOSHUA WILLIAMSON SCRIPT
RAFA SANDOVAL PENCILS
JORDI TARRAGONA INKS
TOMEU MOREY and HI-FI COLORS STEVE WANDS LETTERS
SANDOVAL, TARRAGONA, MOREY COVER
ANDREW MARINO ASSISTANT EDITOR
PAUL KAMINSKI EDITOR
MARIE JAVINS GROUP EDITOR

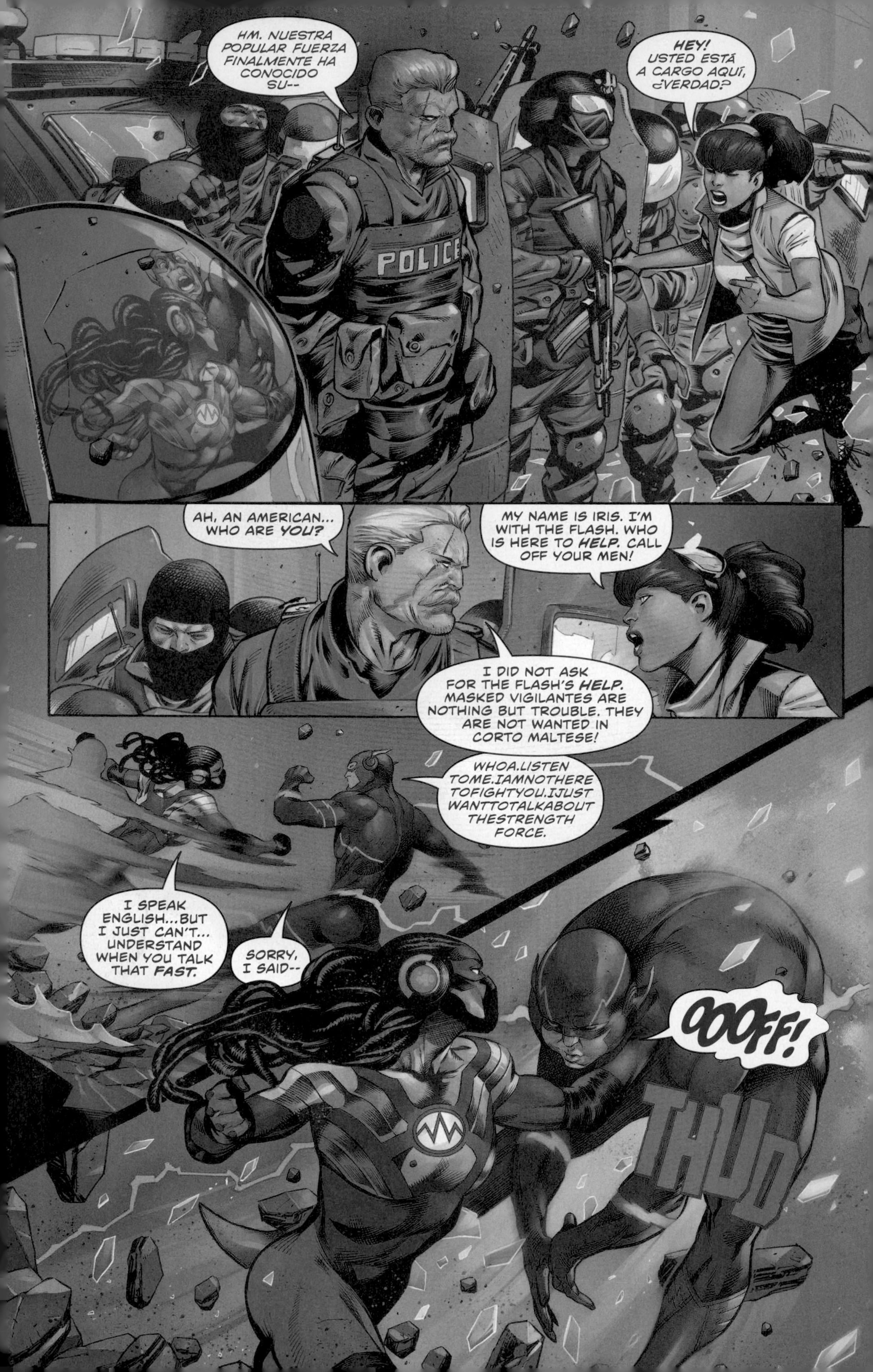
HM. NUESTRA POPULAR FUERZA FINALMENTE HA CONOCIDO SU--
HEY! USTED ESTÁ A CARGO AQUÍ, ¿VERDAD?
POLICE
AH, AN AMERICAN... WHO ARE YOU?
MY NAME IS IRIS. I'M WITH THE FLASH. WHO IS HERE TO HELP. CALL OFF YOUR MEN!
I DID NOT ASK FOR THE FLASH'S HELP. MASKED VIGILANTES ARE NOTHING BUT TROUBLE. THEY ARE NOT WANTED IN CORTO MALTESE!
WHOA.LISTEN TOME.IAMNOTHERE TOFIGHTYOU.IJUST WANTTOTALKABOUT THESTRENGTH FORCE.
I SPEAK ENGLISH...BUT I JUST CAN'T... UNDERSTAND WHEN YOU TALK THAT FAST.
SORRY, I SAID--
OOOFF!
THUD

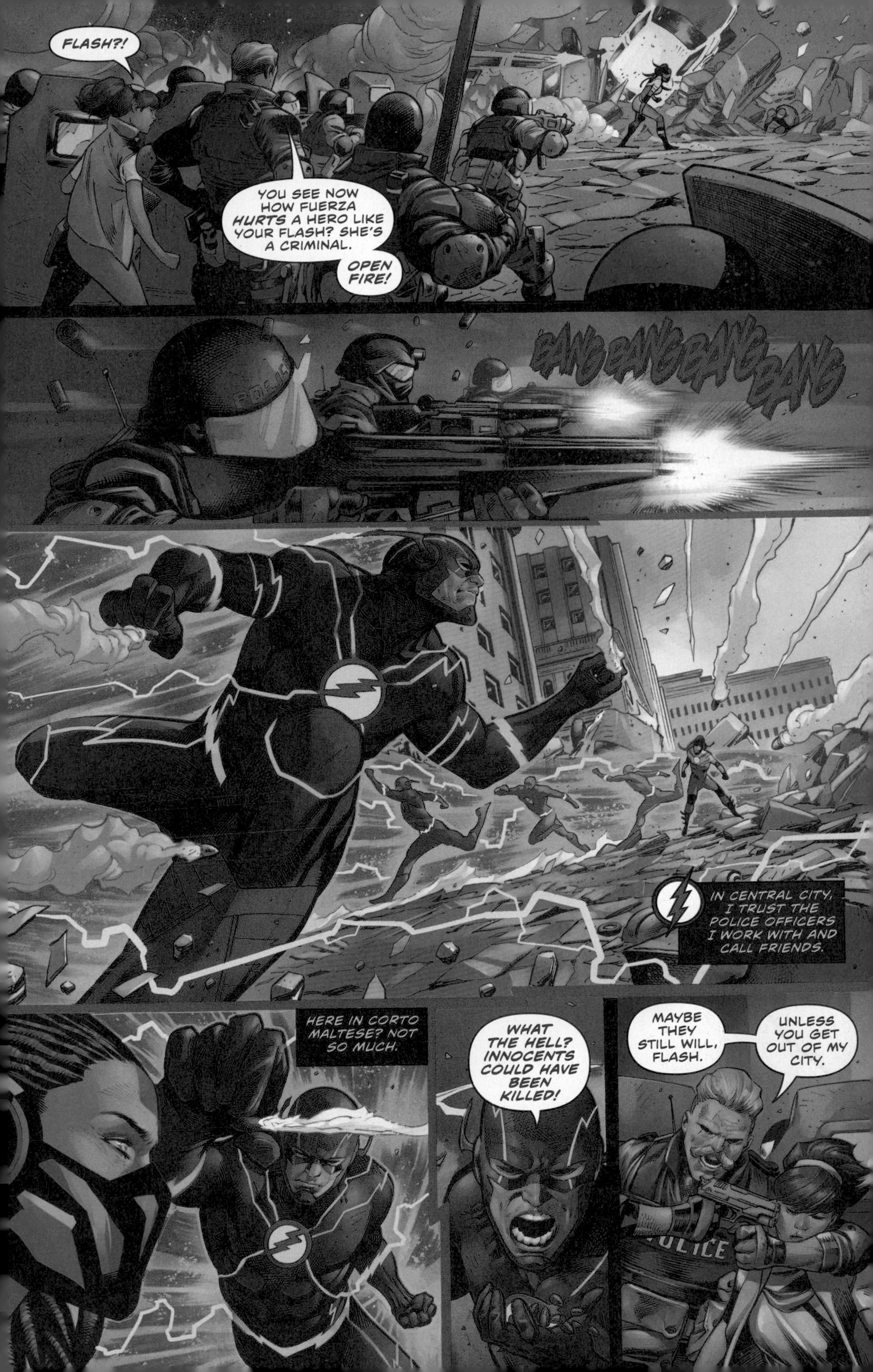
FLASH?!
YOU SEE NOW HOW FUERZA HURTS A HERO LIKE YOUR FLASH? SHE'S A CRIMINAL.
OPEN FIRE!
BANG BANG BANG BANG BANG
IN CENTRAL CITY, I TRUST THE POLICE OFFICERS I WORK WITH AND CALL FRIENDS.
HERE IN CORTO MALTESE? NOT SO MUCH.
WHAT THE HELL? INNOCENTS COULD HAVE BEEN KILLED!
MAYBE THEY STILL WILL, FLASH.
UNLESS YOU GET OUT OF MY CITY.
POLICE

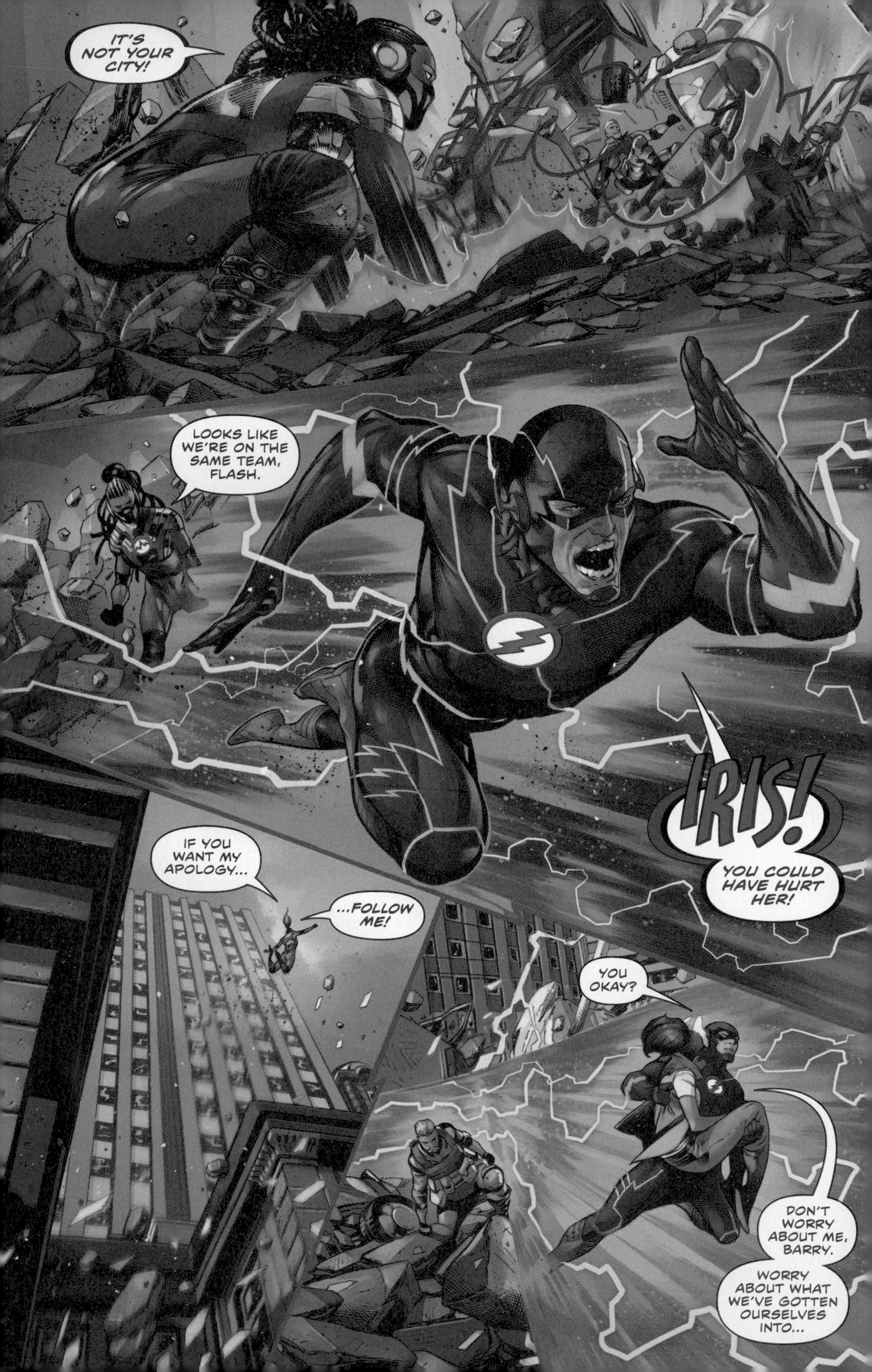
IT'S NOT YOUR CITY!
LOOKS LIKE WE'RE ON THE SAME TEAM, FLASH.
IRIS!
YOU COULD HAVE HURT HER!
IF YOU WANT MY APOLOGY...
...FOLLOW ME!
YOU OKAY?
DON'T WORRY ABOUT ME, BARRY.
WORRY ABOUT WHAT WE'VE GOTTEN OURSELVES INTO...

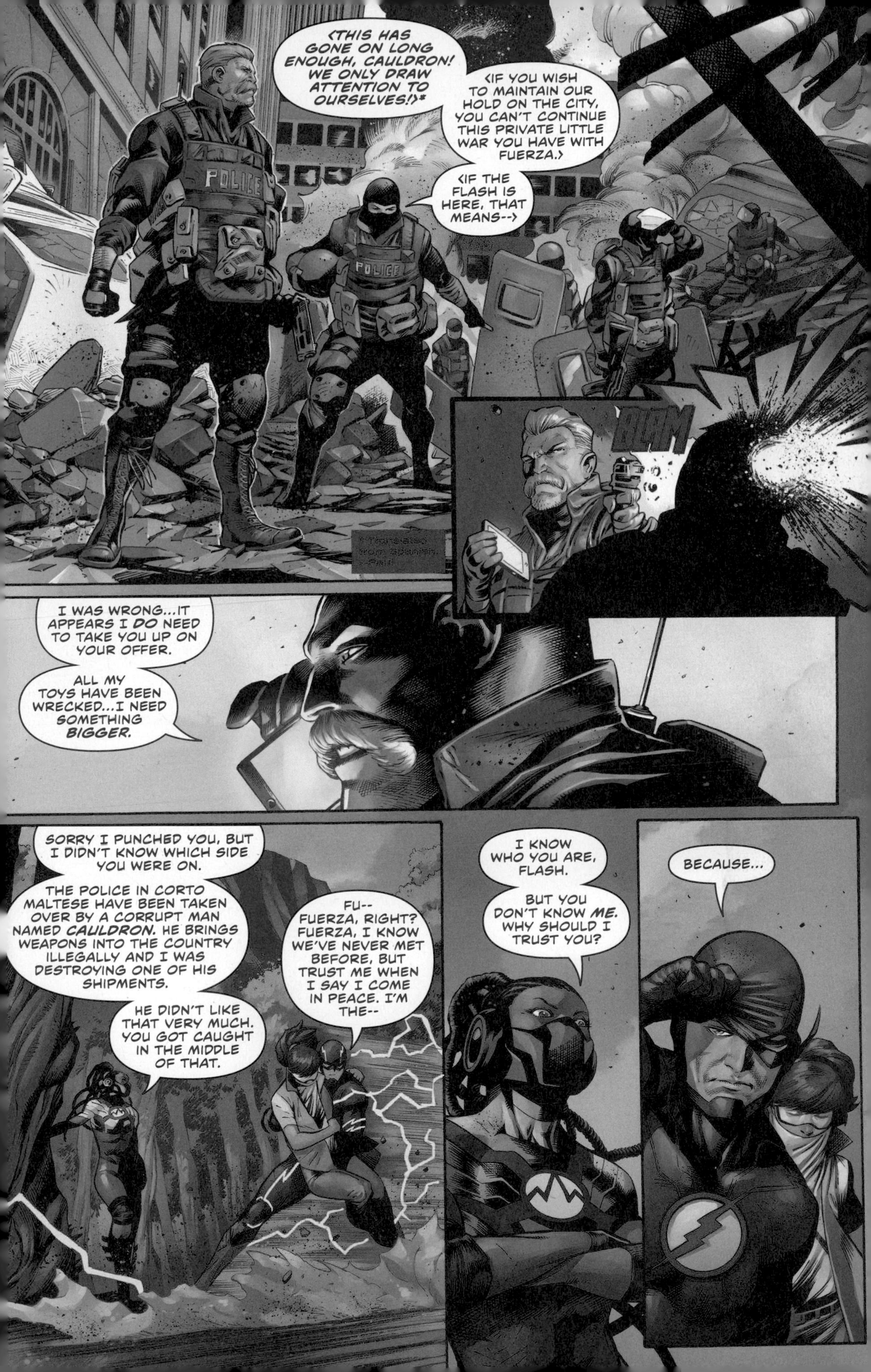

<THIS HAS GONE ON LONG ENOUGH, CAULDRON! WE ONLY DRAW ATTENTION TO OURSELVES!>*
<IF YOU WISH TO MAINTAIN OUR HOLD ON THE CITY, YOU CAN'T CONTINUE THIS PRIVATE LITTLE WAR YOU HAVE WITH FUERZA.>
<IF THE FLASH IS HERE, THAT MEANS-->
*Translated from Spanish. --Paul
BLAM
I WAS WRONG...IT APPEARS I DO NEED TO TAKE YOU UP ON YOUR OFFER.
ALL MY TOYS HAVE BEEN WRECKED...I NEED SOMETHING BIGGER.
SORRY I PUNCHED YOU, BUT I DIDN'T KNOW WHICH SIDE YOU WERE ON.
THE POLICE IN CORTO MALTESE HAVE BEEN TAKEN OVER BY A CORRUPT MAN NAMED CAULDRON. HE BRINGS WEAPONS INTO THE COUNTRY ILLEGALLY AND I WAS DESTROYING ONE OF HIS SHIPMENTS.
HE DIDN'T LIKE THAT VERY MUCH. YOU GOT CAUGHT IN THE MIDDLE OF THAT.
FU-- FUERZA, RIGHT? FUERZA, I KNOW WE'VE NEVER MET BEFORE, BUT TRUST ME WHEN I SAY I COME IN PEACE. I'M THE--
I KNOW WHO YOU ARE, FLASH.
BUT YOU DON'T KNOW ME. WHY SHOULD I TRUST YOU?
BECAUSE...

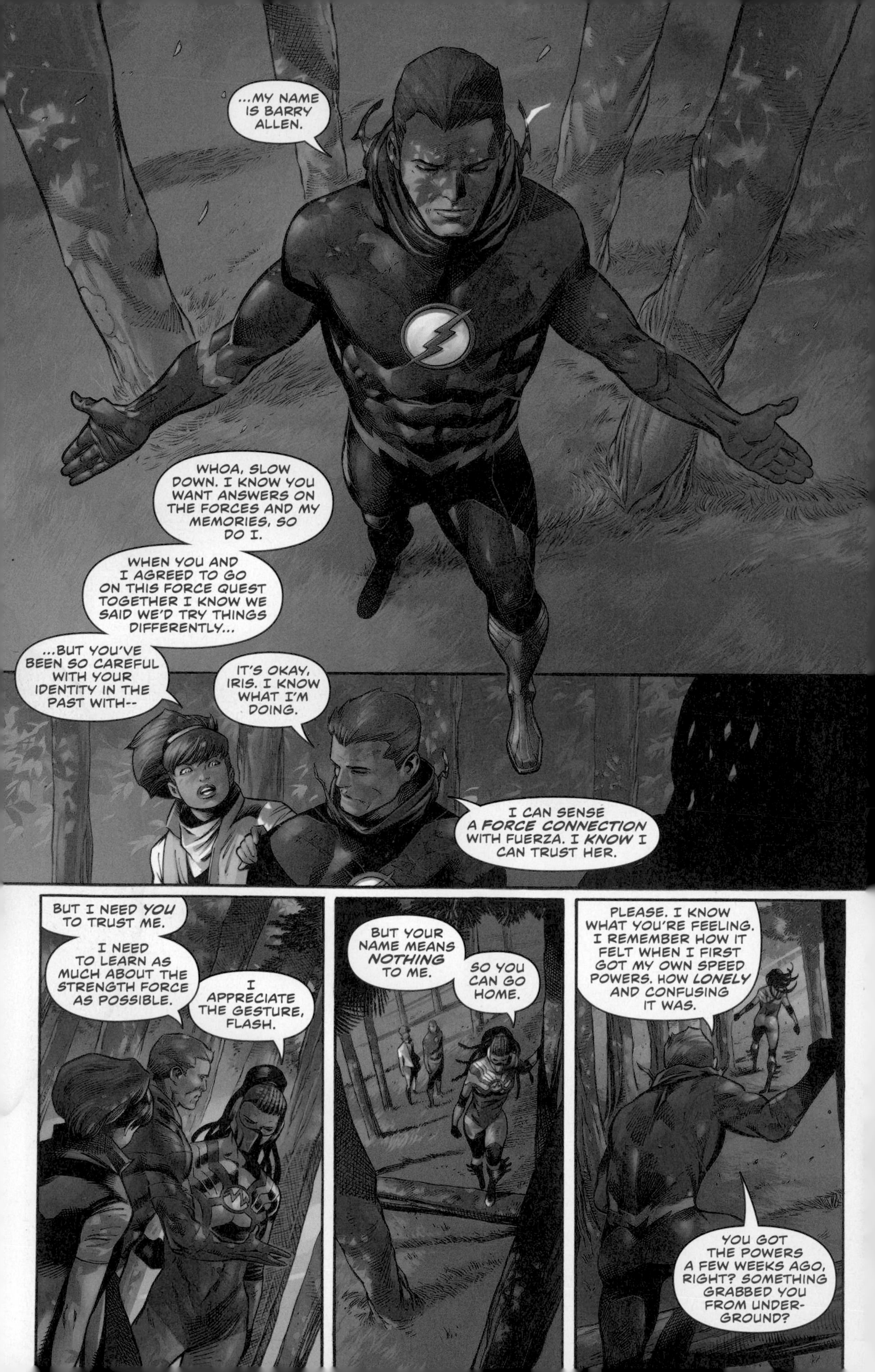
...MY NAME IS BARRY ALLEN.
WHOA, SLOW DOWN. I KNOW YOU WANT ANSWERS ON THE FORCES AND MY MEMORIES, SO DO I.
WHEN YOU AND I AGREED TO GO ON THIS FORCE QUEST TOGETHER I KNOW WE SAID WE'D TRY THINGS DIFFERENTLY...
...BUT YOU'VE BEEN SO CAREFUL WITH YOUR IDENTITY IN THE PAST WITH--
IT'S OKAY, IRIS. I KNOW WHAT I'M DOING.
I CAN SENSE A *FORCE CONNECTION* WITH FUERZA. I *KNOW* I CAN TRUST HER.
BUT I NEED *YOU* TO TRUST ME.
I NEED TO LEARN AS MUCH ABOUT THE STRENGTH FORCE AS POSSIBLE.
I APPRECIATE THE GESTURE, FLASH.
BUT YOUR NAME MEANS *NOTHING* TO ME.
SO YOU CAN GO HOME.
PLEASE. I KNOW WHAT YOU'RE FEELING. I REMEMBER HOW IT FELT WHEN I FIRST GOT MY OWN SPEED POWERS. HOW *LONELY* AND CONFUSING IT WAS.
YOU GOT THE POWERS A FEW WEEKS AGO, RIGHT? SOMETHING GRABBED YOU FROM UNDER-GROUND?

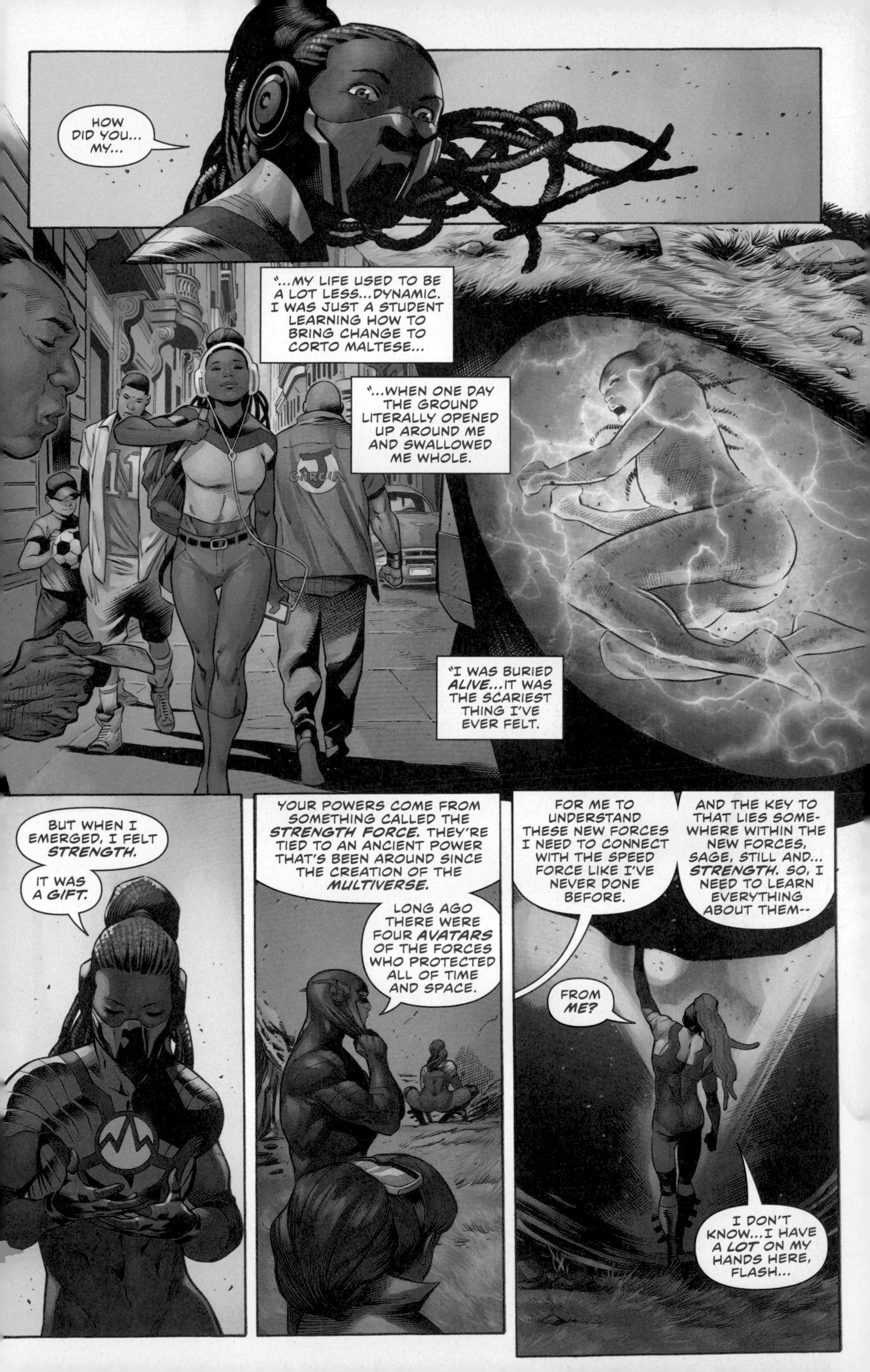
HOW DID YOU... MY...
"...MY LIFE USED TO BE A LOT LESS...DYNAMIC. I WAS JUST A STUDENT LEARNING HOW TO BRING CHANGE TO CORTO MALTESE...
"...WHEN ONE DAY THE GROUND LITERALLY OPENED UP AROUND ME AND SWALLOWED ME WHOLE.
"I WAS BURIED ALIVE...IT WAS THE SCARIEST THING I'VE EVER FELT.
BUT WHEN I EMERGED, I FELT STRENGTH.
IT WAS A GIFT.
YOUR POWERS COME FROM SOMETHING CALLED THE STRENGTH FORCE. THEY'RE TIED TO AN ANCIENT POWER THAT'S BEEN AROUND SINCE THE CREATION OF THE MULTIVERSE.
LONG AGO THERE WERE FOUR AVATARS OF THE FORCES WHO PROTECTED ALL OF TIME AND SPACE.
FOR ME TO UNDERSTAND THESE NEW FORCES I NEED TO CONNECT WITH THE SPEED FORCE LIKE I'VE NEVER DONE BEFORE.
AND THE KEY TO THAT LIES SOMEWHERE WITHIN THE NEW FORCES, SAGE, STILL AND... STRENGTH. SO, I NEED TO LEARN EVERYTHING ABOUT THEM--
FROM ME?
I DON'T KNOW...I HAVE A LOT ON MY HANDS HERE, FLASH...

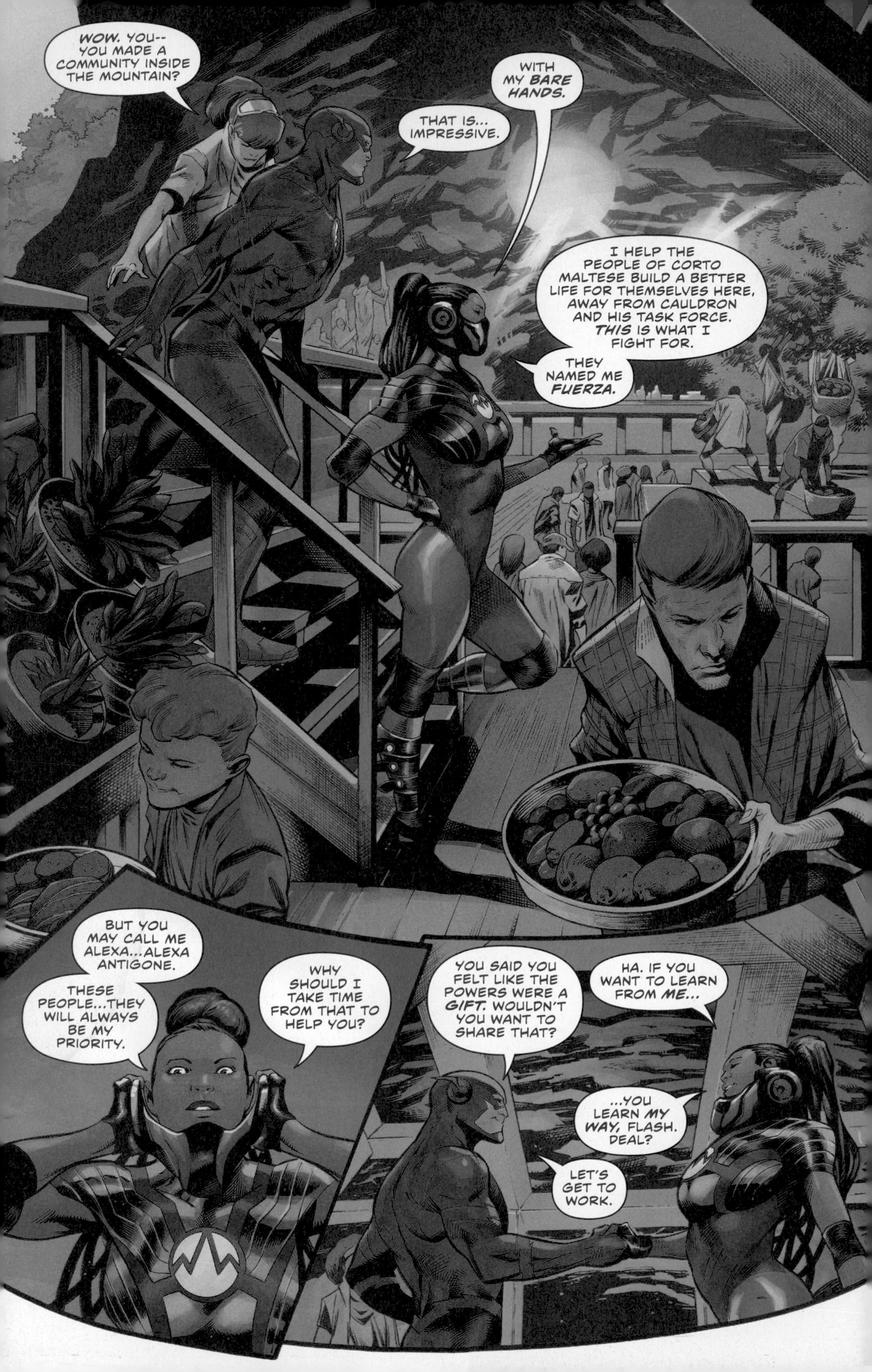
WOW. YOU-- YOU MADE A COMMUNITY INSIDE THE MOUNTAIN?
THAT IS... IMPRESSIVE.
WITH MY BARE HANDS.
I HELP THE PEOPLE OF CORTO MALTESE BUILD A BETTER LIFE FOR THEMSELVES HERE, AWAY FROM CAULDRON AND HIS TASK FORCE. THIS IS WHAT I FIGHT FOR.
THEY NAMED ME FUERZA.
BUT YOU MAY CALL ME ALEXA...ALEXA ANTIGONE.
THESE PEOPLE...THEY WILL ALWAYS BE MY PRIORITY.
WHY SHOULD I TAKE TIME FROM THAT TO HELP YOU?
YOU SAID YOU FELT LIKE THE POWERS WERE A GIFT. WOULDN'T YOU WANT TO SHARE THAT?
HA. IF YOU WANT TO LEARN FROM ME...
...YOU LEARN MY WAY, FLASH. DEAL?
LET'S GET TO WORK.

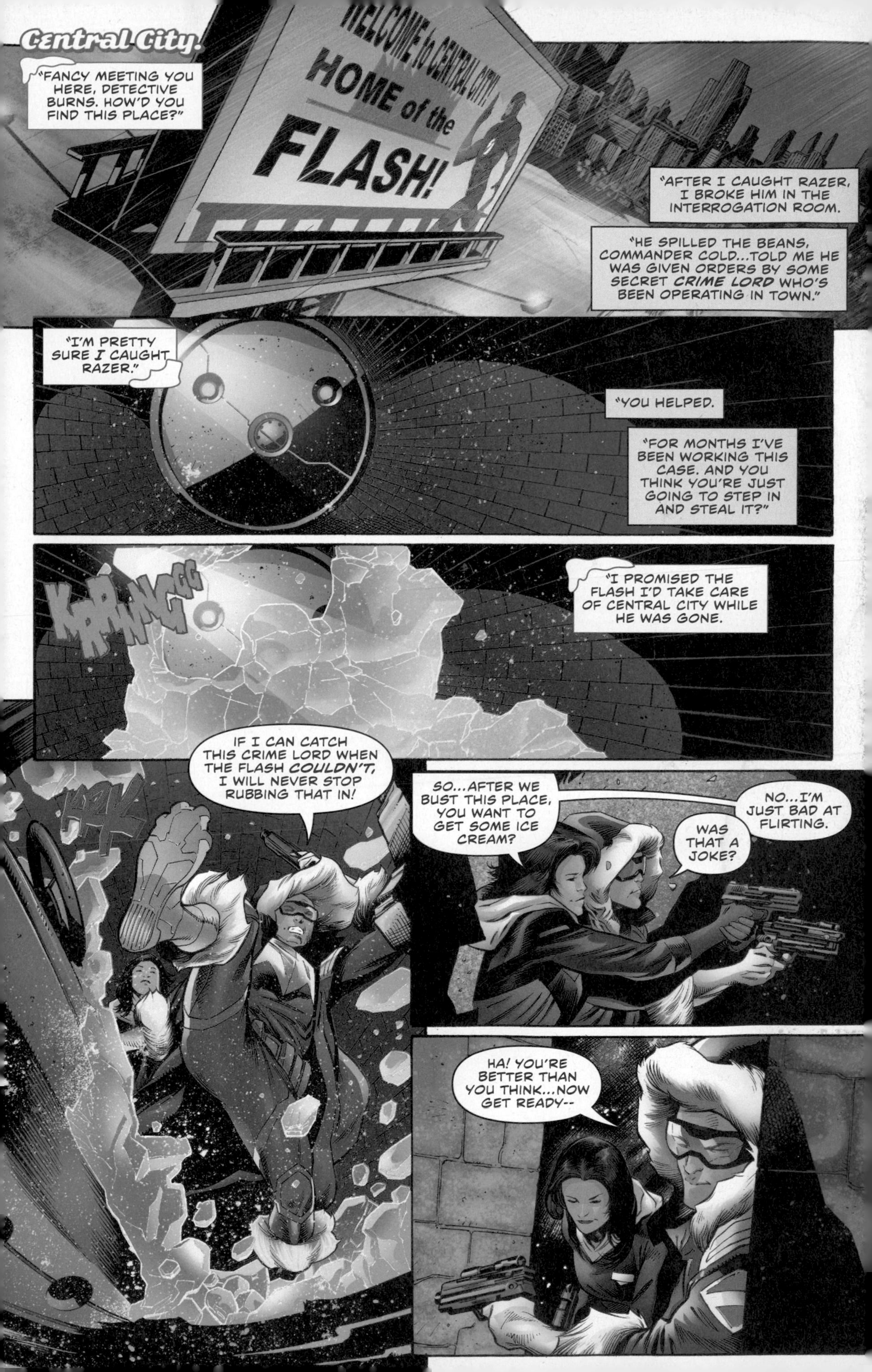
Central City.
"FANCY MEETING YOU HERE, DETECTIVE BURNS. HOW'D YOU FIND THIS PLACE?"
WELCOME to CENTRAL CITY HOME of the FLASH!
"AFTER I CAUGHT RAZER, I BROKE HIM IN THE INTERROGATION ROOM.
"HE SPILLED THE BEANS, COMMANDER COLD...TOLD ME HE WAS GIVEN ORDERS BY SOME SECRET CRIME LORD WHO'S BEEN OPERATING IN TOWN."
"I'M PRETTY SURE I CAUGHT RAZER."
"YOU HELPED.
"FOR MONTHS I'VE BEEN WORKING THIS CASE. AND YOU THINK YOU'RE JUST GOING TO STEP IN AND STEAL IT?"
KRRANNGGG
"I PROMISED THE FLASH I'D TAKE CARE OF CENTRAL CITY WHILE HE WAS GONE.
IF I CAN CATCH THIS CRIME LORD WHEN THE FLASH COULDN'T, I WILL NEVER STOP RUBBING THAT IN!
SO...AFTER WE BUST THIS PLACE, YOU WANT TO GET SOME ICE CREAM?
WAS THAT A JOKE?
NO...I'M JUST BAD AT FLIRTING.
HA! YOU'RE BETTER THAN YOU THINK...NOW GET READY--

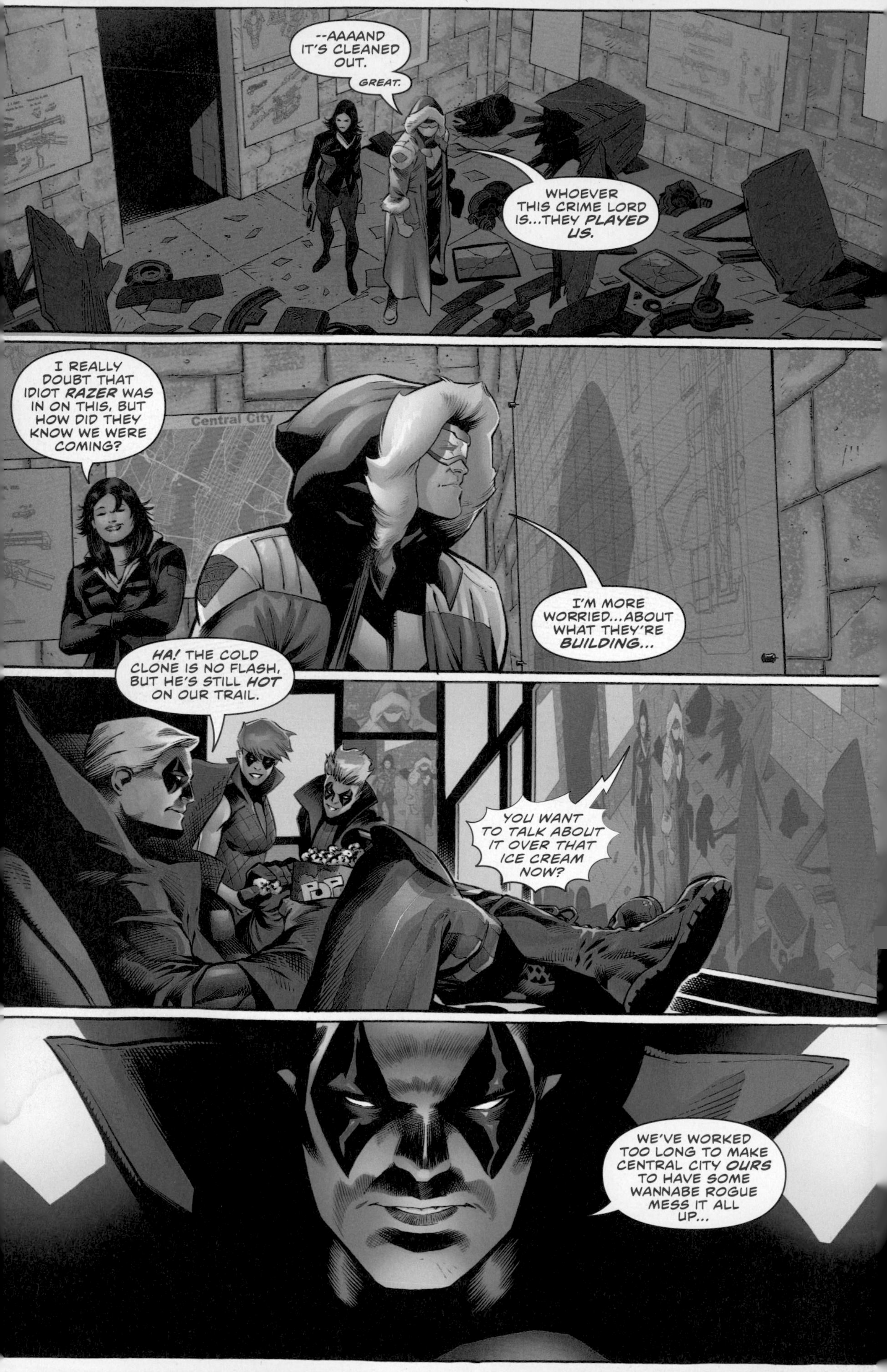
--AAAAND IT'S CLEANED OUT.
GREAT.
WHOEVER THIS CRIME LORD IS...THEY PLAYED US.
I REALLY DOUBT THAT IDIOT RAZER WAS IN ON THIS, BUT HOW DID THEY KNOW WE WERE COMING?
Central City
I'M MORE WORRIED...ABOUT WHAT THEY'RE BUILDING...
HA! THE COLD CLONE IS NO FLASH, BUT HE'S STILL HOT ON OUR TRAIL.
YOU WANT TO TALK ABOUT IT OVER THAT ICE CREAM NOW?
POP
WE'VE WORKED TOO LONG TO MAKE CENTRAL CITY OURS TO HAVE SOME WANNABE ROGUE MESS IT ALL UP...

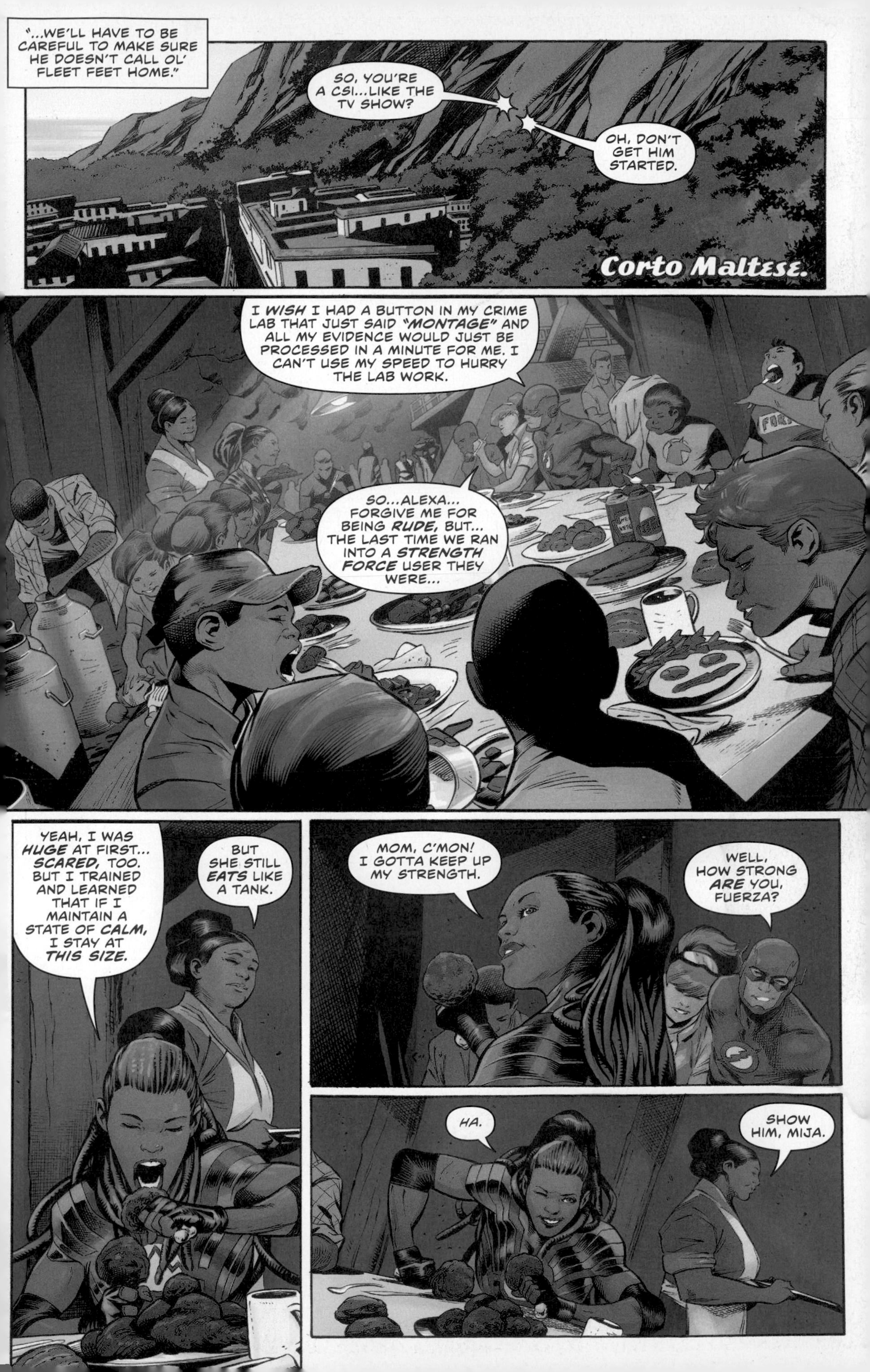
"...WE'LL HAVE TO BE CAREFUL TO MAKE SURE HE DOESN'T CALL OL' FLEET FEET HOME."
SO, YOU'RE A CSI...LIKE THE TV SHOW?
OH, DON'T GET HIM STARTED.
Corto Maltese.
I WISH I HAD A BUTTON IN MY CRIME LAB THAT JUST SAID "MONTAGE" AND ALL MY EVIDENCE WOULD JUST BE PROCESSED IN A MINUTE FOR ME. I CAN'T USE MY SPEED TO HURRY THE LAB WORK.
SO...ALEXA... FORGIVE ME FOR BEING RUDE, BUT... THE LAST TIME WE RAN INTO A STRENGTH FORCE USER THEY WERE...
YEAH, I WAS HUGE AT FIRST... SCARED, TOO. BUT I TRAINED AND LEARNED THAT IF I MAINTAIN A STATE OF CALM, I STAY AT THIS SIZE.
BUT SHE STILL EATS LIKE A TANK.
MOM, C'MON! I GOTTA KEEP UP MY STRENGTH.
WELL, HOW STRONG ARE YOU, FUERZA?
HA.
SHOW HIM, MIJA.

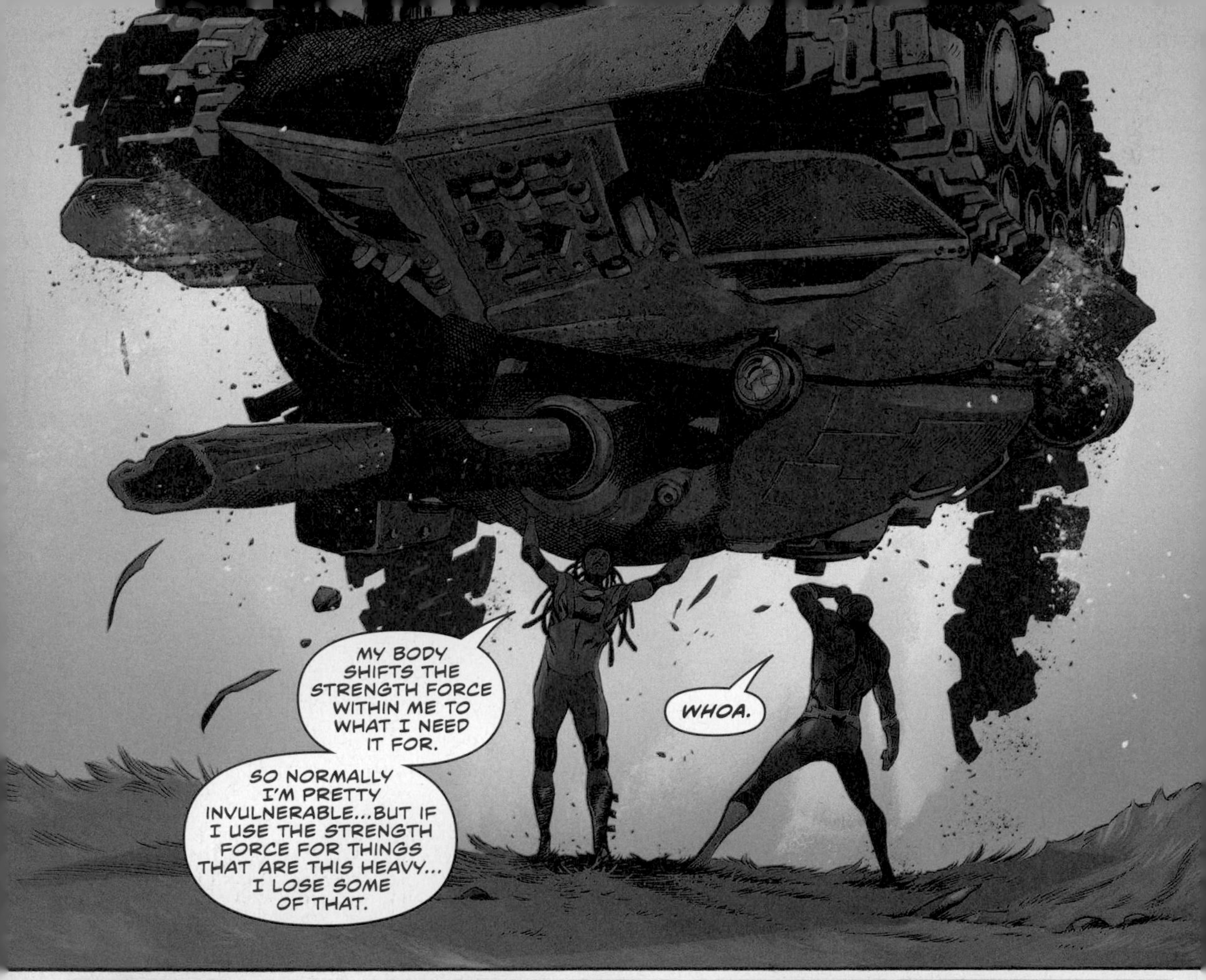
MY BODY SHIFTS THE STRENGTH FORCE WITHIN ME TO WHAT I NEED IT FOR.
SO NORMALLY I'M PRETTY INVULNERABLE...BUT IF I USE THE STRENGTH FORCE FOR THINGS THAT ARE THIS HEAVY... I LOSE SOME OF THAT.
WHOA.

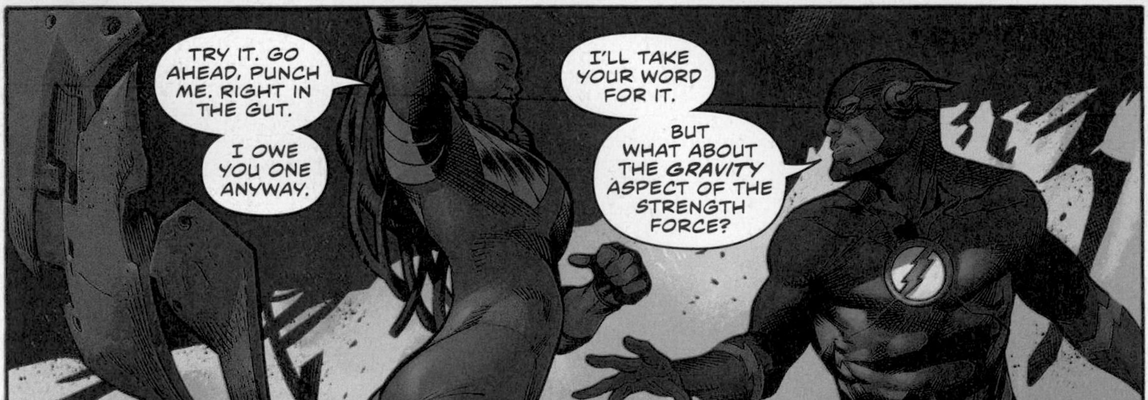
TRY IT. GO AHEAD, PUNCH ME. RIGHT IN THE GUT.
I OWE YOU ONE ANYWAY.
I'LL TAKE YOUR WORD FOR IT.
BUT WHAT ABOUT THE GRAVITY ASPECT OF THE STRENGTH FORCE?

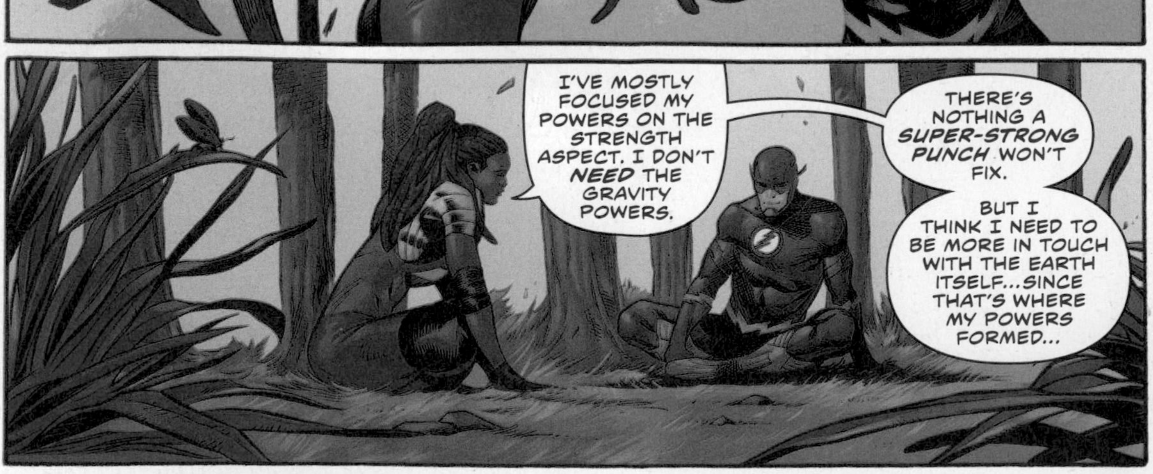
I'VE MOSTLY FOCUSED MY POWERS ON THE STRENGTH ASPECT. I DON'T NEED THE GRAVITY POWERS.
THERE'S NOTHING A SUPER-STRONG PUNCH WON'T FIX.
BUT I THINK I NEED TO BE MORE IN TOUCH WITH THE EARTH ITSELF...SINCE THAT'S WHERE MY POWERS FORMED...

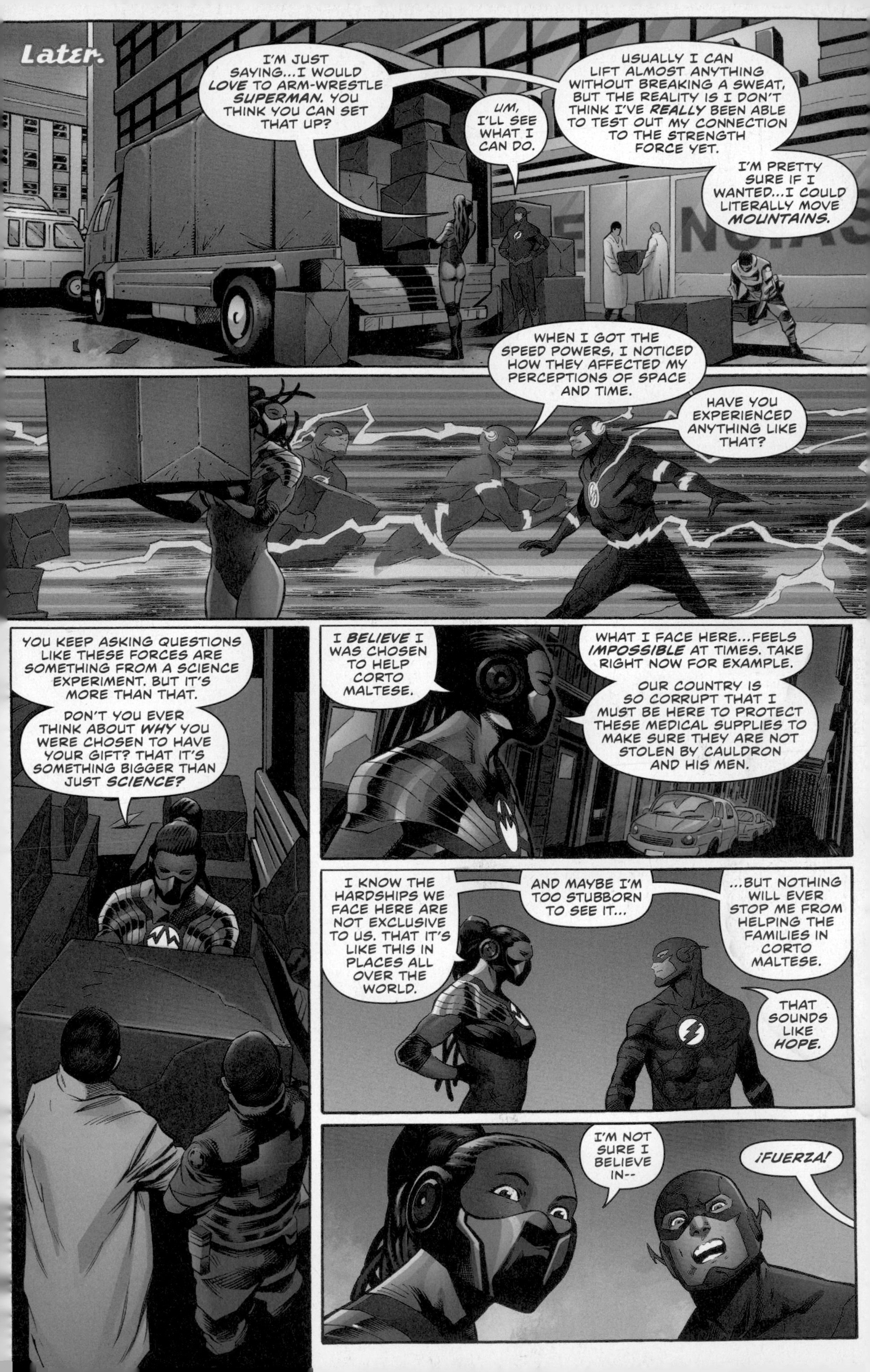
Later.
I'M JUST SAYING...I WOULD LOVE TO ARM-WRESTLE SUPERMAN. YOU THINK YOU CAN SET THAT UP?
UM, I'LL SEE WHAT I CAN DO.
USUALLY I CAN LIFT ALMOST ANYTHING WITHOUT BREAKING A SWEAT, BUT THE REALITY IS I DON'T THINK I'VE REALLY BEEN ABLE TO TEST OUT MY CONNECTION TO THE STRENGTH FORCE YET.
I'M PRETTY SURE IF I WANTED...I COULD LITERALLY MOVE MOUNTAINS.
WHEN I GOT THE SPEED POWERS, I NOTICED HOW THEY AFFECTED MY PERCEPTIONS OF SPACE AND TIME.
HAVE YOU EXPERIENCED ANYTHING LIKE THAT?
YOU KEEP ASKING QUESTIONS LIKE THESE FORCES ARE SOMETHING FROM A SCIENCE EXPERIMENT. BUT IT'S MORE THAN THAT.
DON'T YOU EVER THINK ABOUT WHY YOU WERE CHOSEN TO HAVE YOUR GIFT? THAT IT'S SOMETHING BIGGER THAN JUST SCIENCE?
I BELIEVE I WAS CHOSEN TO HELP CORTO MALTESE.
WHAT I FACE HERE...FEELS IMPOSSIBLE AT TIMES. TAKE RIGHT NOW FOR EXAMPLE.
OUR COUNTRY IS SO CORRUPT THAT I MUST BE HERE TO PROTECT THESE MEDICAL SUPPLIES TO MAKE SURE THEY ARE NOT STOLEN BY CAULDRON AND HIS MEN.
I KNOW THE HARDSHIPS WE FACE HERE ARE NOT EXCLUSIVE TO US. THAT IT'S LIKE THIS IN PLACES ALL OVER THE WORLD.
AND MAYBE I'M TOO STUBBORN TO SEE IT...
...BUT NOTHING WILL EVER STOP ME FROM HELPING THE FAMILIES IN CORTO MALTESE.
THAT SOUNDS LIKE HOPE.
I'M NOT SURE I BELIEVE IN--
¡FUERZA!

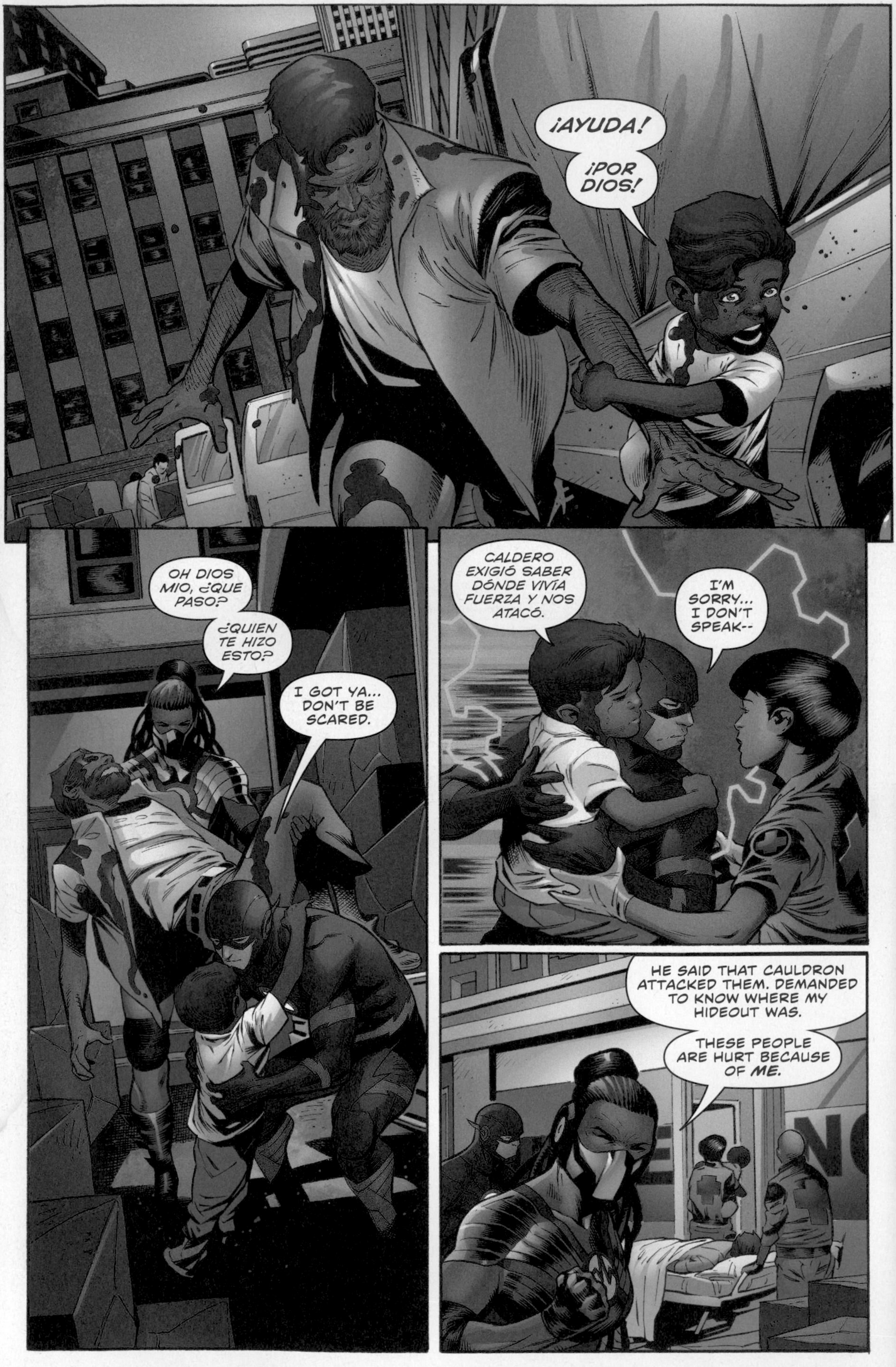
¡AYUDA!
¡POR DIOS!
OH DIOS MIO, ¿QUE PASO?
¿QUIEN TE HIZO ESTO?
I GOT YA... DON'T BE SCARED.
CALDERO EXIGIÓ SABER DÓNDE VIVÍA FUERZA Y NOS ATACÓ.
I'M SORRY... I DON'T SPEAK--
HE SAID THAT CALDRON ATTACKED THEM. DEMANDED TO KNOW WHERE MY HIDEOUT WAS.
THESE PEOPLE ARE HURT BECAUSE OF ME.

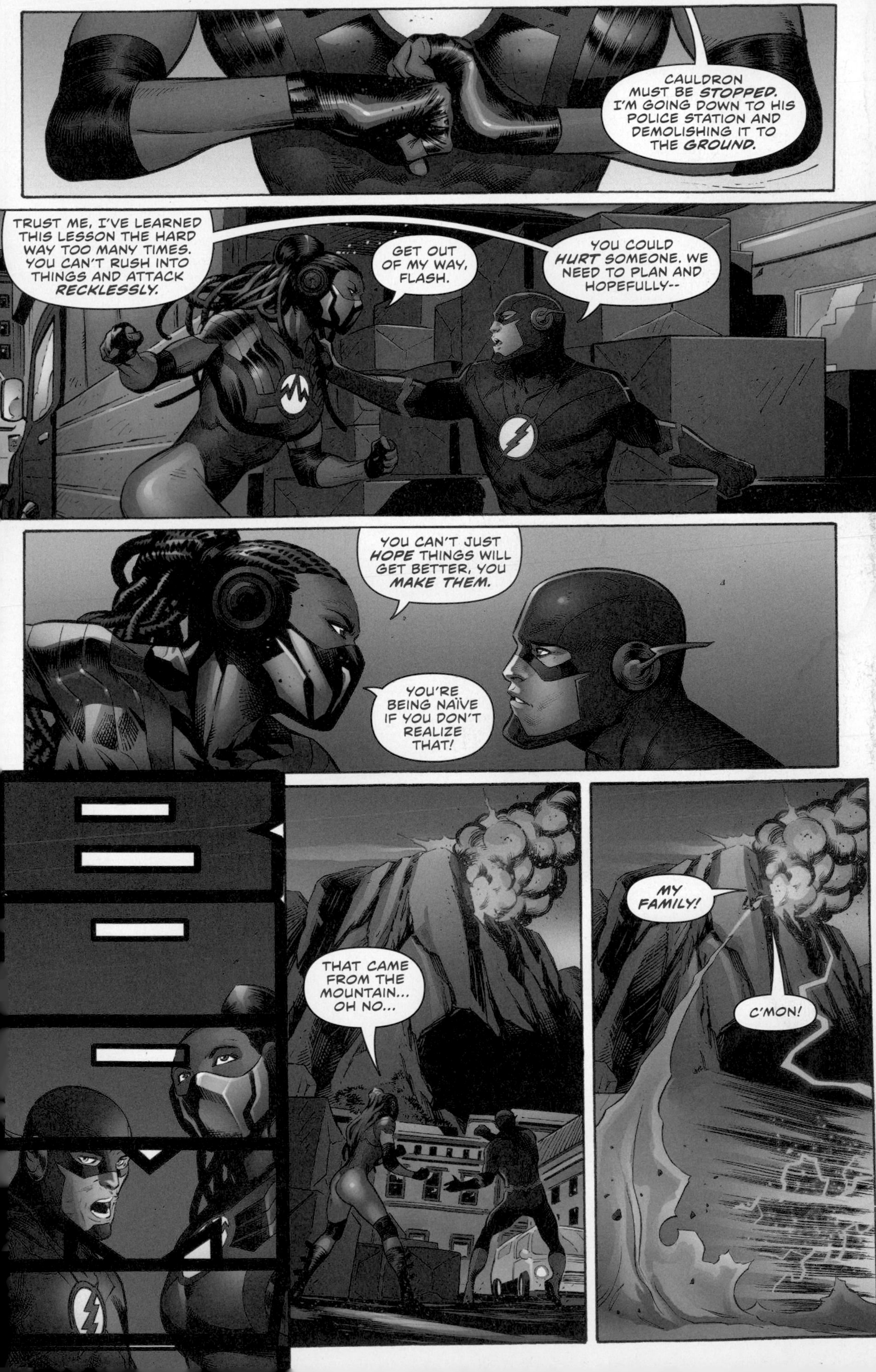
CAULDRON MUST BE STOPPED. I'M GOING DOWN TO HIS POLICE STATION AND DEMOLISHING IT TO THE GROUND.
TRUST ME, I'VE LEARNED THIS LESSON THE HARD WAY TOO MANY TIMES. YOU CAN'T RUSH INTO THINGS AND ATTACK RECKLESSLY.
GET OUT OF MY WAY, FLASH.
YOU COULD HURT SOMEONE. WE NEED TO PLAN AND HOPEFULLY--
YOU CAN'T JUST HOPE THINGS WILL GET BETTER, YOU MAKE THEM.
YOU'RE BEING NAÏVE IF YOU DON'T REALIZE THAT!
THAT CAME FROM THE MOUNTAIN... OH NO...
MY FAMILY!
C'MON!

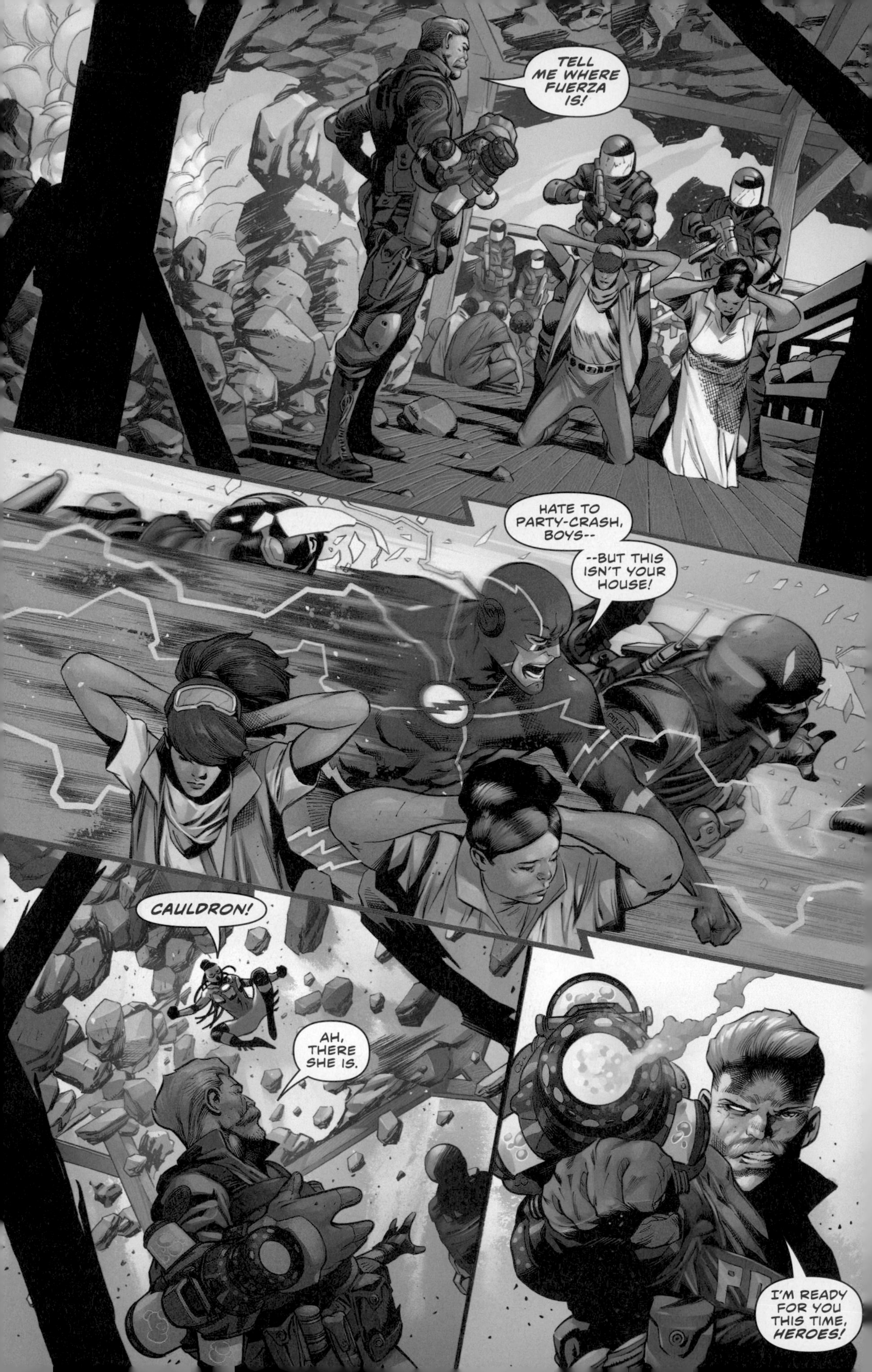
TELL ME WHERE FUERZA IS!
HATE TO PARTY-CRASH, BOYS--
--BUT THIS ISN'T YOUR HOUSE!
CAULDRON!
AH, THERE SHE IS.
I'M READY FOR YOU THIS TIME, HEROES!

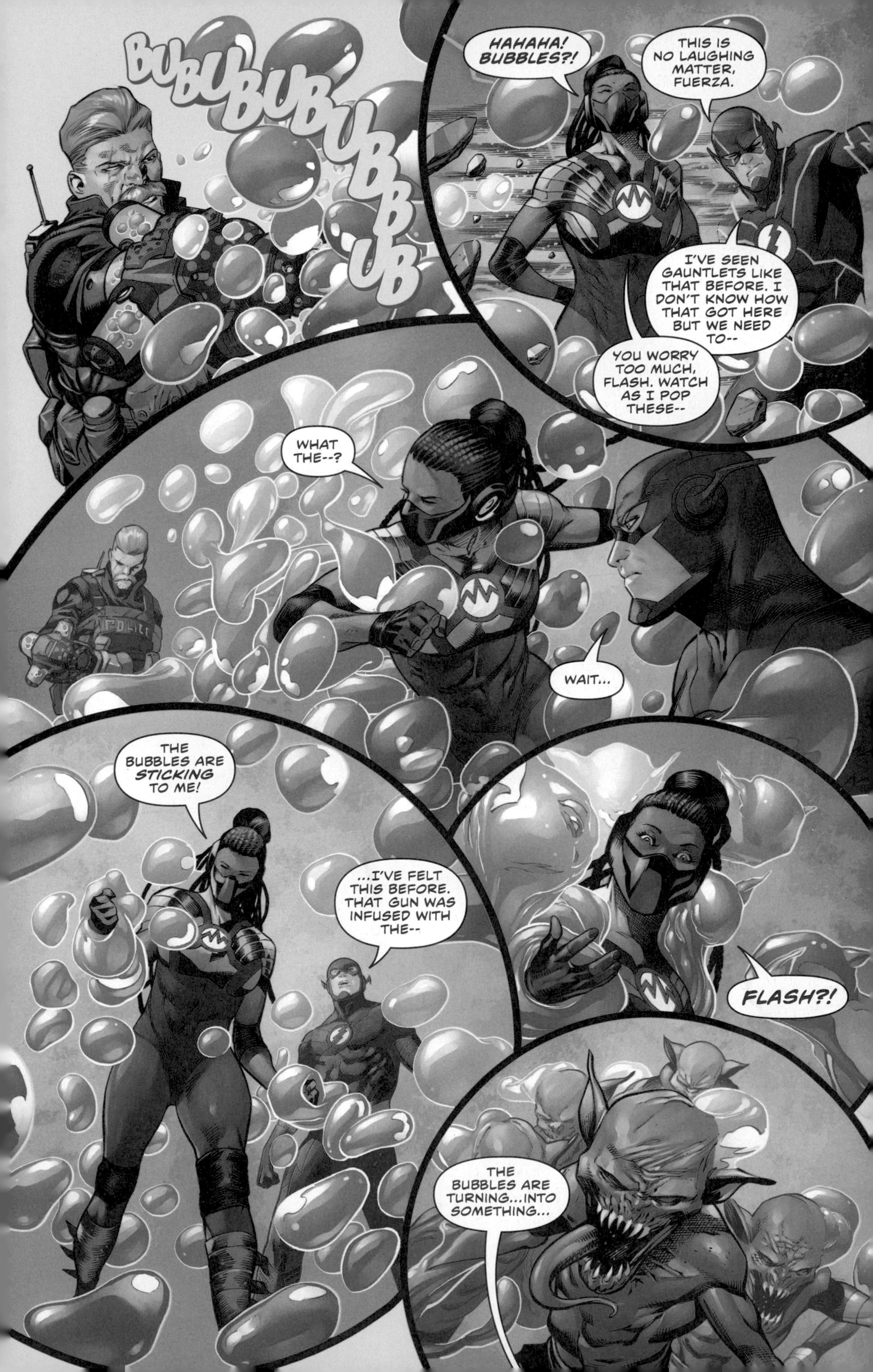

BUBUBUBUBUBBBUB
HAHAHA! BUBBLES?!
THIS IS NO LAUGHING MATTER, FUERZA.
I'VE SEEN GAUNTLETS LIKE THAT BEFORE. I DON'T KNOW HOW THAT GOT HERE BUT WE NEED TO--
YOU WORRY TOO MUCH, FLASH. WATCH AS I POP THESE--
WHAT THE--?
WAIT...
THE BUBBLES ARE STICKING TO ME!
...I'VE FELT THIS BEFORE. THAT GUN WAS INFUSED WITH THE--
FLASH?!
THE BUBBLES ARE TURNING...INTO SOMETHING...

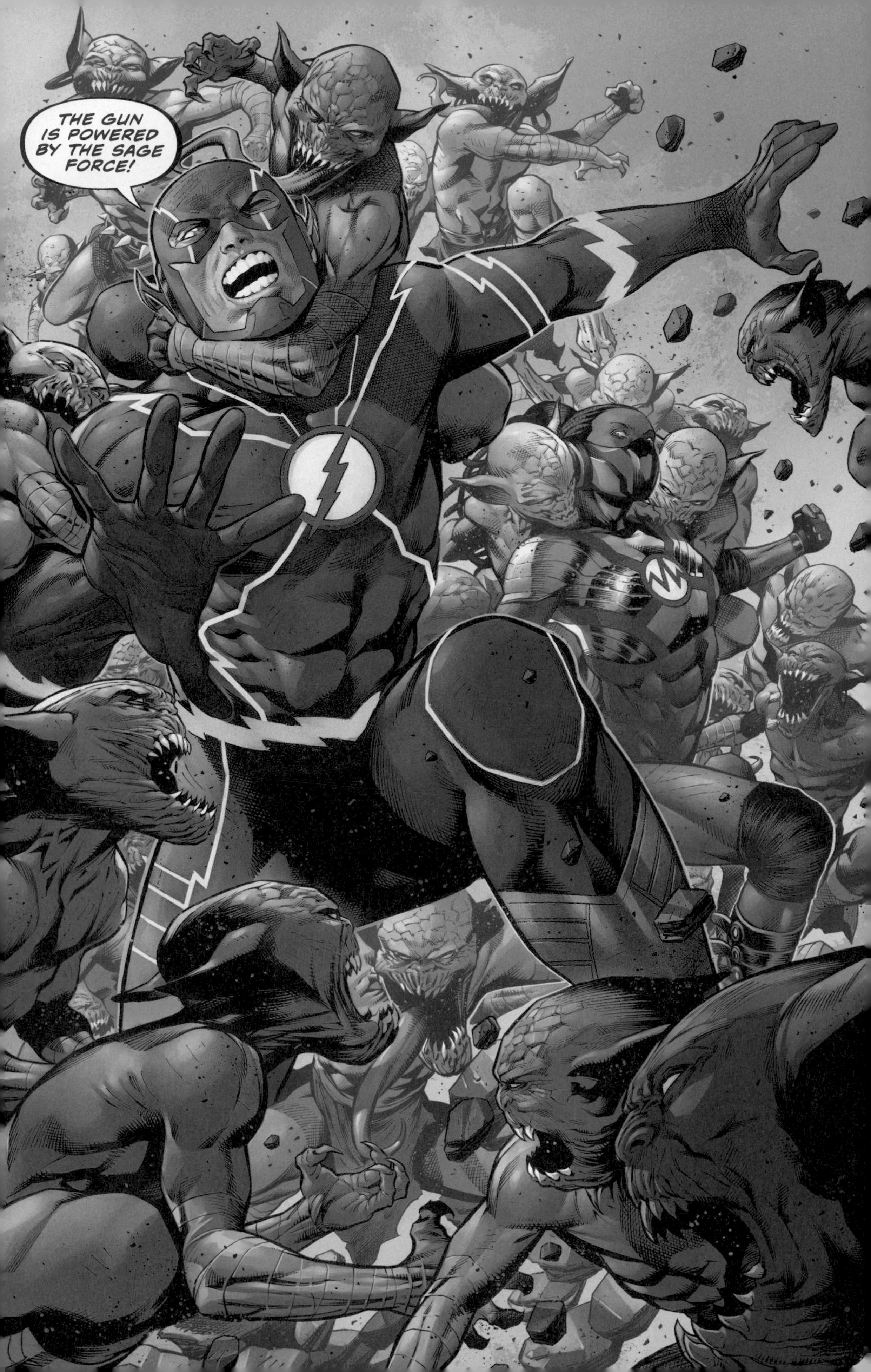
THE GUN IS POWERED BY THE SAGE FORCE!

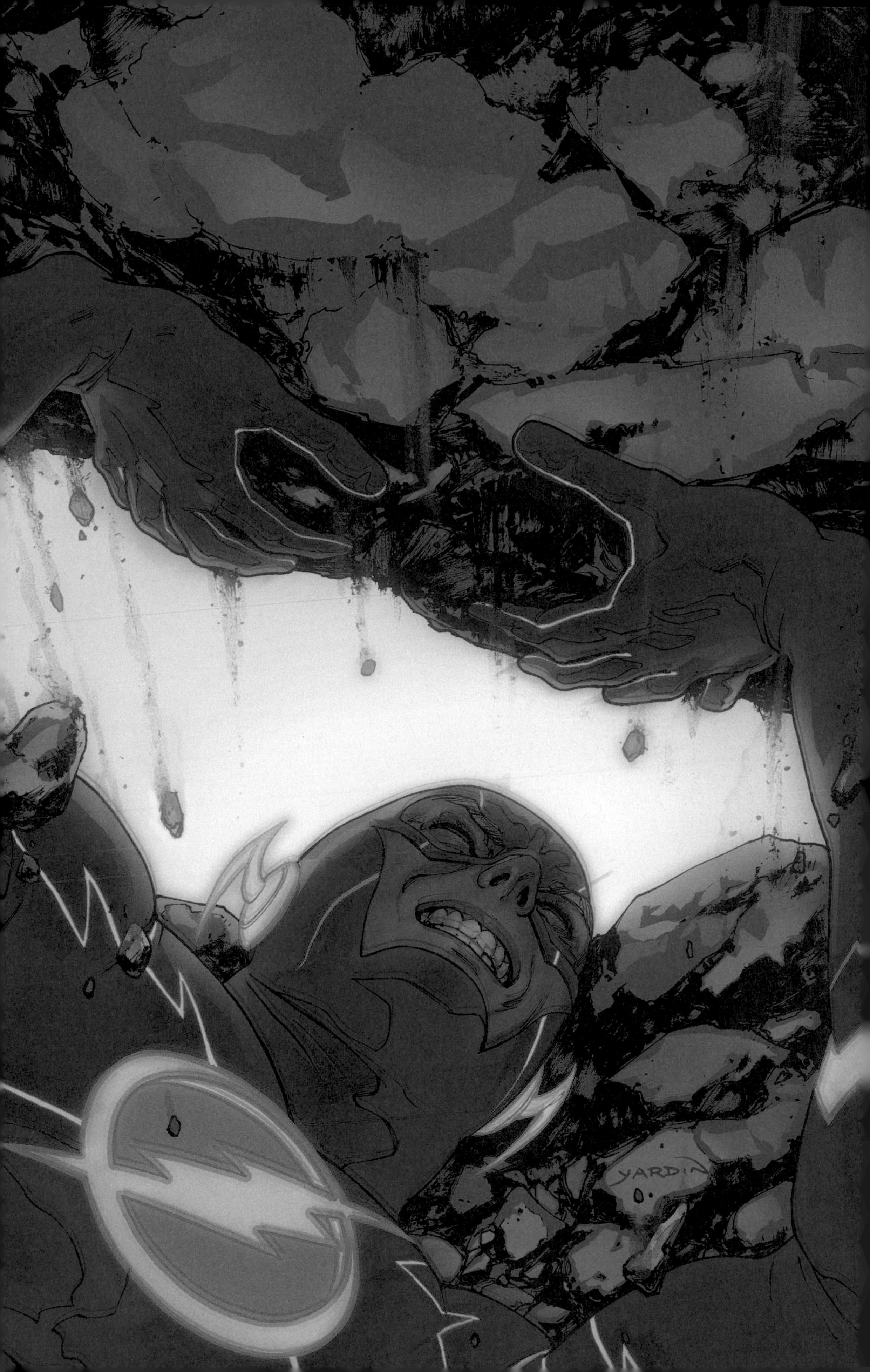
YARDIN

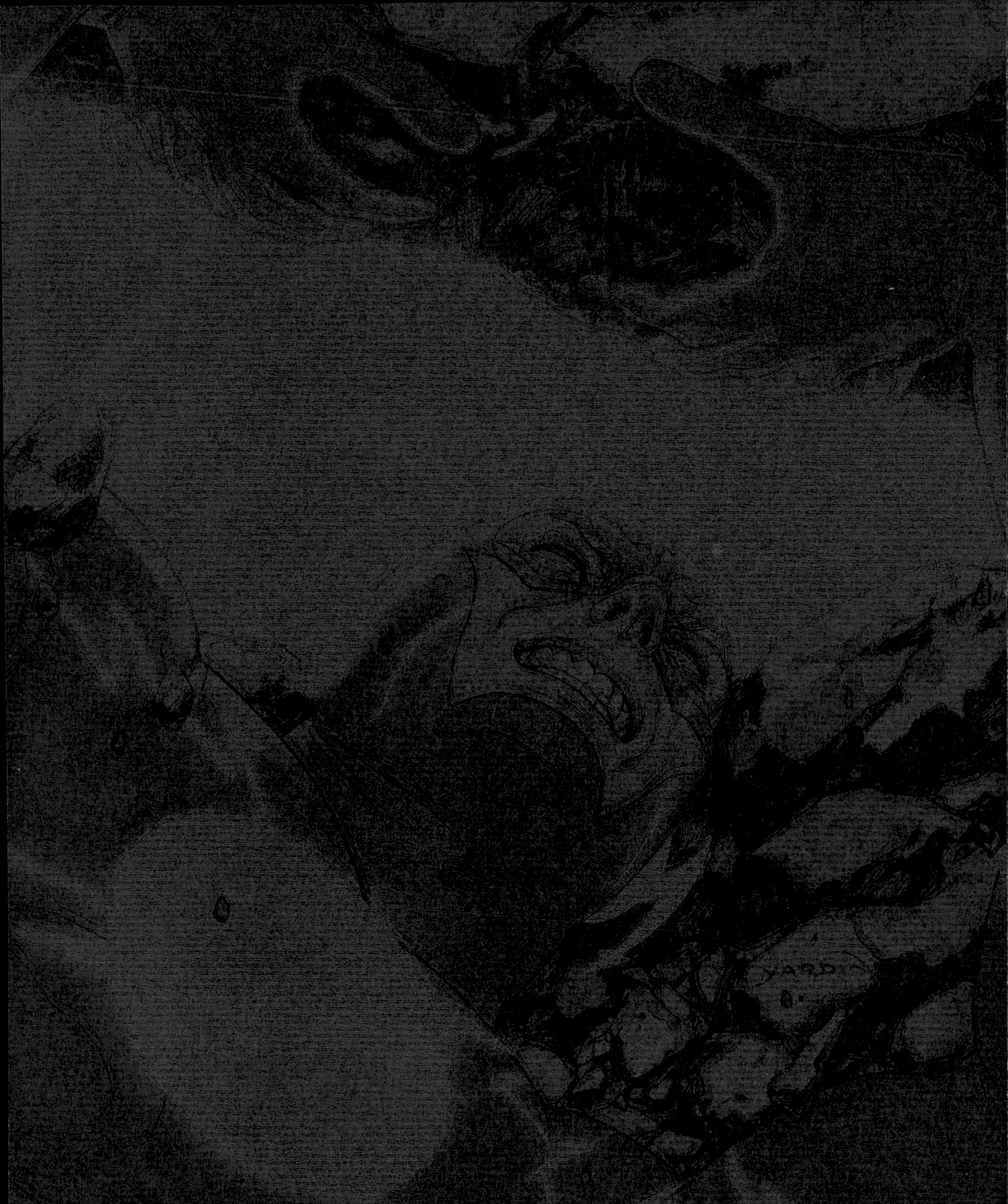

THE FLASH
#61

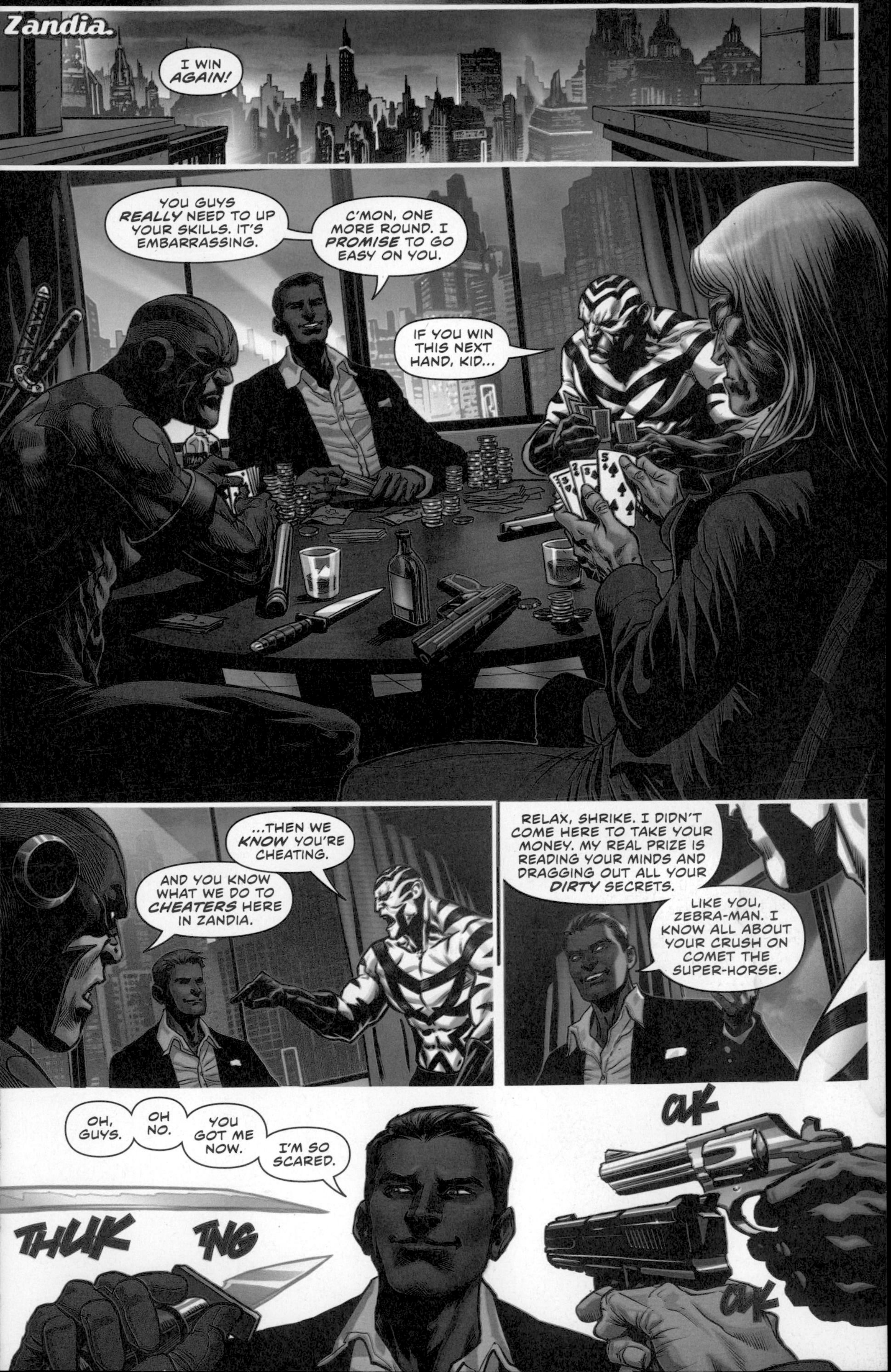
Zandia.
I WIN AGAIN!
YOU GUYS REALLY NEED TO UP YOUR SKILLS. IT'S EMBARRASSING.
C'MON, ONE MORE ROUND. I PROMISE TO GO EASY ON YOU.
IF YOU WIN THIS NEXT HAND, KID...
...THEN WE KNOW YOU'RE CHEATING.
AND YOU KNOW WHAT WE DO TO CHEATERS HERE IN ZANDIA.
RELAX, SHRIKE. I DIDN'T COME HERE TO TAKE YOUR MONEY. MY REAL PRIZE IS READING YOUR MINDS AND DRAGGING OUT ALL YOUR DIRTY SECRETS.
LIKE YOU, ZEBRA-MAN. I KNOW ALL ABOUT YOUR CRUSH ON COMET THE SUPER-HORSE.
OH, GUYS.
OH NO.
YOU GOT ME NOW.
I'M SO SCARED.
CLIK
THUK
TNG
CLIK

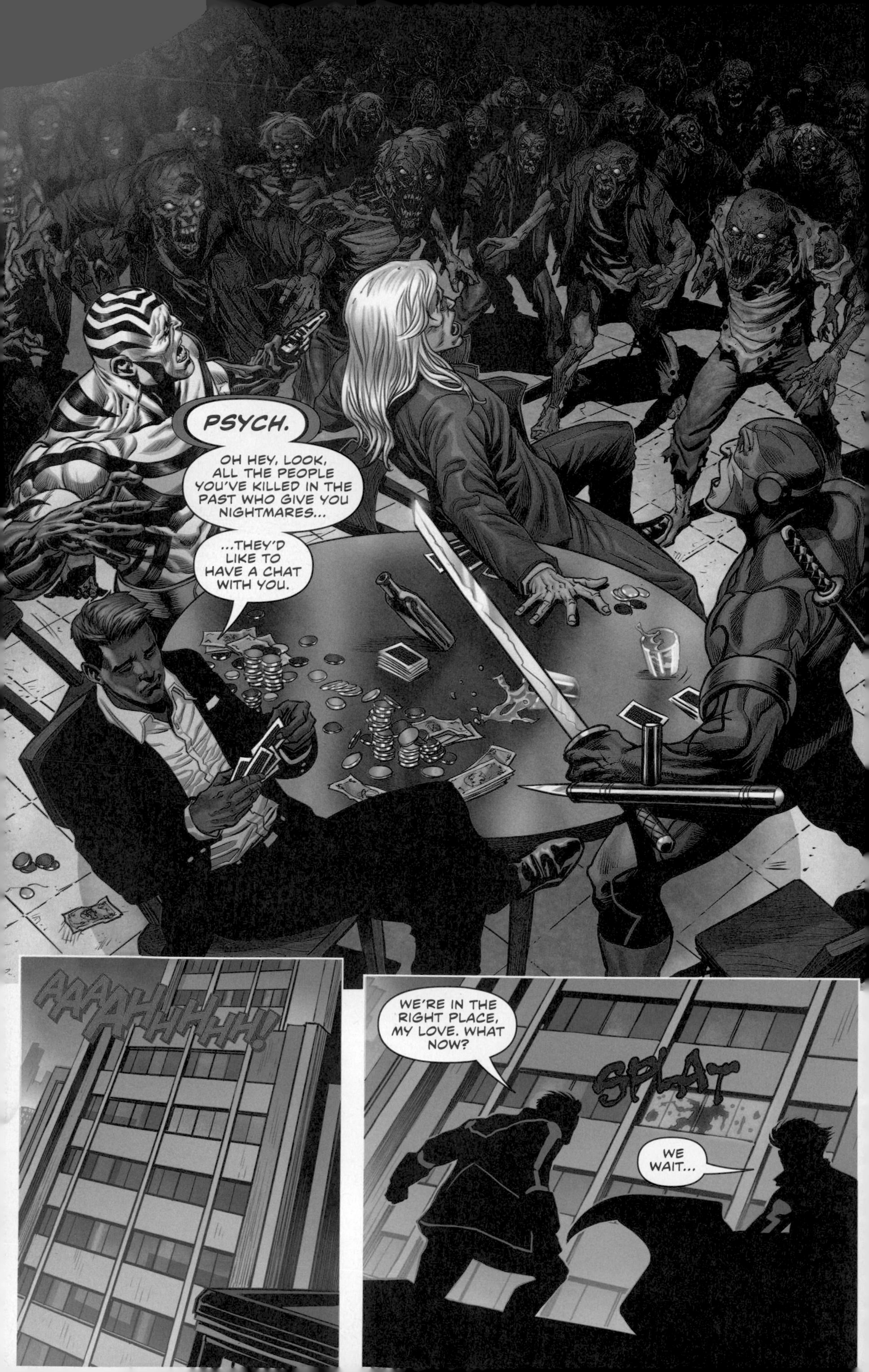
PSYCH.
OH HEY, LOOK, ALL THE PEOPLE YOU'VE KILLED IN THE PAST WHO GIVE YOU NIGHTMARES...
...THEY'D LIKE TO HAVE A CHAT WITH YOU.
AAAAHHHHHH!
WE'RE IN THE RIGHT PLACE, MY LOVE. WHAT NOW?
SPLAT
WE WAIT...

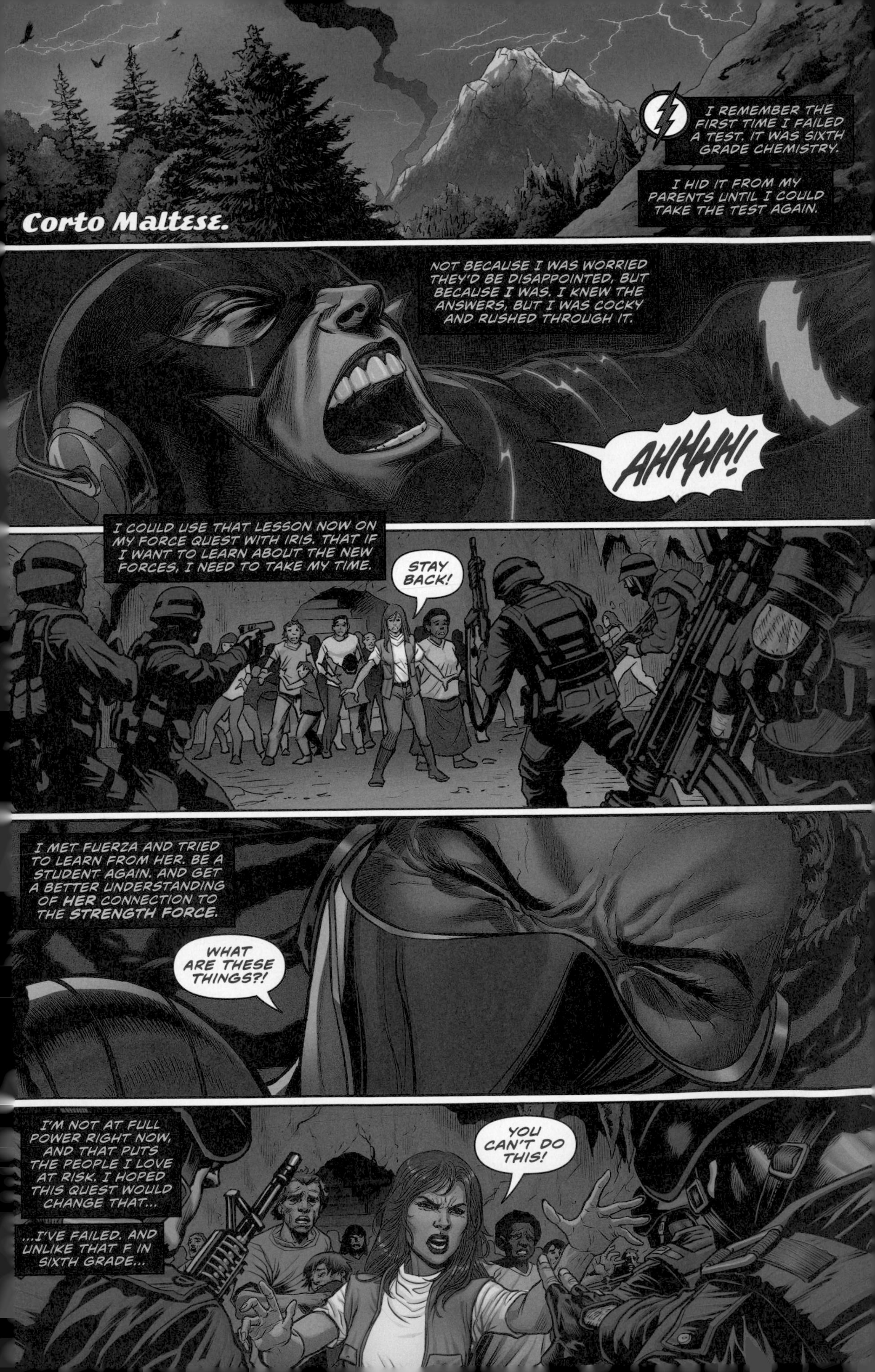
Corto Maltese.
I REMEMBER THE FIRST TIME I FAILED A TEST. IT WAS SIXTH GRADE CHEMISTRY.
I HID IT FROM MY PARENTS UNTIL I COULD TAKE THE TEST AGAIN.
NOT BECAUSE I WAS WORRIED THEY'D BE DISAPPOINTED, BUT BECAUSE I WAS. I KNEW THE ANSWERS, BUT I WAS COCKY AND RUSHED THROUGH IT.
AHHHH!
I COULD USE THAT LESSON NOW ON MY FORCE QUEST WITH IRIS. THAT IF I WANT TO LEARN ABOUT THE NEW FORCES, I NEED TO TAKE MY TIME.
STAY BACK!
I MET FUERZA AND TRIED TO LEARN FROM HER. BE A STUDENT AGAIN. AND GET A BETTER UNDERSTANDING OF HER CONNECTION TO THE STRENGTH FORCE.
WHAT ARE THESE THINGS?!
I'M NOT AT FULL POWER RIGHT NOW, AND THAT PUTS THE PEOPLE I LOVE AT RISK. I HOPED THIS QUEST WOULD CHANGE THAT...
YOU CAN'T DO THIS!
...I'VE FAILED. AND UNLIKE THAT F IN SIXTH GRADE...

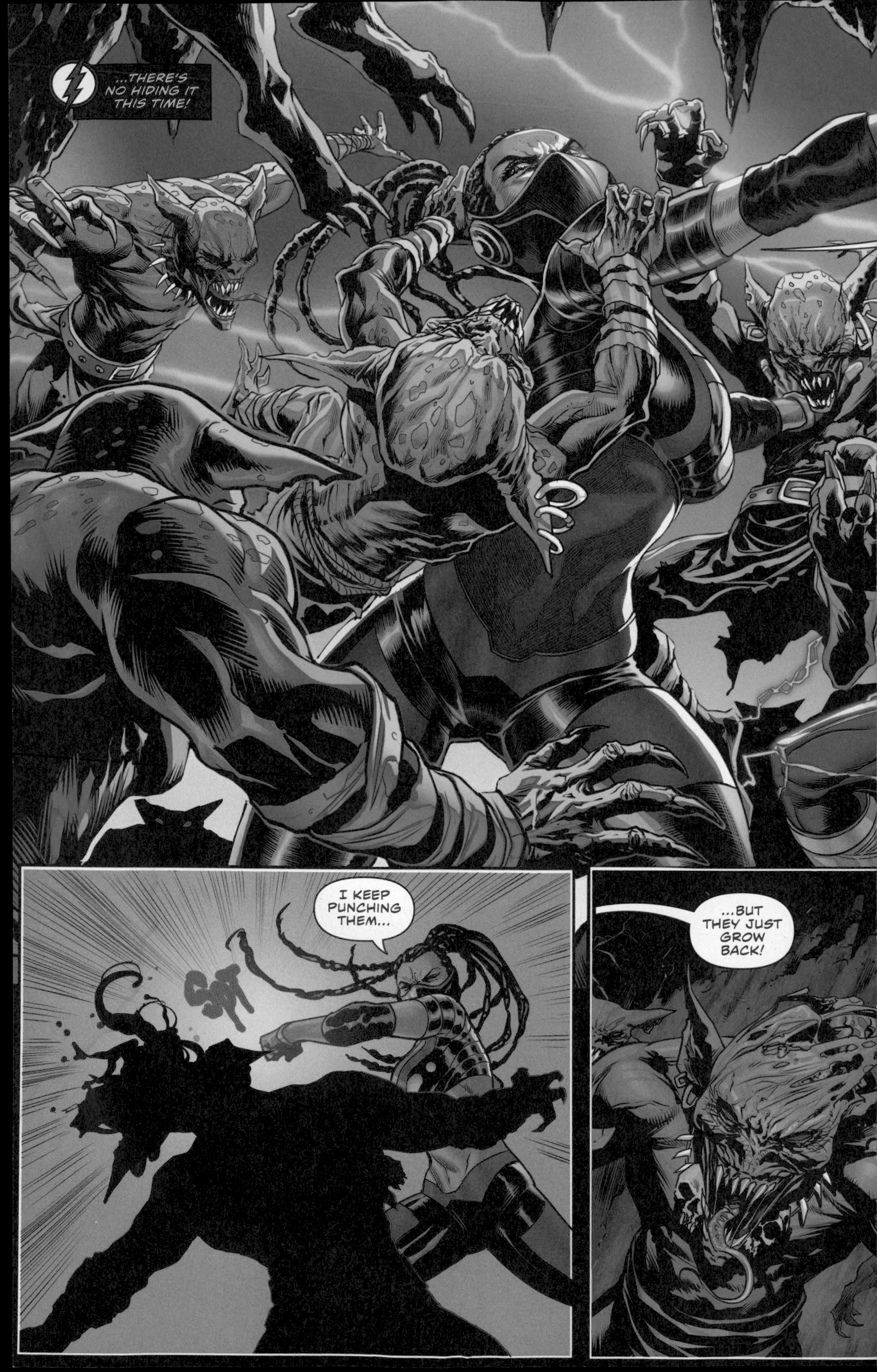
...THERE'S NO HIDING IT THIS TIME!
I KEEP PUNCHING THEM...
...BUT THEY JUST GROW BACK!

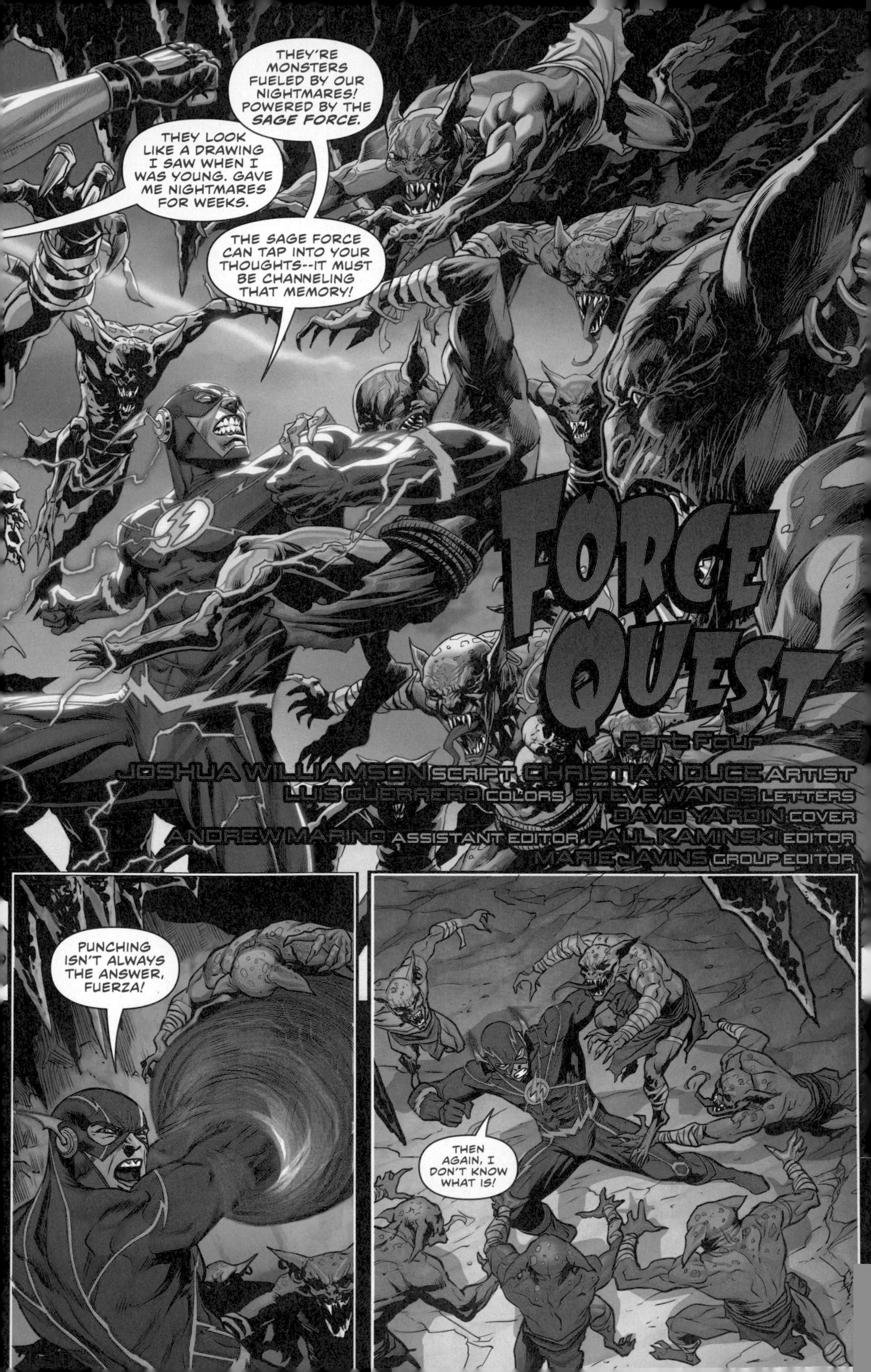
THEY'RE MONSTERS FUELED BY OUR NIGHTMARES! POWERED BY THE SAGE FORCE.
THEY LOOK LIKE A DRAWING I SAW WHEN I WAS YOUNG. GAVE ME NIGHTMARES FOR WEEKS.
THE SAGE FORCE CAN TAP INTO YOUR THOUGHTS--IT MUST BE CHANNELING THAT MEMORY!
FORCE QUEST
Part Four
JOSHUA WILLIAMSON SCRIPT CHRISTIAN DUCE ARTIST
LUIS GUERRERO COLORS STEVE WANDS LETTERS
DAVID YARDIN COVER
ANDREW MARINO ASSISTANT EDITOR PAUL KAMINSKI EDITOR
MARIE JAVINS GROUP EDITOR
PUNCHING ISN'T ALWAYS THE ANSWER, FUERZA!
THEN AGAIN, I DON'T KNOW WHAT IS!

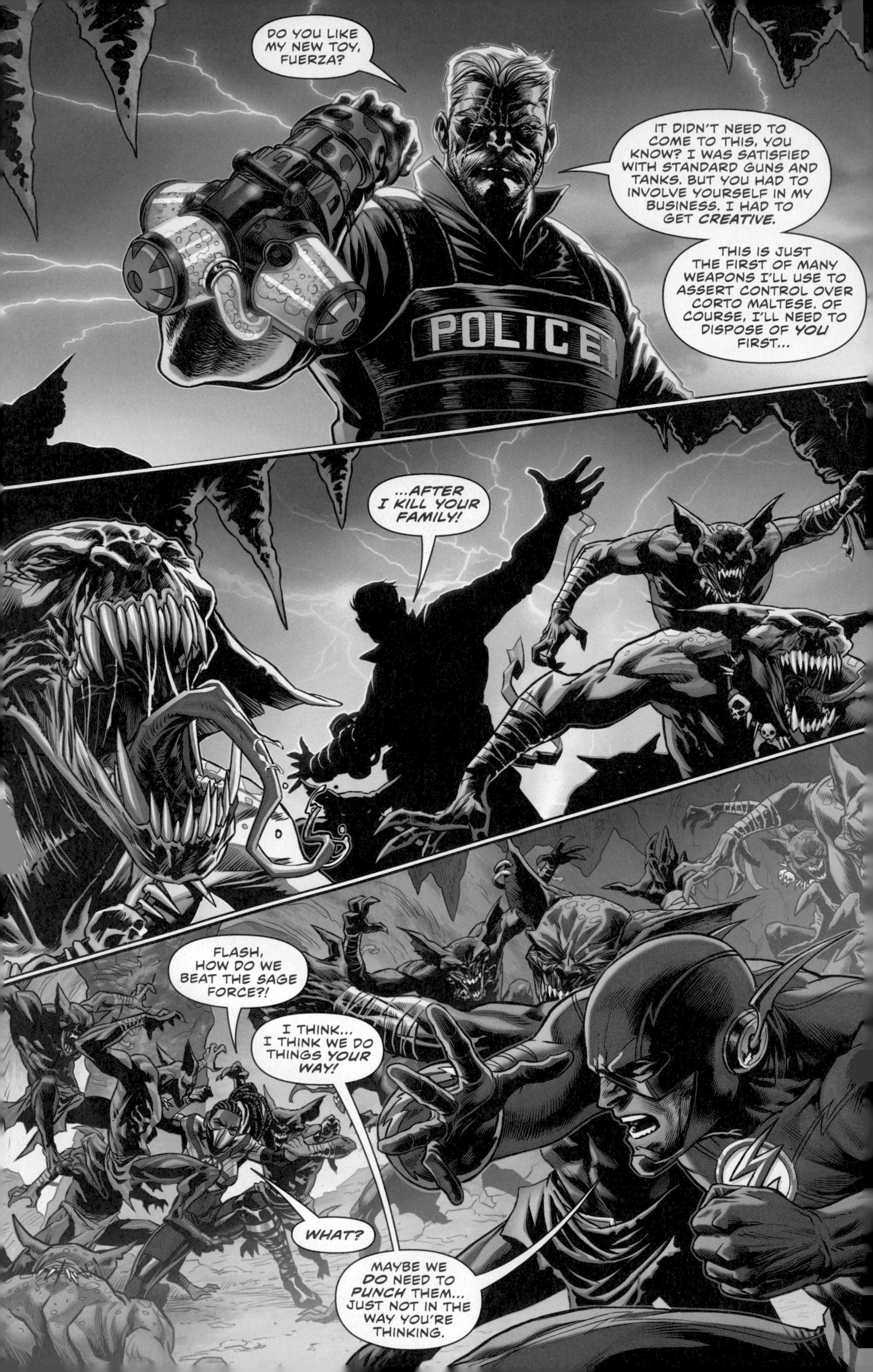
DO YOU LIKE MY NEW TOY, FUERZA?
IT DIDN'T NEED TO COME TO THIS, YOU KNOW? I WAS SATISFIED WITH STANDARD GUNS AND TANKS. BUT YOU HAD TO INVOLVE YOURSELF IN MY BUSINESS. I HAD TO GET *CREATIVE*.
THIS IS JUST THE FIRST OF MANY WEAPONS I'LL USE TO ASSERT CONTROL OVER CORTO MALTESE. OF COURSE, I'LL NEED TO DISPOSE OF *YOU* FIRST...
POLICE
...AFTER I KILL YOUR FAMILY!
FLASH, HOW DO WE BEAT THE SAGE FORCE?!
I THINK... I THINK WE DO THINGS *YOUR WAY!*
WHAT?
MAYBE WE *DO* NEED TO *PUNCH* THEM... JUST NOT IN THE WAY YOU'RE THINKING.

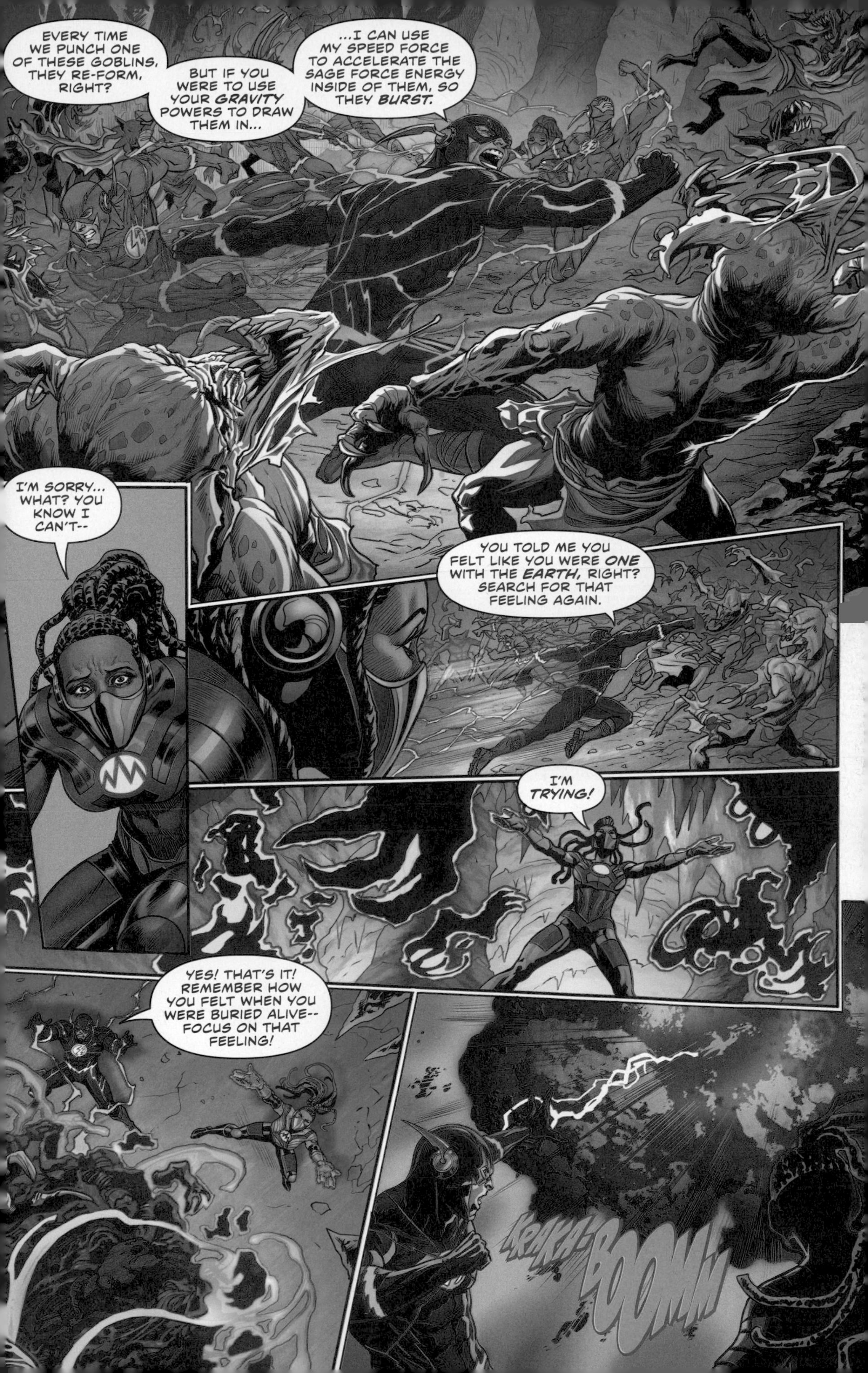
EVERY TIME WE PUNCH ONE OF THESE GOBLINS, THEY RE-FORM, RIGHT?
BUT IF YOU WERE TO USE YOUR GRAVITY POWERS TO DRAW THEM IN...
...I CAN USE MY SPEED FORCE TO ACCELERATE THE SAGE FORCE ENERGY INSIDE OF THEM, SO THEY BURST.
I'M SORRY... WHAT? YOU KNOW I CAN'T--
YOU TOLD ME YOU FELT LIKE YOU WERE ONE WITH THE EARTH, RIGHT? SEARCH FOR THAT FEELING AGAIN.
I'M TRYING!
YES! THAT'S IT! REMEMBER HOW YOU FELT WHEN YOU WERE BURIED ALIVE-- FOCUS ON THAT FEELING!
KRAKA-BOOMM

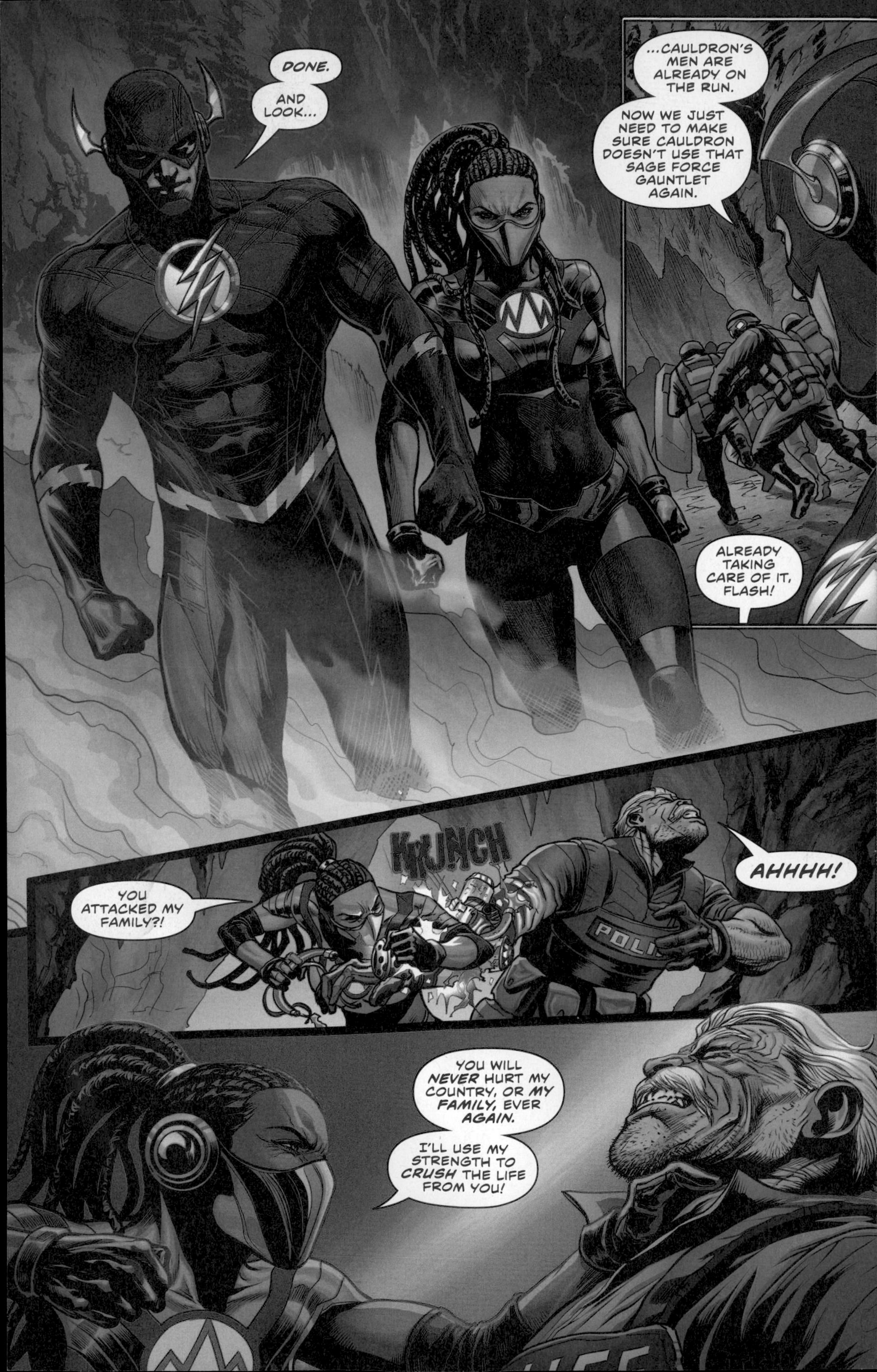
DONE.
AND LOOK...
...CAULDRON'S MEN ARE ALREADY ON THE RUN.
NOW WE JUST NEED TO MAKE SURE CAULDRON DOESN'T USE THAT SAGE FORCE GAUNTLET AGAIN.
ALREADY TAKING CARE OF IT, FLASH!
KKUNCH
YOU ATTACKED MY FAMILY?!
AHHHH!
YOU WILL NEVER HURT MY COUNTRY, OR MY FAMILY, EVER AGAIN.
I'LL USE MY STRENGTH TO CRUSH THE LIFE FROM YOU!

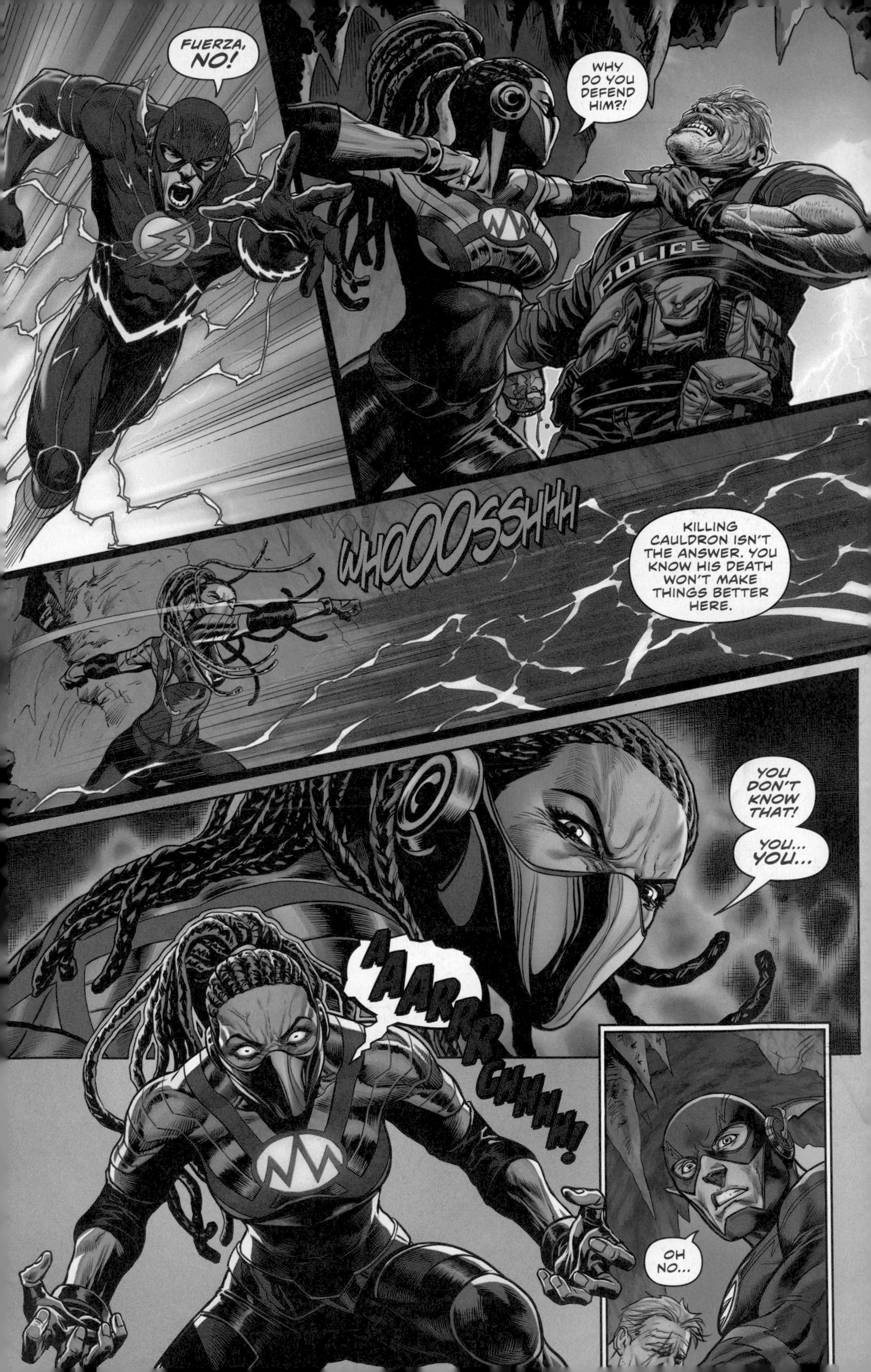

FUERZA, NO!
WHY DO YOU DEFEND HIM?!
POLICE
WHOOOOSSHHH
KILLING CAULDRON ISN'T THE ANSWER. YOU KNOW HIS DEATH WON'T MAKE THINGS BETTER HERE.
YOU DON'T KNOW THAT!
YOU... YOU...
AAARRRGHHHH!
OH NO...

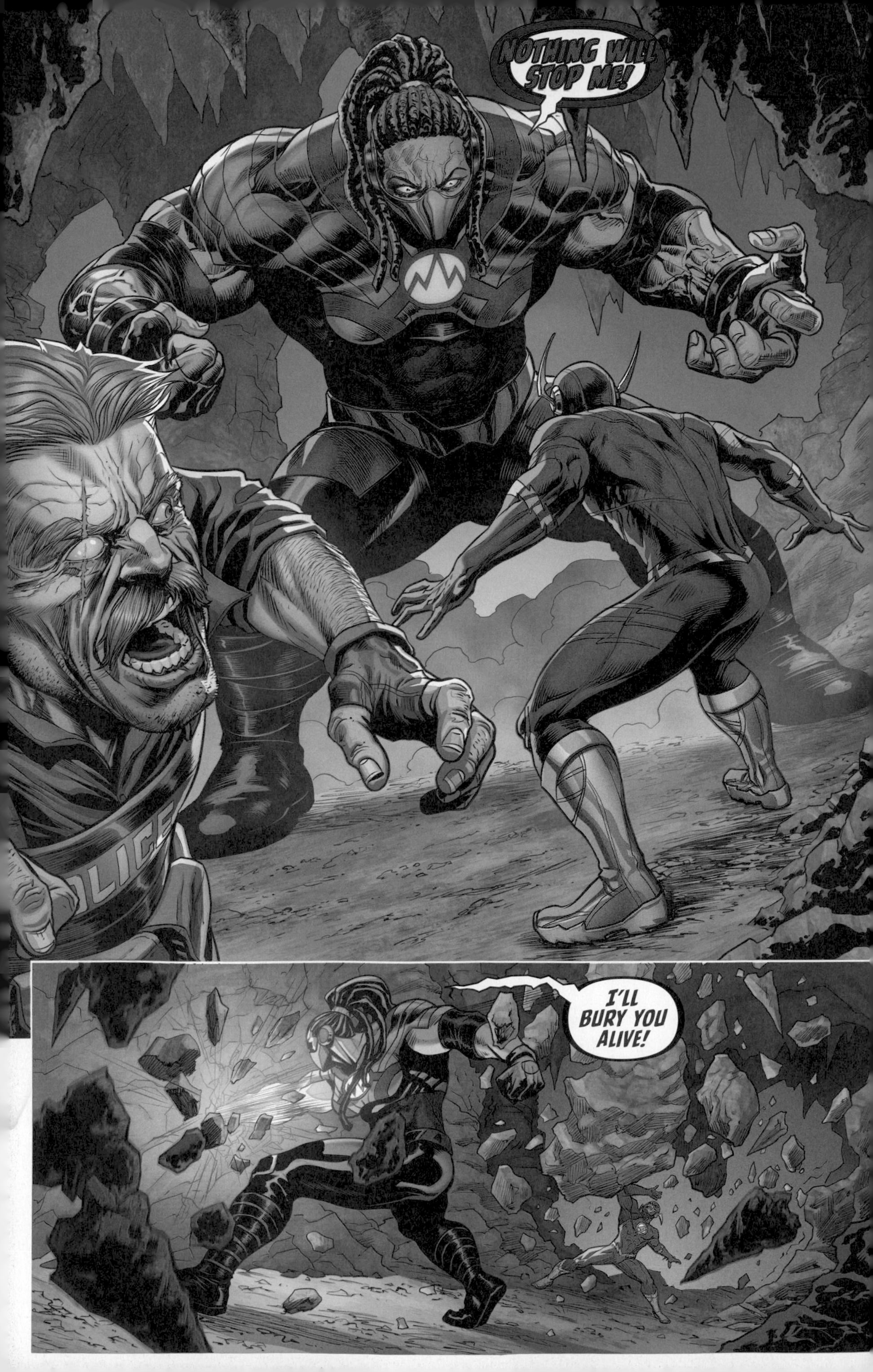
NOTHING WILL STOP ME!
POLICE
I'LL BURY YOU ALIVE!

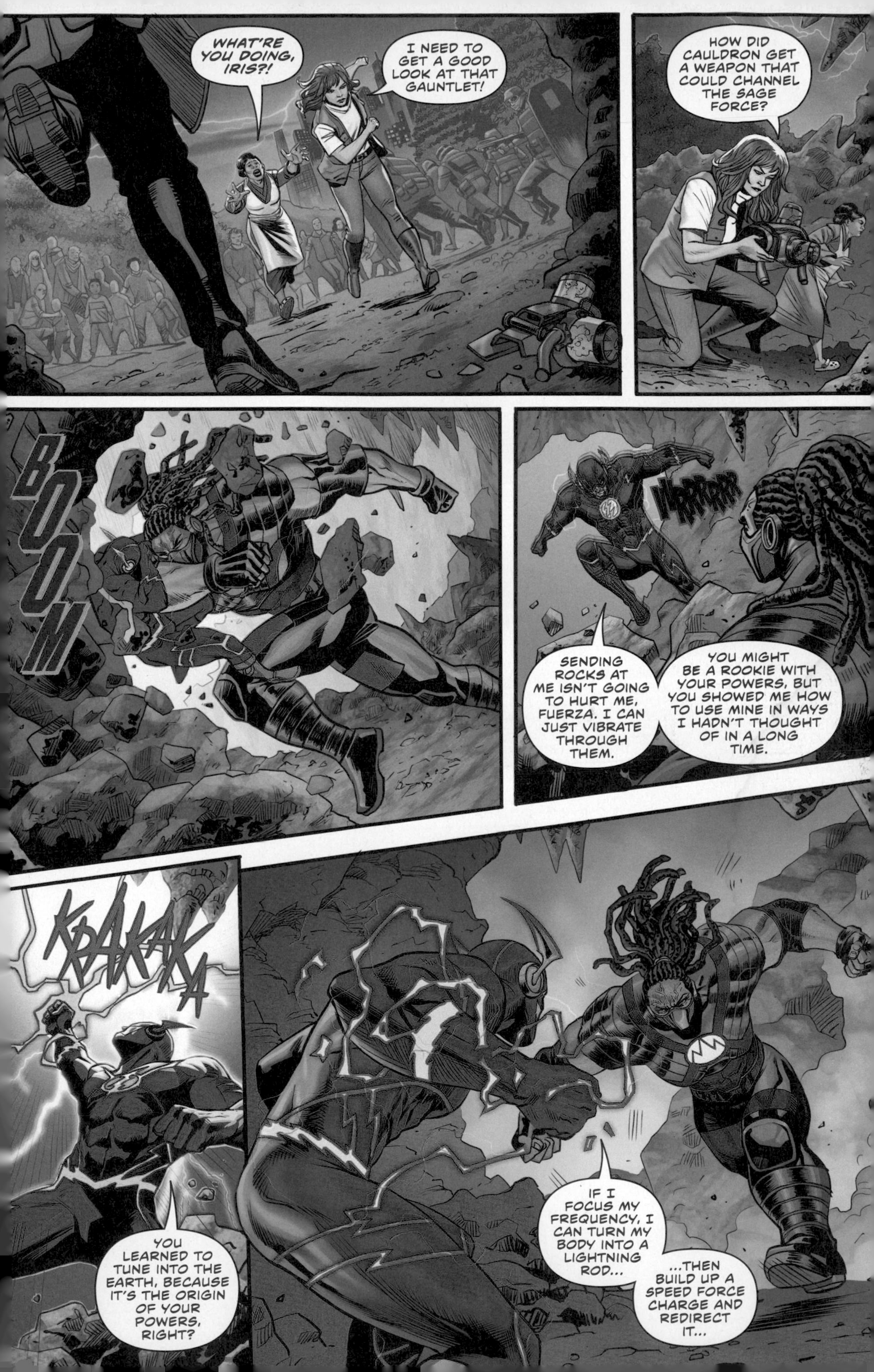
WHAT'RE YOU DOING, IRIS?!
I NEED TO GET A GOOD LOOK AT THAT GAUNTLET!
HOW DID CAULDRON GET A WEAPON THAT COULD CHANNEL THE SAGE FORCE?
BOOOM
VRRRRRRR
SENDING ROCKS AT ME ISN'T GOING TO HURT ME, FUERZA. I CAN JUST VIBRATE THROUGH THEM.
YOU MIGHT BE A ROOKIE WITH YOUR POWERS, BUT YOU SHOWED ME HOW TO USE MINE IN WAYS I HADN'T THOUGHT OF IN A LONG TIME.
KRAKAKAKA
YOU LEARNED TO TUNE INTO THE EARTH, BECAUSE IT'S THE ORIGIN OF YOUR POWERS, RIGHT?
IF I FOCUS MY FREQUENCY, I CAN TURN MY BODY INTO A LIGHTNING ROD...
...THEN BUILD UP A SPEED FORCE CHARGE AND REDIRECT IT...

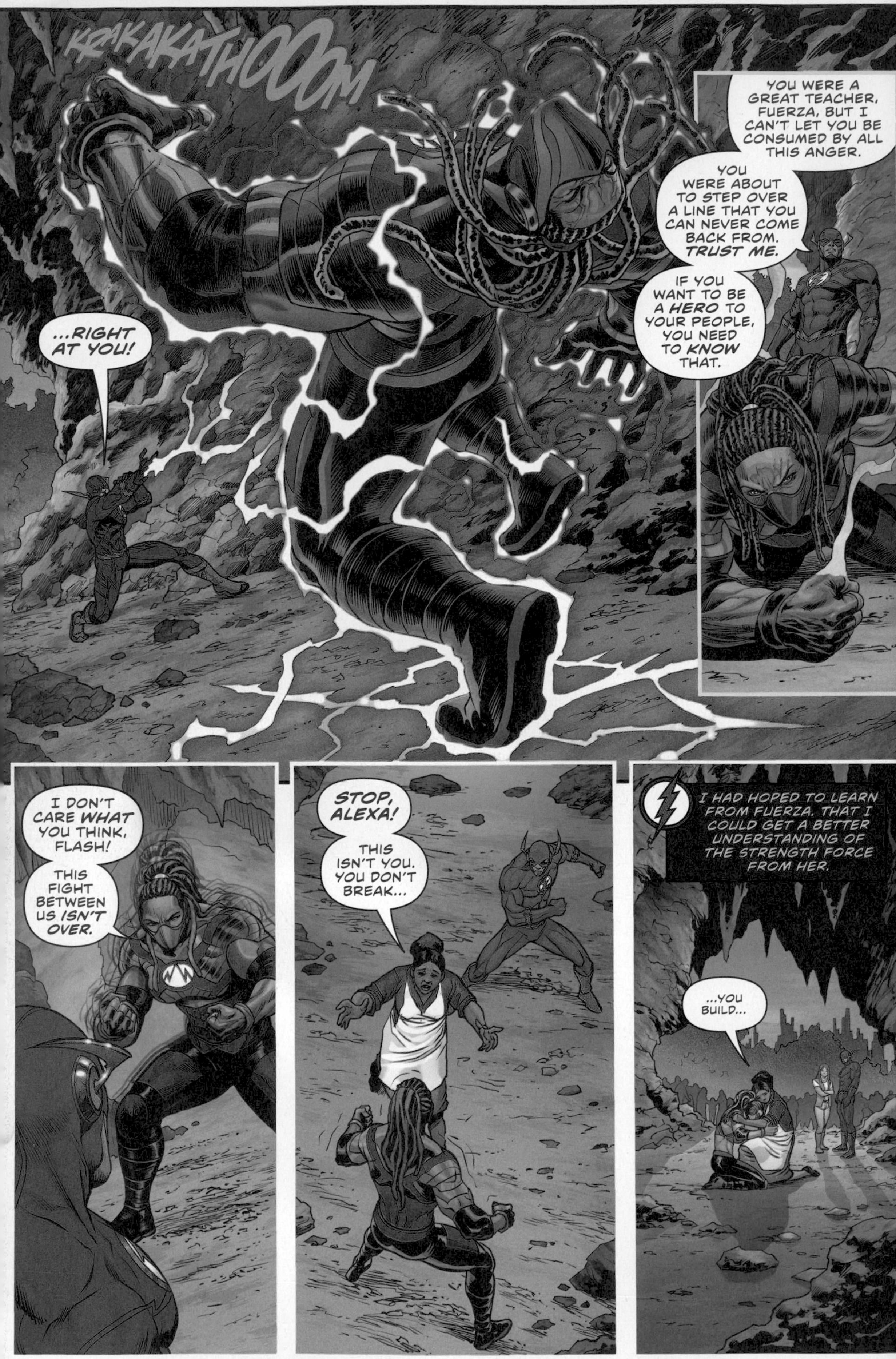
KRAKAKATHOOOOM
...RIGHT AT YOU!
YOU WERE A GREAT TEACHER, FUERZA, BUT I CAN'T LET YOU BE CONSUMED BY ALL THIS ANGER.
YOU WERE ABOUT TO STEP OVER A LINE THAT YOU CAN NEVER COME BACK FROM. TRUST ME.
IF YOU WANT TO BE A HERO TO YOUR PEOPLE, YOU NEED TO KNOW THAT.
I DON'T CARE WHAT YOU THINK, FLASH!
THIS FIGHT BETWEEN US ISN'T OVER.
STOP, ALEXA!
THIS ISN'T YOU. YOU DON'T BREAK...
I HAD HOPED TO LEARN FROM FUERZA. THAT I COULD GET A BETTER UNDERSTANDING OF THE STRENGTH FORCE FROM HER.
...YOU BUILD...

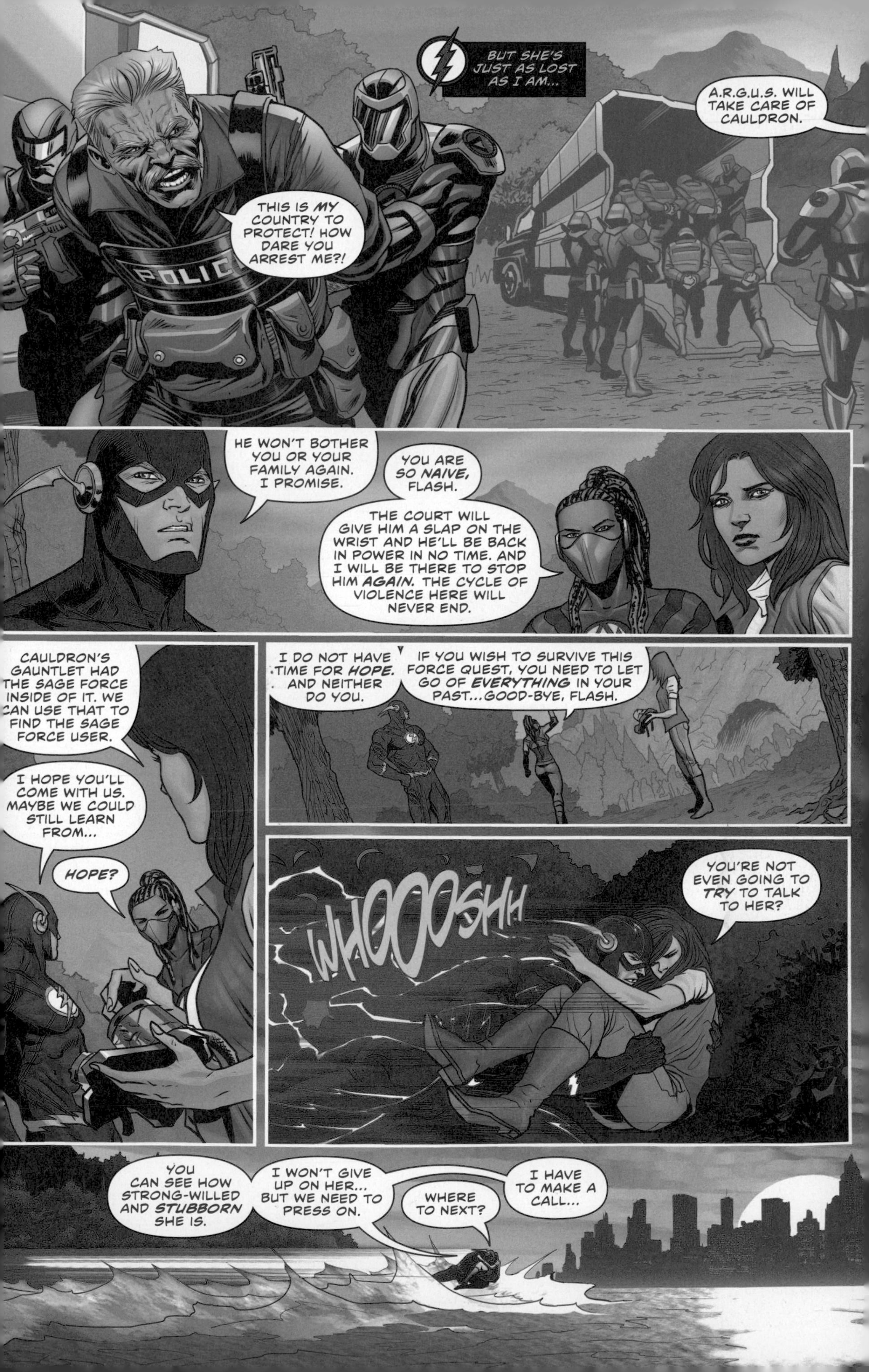
BUT SHE'S JUST AS LOST AS I AM...
THIS IS MY COUNTRY TO PROTECT! HOW DARE YOU ARREST ME?!
A.R.G.U.S. WILL TAKE CARE OF CAULDRON.
HE WON'T BOTHER YOU OR YOUR FAMILY AGAIN. I PROMISE.
YOU ARE SO NAIVE, FLASH.
THE COURT WILL GIVE HIM A SLAP ON THE WRIST AND HE'LL BE BACK IN POWER IN NO TIME. AND I WILL BE THERE TO STOP HIM AGAIN. THE CYCLE OF VIOLENCE HERE WILL NEVER END.
CAULDRON'S GAUNTLET HAD THE SAGE FORCE INSIDE OF IT. WE CAN USE THAT TO FIND THE SAGE FORCE USER.
I HOPE YOU'LL COME WITH US. MAYBE WE COULD STILL LEARN FROM...
HOPE?
I DO NOT HAVE TIME FOR HOPE. AND NEITHER DO YOU.
IF YOU WISH TO SURVIVE THIS FORCE QUEST, YOU NEED TO LET GO OF EVERYTHING IN YOUR PAST...GOOD-BYE, FLASH.
WHOOOSHH
YOU'RE NOT EVEN GOING TO TRY TO TALK TO HER?
YOU CAN SEE HOW STRONG-WILLED AND STUBBORN SHE IS.
I WON'T GIVE UP ON HER... BUT WE NEED TO PRESS ON.
WHERE TO NEXT?
I HAVE TO MAKE A CALL...

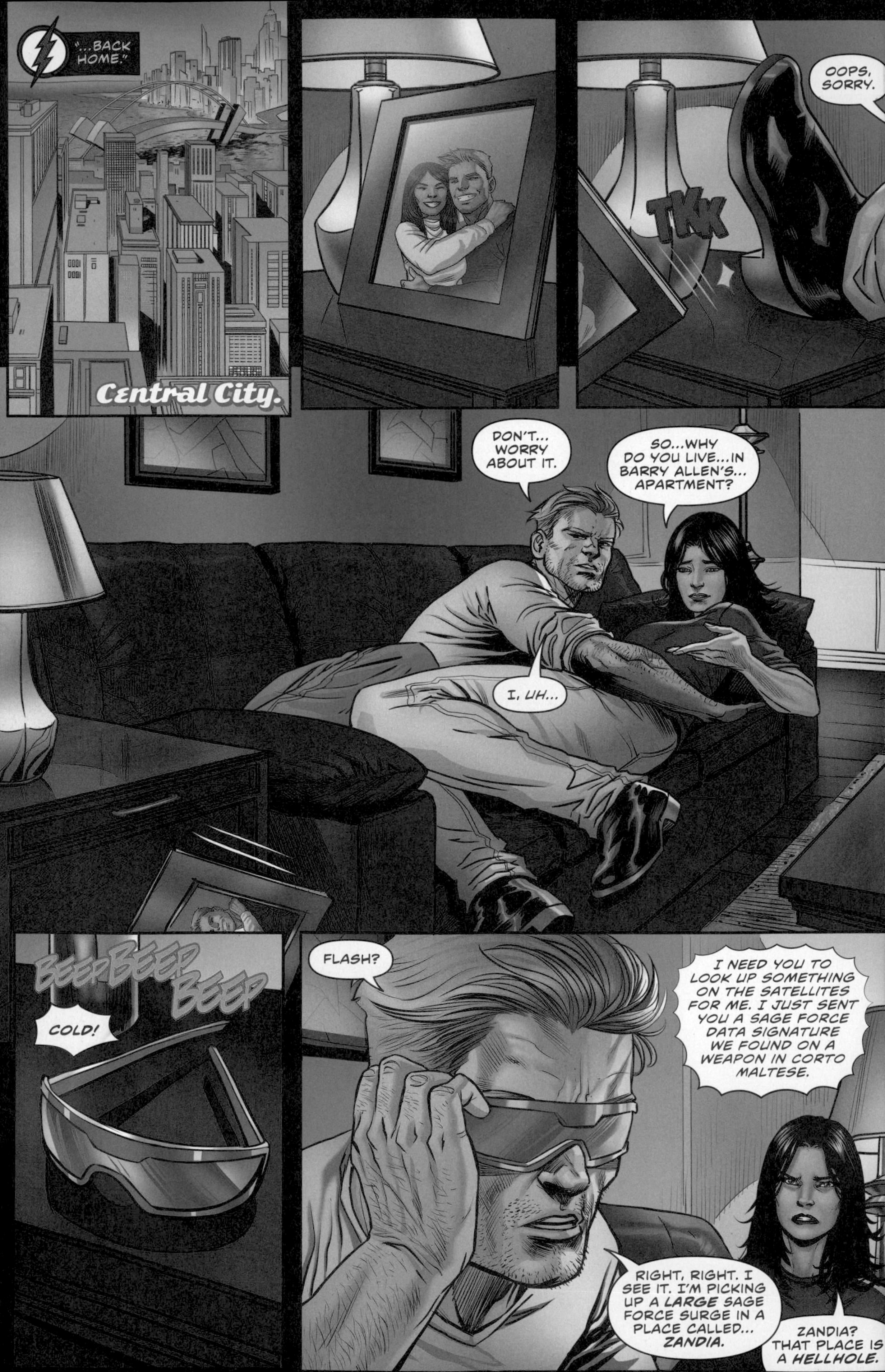
"...BACK HOME."
Central City.
TKK
OOPS, SORRY.
DON'T... WORRY ABOUT IT.
SO...WHY DO YOU LIVE...IN BARRY ALLEN'S... APARTMENT?
I, UH...
BEEP BEEP BEEP
COLD!
FLASH?
I NEED YOU TO LOOK UP SOMETHING ON THE SATELLITES FOR ME. I JUST SENT YOU A SAGE FORCE DATA SIGNATURE WE FOUND ON A WEAPON IN CORTO MALTESE.
RIGHT, RIGHT. I SEE IT. I'M PICKING UP A LARGE SAGE FORCE SURGE IN A PLACE CALLED... ZANDIA.
ZANDIA? THAT PLACE IS A HELLHOLE.

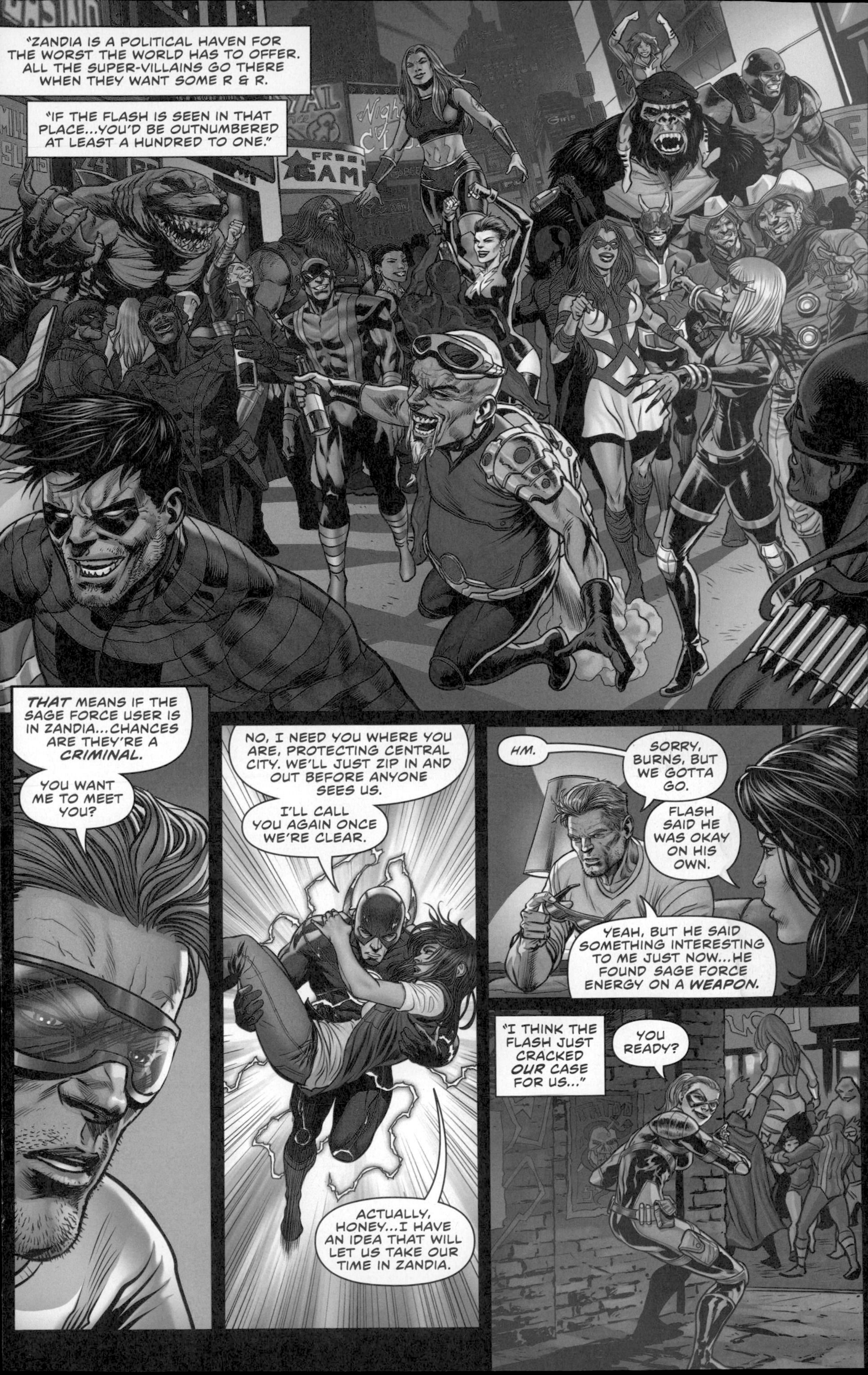
"ZANDIA IS A POLITICAL HAVEN FOR THE WORST THE WORLD HAS TO OFFER. ALL THE SUPER-VILLAINS GO THERE WHEN THEY WANT SOME R & R.
"IF THE FLASH IS SEEN IN THAT PLACE...YOU'D BE OUTNUMBERED AT LEAST A HUNDRED TO ONE."
THAT MEANS IF THE SAGE FORCE USER IS IN ZANDIA...CHANCES ARE THEY'RE A CRIMINAL.
YOU WANT ME TO MEET YOU?
NO, I NEED YOU WHERE YOU ARE, PROTECTING CENTRAL CITY. WE'LL JUST ZIP IN AND OUT BEFORE ANYONE SEES US.
I'LL CALL YOU AGAIN ONCE WE'RE CLEAR.
ACTUALLY, HONEY...I HAVE AN IDEA THAT WILL LET US TAKE OUR TIME IN ZANDIA.
HM.
SORRY, BURNS, BUT WE GOTTA GO.
FLASH SAID HE WAS OKAY ON HIS OWN.
YEAH, BUT HE SAID SOMETHING INTERESTING TO ME JUST NOW...HE FOUND SAGE FORCE ENERGY ON A WEAPON.
"I THINK THE FLASH JUST CRACKED OUR CASE FOR US..."
YOU READY?

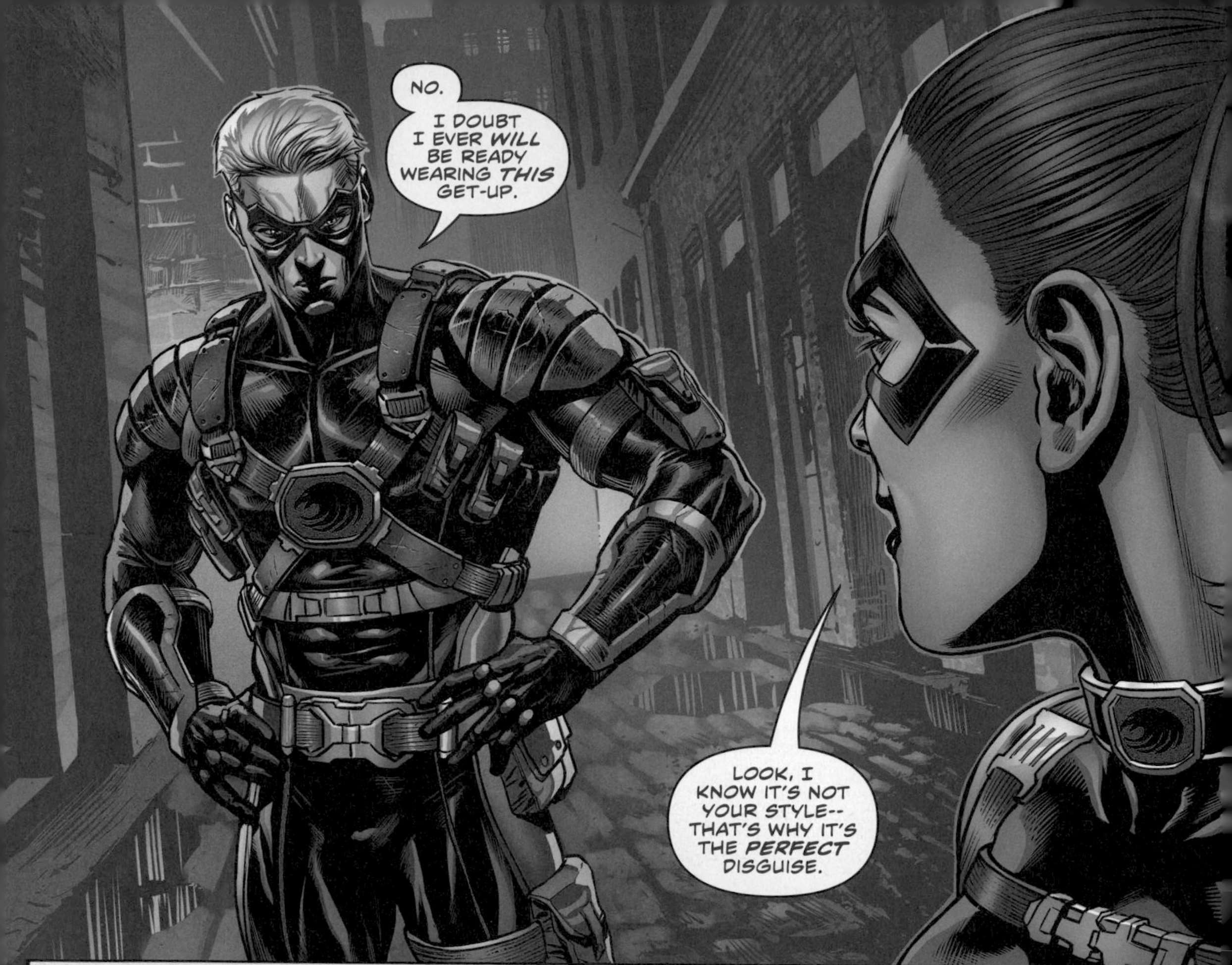
NO.
I DOUBT I EVER WILL BE READY WEARING THIS GET-UP.
LOOK, I KNOW IT'S NOT YOUR STYLE--THAT'S WHY IT'S THE PERFECT DISGUISE.

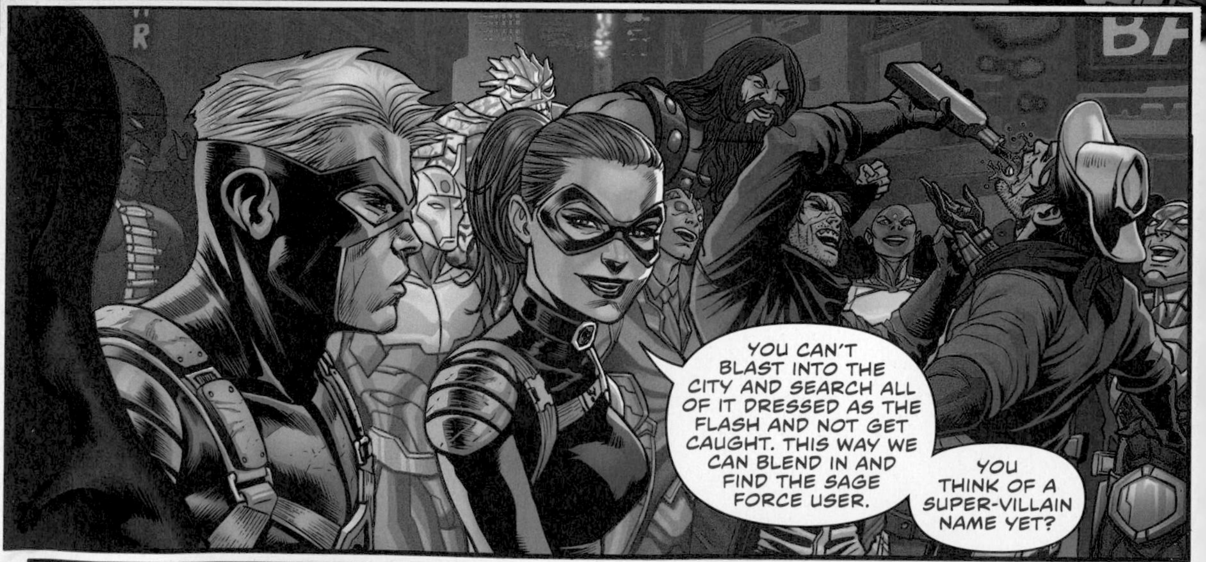
YOU CAN'T BLAST INTO THE CITY AND SEARCH ALL OF IT DRESSED AS THE FLASH AND NOT GET CAUGHT. THIS WAY WE CAN BLEND IN AND FIND THE SAGE FORCE USER.
YOU THINK OF A SUPER-VILLAIN NAME YET?

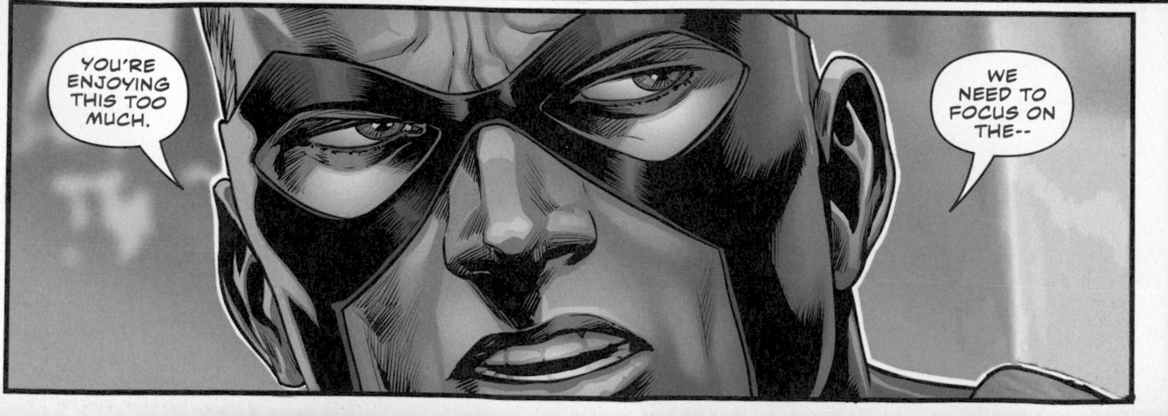
YOU'RE ENJOYING THIS TOO MUCH.
WE NEED TO FOCUS ON THE--

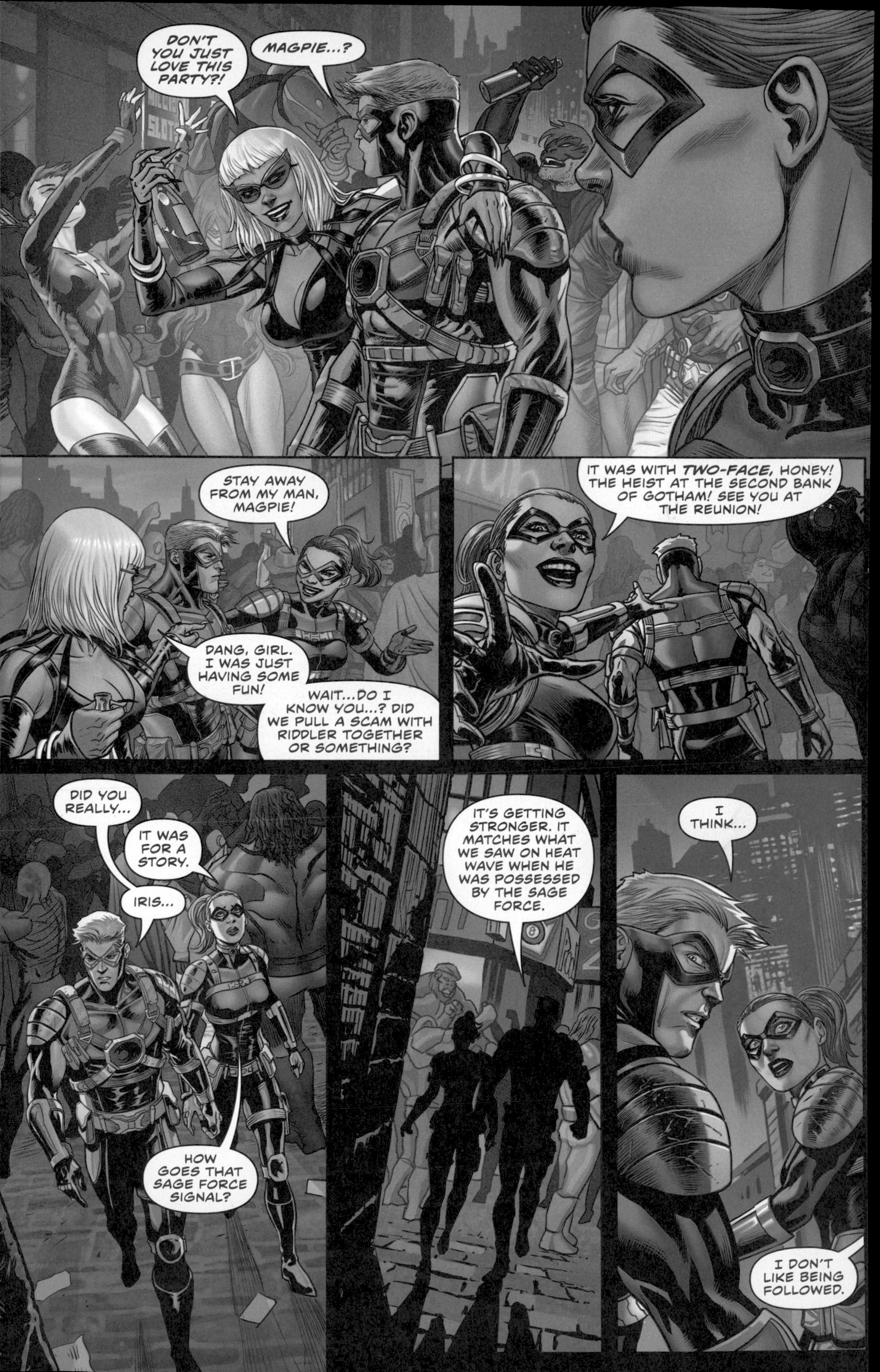
DON'T YOU JUST LOVE THIS PARTY?!
MAGPIE...?
MILLION SLOTS
STAY AWAY FROM MY MAN, MAGPIE!
DANG, GIRL. I WAS JUST HAVING SOME FUN!
WAIT...DO I KNOW YOU...? DID WE PULL A SCAM WITH RIDDLER TOGETHER OR SOMETHING?
IT WAS WITH **TWO-FACE,** HONEY! THE HEIST AT THE SECOND BANK OF GOTHAM! SEE YOU AT THE REUNION!
DID YOU REALLY...
IT WAS FOR A STORY.
IRIS...
HOW GOES THAT SAGE FORCE SIGNAL?
IT'S GETTING STRONGER. IT MATCHES WHAT WE SAW ON HEAT WAVE WHEN HE WAS POSSESSED BY THE SAGE FORCE.
I THINK...
I DON'T LIKE BEING FOLLOWED.

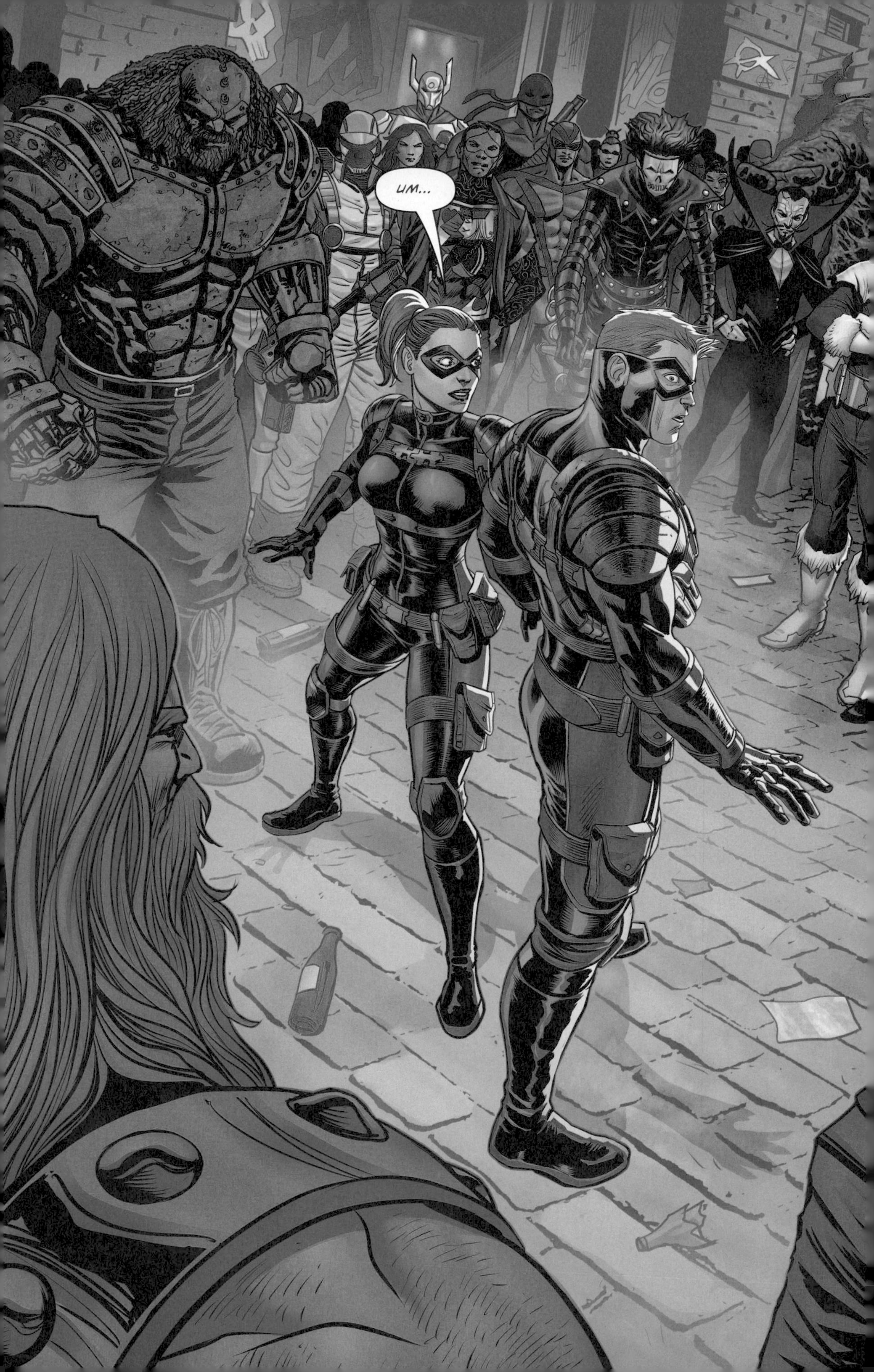
UM...

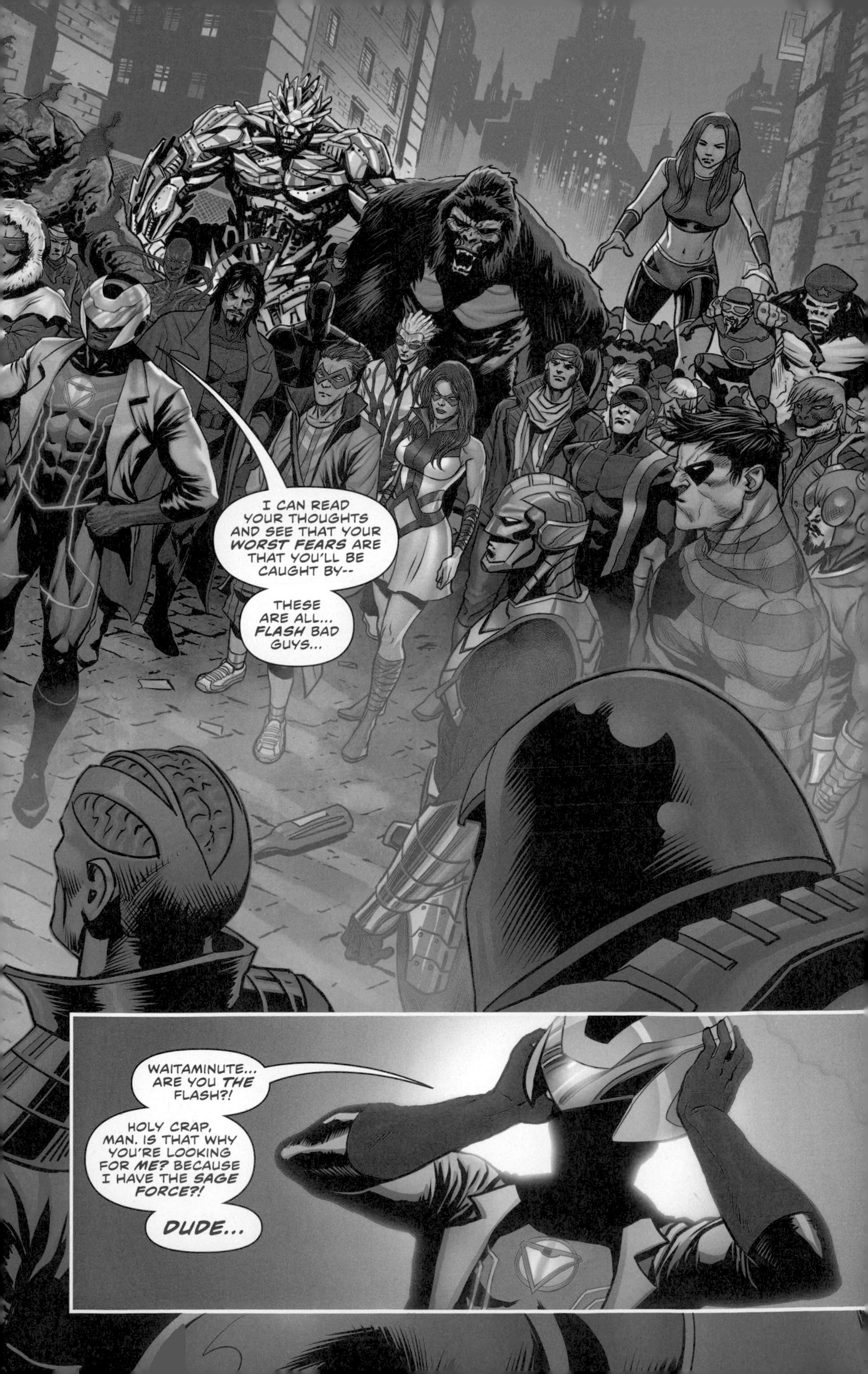
I CAN READ YOUR THOUGHTS AND SEE THAT YOUR *WORST FEARS* ARE THAT YOU'LL BE CAUGHT BY--
THESE ARE ALL... *FLASH* BAD GUYS...
WAITAMINUTE... ARE YOU *THE* FLASH?!
HOLY CRAP, MAN. IS THAT WHY YOU'RE LOOKING FOR *ME?* BECAUSE I HAVE THE *SAGE FORCE?!*
DUDE...

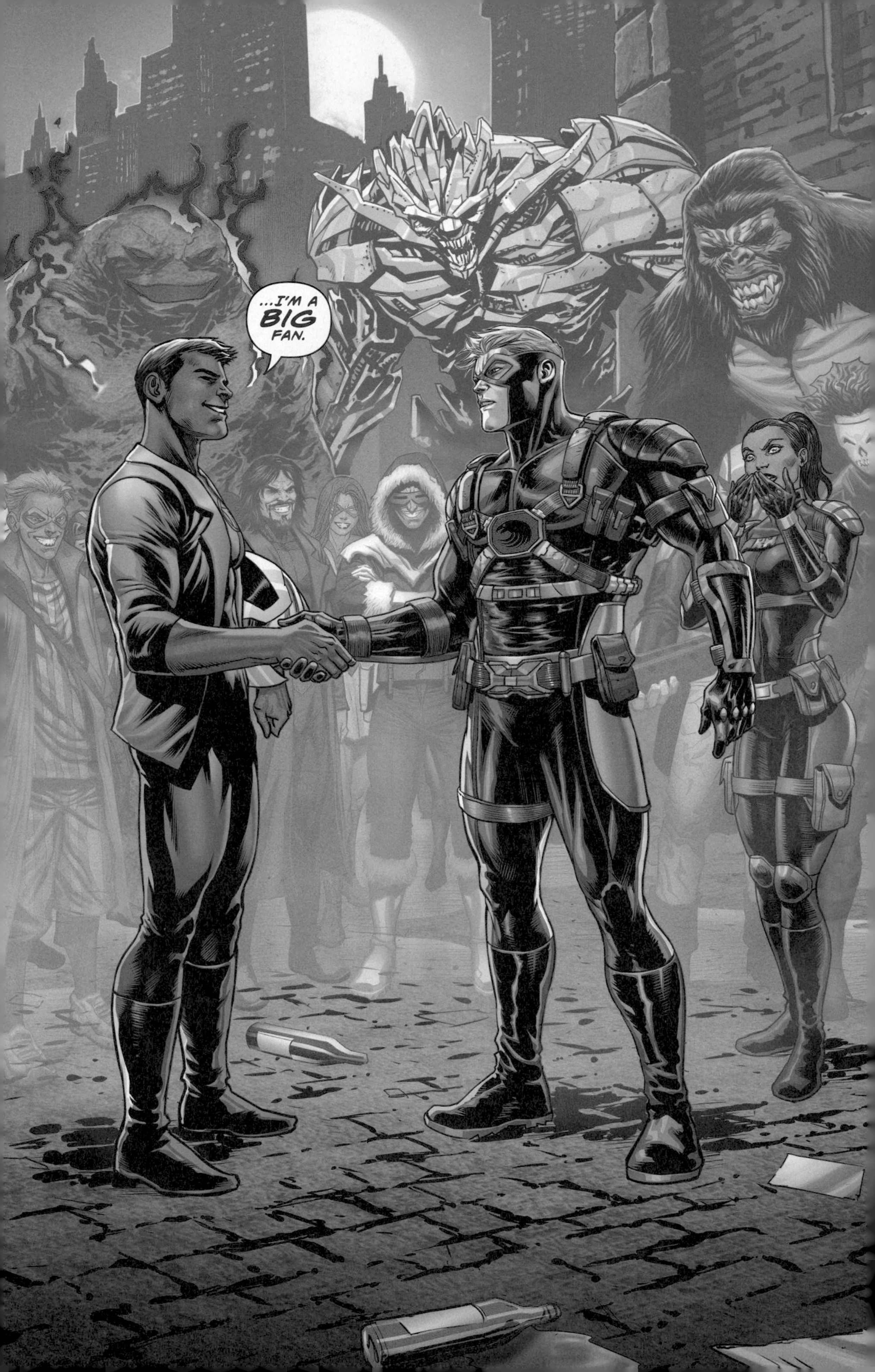
...I'M A BIG FAN.

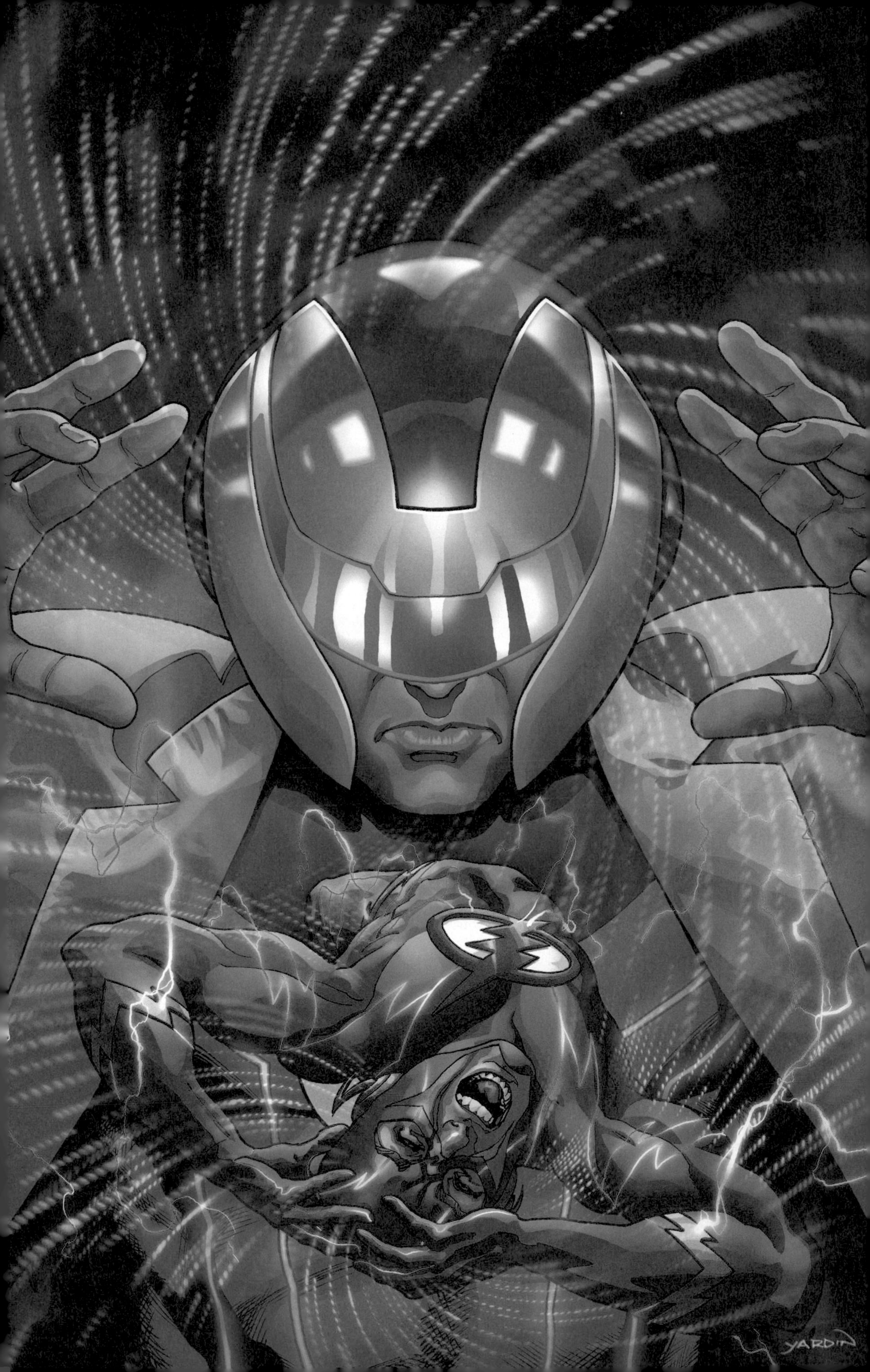
YARDIN

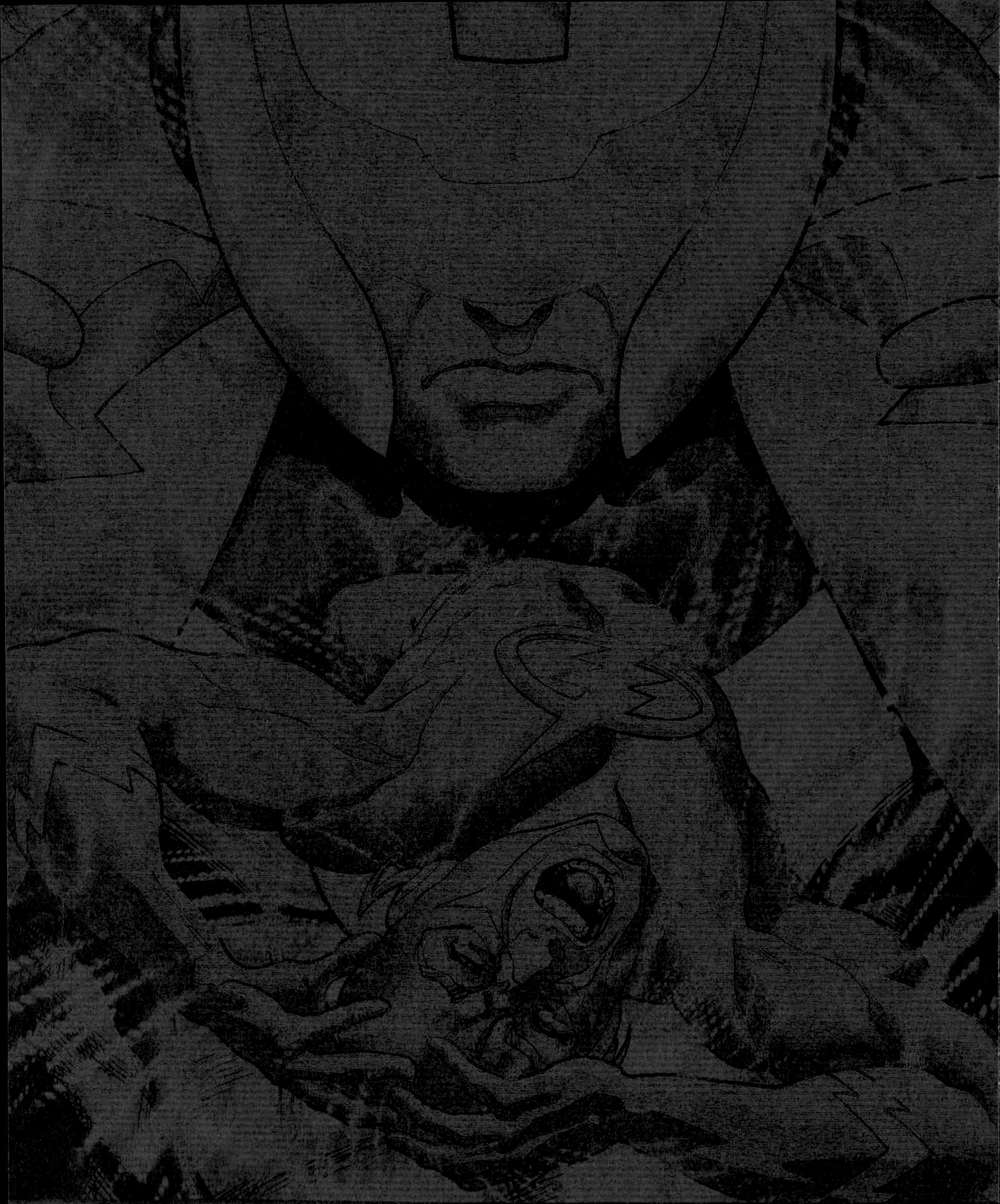

THE FLASH

#62

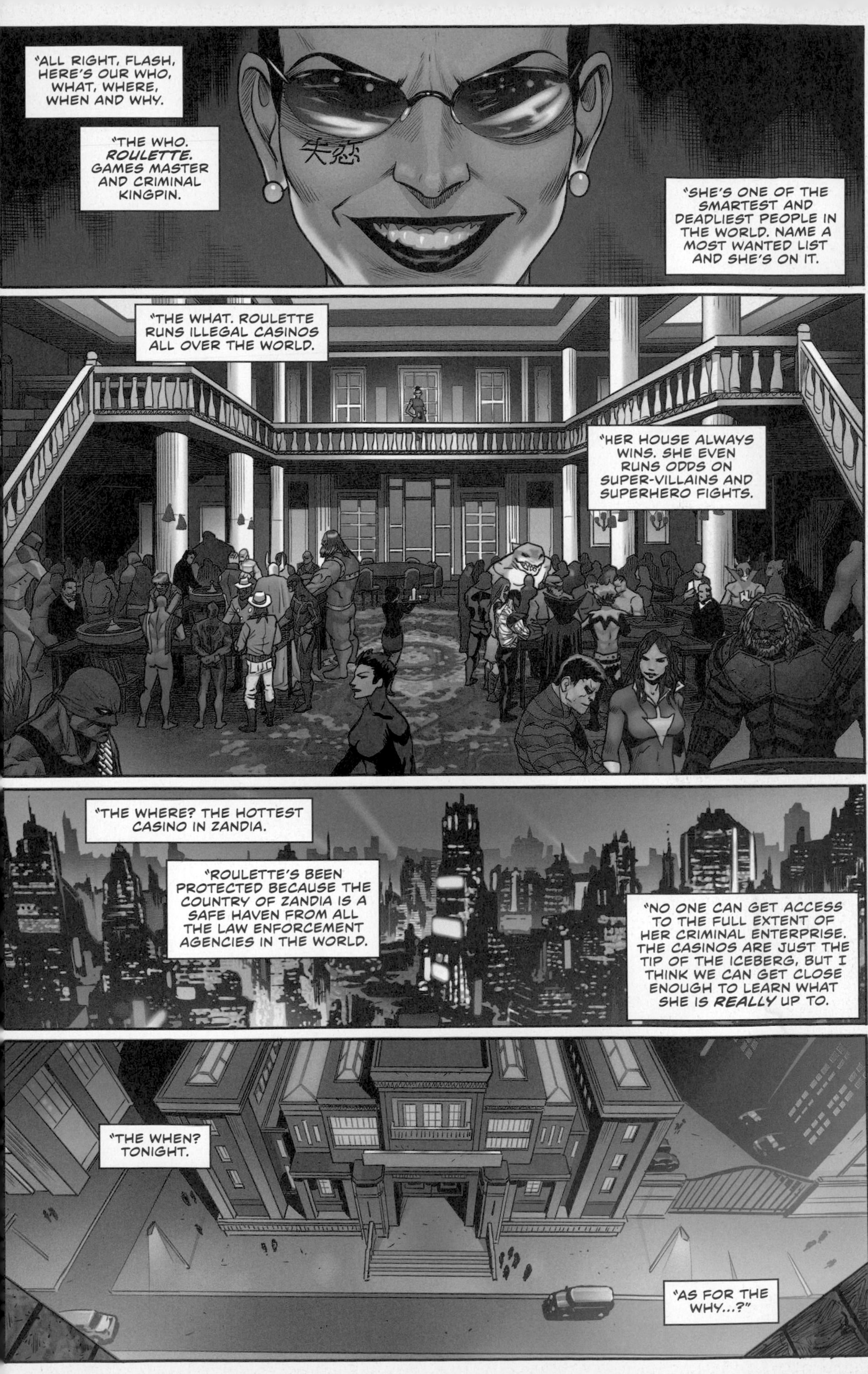
"ALL RIGHT, FLASH, HERE'S OUR WHO, WHAT, WHERE, WHEN AND WHY.
"THE WHO. ***ROULETTE.*** GAMES MASTER AND CRIMINAL KINGPIN.
"SHE'S ONE OF THE SMARTEST AND DEADLIEST PEOPLE IN THE WORLD. NAME A MOST WANTED LIST AND SHE'S ON IT.
"THE WHAT. ROULETTE RUNS ILLEGAL CASINOS ALL OVER THE WORLD.
"HER HOUSE ALWAYS WINS. SHE EVEN RUNS ODDS ON SUPER-VILLAINS AND SUPERHERO FIGHTS.
"THE WHERE? THE HOTTEST CASINO IN ZANDIA.
"ROULETTE'S BEEN PROTECTED BECAUSE THE COUNTRY OF ZANDIA IS A SAFE HAVEN FROM ALL THE LAW ENFORCEMENT AGENCIES IN THE WORLD.
"NO ONE CAN GET ACCESS TO THE FULL EXTENT OF HER CRIMINAL ENTERPRISE. THE CASINOS ARE JUST THE TIP OF THE ICEBERG, BUT I THINK WE CAN GET CLOSE ENOUGH TO LEARN WHAT SHE IS ***REALLY*** UP TO.
"THE WHEN? TONIGHT.
"AS FOR THE WHY...?"

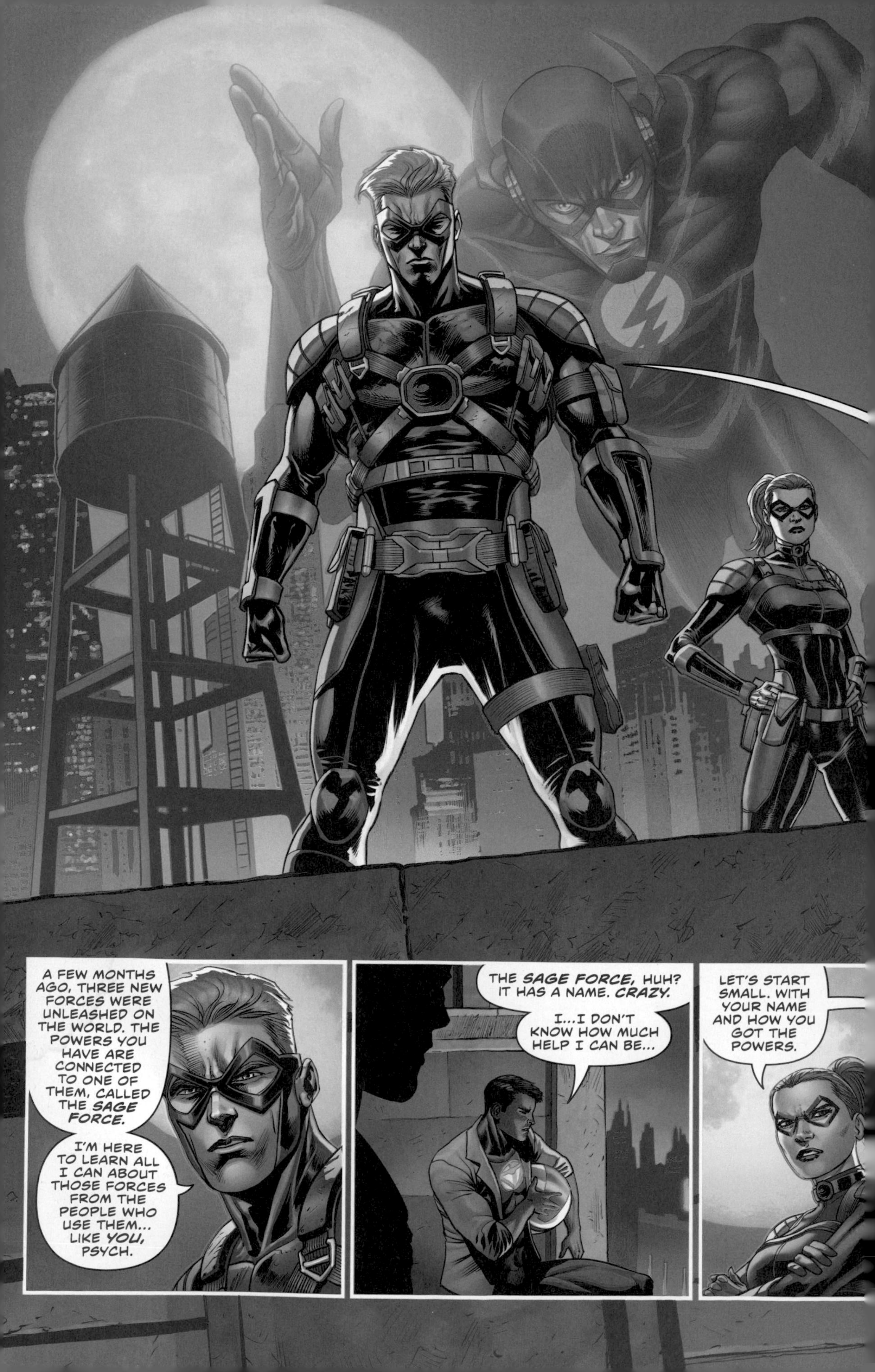
A FEW MONTHS AGO, THREE NEW FORCES WERE UNLEASHED ON THE WORLD. THE POWERS YOU HAVE ARE CONNECTED TO ONE OF THEM, CALLED THE *SAGE FORCE*.
I'M HERE TO LEARN ALL I CAN ABOUT THOSE FORCES FROM THE PEOPLE WHO USE THEM... LIKE *YOU*, PSYCH.
THE *SAGE FORCE*, HUH? IT HAS A NAME. *CRAZY*.
I...I DON'T KNOW HOW MUCH HELP I CAN BE...
LET'S START SMALL. WITH YOUR NAME AND HOW YOU GOT THE POWERS.

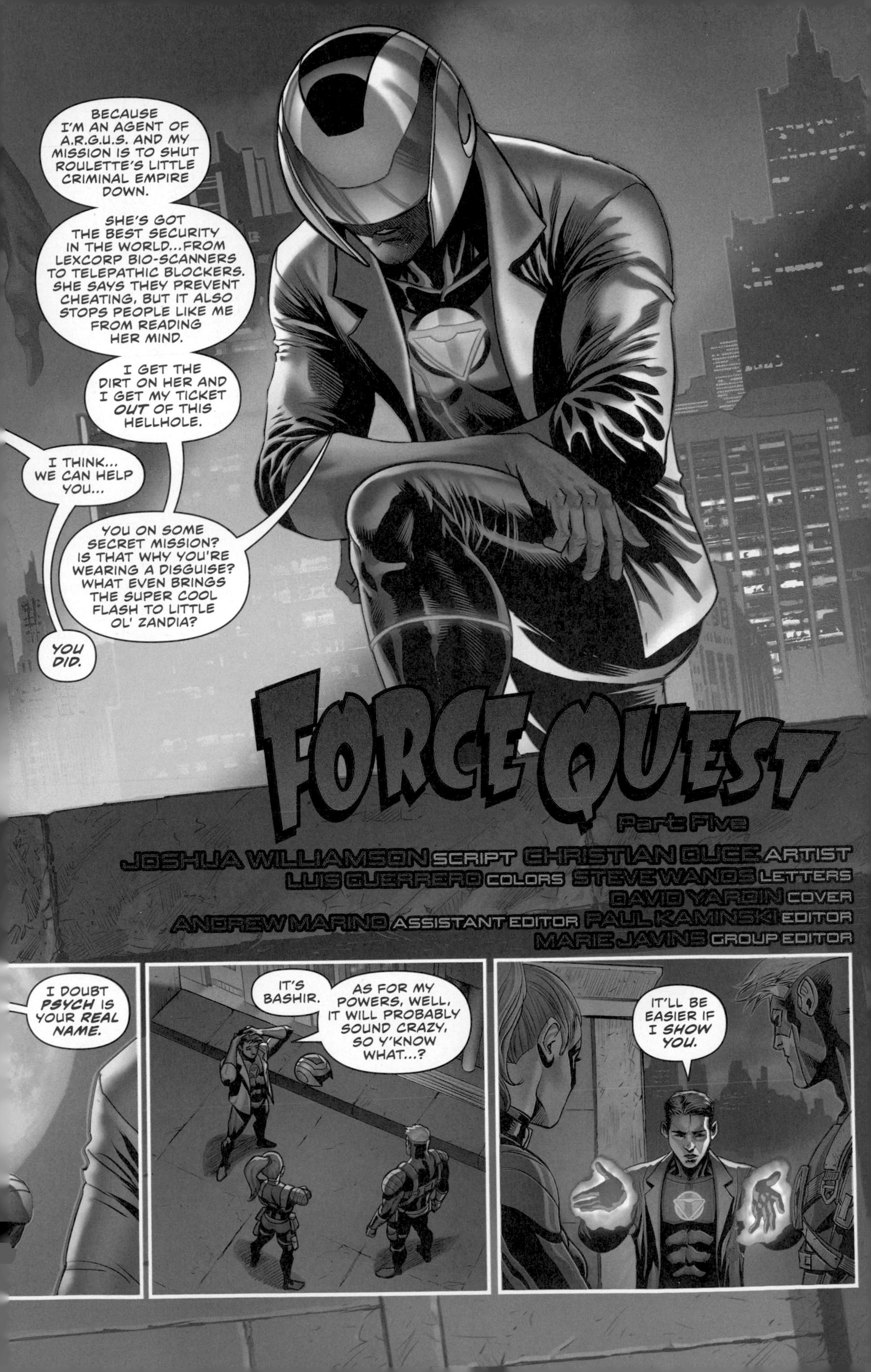
BECAUSE I'M AN AGENT OF A.R.G.U.S. AND MY MISSION IS TO SHUT ROULETTE'S LITTLE CRIMINAL EMPIRE DOWN.
SHE'S GOT THE BEST SECURITY IN THE WORLD...FROM LEXCORP BIO-SCANNERS TO TELEPATHIC BLOCKERS. SHE SAYS THEY PREVENT CHEATING, BUT IT ALSO STOPS PEOPLE LIKE ME FROM READING HER MIND.
I GET THE DIRT ON HER AND I GET MY TICKET *OUT* OF THIS HELLHOLE.
I THINK... WE CAN HELP YOU...
YOU ON SOME SECRET MISSION? IS THAT WHY YOU'RE WEARING A DISGUISE? WHAT EVEN BRINGS THE SUPER COOL FLASH TO LITTLE OL' ZANDIA?
YOU DID.
FORCE QUEST
Part Five
JOSHUA WILLIAMSON SCRIPT CHRISTIAN DUCE ARTIST
LUIS GUERRERO COLORS STEVE WANDS LETTERS
DAVID YARDIN COVER
ANDREW MARINO ASSISTANT EDITOR PAUL KAMINSKI EDITOR
MARIE JAVINS GROUP EDITOR
I DOUBT *PSYCH* IS YOUR *REAL NAME.*
IT'S BASHIR.
AS FOR MY POWERS, WELL, IT WILL PROBABLY SOUND CRAZY, SO Y'KNOW WHAT...?
IT'LL BE EASIER IF I *SHOW* YOU.

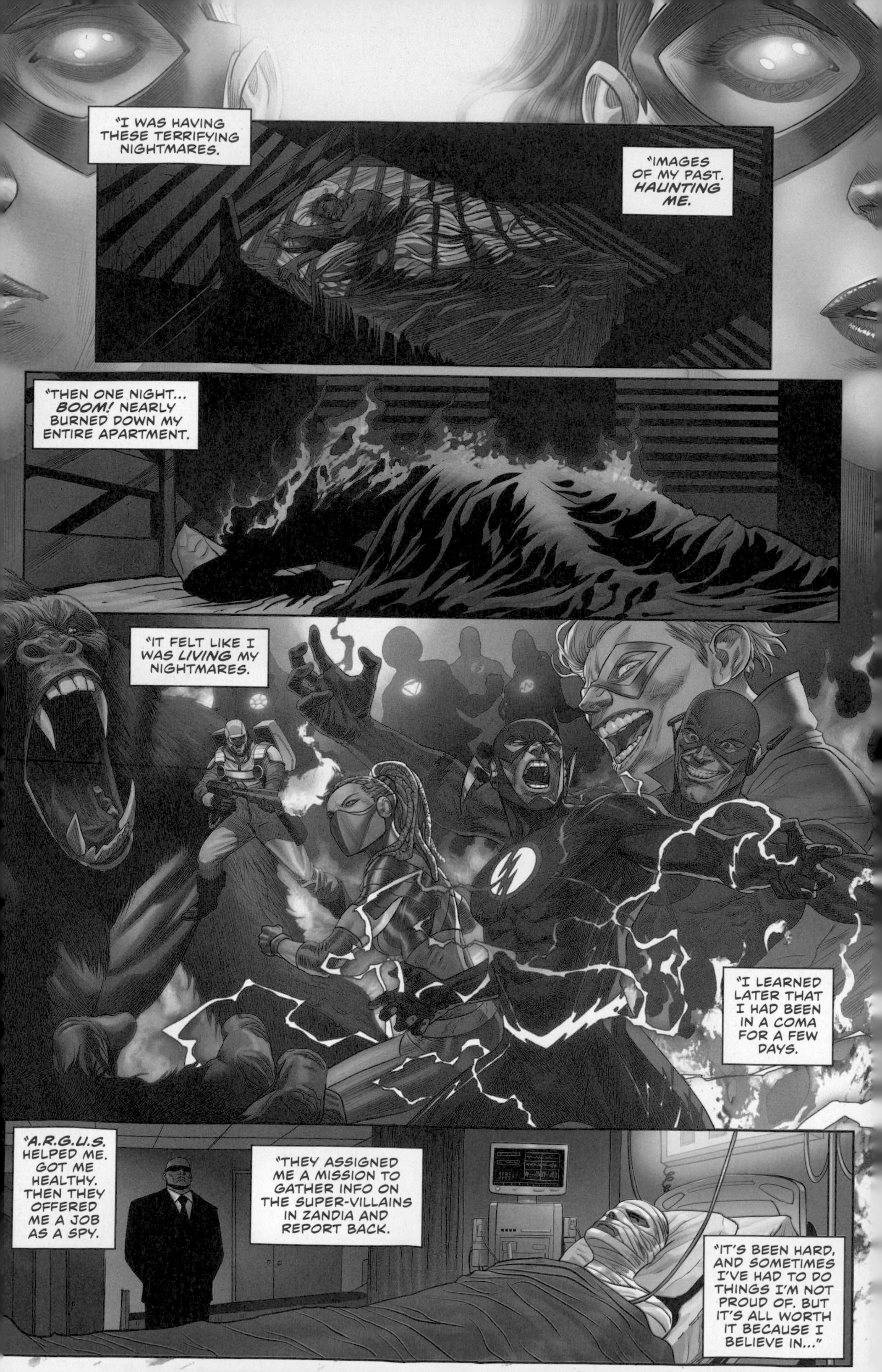
"I WAS HAVING THESE TERRIFYING NIGHTMARES.
"IMAGES OF MY PAST. *HAUNTING* ME.
"THEN ONE NIGHT... *BOOM!* NEARLY BURNED DOWN MY ENTIRE APARTMENT.
"IT FELT LIKE I WAS *LIVING* MY NIGHTMARES.
"I LEARNED LATER THAT I HAD BEEN IN A COMA FOR A FEW DAYS.
"*A.R.G.U.S.* HELPED ME. GOT ME HEALTHY. THEN THEY OFFERED ME A JOB AS A SPY.
"THEY ASSIGNED ME A MISSION TO GATHER INFO ON THE SUPER-VILLAINS IN ZANDIA AND REPORT BACK.
"IT'S BEEN HARD, AND SOMETIMES I'VE HAD TO DO THINGS I'M NOT PROUD OF. BUT IT'S ALL WORTH IT BECAUSE I BELIEVE IN..."

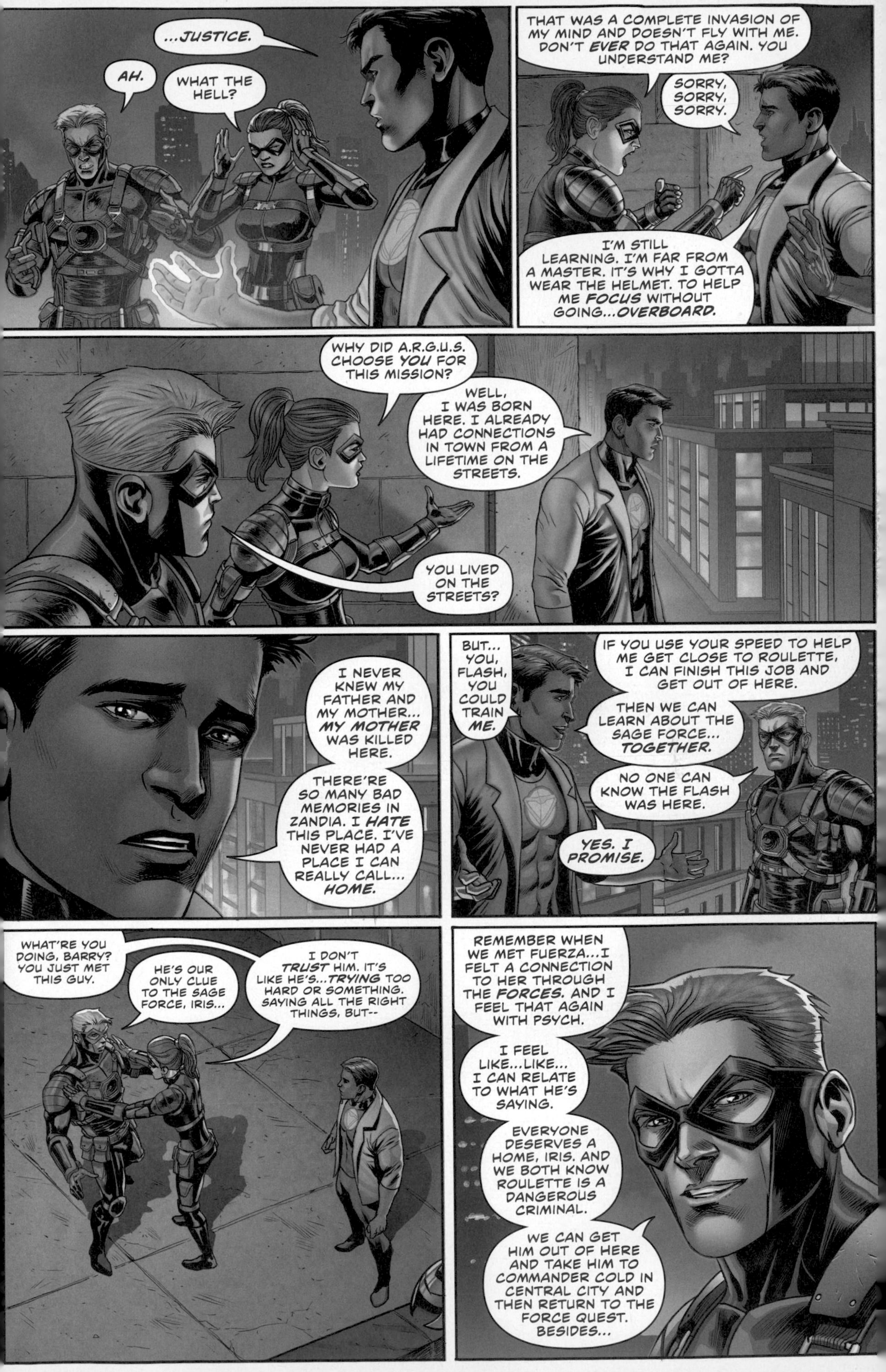
...JUSTICE.
AH.
WHAT THE HELL?
THAT WAS A COMPLETE INVASION OF MY MIND AND DOESN'T FLY WITH ME. DON'T EVER DO THAT AGAIN. YOU UNDERSTAND ME?
SORRY, SORRY, SORRY.
I'M STILL LEARNING. I'M FAR FROM A MASTER. IT'S WHY I GOTTA WEAR THE HELMET. TO HELP ME FOCUS WITHOUT GOING...OVERBOARD.
WHY DID A.R.G.U.S. CHOOSE YOU FOR THIS MISSION?
WELL, I WAS BORN HERE. I ALREADY HAD CONNECTIONS IN TOWN FROM A LIFETIME ON THE STREETS.
YOU LIVED ON THE STREETS?
I NEVER KNEW MY FATHER AND MY MOTHER... MY MOTHER WAS KILLED HERE.
THERE'RE SO MANY BAD MEMORIES IN ZANDIA. I HATE THIS PLACE. I'VE NEVER HAD A PLACE I CAN REALLY CALL... HOME.
BUT... YOU, FLASH, YOU COULD TRAIN ME.
IF YOU USE YOUR SPEED TO HELP ME GET CLOSE TO ROULETTE, I CAN FINISH THIS JOB AND GET OUT OF HERE.
THEN WE CAN LEARN ABOUT THE SAGE FORCE... TOGETHER.
NO ONE CAN KNOW THE FLASH WAS HERE.
YES. I PROMISE.
WHAT'RE YOU DOING, BARRY? YOU JUST MET THIS GUY.
HE'S OUR ONLY CLUE TO THE SAGE FORCE, IRIS...
I DON'T TRUST HIM. IT'S LIKE HE'S...TRYING TOO HARD OR SOMETHING. SAYING ALL THE RIGHT THINGS, BUT--
REMEMBER WHEN WE MET FUERZA...I FELT A CONNECTION TO HER THROUGH THE FORCES. AND I FEEL THAT AGAIN WITH PSYCH.
I FEEL LIKE...LIKE... I CAN RELATE TO WHAT HE'S SAYING.
EVERYONE DESERVES A HOME, IRIS. AND WE BOTH KNOW ROULETTE IS A DANGEROUS CRIMINAL.
WE CAN GET HIM OUT OF HERE AND TAKE HIM TO COMMANDER COLD IN CENTRAL CITY AND THEN RETURN TO THE FORCE QUEST. BESIDES...

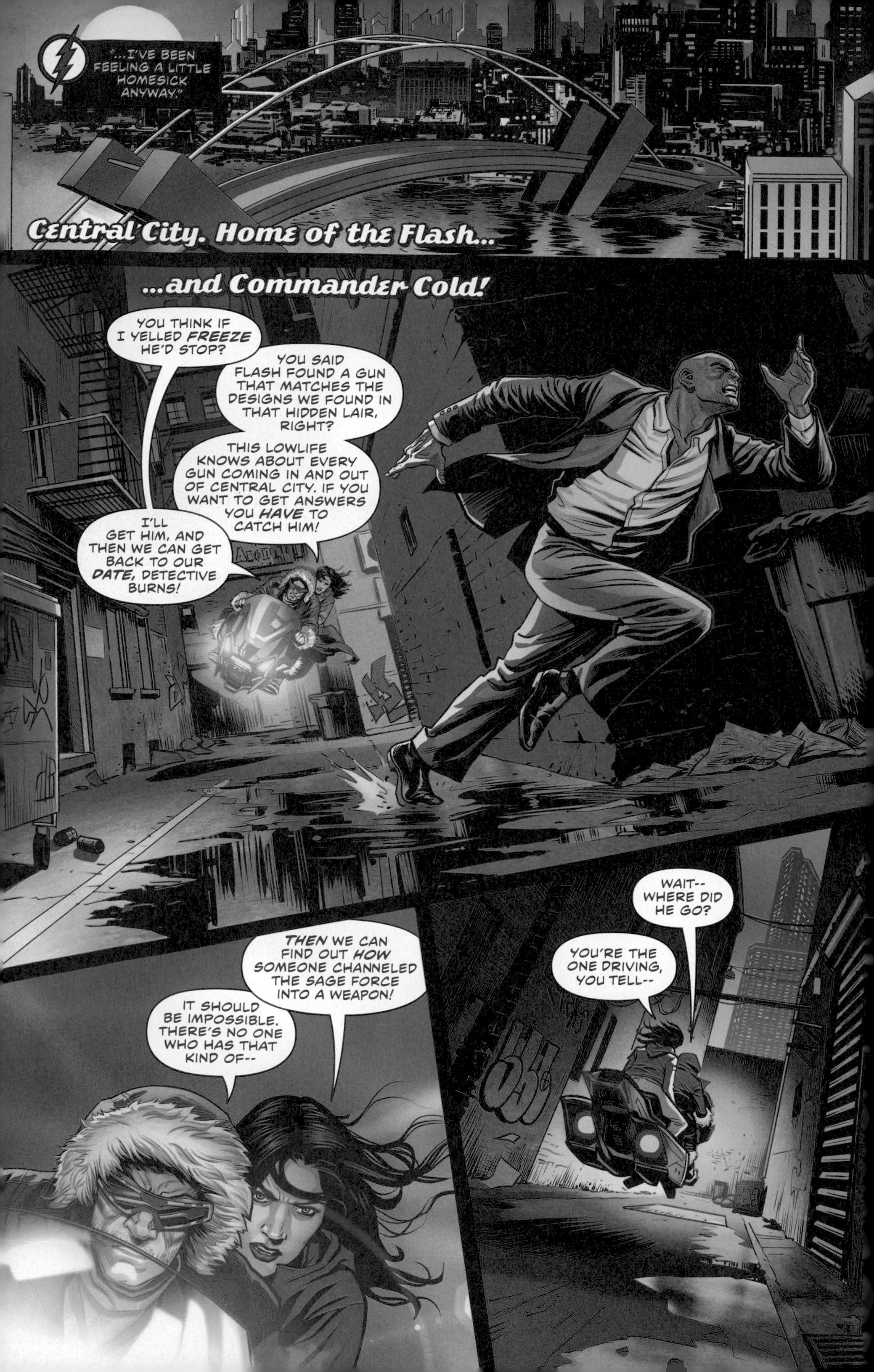
"...I'VE BEEN FEELING A LITTLE HOMESICK ANYWAY."
Central City. Home of the Flash...
...and Commander Cold!
YOU THINK IF I YELLED FREEZE HE'D STOP?
YOU SAID FLASH FOUND A GUN THAT MATCHES THE DESIGNS WE FOUND IN THAT HIDDEN LAIR, RIGHT?
THIS LOWLIFE KNOWS ABOUT EVERY GUN COMING IN AND OUT OF CENTRAL CITY. IF YOU WANT TO GET ANSWERS YOU HAVE TO CATCH HIM!
I'LL GET HIM, AND THEN WE CAN GET BACK TO OUR DATE, DETECTIVE BURNS!
THEN WE CAN FIND OUT HOW SOMEONE CHANNELED THE SAGE FORCE INTO A WEAPON!
IT SHOULD BE IMPOSSIBLE. THERE'S NO ONE WHO HAS THAT KIND OF--
WAIT-- WHERE DID HE GO?
YOU'RE THE ONE DRIVING, YOU TELL--

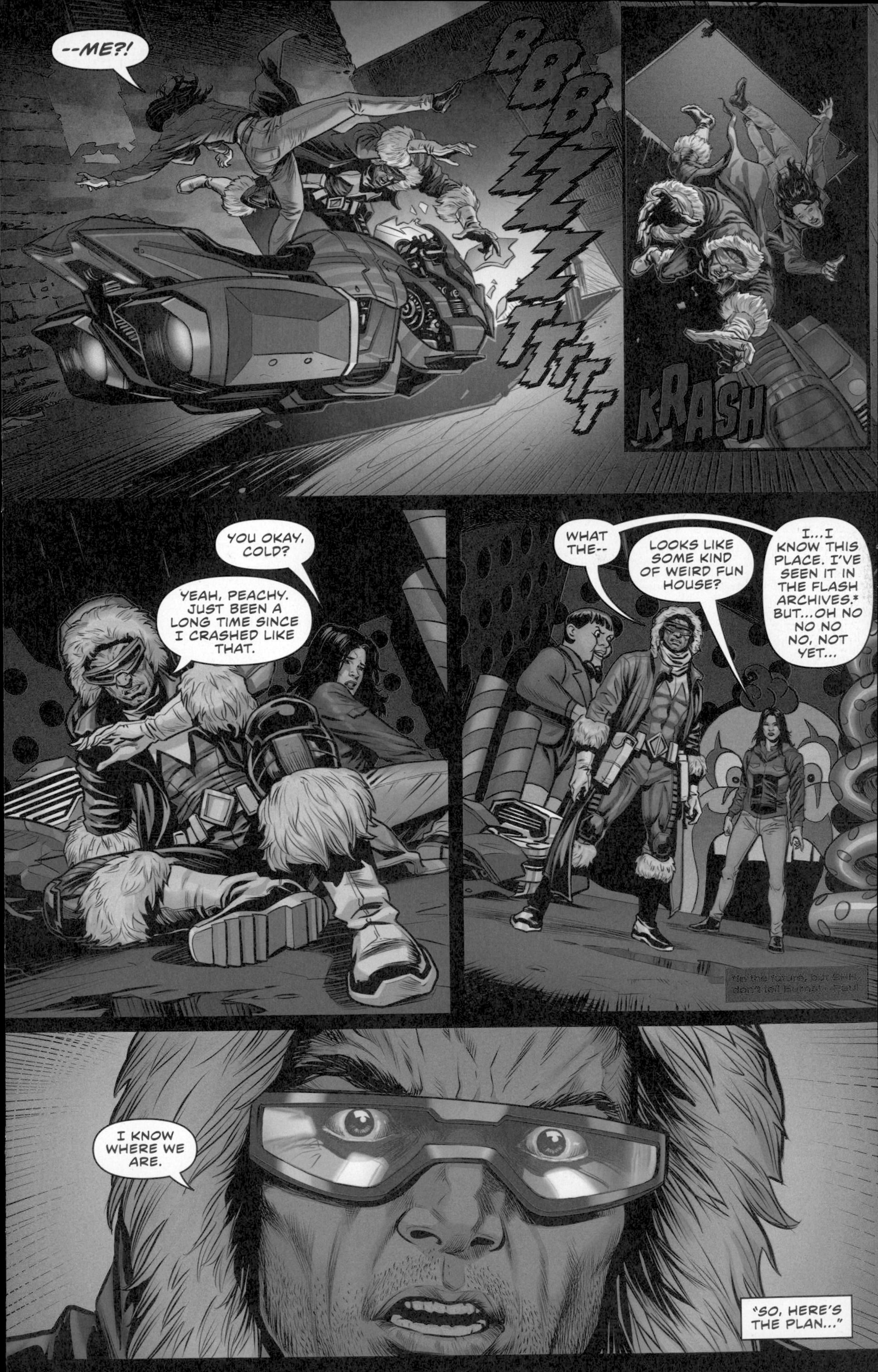
--ME?!
BBBZZZZZTTTTTT
KRASH
YOU OKAY, COLD?
YEAH, PEACHY. JUST BEEN A LONG TIME SINCE I CRASHED LIKE THAT.
WHAT THE--
LOOKS LIKE SOME KIND OF WEIRD FUN HOUSE?
I...I KNOW THIS PLACE. I'VE SEEN IT IN THE FLASH ARCHIVES.* BUT...OH NO NO NO NO, NOT YET...
*In the future, but SHH, don't tell Burns! --Paul
I KNOW WHERE WE ARE.
"SO, HERE'S THE PLAN..."

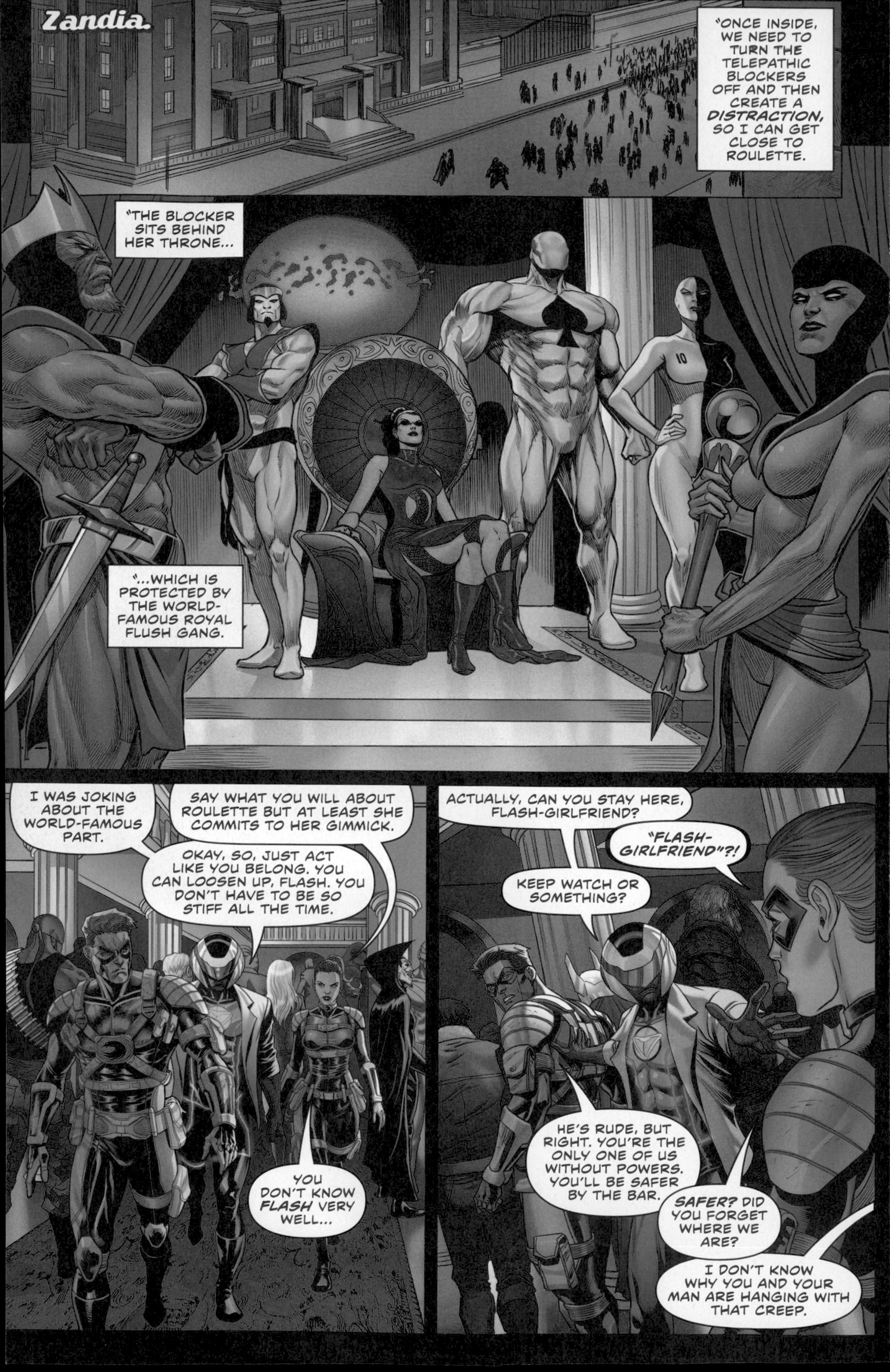

Zandia.
"ONCE INSIDE, WE NEED TO TURN THE TELEPATHIC BLOCKERS OFF AND THEN CREATE A DISTRACTION, SO I CAN GET CLOSE TO ROULETTE.
"THE BLOCKER SITS BEHIND HER THRONE...
"...WHICH IS PROTECTED BY THE WORLD-FAMOUS ROYAL FLUSH GANG.
I WAS JOKING ABOUT THE WORLD-FAMOUS PART.
SAY WHAT YOU WILL ABOUT ROULETTE BUT AT LEAST SHE COMMITS TO HER GIMMICK.
OKAY, SO, JUST ACT LIKE YOU BELONG. YOU CAN LOOSEN UP, FLASH. YOU DON'T HAVE TO BE SO STIFF ALL THE TIME.
YOU DON'T KNOW FLASH VERY WELL...
ACTUALLY, CAN YOU STAY HERE, FLASH-GIRLFRIEND?
"FLASH-GIRLFRIEND"?!
KEEP WATCH OR SOMETHING?
HE'S RUDE, BUT RIGHT. YOU'RE THE ONLY ONE OF US WITHOUT POWERS. YOU'LL BE SAFER BY THE BAR.
SAFER? DID YOU FORGET WHERE WE ARE?
I DON'T KNOW WHY YOU AND YOUR MAN ARE HANGING WITH THAT CREEP.

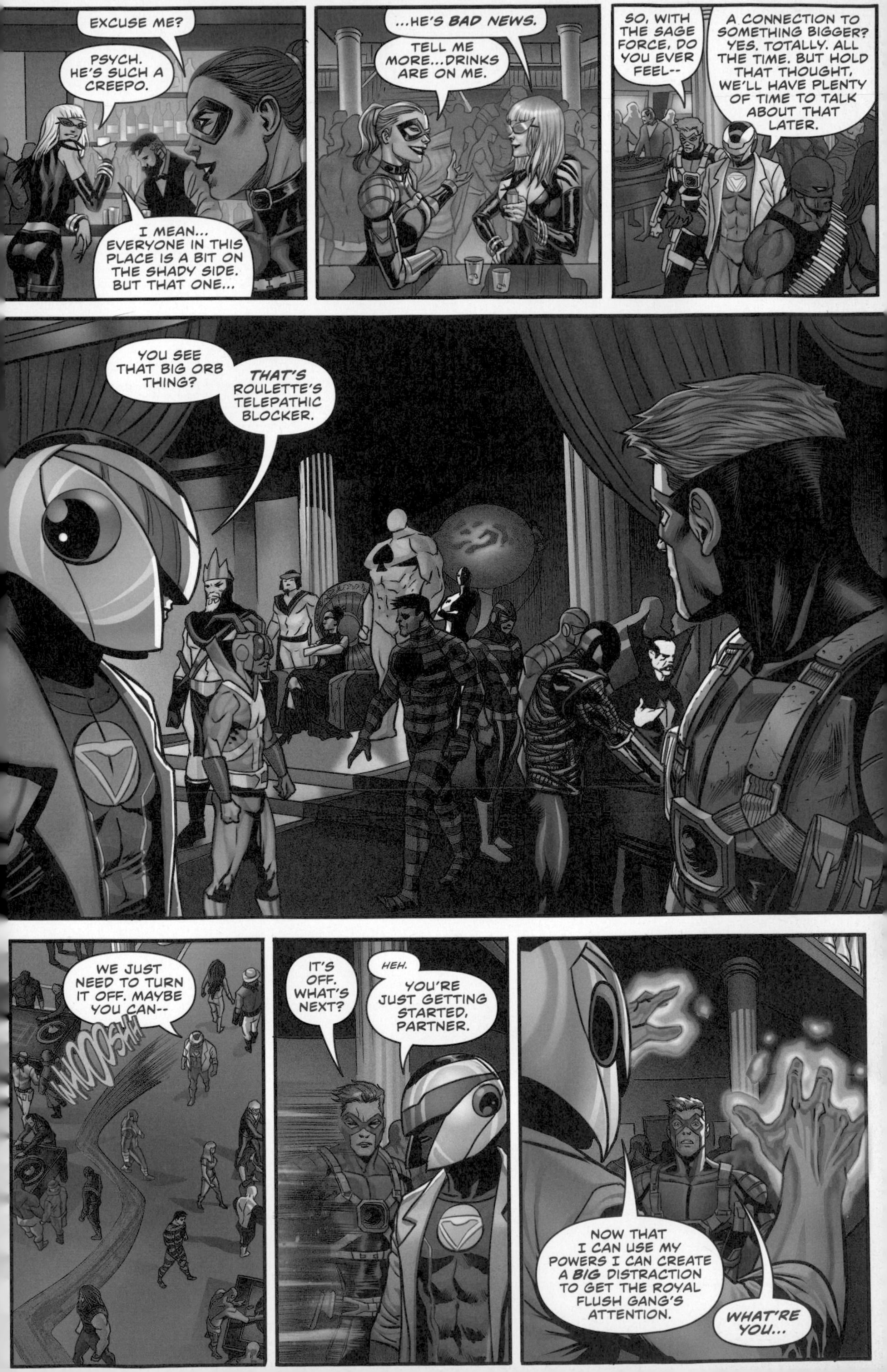
EXCUSE ME?
PSYCH. HE'S SUCH A CREEPO.
I MEAN... EVERYONE IN THIS PLACE IS A BIT ON THE SHADY SIDE. BUT THAT ONE...
...HE'S BAD NEWS.
TELL ME MORE...DRINKS ARE ON ME.
SO, WITH THE SAGE FORCE, DO YOU EVER FEEL--
A CONNECTION TO SOMETHING BIGGER? YES. TOTALLY. ALL THE TIME. BUT HOLD THAT THOUGHT, WE'LL HAVE PLENTY OF TIME TO TALK ABOUT THAT LATER.
YOU SEE THAT BIG ORB THING?
THAT'S ROULETTE'S TELEPATHIC BLOCKER.
WE JUST NEED TO TURN IT OFF. MAYBE YOU CAN--
WHOOSH
IT'S OFF. WHAT'S NEXT?
HEH.
YOU'RE JUST GETTING STARTED, PARTNER.
NOW THAT I CAN USE MY POWERS I CAN CREATE A BIG DISTRACTION TO GET THE ROYAL FLUSH GANG'S ATTENTION.
WHAT'RE YOU...

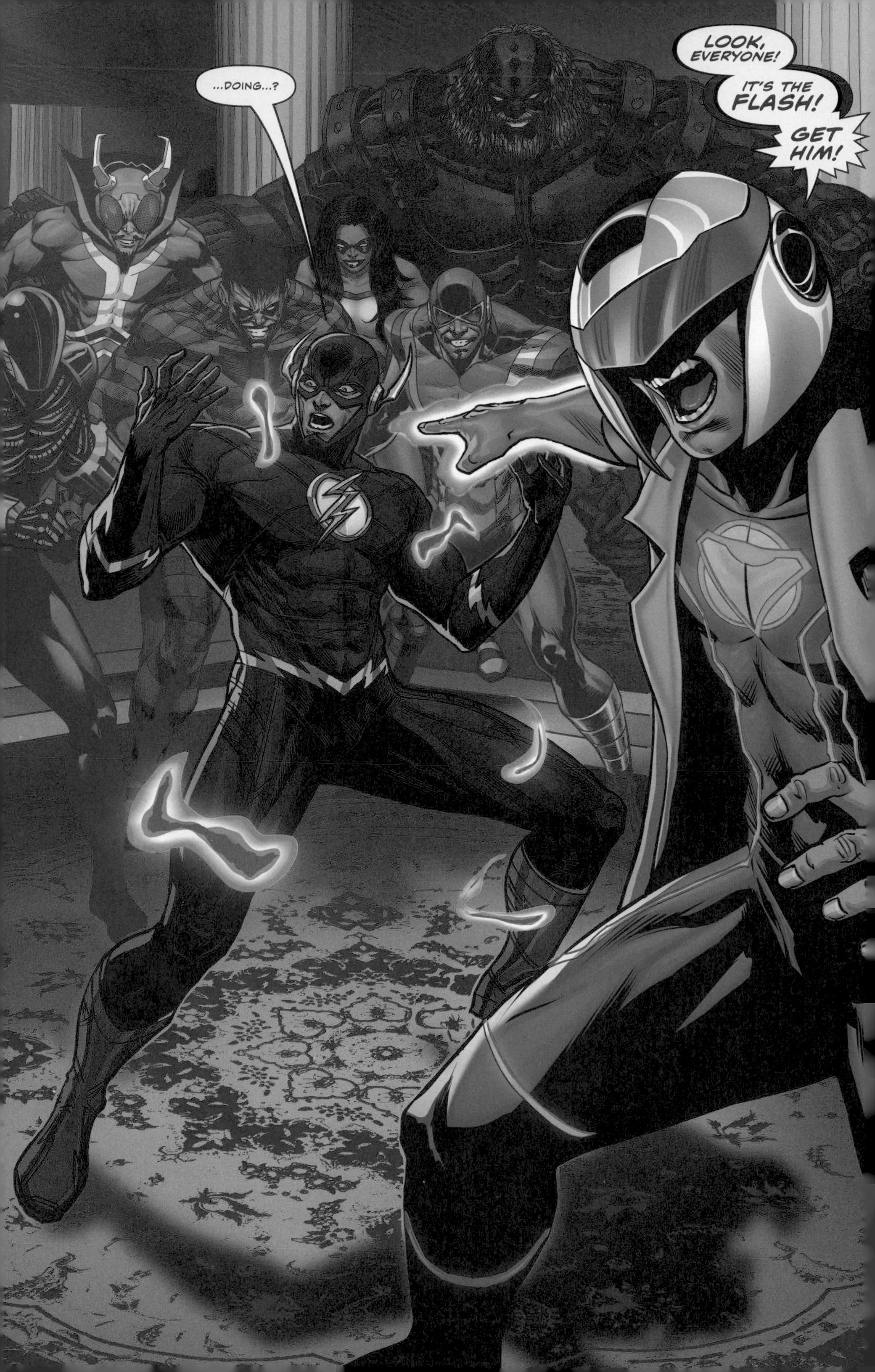
LOOK, EVERYONE!
IT'S THE FLASH!
GET HIM!
...DOING...?

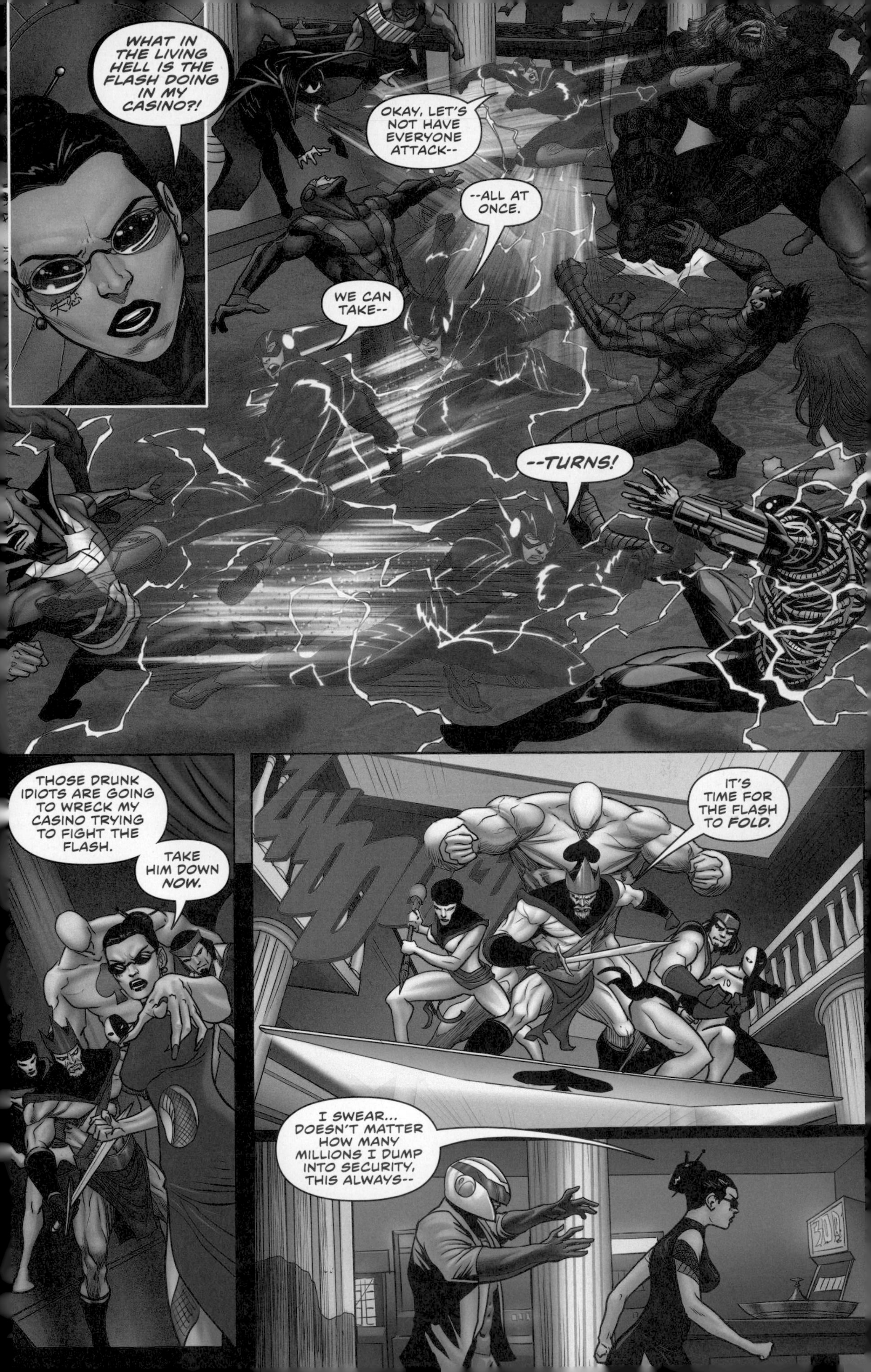
WHAT IN THE LIVING HELL IS THE FLASH DOING IN MY CASINO?!
OKAY, LET'S NOT HAVE EVERYONE ATTACK--
--ALL AT ONCE.
WE CAN TAKE--
--TURNS!
THOSE DRUNK IDIOTS ARE GOING TO WRECK MY CASINO TRYING TO FIGHT THE FLASH.
TAKE HIM DOWN NOW.
IT'S TIME FOR THE FLASH TO FOLD.
I SWEAR... DOESN'T MATTER HOW MANY MILLIONS I DUMP INTO SECURITY, THIS ALWAYS--

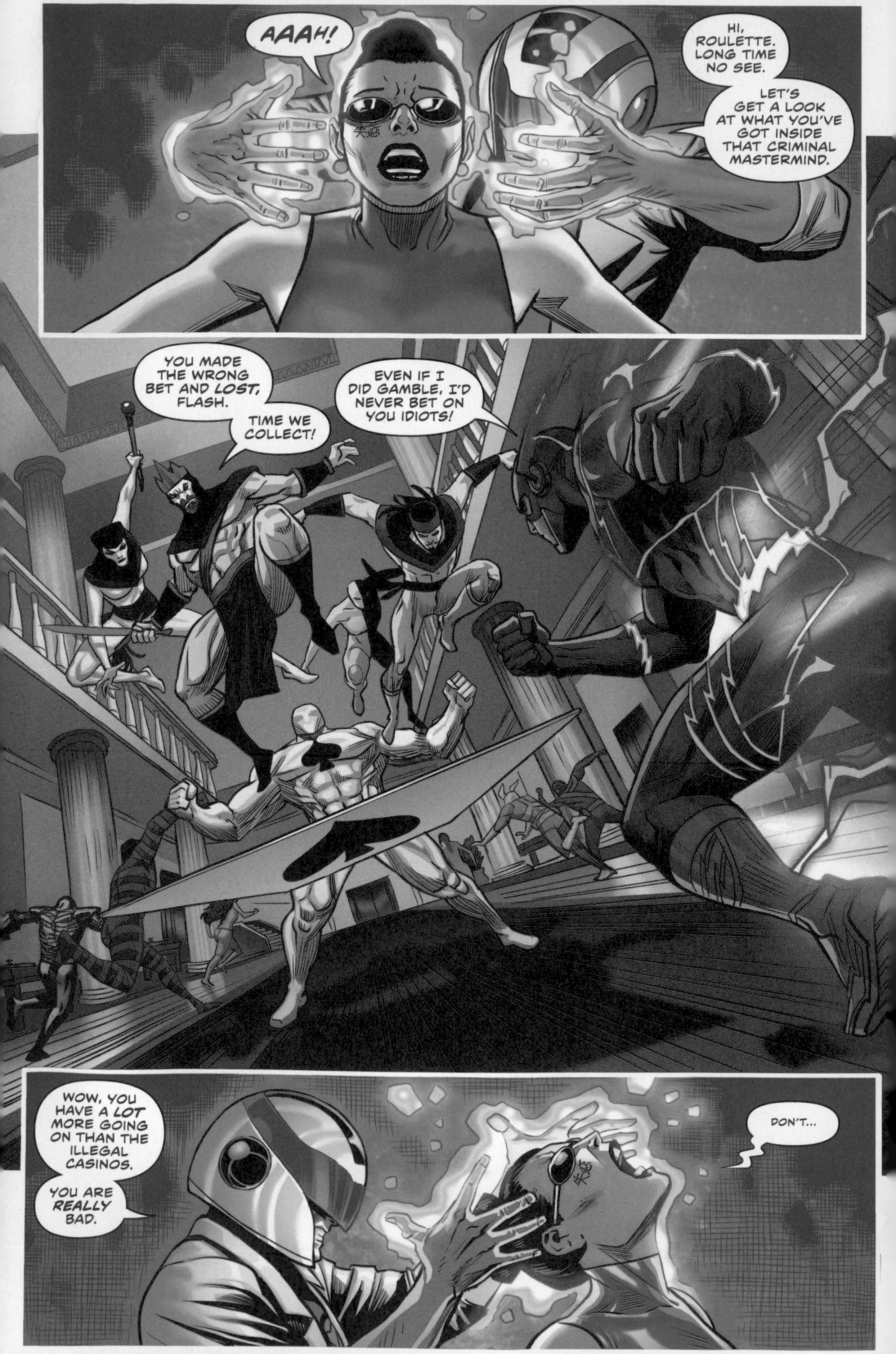
AAAH!
HI, ROULETTE. LONG TIME NO SEE.
LET'S GET A LOOK AT WHAT YOU'VE GOT INSIDE THAT CRIMINAL MASTERMIND.
YOU MADE THE WRONG BET AND LOST, FLASH.
TIME WE COLLECT!
EVEN IF I DID GAMBLE, I'D NEVER BET ON YOU IDIOTS!
WOW, YOU HAVE A LOT MORE GOING ON THAN THE ILLEGAL CASINOS.
YOU ARE REALLY BAD.
DON'T...

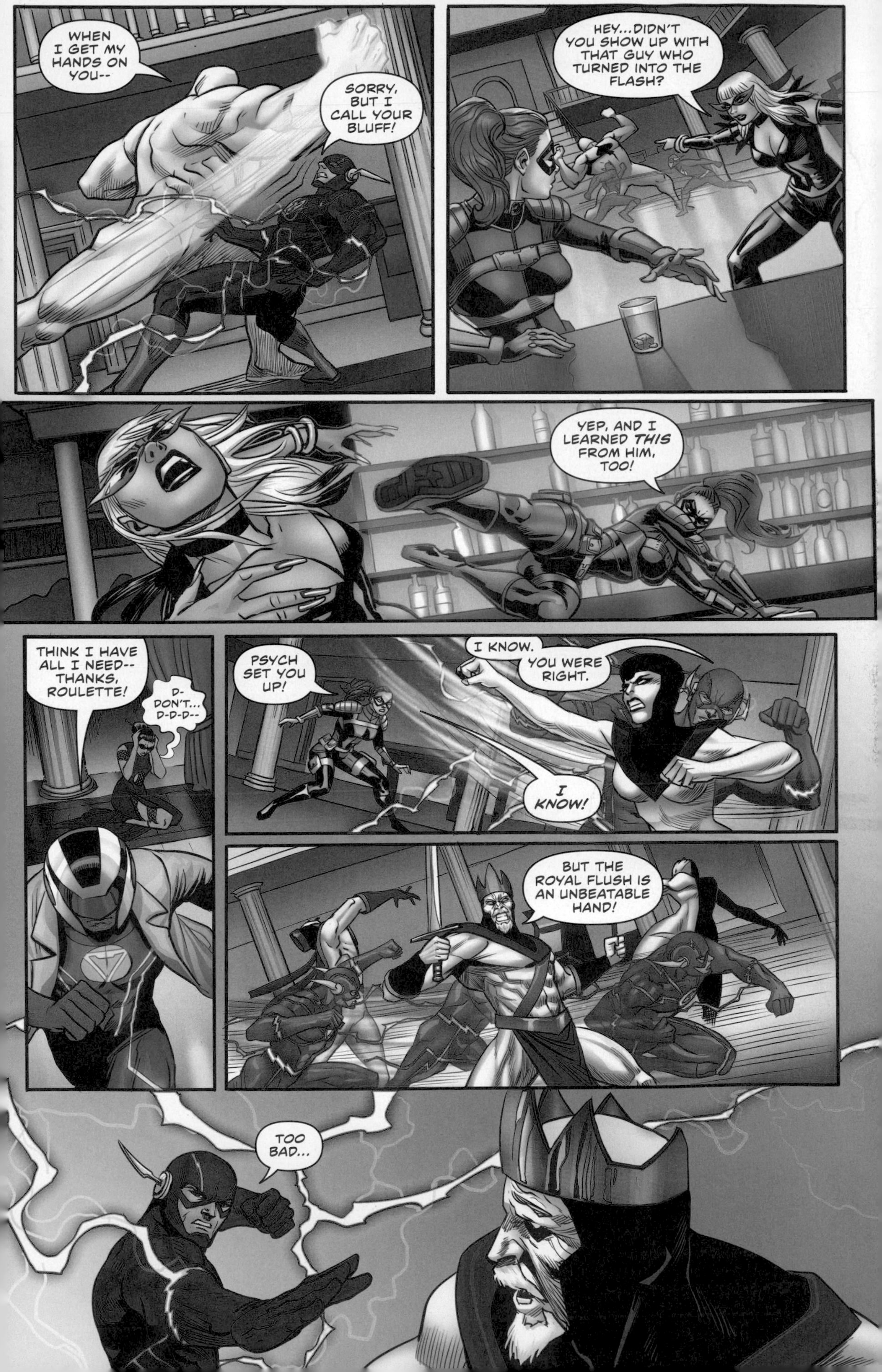

WHEN I GET MY HANDS ON YOU--
SORRY, BUT I CALL YOUR BLUFF!
HEY...DIDN'T YOU SHOW UP WITH THAT GUY WHO TURNED INTO THE FLASH?
YEP, AND I LEARNED THIS FROM HIM, TOO!
THINK I HAVE ALL I NEED--THANKS, ROULETTE!
D-DON'T... D-D-D--
PSYCH SET YOU UP!
I KNOW.
YOU WERE RIGHT.
I KNOW!
BUT THE ROYAL FLUSH IS AN UNBEATABLE HAND!
TOO BAD...

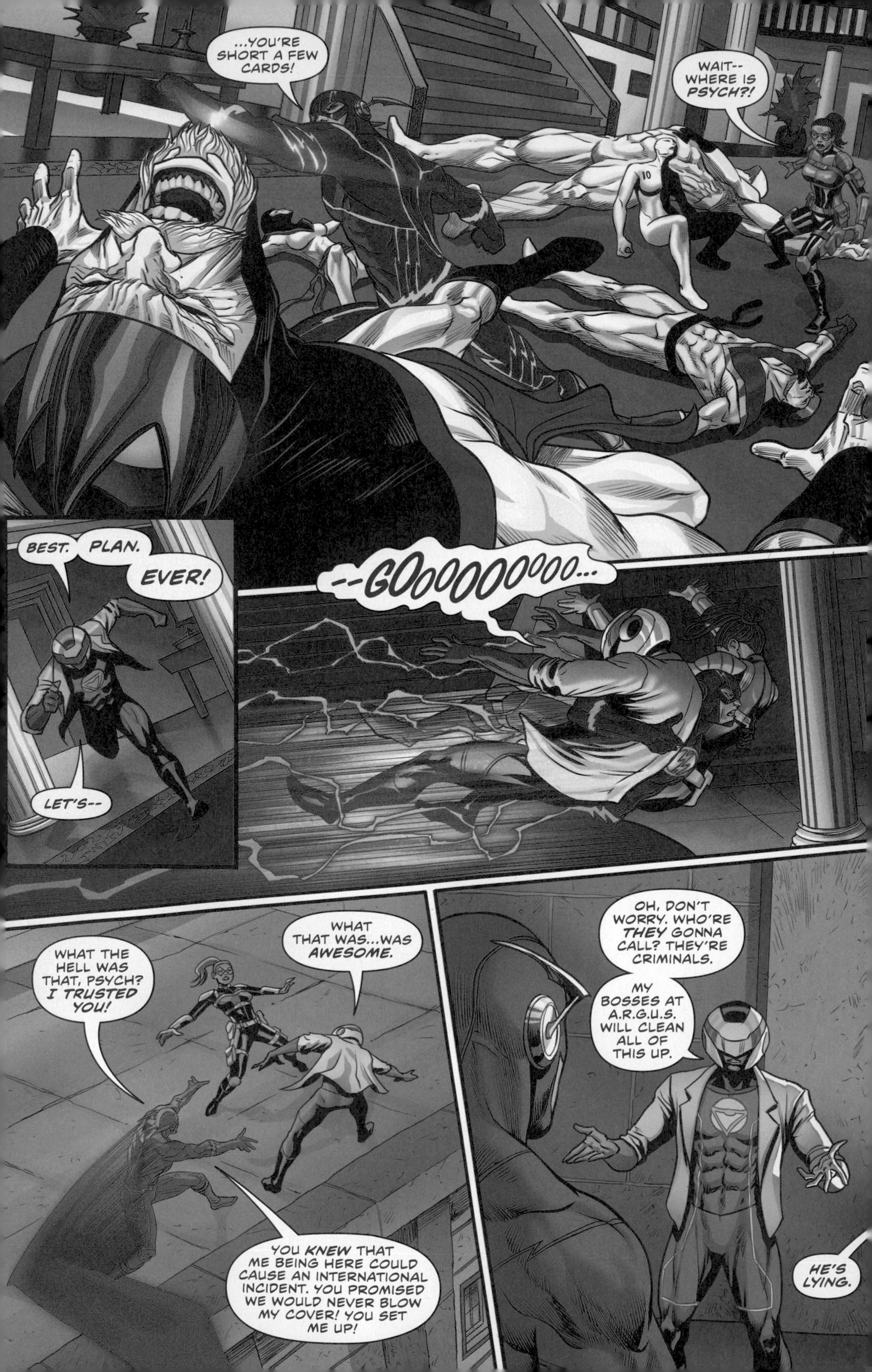
...YOU'RE SHORT A FEW CARDS!
WAIT-- WHERE IS PSYCH?!
BEST. PLAN. EVER!
LET'S--
--GOOOOOOOOO...
WHAT THE HELL WAS THAT, PSYCH? I TRUSTED YOU!
WHAT THAT WAS...WAS AWESOME.
YOU KNEW THAT ME BEING HERE COULD CAUSE AN INTERNATIONAL INCIDENT. YOU PROMISED WE WOULD NEVER BLOW MY COVER! YOU SET ME UP!
OH, DON'T WORRY. WHO'RE THEY GONNA CALL? THEY'RE CRIMINALS.
MY BOSSES AT A.R.G.U.S. WILL CLEAN ALL OF THIS UP.
HE'S LYING.

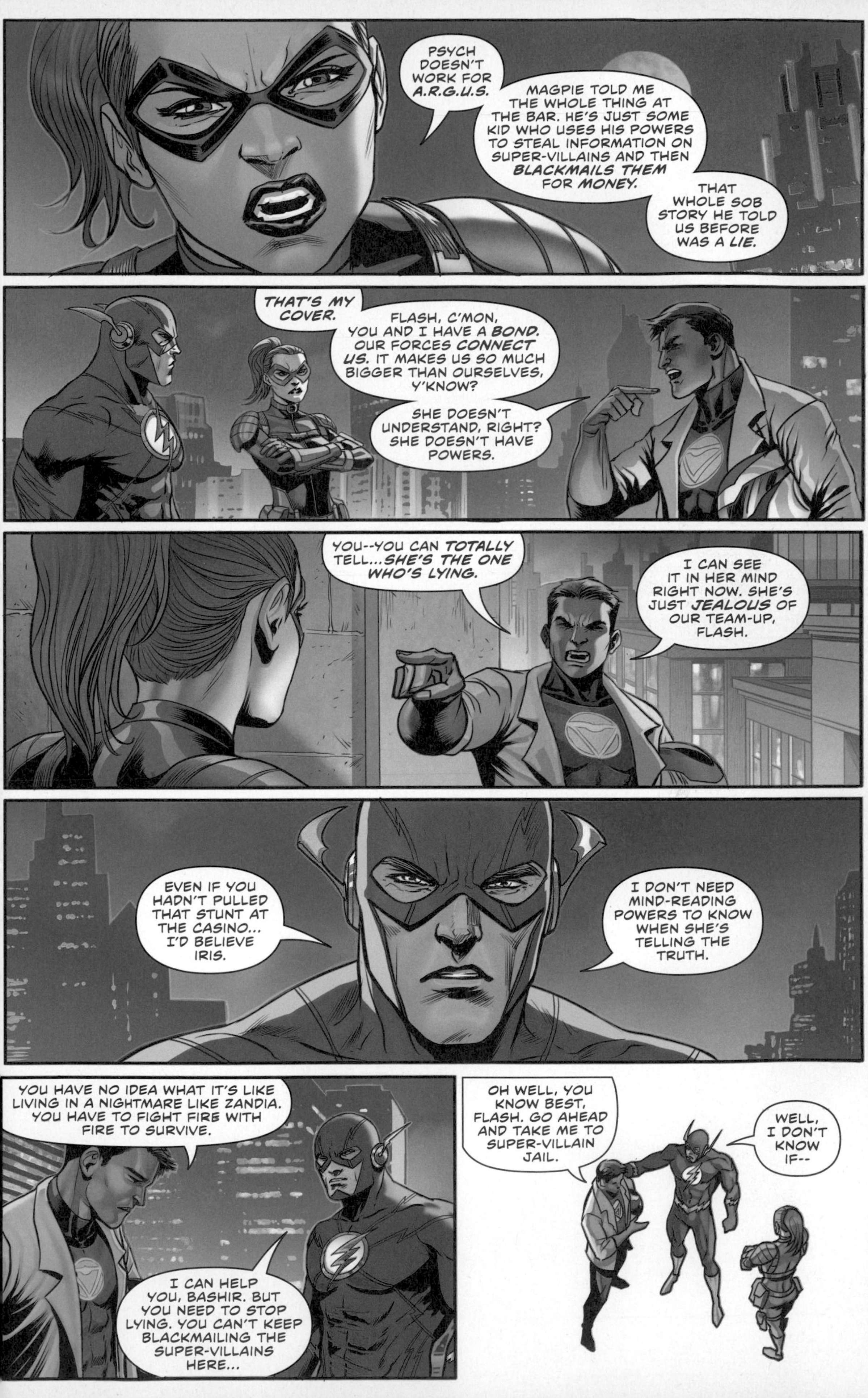
PSYCH DOESN'T WORK FOR *A.R.G.U.S.*
MAGPIE TOLD ME THE WHOLE THING AT THE BAR. HE'S JUST SOME KID WHO USES HIS POWERS TO STEAL INFORMATION ON SUPER-VILLAINS AND THEN ***BLACKMAILS THEM*** FOR *MONEY.*
THAT WHOLE SOB STORY HE TOLD US BEFORE WAS A *LIE.*
THAT'S MY COVER.
FLASH, C'MON, YOU AND I HAVE A *BOND.* OUR FORCES *CONNECT US.* IT MAKES US SO MUCH BIGGER THAN OURSELVES, Y'KNOW?
SHE DOESN'T UNDERSTAND, RIGHT? SHE DOESN'T HAVE POWERS.
YOU--YOU CAN *TOTALLY* TELL...*SHE'S THE ONE WHO'S LYING.*
I CAN SEE IT IN HER MIND RIGHT NOW. SHE'S JUST ***JEALOUS*** OF OUR TEAM-UP, FLASH.
EVEN IF YOU HADN'T PULLED THAT STUNT AT THE CASINO... I'D BELIEVE IRIS.
I DON'T NEED MIND-READING POWERS TO KNOW WHEN SHE'S TELLING THE TRUTH.
YOU HAVE NO IDEA WHAT IT'S LIKE LIVING IN A NIGHTMARE LIKE ZANDIA. YOU HAVE TO FIGHT FIRE WITH FIRE TO SURVIVE.
I CAN HELP YOU, BASHIR. BUT YOU NEED TO STOP LYING. YOU CAN'T KEEP BLACKMAILING THE SUPER-VILLAINS HERE...
OH WELL, YOU KNOW BEST, FLASH. GO AHEAD AND TAKE ME TO SUPER-VILLAIN JAIL.
WELL, I DON'T KNOW IF--

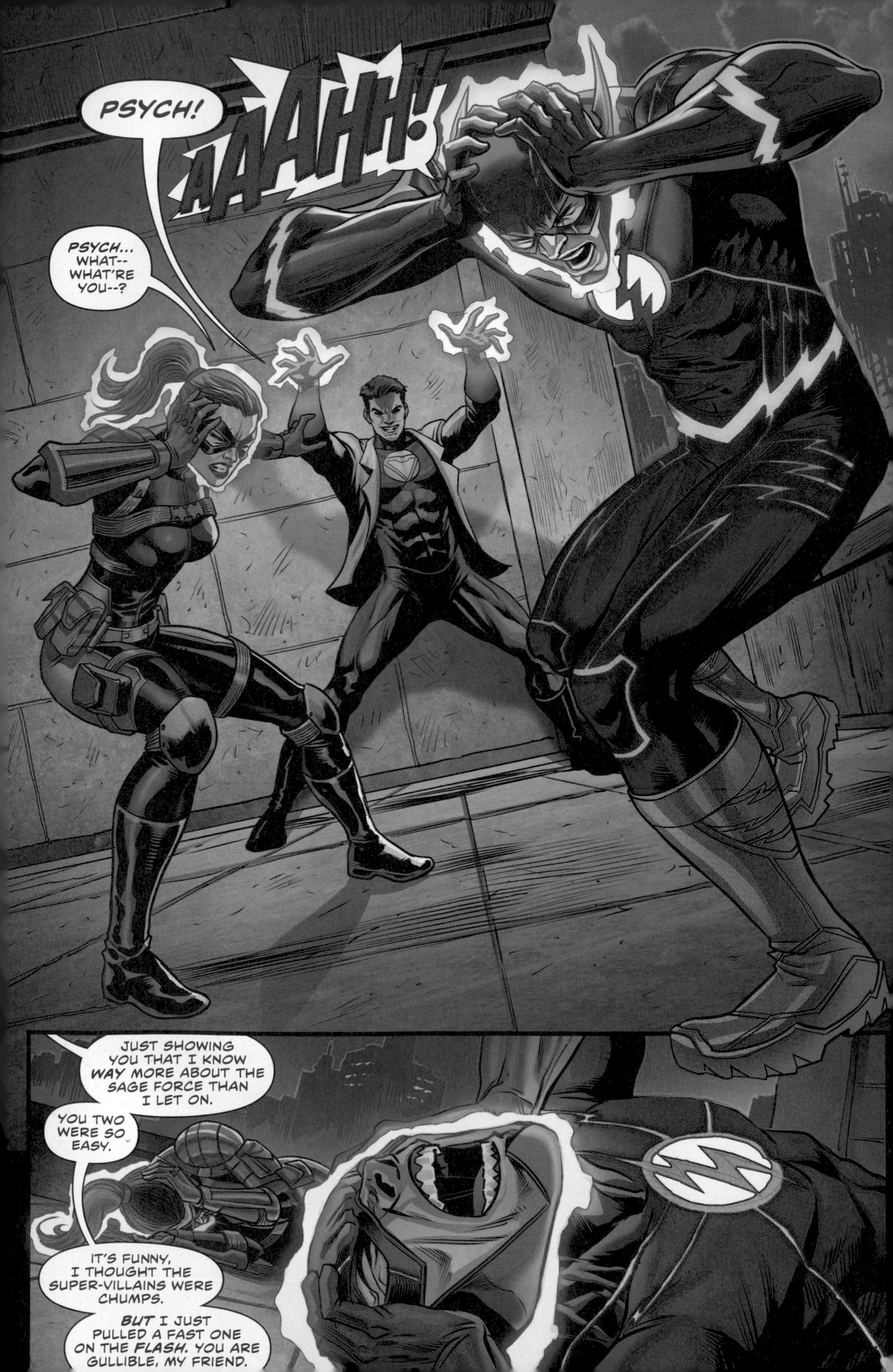
PSYCH!
AAAHH!
PSYCH... WHAT-- WHAT'RE YOU--?
JUST SHOWING YOU THAT I KNOW WAY MORE ABOUT THE SAGE FORCE THAN I LET ON.
YOU TWO WERE SO EASY.
IT'S FUNNY, I THOUGHT THE SUPER-VILLAINS WERE CHUMPS.
BUT I JUST PULLED A FAST ONE ON THE FLASH. YOU ARE GULLIBLE, MY FRIEND.

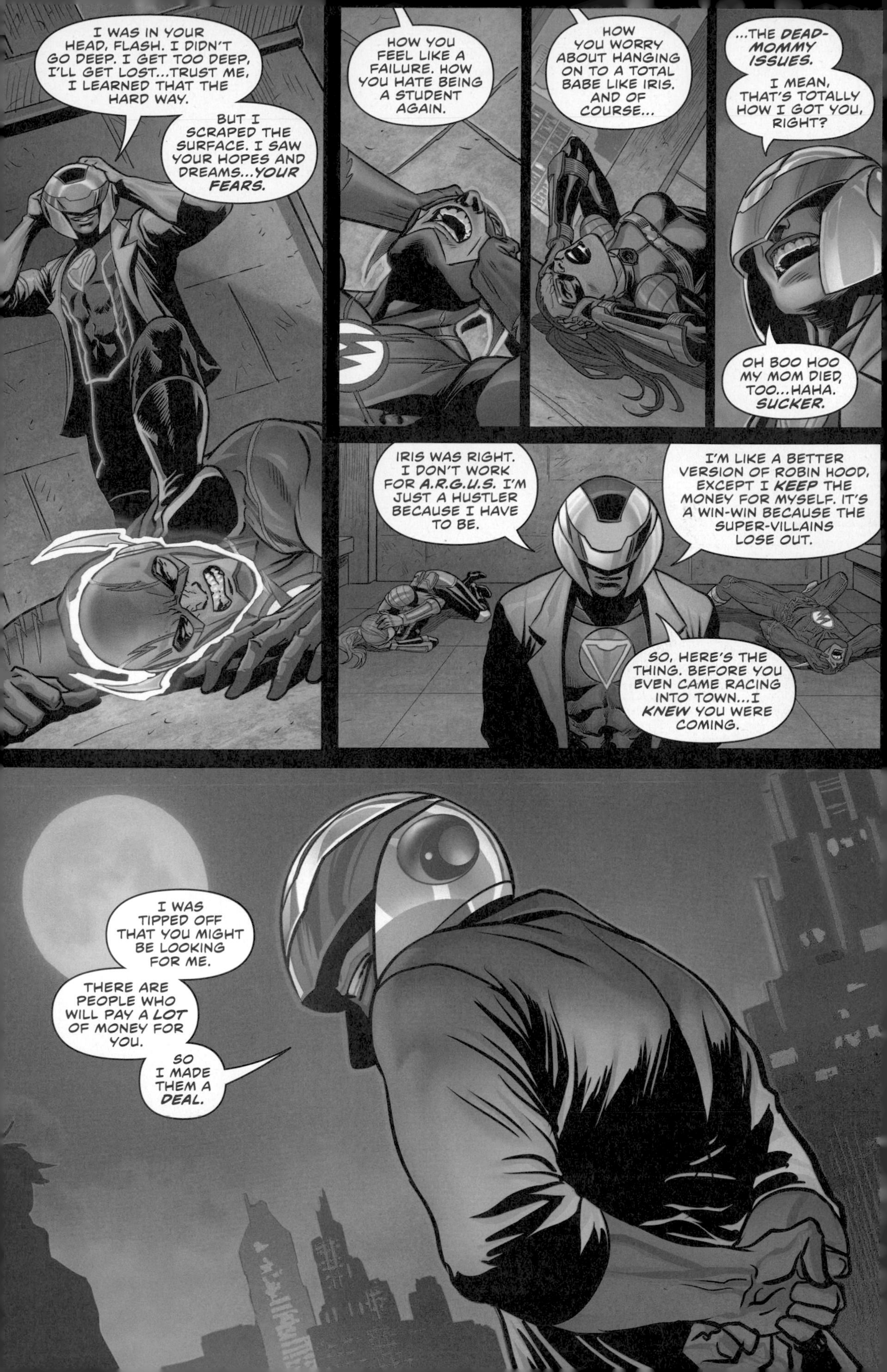
I WAS IN YOUR HEAD, FLASH. I DIDN'T GO DEEP. I GET TOO DEEP, I'LL GET LOST...TRUST ME, I LEARNED THAT THE HARD WAY.
BUT I SCRAPED THE SURFACE. I SAW YOUR HOPES AND DREAMS...*YOUR FEARS.*
HOW YOU FEEL LIKE A FAILURE. HOW YOU HATE BEING A STUDENT AGAIN.
HOW YOU WORRY ABOUT HANGING ON TO A TOTAL BABE LIKE IRIS. AND OF COURSE...
...THE *DEAD-MOMMY ISSUES.*
I MEAN, THAT'S TOTALLY HOW I GOT YOU, RIGHT?
OH BOO HOO MY MOM DIED, TOO...HAHA. *SUCKER.*
IRIS WAS RIGHT. I DON'T WORK FOR *A.R.G.U.S.* I'M JUST A HUSTLER BECAUSE I HAVE TO BE.
I'M LIKE A BETTER VERSION OF ROBIN HOOD, EXCEPT I *KEEP* THE MONEY FOR MYSELF. IT'S A WIN-WIN BECAUSE THE SUPER-VILLAINS LOSE OUT.
SO, HERE'S THE THING. BEFORE YOU EVEN CAME RACING INTO TOWN...I *KNEW* YOU WERE COMING.
I WAS TIPPED OFF THAT YOU MIGHT BE LOOKING FOR ME.
THERE ARE PEOPLE WHO WILL PAY A *LOT* OF MONEY FOR YOU.
SO I MADE THEM A *DEAL.*

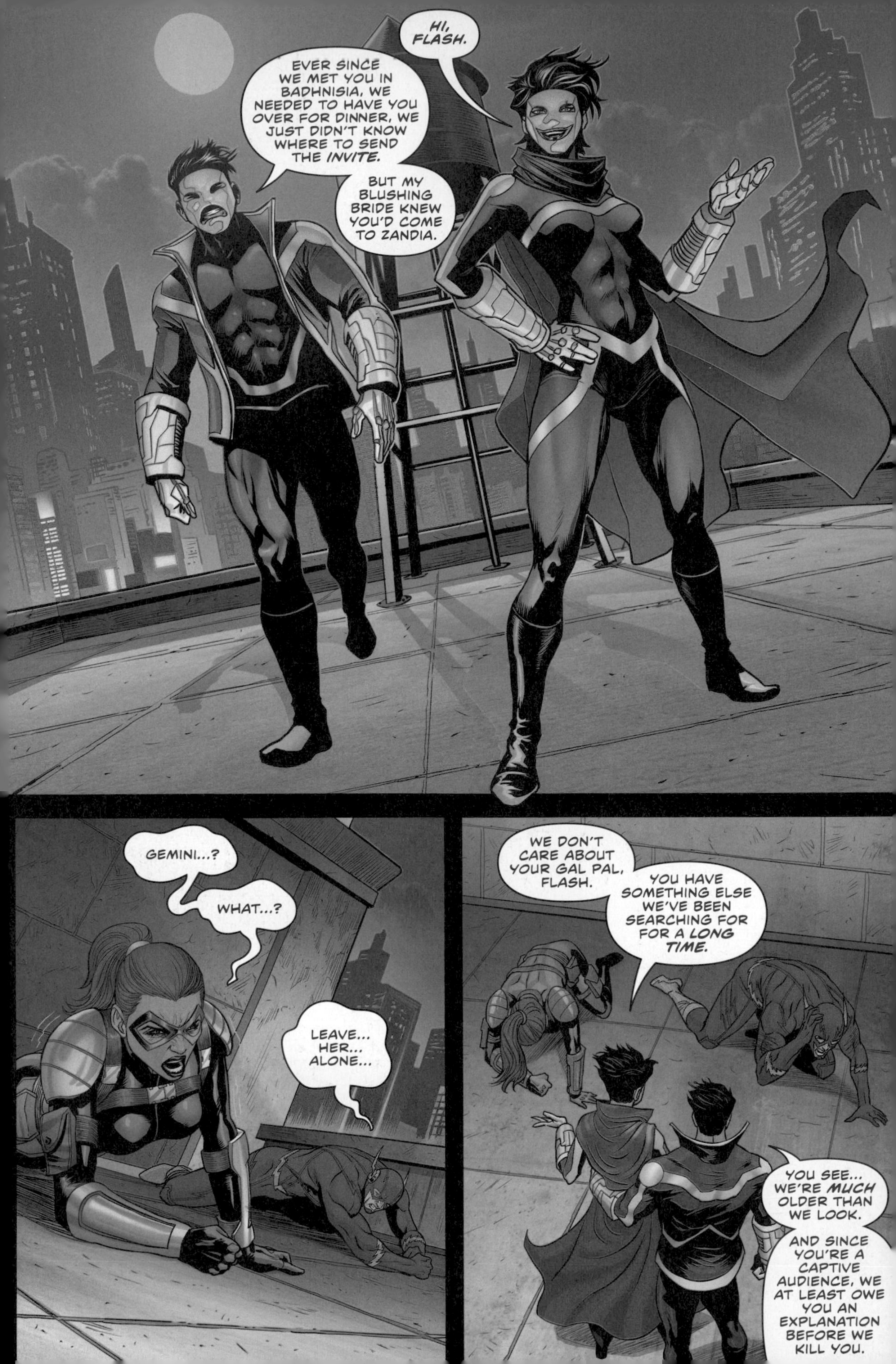
HI, FLASH.
EVER SINCE WE MET YOU IN BADHNISIA, WE NEEDED TO HAVE YOU OVER FOR DINNER, WE JUST DIDN'T KNOW WHERE TO SEND THE INVITE.
BUT MY BLUSHING BRIDE KNEW YOU'D COME TO ZANDIA.
GEMINI...?
WHAT...?
LEAVE... HER... ALONE...
WE DON'T CARE ABOUT YOUR GAL PAL, FLASH.
YOU HAVE SOMETHING ELSE WE'VE BEEN SEARCHING FOR FOR A LONG TIME.
YOU SEE... WE'RE MUCH OLDER THAN WE LOOK.
AND SINCE YOU'RE A CAPTIVE AUDIENCE, WE AT LEAST OWE YOU AN EXPLANATION BEFORE WE KILL YOU.

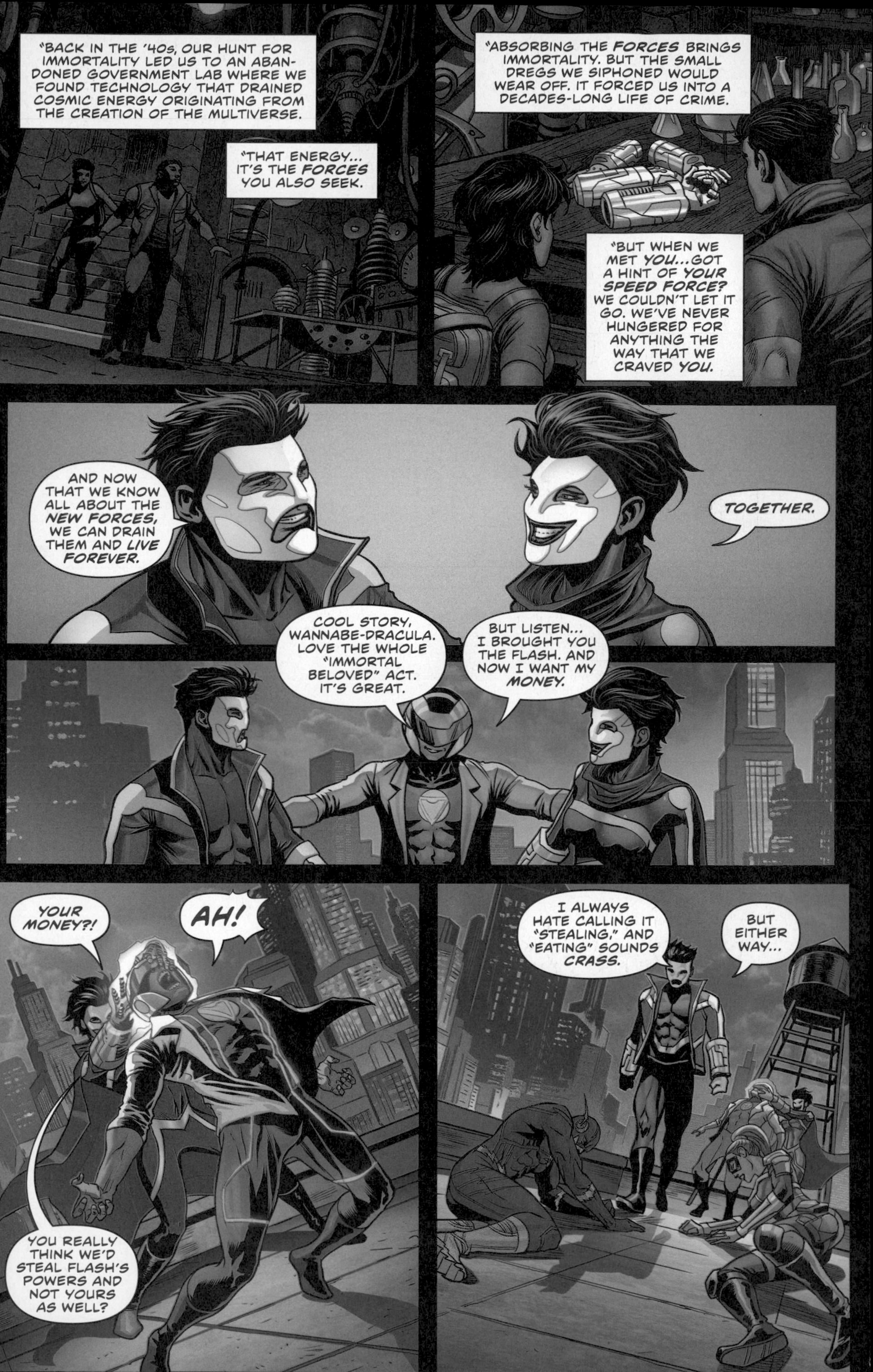
"BACK IN THE '40s, OUR HUNT FOR IMMORTALITY LED US TO AN ABANDONED GOVERNMENT LAB WHERE WE FOUND TECHNOLOGY THAT DRAINED COSMIC ENERGY ORIGINATING FROM THE CREATION OF THE MULTIVERSE.
"THAT ENERGY... IT'S THE FORCES YOU ALSO SEEK.
"ABSORBING THE FORCES BRINGS IMMORTALITY. BUT THE SMALL DREGS WE SIPHONED WOULD WEAR OFF. IT FORCED US INTO A DECADES-LONG LIFE OF CRIME.
"BUT WHEN WE MET YOU...GOT A HINT OF YOUR SPEED FORCE? WE COULDN'T LET IT GO. WE'VE NEVER HUNGERED FOR ANYTHING THE WAY THAT WE CRAVED YOU.
AND NOW THAT WE KNOW ALL ABOUT THE NEW FORCES, WE CAN DRAIN THEM AND LIVE FOREVER.
TOGETHER.
COOL STORY, WANNABE-DRACULA. LOVE THE WHOLE "IMMORTAL BELOVED" ACT. IT'S GREAT.
BUT LISTEN... I BROUGHT YOU THE FLASH. AND NOW I WANT MY MONEY.
YOUR MONEY?!
AH!
YOU REALLY THINK WE'D STEAL FLASH'S POWERS AND NOT YOURS AS WELL?
I ALWAYS HATE CALLING IT "STEALING," AND "EATING" SOUNDS CRASS.
BUT EITHER WAY...

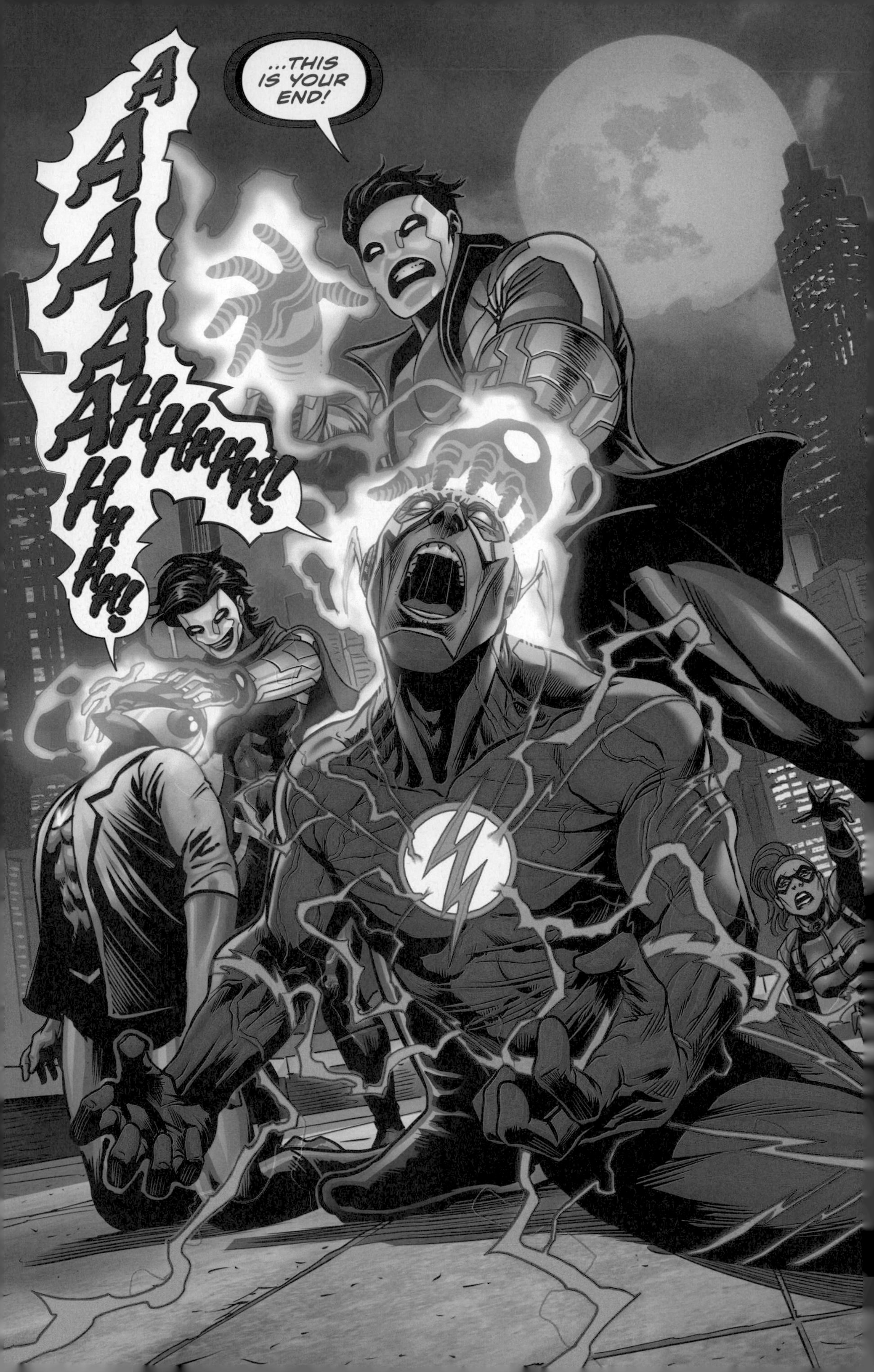
...THIS IS YOUR END!
AAAAAAHHHHHA!
HHAH!!

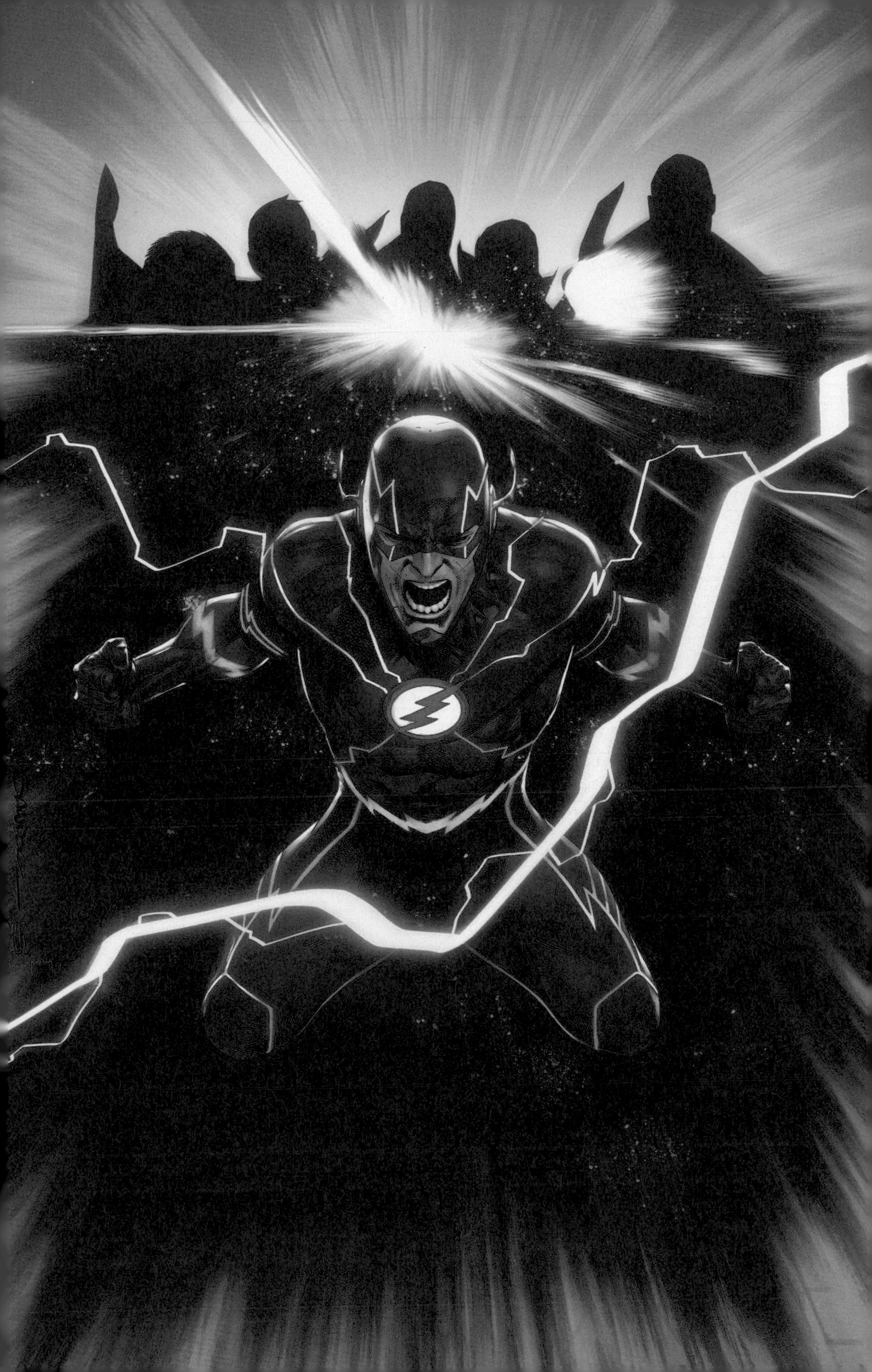

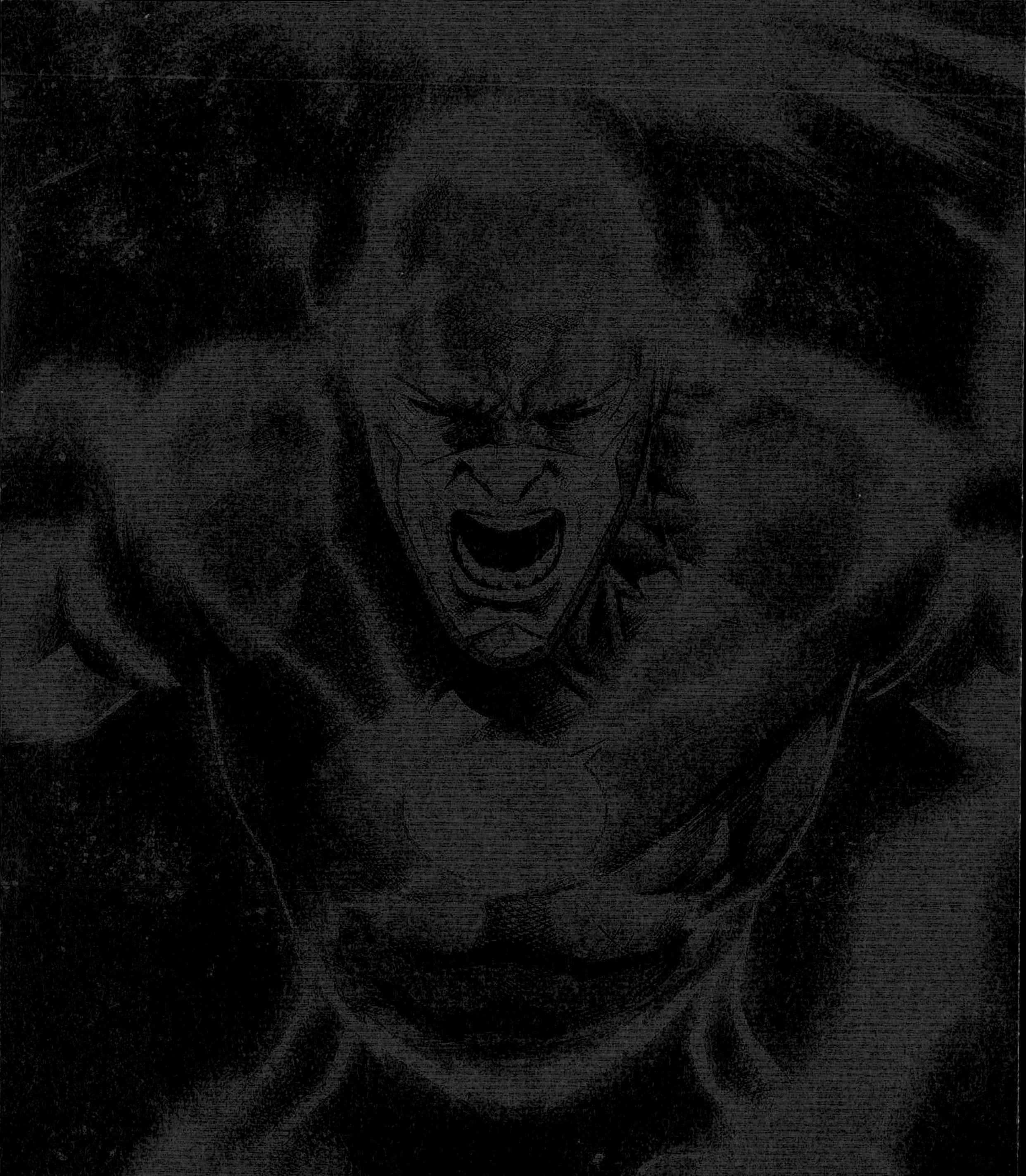

THE FLASH

#63

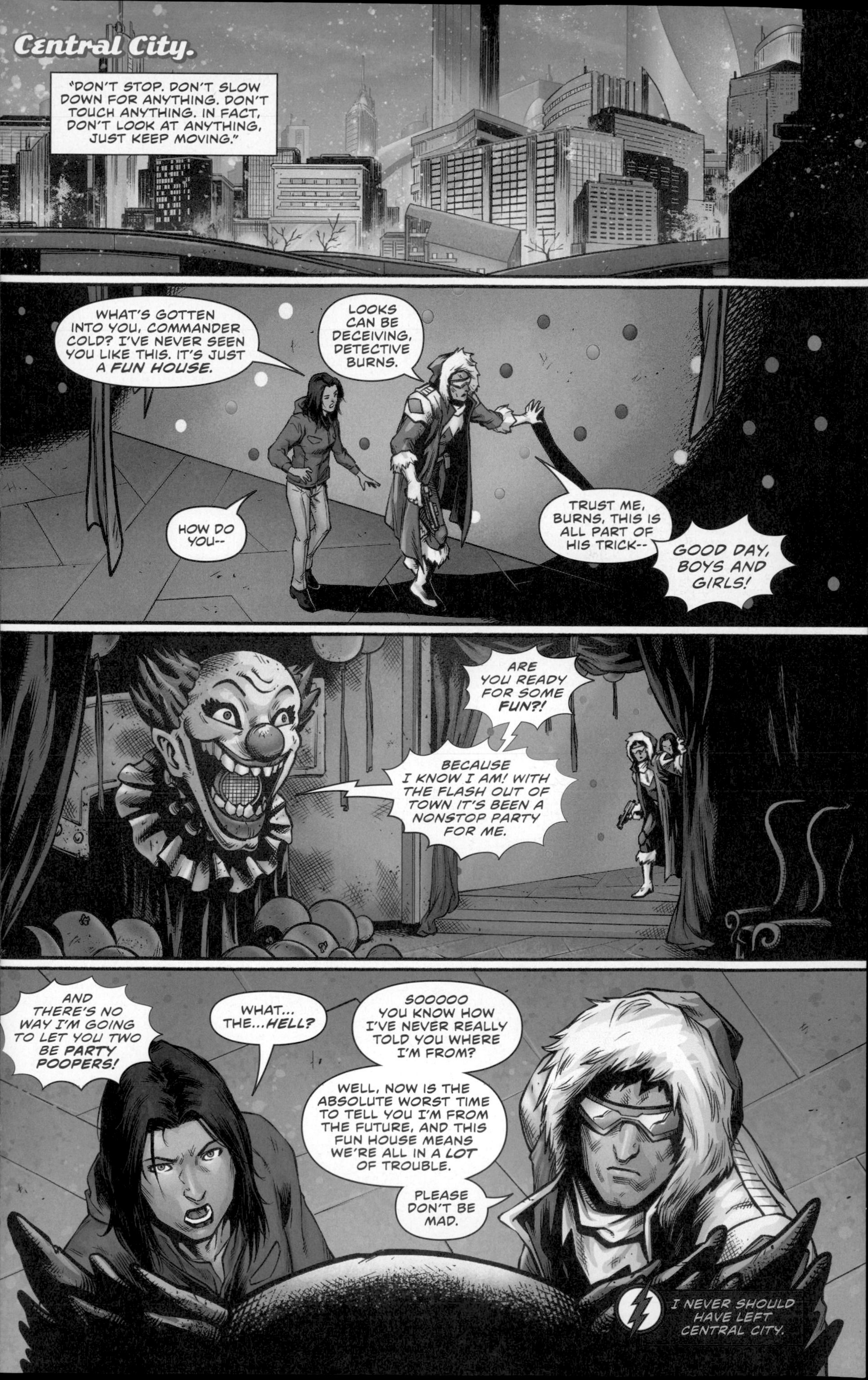
Central City.
"DON'T STOP. DON'T SLOW DOWN FOR ANYTHING. DON'T TOUCH ANYTHING. IN FACT, DON'T LOOK AT ANYTHING, JUST KEEP MOVING."
WHAT'S GOTTEN INTO YOU, COMMANDER COLD? I'VE NEVER SEEN YOU LIKE THIS. IT'S JUST A FUN HOUSE.
LOOKS CAN BE DECEIVING, DETECTIVE BURNS.
HOW DO YOU--
TRUST ME, BURNS, THIS IS ALL PART OF HIS TRICK--
GOOD DAY, BOYS AND GIRLS!
ARE YOU READY FOR SOME FUN?!
BECAUSE I KNOW I AM! WITH THE FLASH OUT OF TOWN IT'S BEEN A NONSTOP PARTY FOR ME.
AND THERE'S NO WAY I'M GOING TO LET YOU TWO BE PARTY POOPERS!
WHAT... THE...HELL?
SOOOOO YOU KNOW HOW I'VE NEVER REALLY TOLD YOU WHERE I'M FROM?
WELL, NOW IS THE ABSOLUTE WORST TIME TO TELL YOU I'M FROM THE FUTURE, AND THIS FUN HOUSE MEANS WE'RE ALL IN A LOT OF TROUBLE.
PLEASE DON'T BE MAD.
I NEVER SHOULD HAVE LEFT CENTRAL CITY.

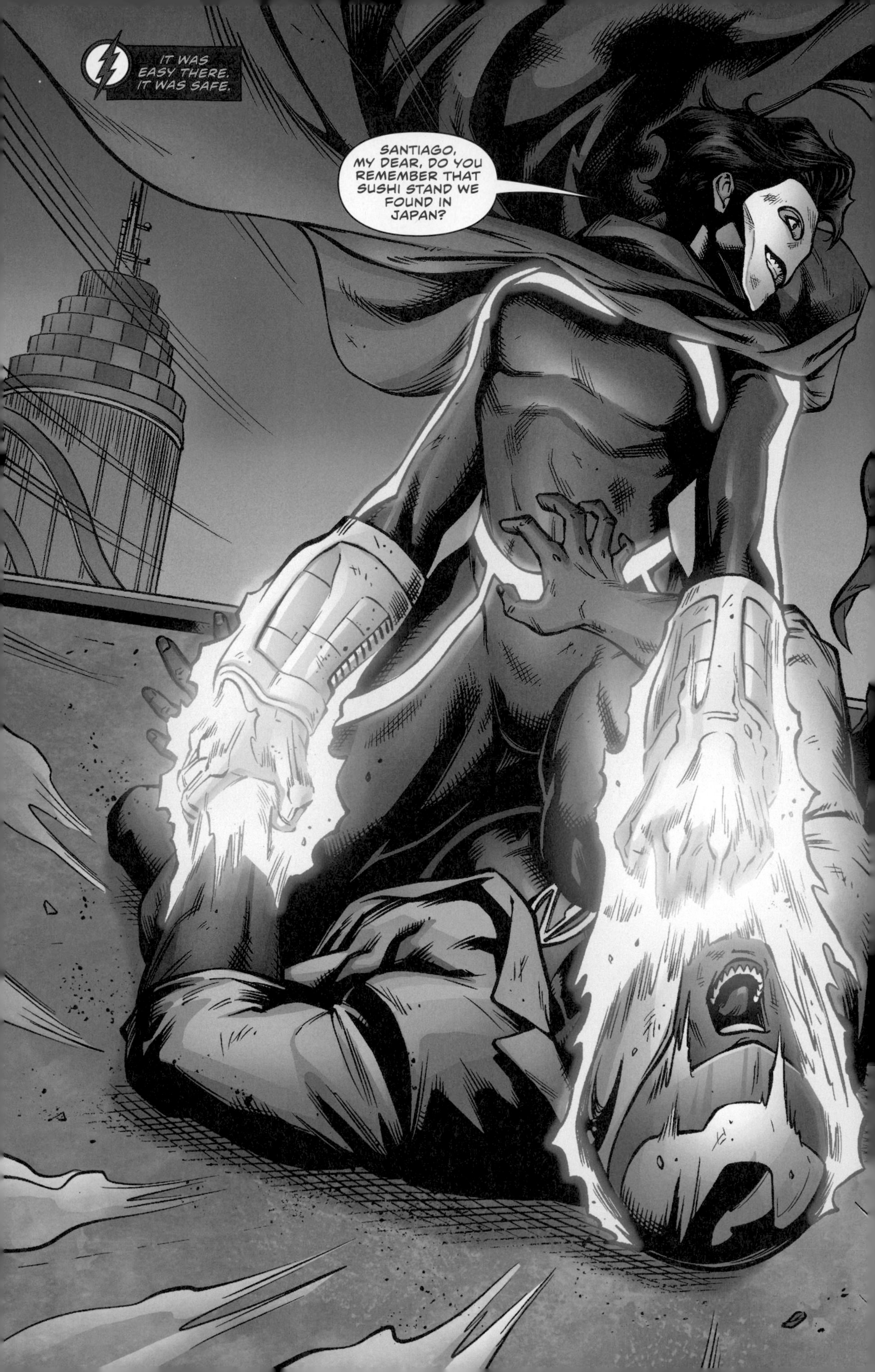
IT WAS EASY THERE. IT WAS SAFE.
SANTIAGO, MY DEAR, DO YOU REMEMBER THAT SUSHI STAND WE FOUND IN JAPAN?

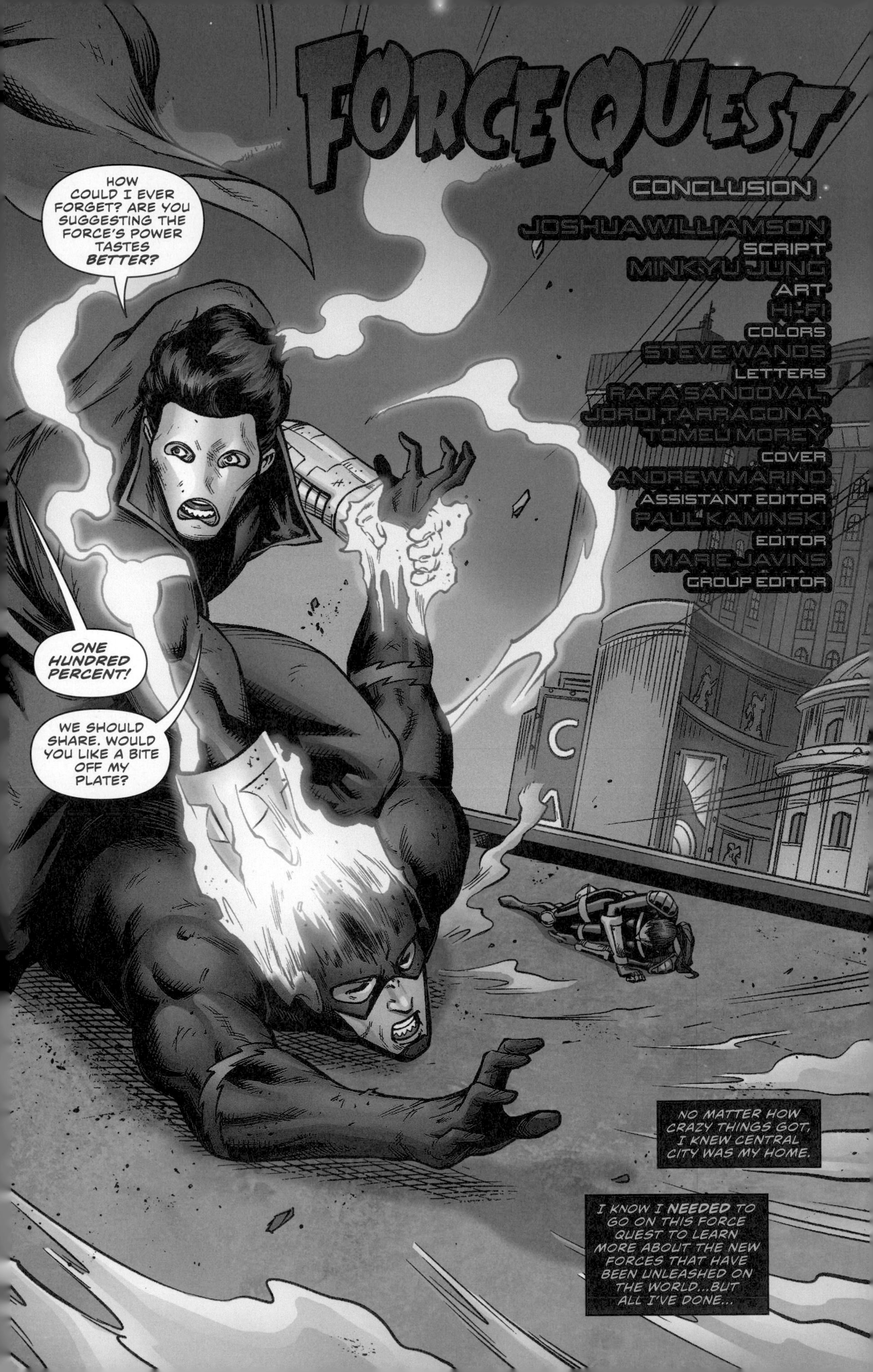
FORCE QUEST
CONCLUSION
JOSHUA WILLIAMSON
SCRIPT
MINKYU JUNG
ART
HI-FI
COLORS
STEVE WANDS
LETTERS
RAFA SANDOVAL, JORDI TARRAGONA, TOMEU MOREY
COVER
ANDREW MARINO
ASSISTANT EDITOR
PAUL KAMINSKI
EDITOR
MARIE JAVINS
GROUP EDITOR
HOW COULD I EVER FORGET? ARE YOU SUGGESTING THE FORCE'S POWER TASTES BETTER?
ONE HUNDRED PERCENT!
WE SHOULD SHARE. WOULD YOU LIKE A BITE OFF MY PLATE?
NO MATTER HOW CRAZY THINGS GOT, I KNEW CENTRAL CITY WAS MY HOME.
I KNOW I NEEDED TO GO ON THIS FORCE QUEST TO LEARN MORE ABOUT THE NEW FORCES THAT HAVE BEEN UNLEASHED ON THE WORLD...BUT ALL I'VE DONE...

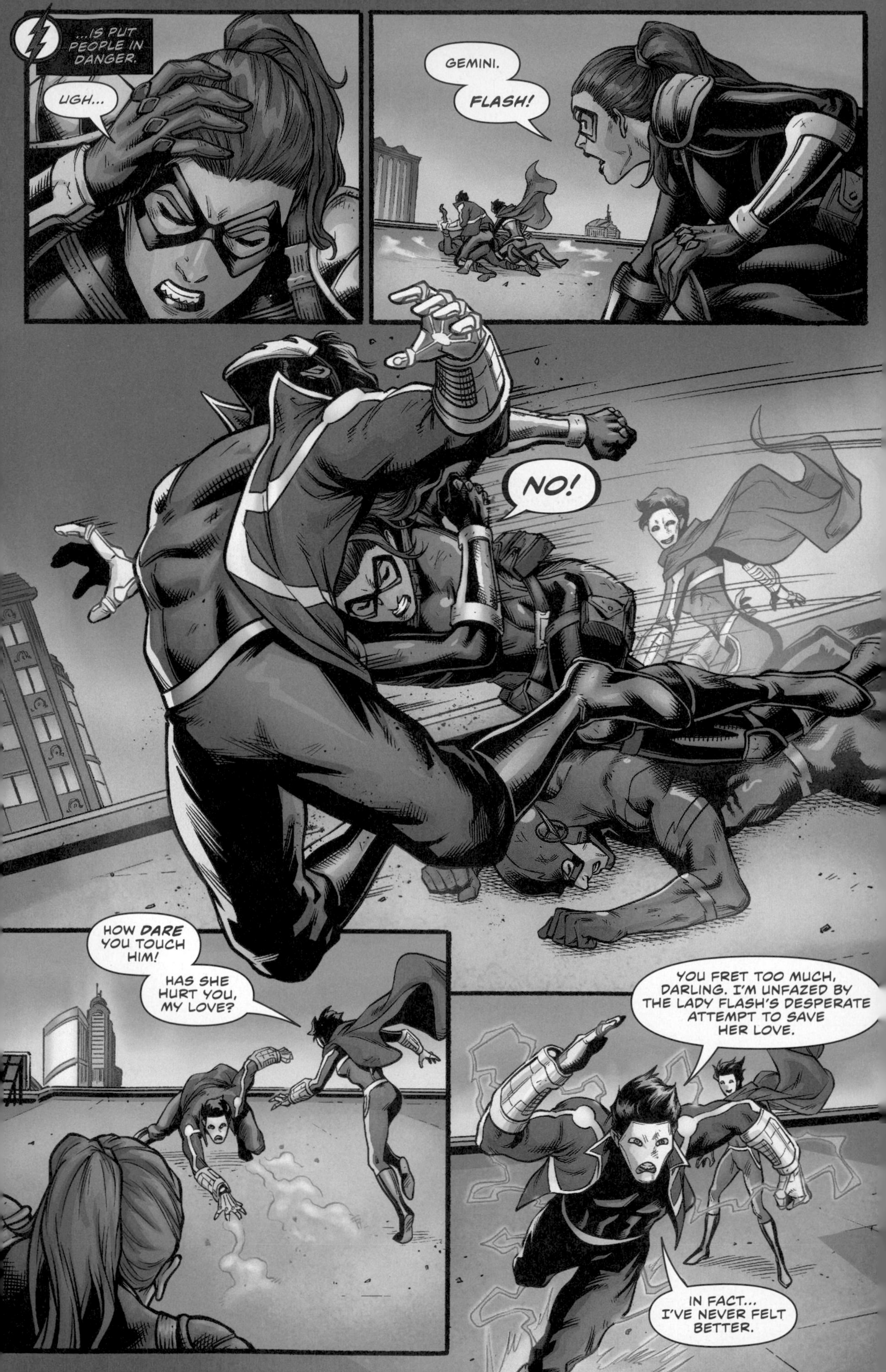
...IS PUT PEOPLE IN DANGER.
UGH...
GEMINI.
FLASH!
NO!
HOW DARE YOU TOUCH HIM!
HAS SHE HURT YOU, MY LOVE?
YOU FRET TOO MUCH, DARLING. I'M UNFAZED BY THE LADY FLASH'S DESPERATE ATTEMPT TO SAVE HER LOVE.
IN FACT... I'VE NEVER FELT BETTER.

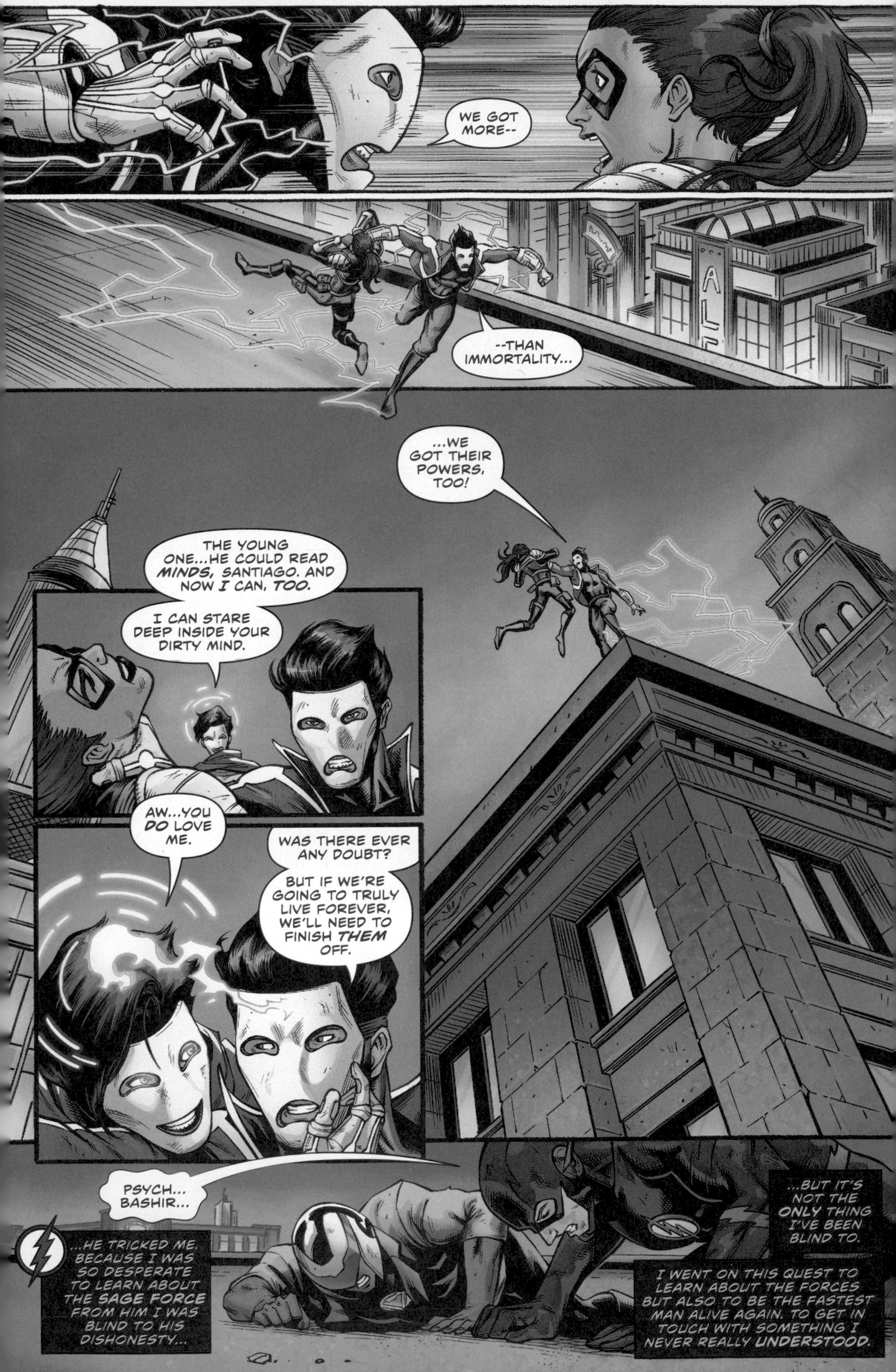
WE GOT MORE--
--THAN IMMORTALITY...
...WE GOT THEIR POWERS, TOO!
THE YOUNG ONE...HE COULD READ MINDS, SANTIAGO. AND NOW I CAN, TOO.
I CAN STARE DEEP INSIDE YOUR DIRTY MIND.
AW...YOU DO LOVE ME.
WAS THERE EVER ANY DOUBT?
BUT IF WE'RE GOING TO TRULY LIVE FOREVER, WE'LL NEED TO FINISH THEM OFF.
PSYCH... BASHIR...
...HE TRICKED ME. BECAUSE I WAS SO DESPERATE TO LEARN ABOUT THE SAGE FORCE FROM HIM I WAS BLIND TO HIS DISHONESTY...
...BUT IT'S NOT THE ONLY THING I'VE BEEN BLIND TO.
I WENT ON THIS QUEST TO LEARN ABOUT THE FORCES BUT ALSO TO BE THE FASTEST MAN ALIVE AGAIN. TO GET IN TOUCH WITH SOMETHING I NEVER REALLY UNDERSTOOD.

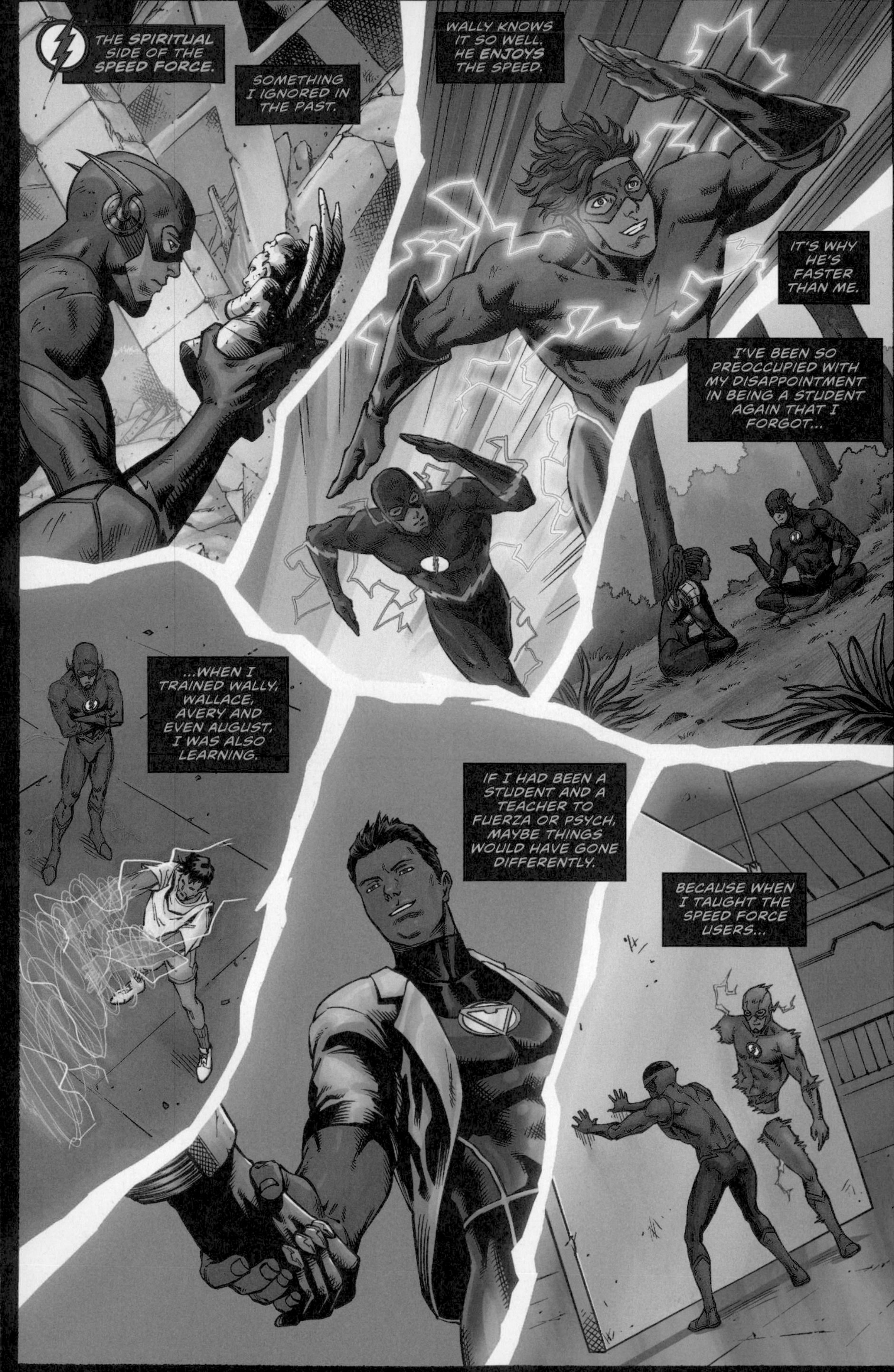
THE SPIRITUAL SIDE OF THE SPEED FORCE.
SOMETHING I IGNORED IN THE PAST.
WALLY KNOWS IT SO WELL. HE ENJOYS THE SPEED.
IT'S WHY HE'S FASTER THAN ME.
I'VE BEEN SO PREOCCUPIED WITH MY DISAPPOINTMENT IN BEING A STUDENT AGAIN THAT I FORGOT...
...WHEN I TRAINED WALLY, WALLACE, AVERY AND EVEN AUGUST, I WAS ALSO LEARNING.
IF I HAD BEEN A STUDENT AND A TEACHER TO FUERZA OR PSYCH, MAYBE THINGS WOULD HAVE GONE DIFFERENTLY.
BECAUSE WHEN I TAUGHT THE SPEED FORCE USERS...

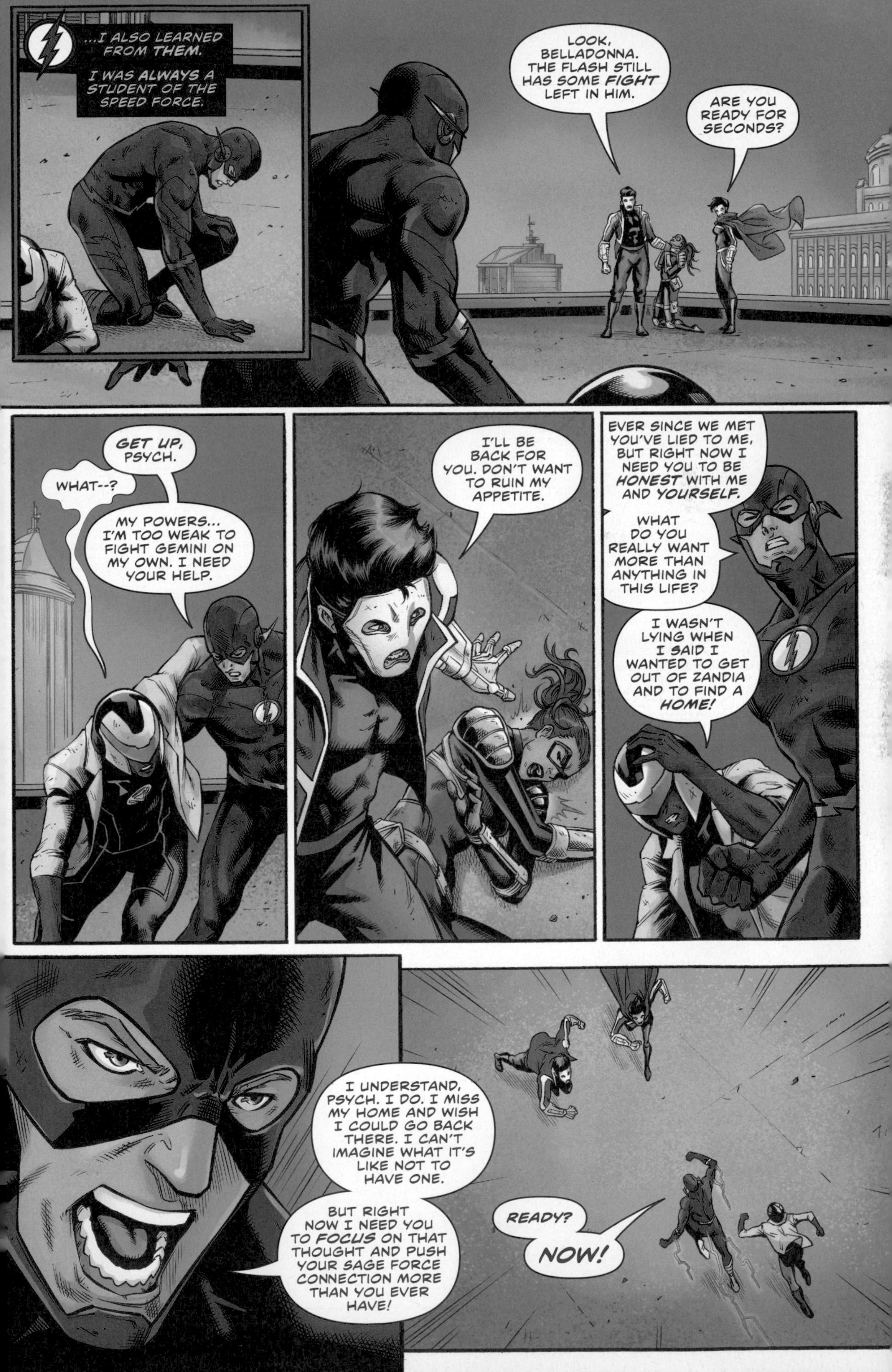
...I ALSO LEARNED FROM THEM.
I WAS ALWAYS A STUDENT OF THE SPEED FORCE.
LOOK, BELLADONNA. THE FLASH STILL HAS SOME FIGHT LEFT IN HIM.
ARE YOU READY FOR SECONDS?
GET UP, PSYCH.
WHAT--?
MY POWERS... I'M TOO WEAK TO FIGHT GEMINI ON MY OWN. I NEED YOUR HELP.
I'LL BE BACK FOR YOU. DON'T WANT TO RUIN MY APPETITE.
EVER SINCE WE MET YOU'VE LIED TO ME, BUT RIGHT NOW I NEED YOU TO BE HONEST WITH ME AND YOURSELF.
WHAT DO YOU REALLY WANT MORE THAN ANYTHING IN THIS LIFE?
I WASN'T LYING WHEN I SAID I WANTED TO GET OUT OF ZANDIA AND TO FIND A HOME!
I UNDERSTAND, PSYCH. I DO. I MISS MY HOME AND WISH I COULD GO BACK THERE. I CAN'T IMAGINE WHAT IT'S LIKE NOT TO HAVE ONE.
BUT RIGHT NOW I NEED YOU TO FOCUS ON THAT THOUGHT AND PUSH YOUR SAGE FORCE CONNECTION MORE THAN YOU EVER HAVE!
READY?
NOW!

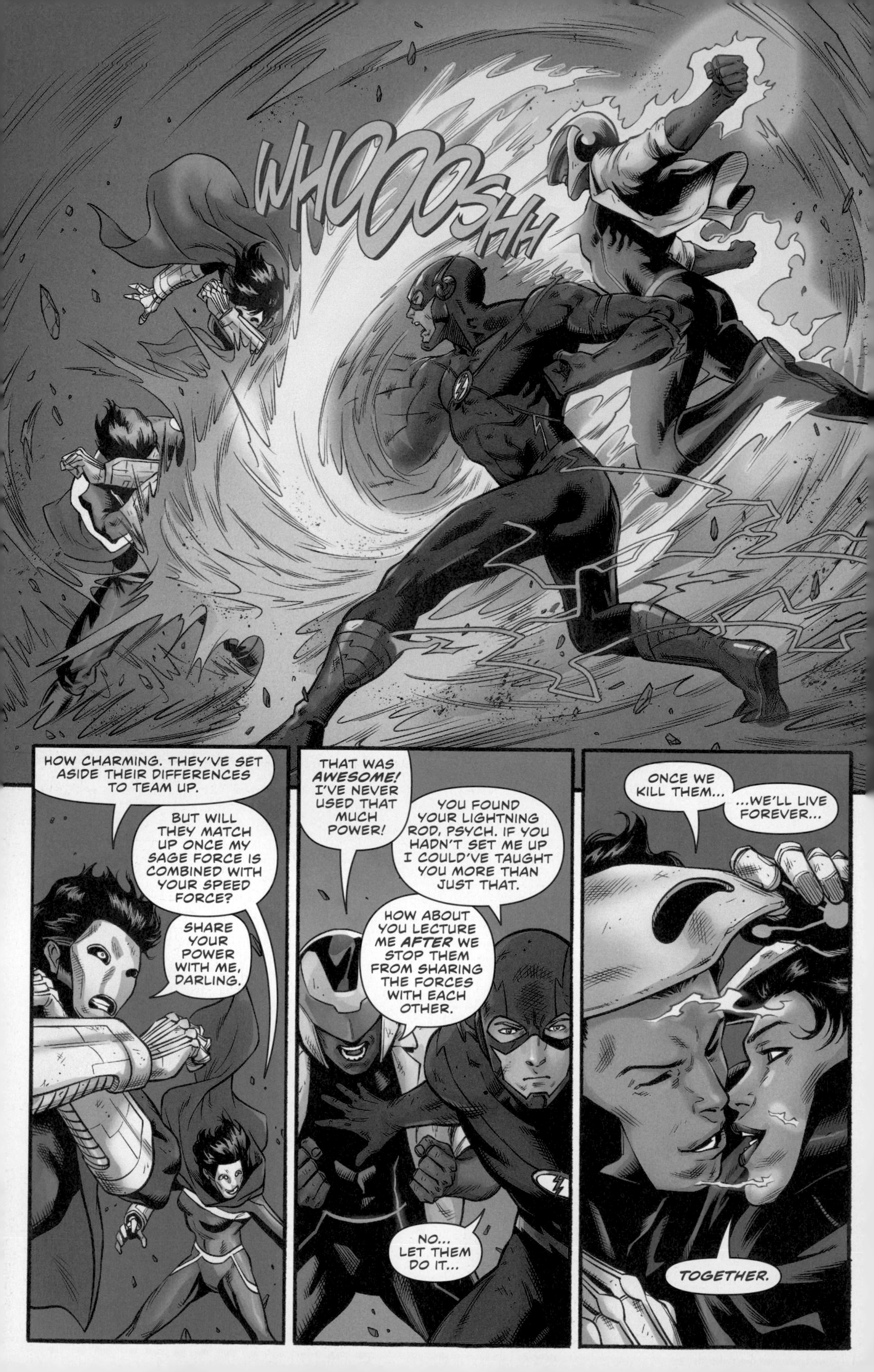
WHOOOOSHH
HOW CHARMING. THEY'VE SET ASIDE THEIR DIFFERENCES TO TEAM UP.
BUT WILL THEY MATCH UP ONCE MY SAGE FORCE IS COMBINED WITH YOUR SPEED FORCE?
SHARE YOUR POWER WITH ME, DARLING.
THAT WAS *AWESOME!* I'VE NEVER USED THAT MUCH POWER!
YOU FOUND YOUR LIGHTNING ROD, PSYCH. IF YOU HADN'T SET ME UP I COULD'VE TAUGHT YOU MORE THAN JUST THAT.
HOW ABOUT YOU LECTURE ME *AFTER* WE STOP THEM FROM SHARING THE FORCES WITH EACH OTHER.
NO... LET THEM DO IT...
ONCE WE KILL THEM...
...WE'LL LIVE FOREVER...
TOGETHER.

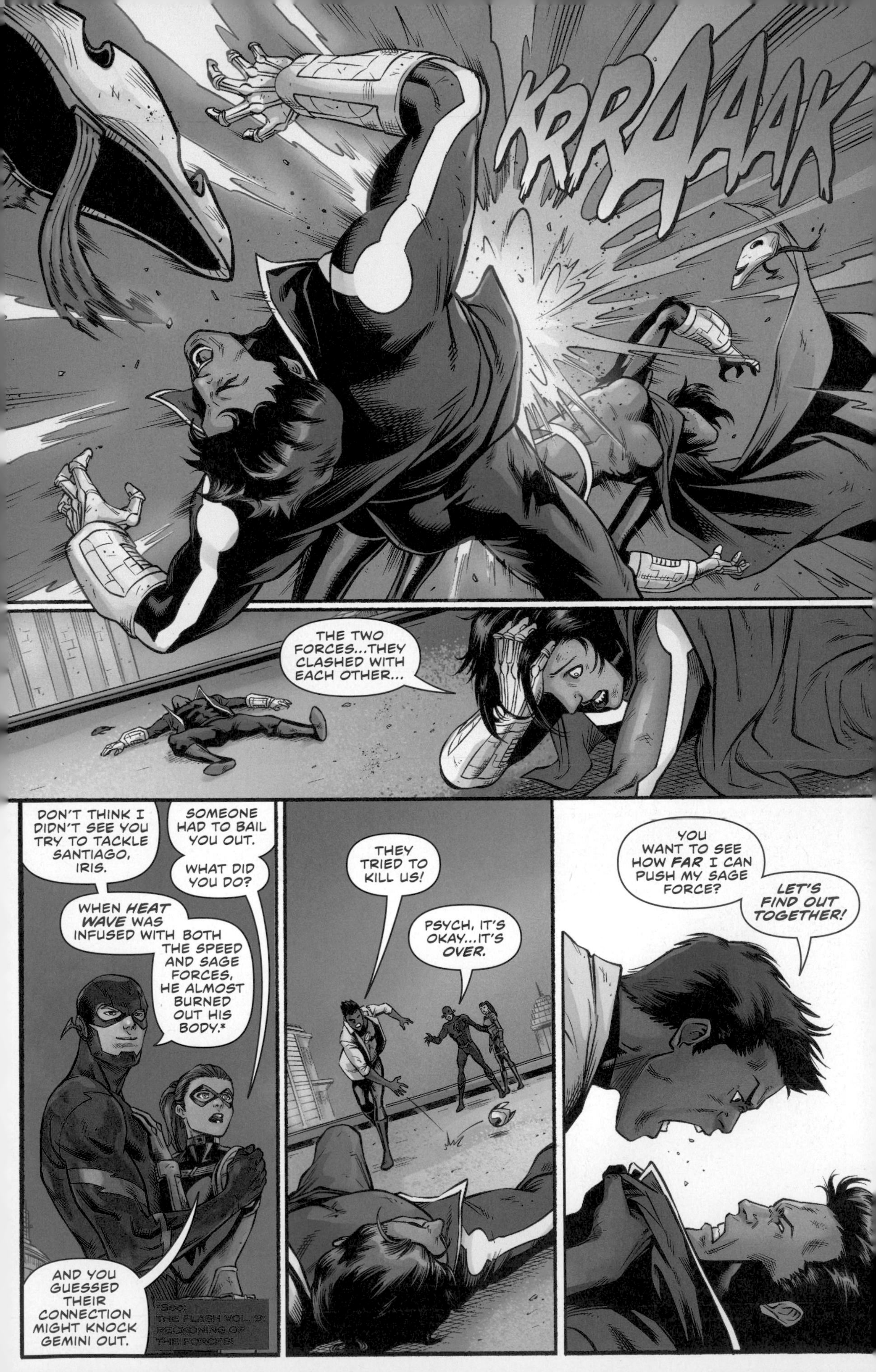
KRRAAAK
THE TWO FORCES...THEY CLASHED WITH EACH OTHER...
DON'T THINK I DIDN'T SEE YOU TRY TO TACKLE SANTIAGO, IRIS.
SOMEONE HAD TO BAIL YOU OUT.
WHAT DID YOU DO?
WHEN HEAT WAVE WAS INFUSED WITH BOTH THE SPEED AND SAGE FORCES, HE ALMOST BURNED OUT HIS BODY.*
AND YOU GUESSED THEIR CONNECTION MIGHT KNOCK GEMINI OUT.
*See: THE FLASH VOL. 9: RECKONING OF THE FORCES!
THEY TRIED TO KILL US!
PSYCH, IT'S OKAY...IT'S OVER.
YOU WANT TO SEE HOW FAR I CAN PUSH MY SAGE FORCE?
LET'S FIND OUT TOGETHER!

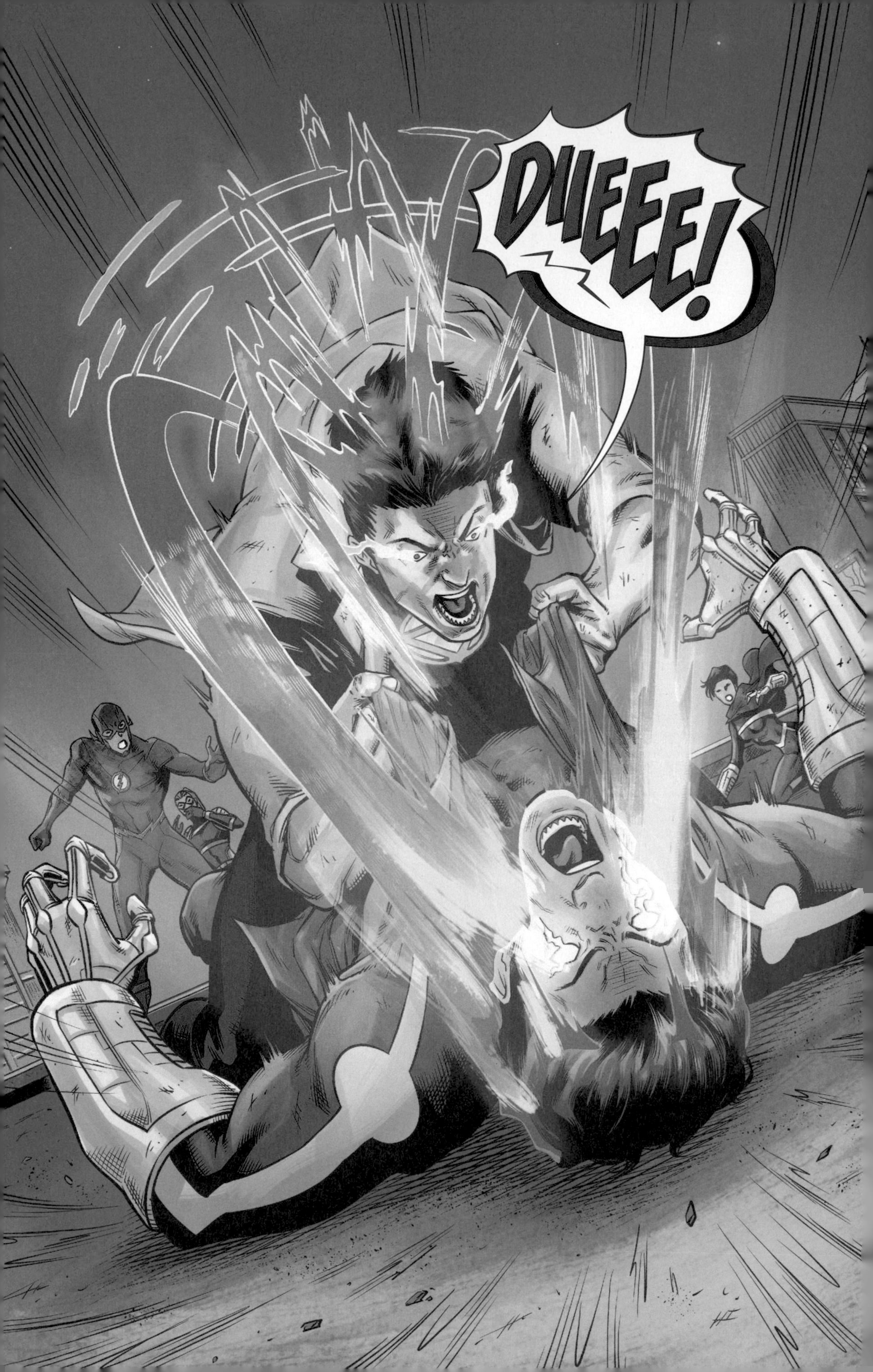
DUEEE!

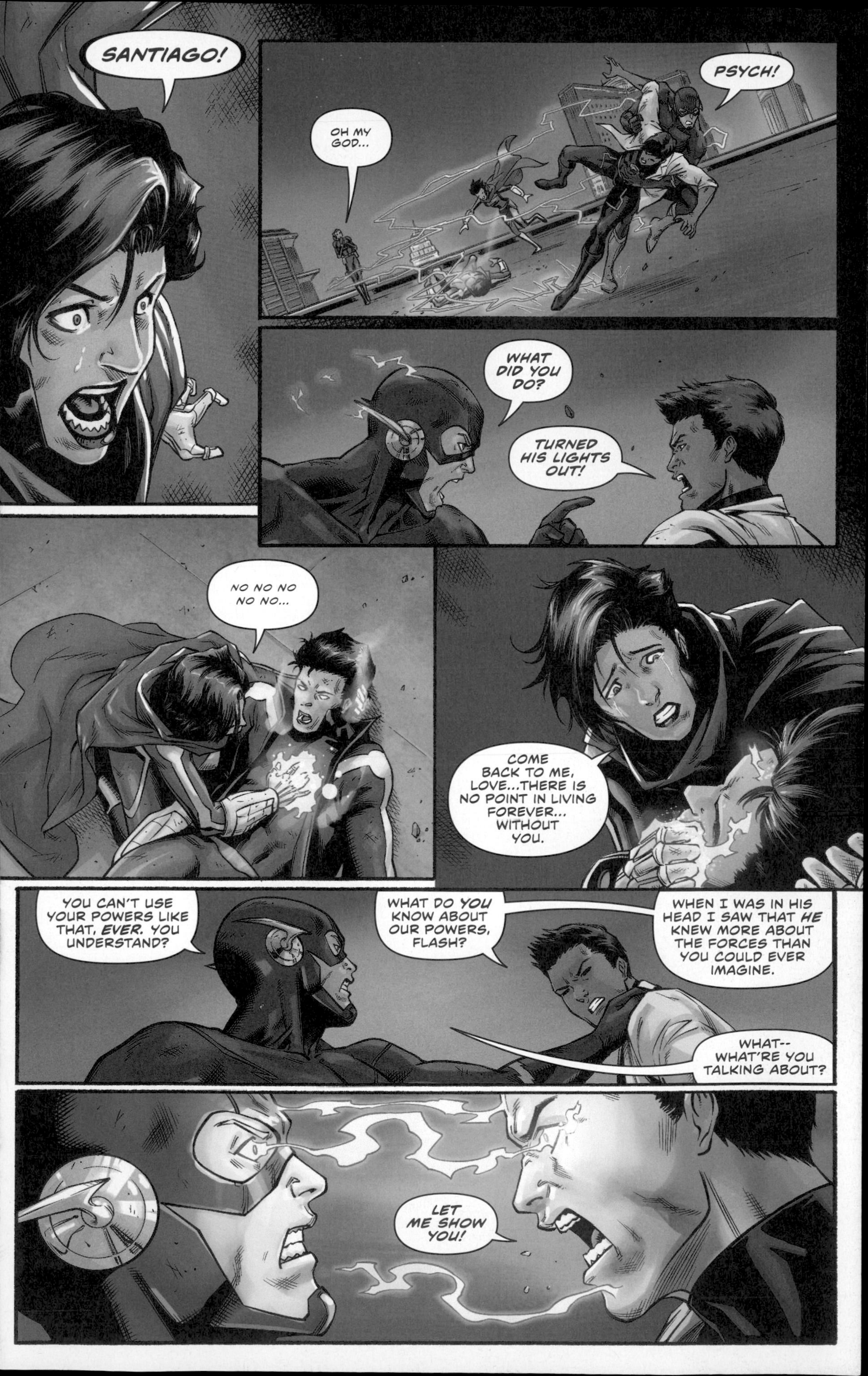
SANTIAGO!
OH MY GOD...
PSYCH!
WHAT DID YOU DO?
TURNED HIS LIGHTS OUT!
NO NO NO NO NO...
COME BACK TO ME, LOVE...THERE IS NO POINT IN LIVING FOREVER... WITHOUT YOU.
YOU CAN'T USE YOUR POWERS LIKE THAT, EVER. YOU UNDERSTAND?
WHAT DO YOU KNOW ABOUT OUR POWERS, FLASH?
WHEN I WAS IN HIS HEAD I SAW THAT HE KNEW MORE ABOUT THE FORCES THAN YOU COULD EVER IMAGINE.
WHAT-- WHAT'RE YOU TALKING ABOUT?
LET ME SHOW YOU!

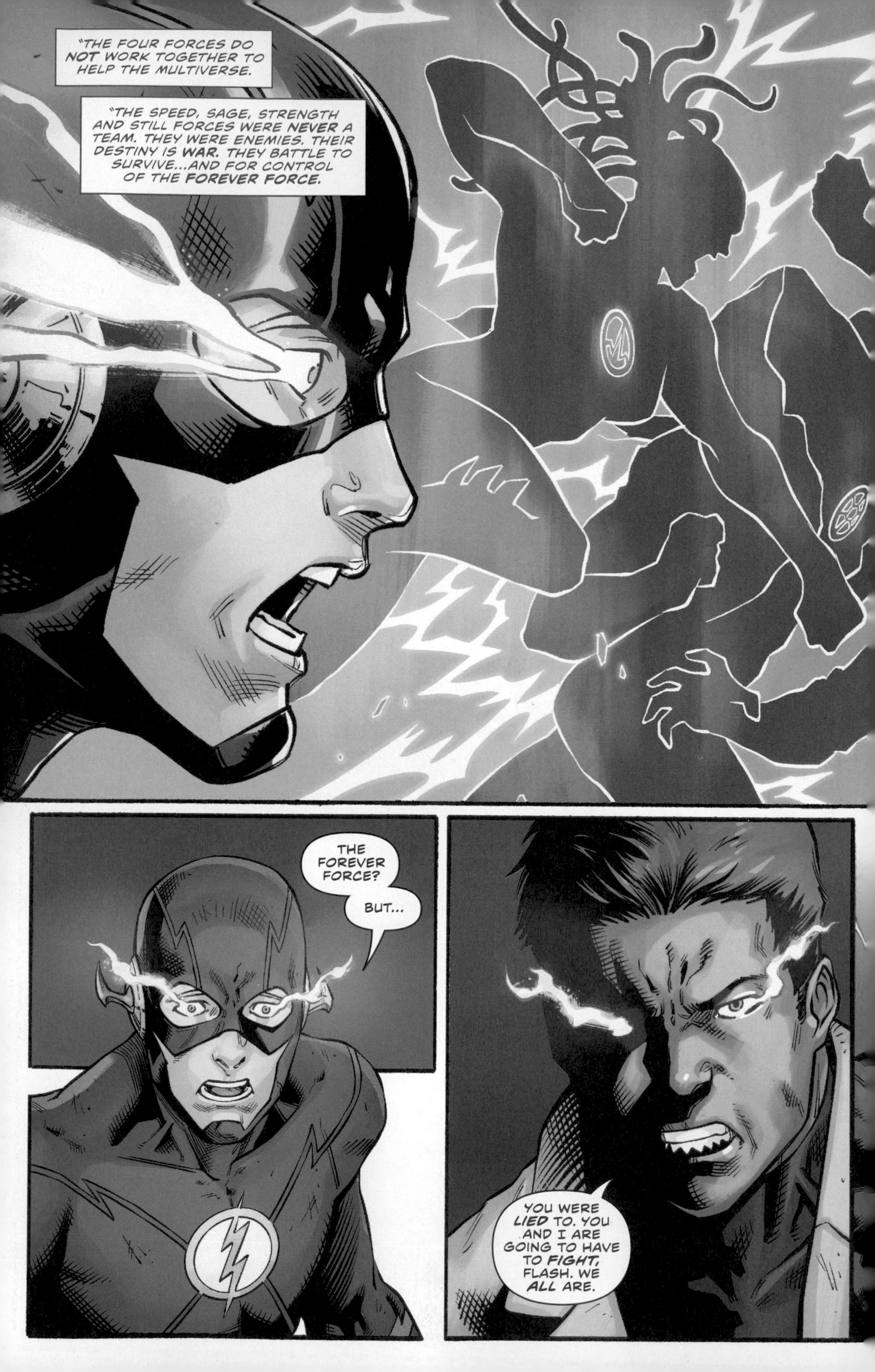
"THE FOUR FORCES DO NOT WORK TOGETHER TO HELP THE MULTIVERSE.
"THE SPEED, SAGE, STRENGTH AND STILL FORCES WERE NEVER A TEAM. THEY WERE ENEMIES. THEIR DESTINY IS WAR. THEY BATTLE TO SURVIVE...AND FOR CONTROL OF THE FOREVER FORCE.
THE FOREVER FORCE?
BUT...
YOU WERE LIED TO. YOU AND I ARE GOING TO HAVE TO FIGHT, FLASH. WE ALL ARE.

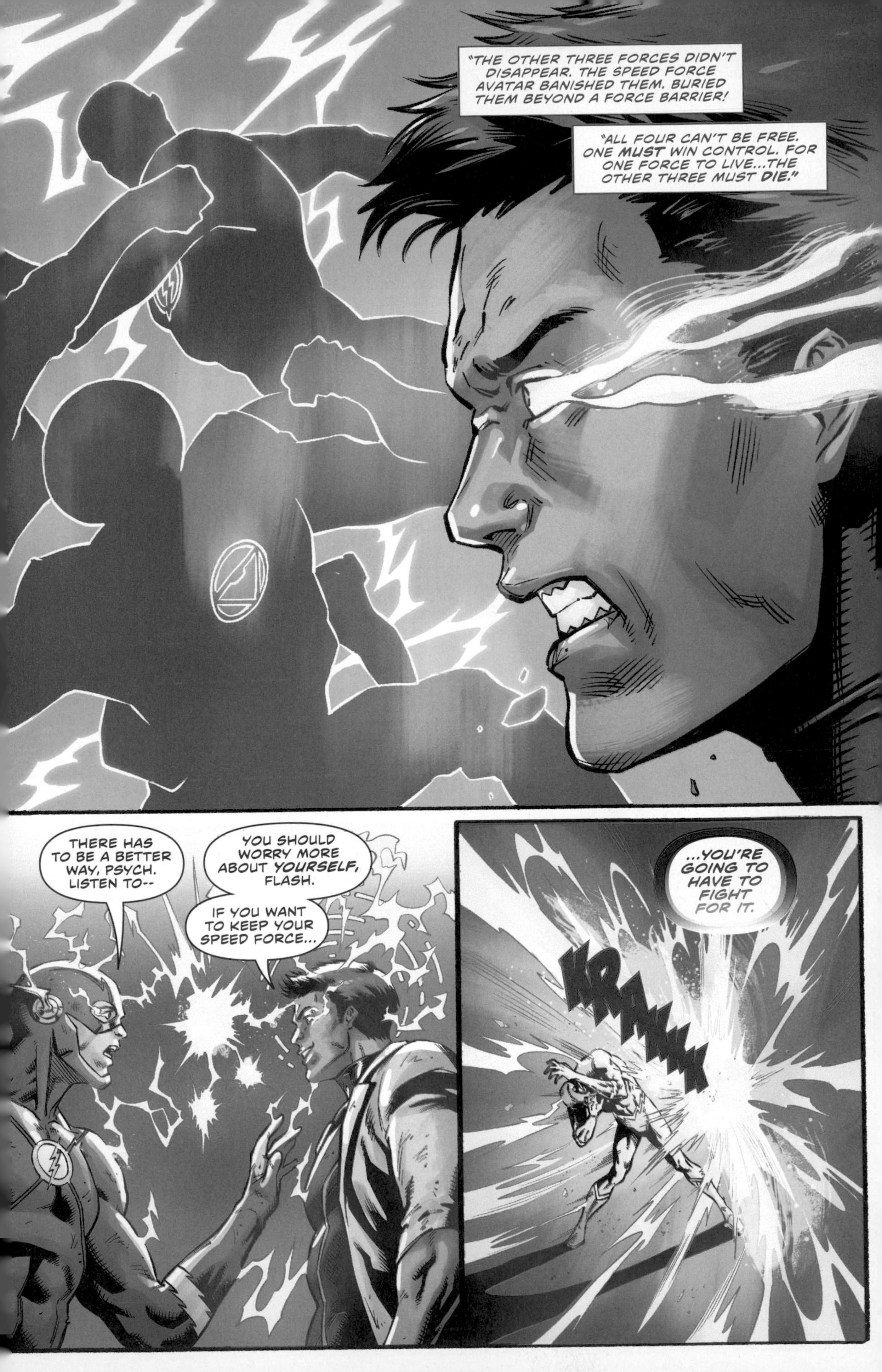
"THE OTHER THREE FORCES DIDN'T DISAPPEAR. THE SPEED FORCE AVATAR BANISHED THEM. BURIED THEM BEYOND A FORCE BARRIER!
"ALL FOUR CAN'T BE FREE. ONE MUST WIN CONTROL. FOR ONE FORCE TO LIVE...THE OTHER THREE MUST DIE."
THERE HAS TO BE A BETTER WAY, PSYCH. LISTEN TO--
YOU SHOULD WORRY MORE ABOUT YOURSELF, FLASH.
IF YOU WANT TO KEEP YOUR SPEED FORCE...
...YOU'RE GOING TO HAVE TO FIGHT FOR IT.
KRAKKK

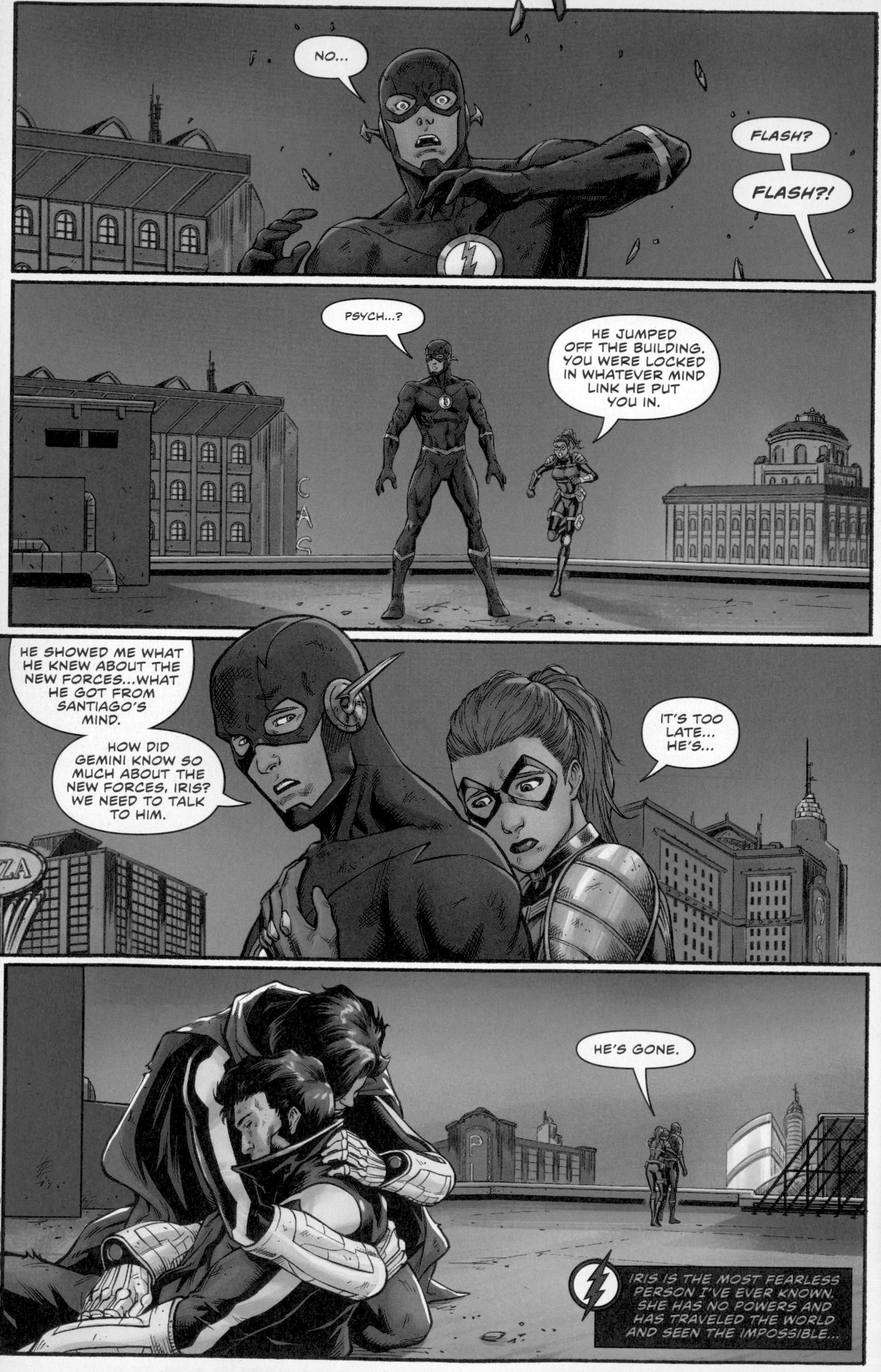
NO...
FLASH?
FLASH?!
PSYCH...?
HE JUMPED OFF THE BUILDING. YOU WERE LOCKED IN WHATEVER MIND LINK HE PUT YOU IN.
CAS
HE SHOWED ME WHAT HE KNEW ABOUT THE NEW FORCES...WHAT HE GOT FROM SANTIAGO'S MIND.
HOW DID GEMINI KNOW SO MUCH ABOUT THE NEW FORCES, IRIS? WE NEED TO TALK TO HIM.
IT'S TOO LATE... HE'S...
ZA
HE'S GONE.
IRIS IS THE MOST FEARLESS PERSON I'VE EVER KNOWN. SHE HAS NO POWERS AND HAS TRAVELED THE WORLD AND SEEN THE IMPOSSIBLE...

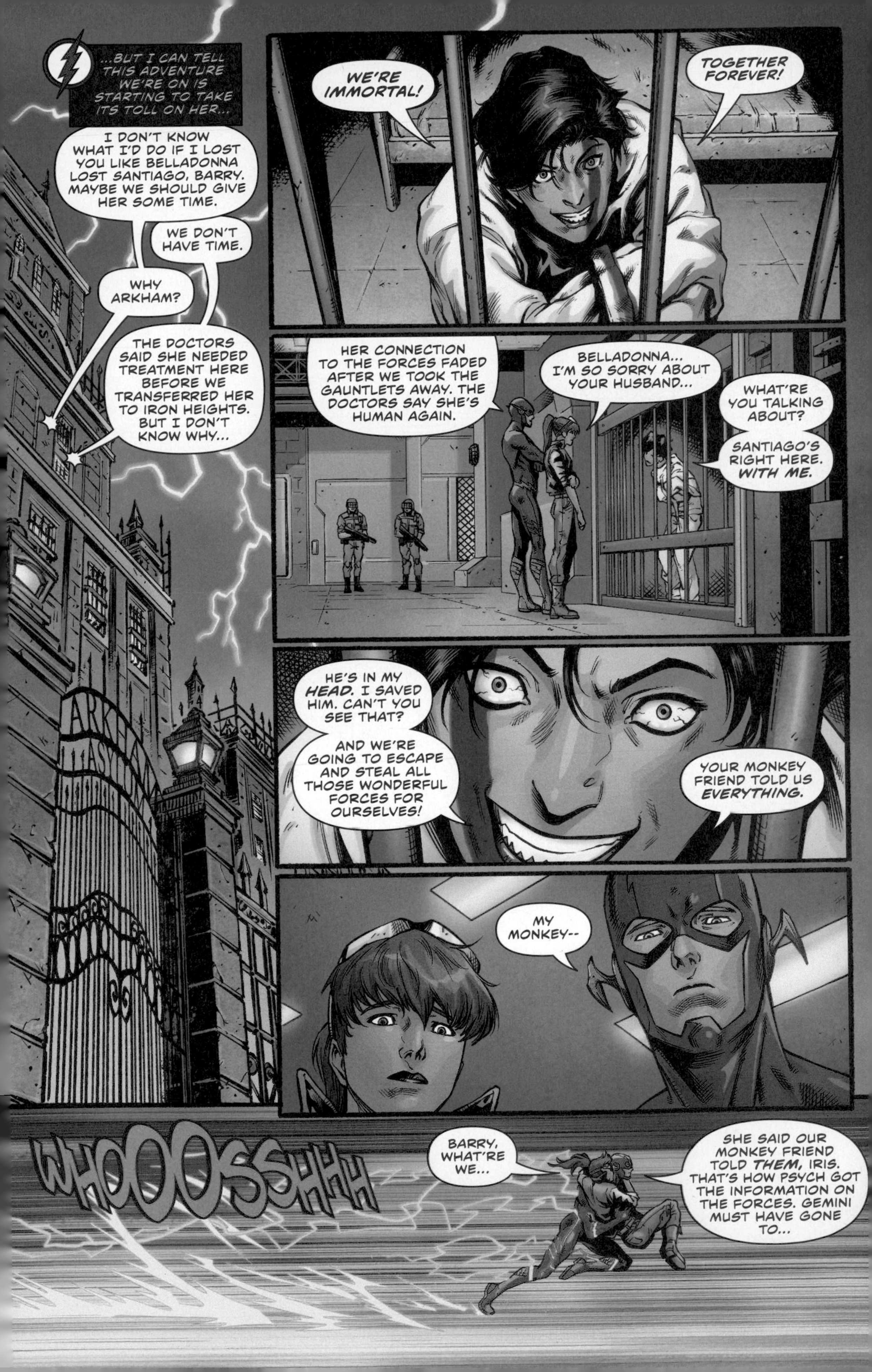
...BUT I CAN TELL THIS ADVENTURE WE'RE ON IS STARTING TO TAKE ITS TOLL ON HER...
I DON'T KNOW WHAT I'D DO IF I LOST YOU LIKE BELLADONNA LOST SANTIAGO, BARRY. MAYBE WE SHOULD GIVE HER SOME TIME.
WE DON'T HAVE TIME.
WHY ARKHAM?
THE DOCTORS SAID SHE NEEDED TREATMENT HERE BEFORE WE TRANSFERRED HER TO IRON HEIGHTS. BUT I DON'T KNOW WHY...
ARKHAM ASYLUM
WE'RE IMMORTAL!
TOGETHER FOREVER!
HER CONNECTION TO THE FORCES FADED AFTER WE TOOK THE GAUNTLETS AWAY. THE DOCTORS SAY SHE'S HUMAN AGAIN.
BELLADONNA... I'M SO SORRY ABOUT YOUR HUSBAND...
WHAT'RE YOU TALKING ABOUT?
SANTIAGO'S RIGHT HERE. WITH ME.
HE'S IN MY HEAD. I SAVED HIM. CAN'T YOU SEE THAT?
AND WE'RE GOING TO ESCAPE AND STEAL ALL THOSE WONDERFUL FORCES FOR OURSELVES!
YOUR MONKEY FRIEND TOLD US EVERYTHING.
MY MONKEY--
WHOOOSSHHH
BARRY, WHAT'RE WE...
SHE SAID OUR MONKEY FRIEND TOLD THEM, IRIS. THAT'S HOW PSYCH GOT THE INFORMATION ON THE FORCES. GEMINI MUST HAVE GONE TO...

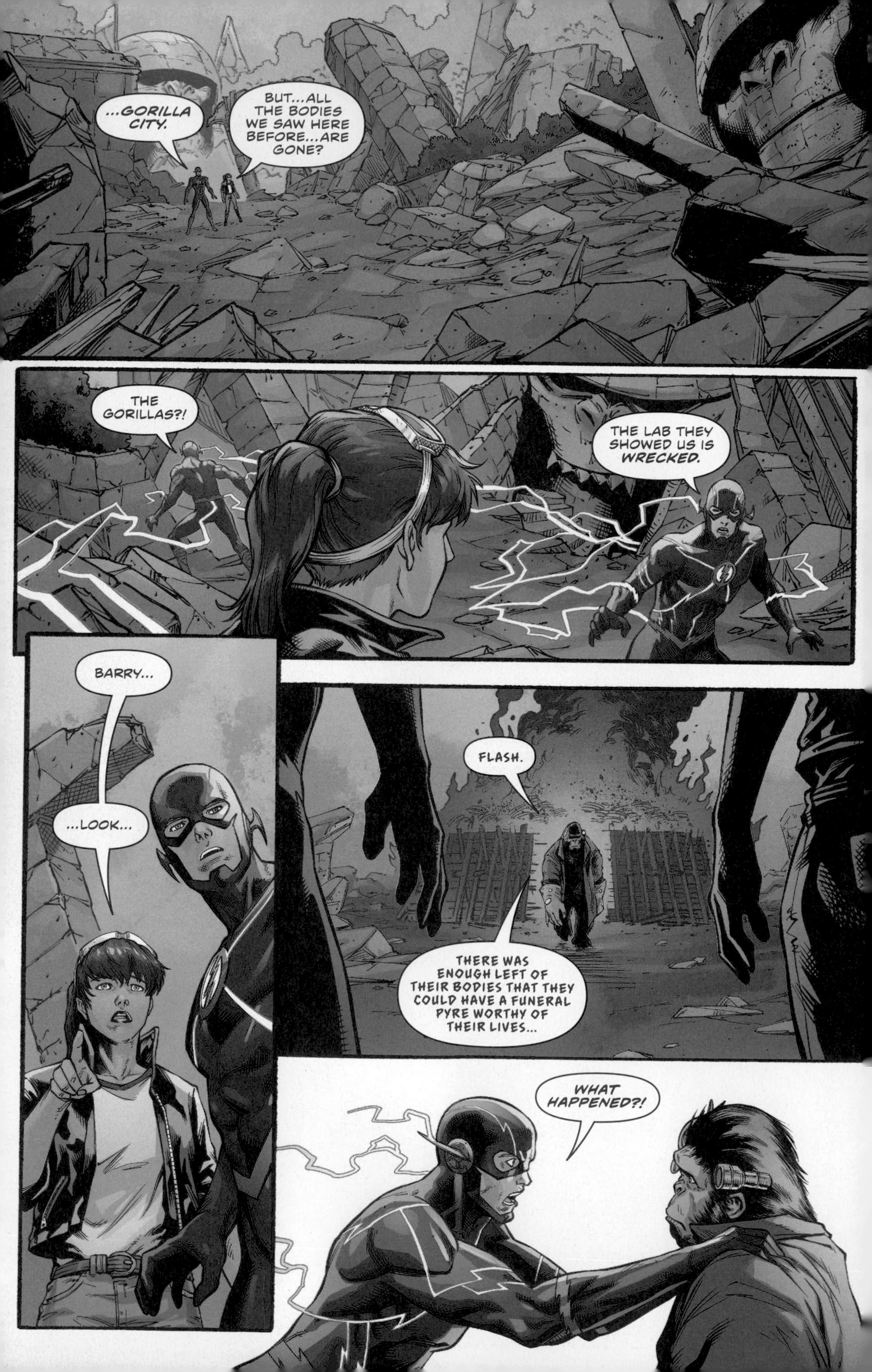
...GORILLA CITY.
BUT...ALL THE BODIES WE SAW HERE BEFORE...ARE GONE?
THE GORILLAS?!
THE LAB THEY SHOWED US IS WRECKED.
BARRY...
...LOOK...
FLASH.
THERE WAS ENOUGH LEFT OF THEIR BODIES THAT THEY COULD HAVE A FUNERAL PYRE WORTHY OF THEIR LIVES...
WHAT HAPPENED?!

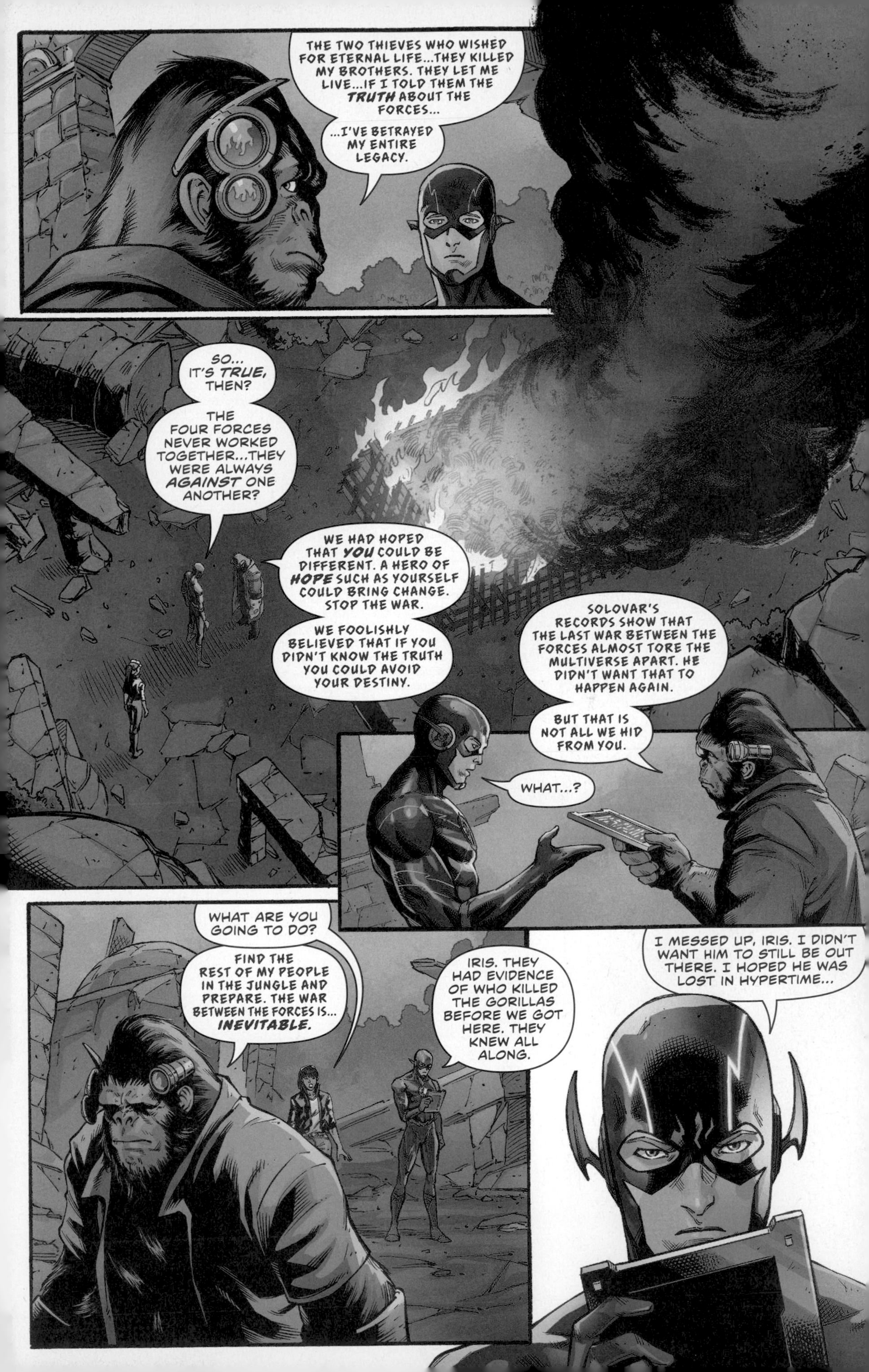
THE TWO THIEVES WHO WISHED FOR ETERNAL LIFE...THEY KILLED MY BROTHERS. THEY LET ME LIVE...IF I TOLD THEM THE TRUTH ABOUT THE FORCES...
...I'VE BETRAYED MY ENTIRE LEGACY.
SO... IT'S TRUE, THEN?
THE FOUR FORCES NEVER WORKED TOGETHER...THEY WERE ALWAYS AGAINST ONE ANOTHER?
WE HAD HOPED THAT YOU COULD BE DIFFERENT. A HERO OF HOPE SUCH AS YOURSELF COULD BRING CHANGE. STOP THE WAR.
WE FOOLISHLY BELIEVED THAT IF YOU DIDN'T KNOW THE TRUTH YOU COULD AVOID YOUR DESTINY.
SOLOVAR'S RECORDS SHOW THAT THE LAST WAR BETWEEN THE FORCES ALMOST TORE THE MULTIVERSE APART. HE DIDN'T WANT THAT TO HAPPEN AGAIN.
BUT THAT IS NOT ALL WE HID FROM YOU.
WHAT...?
WHAT ARE YOU GOING TO DO?
FIND THE REST OF MY PEOPLE IN THE JUNGLE AND PREPARE. THE WAR BETWEEN THE FORCES IS... INEVITABLE.
IRIS. THEY HAD EVIDENCE OF WHO KILLED THE GORILLAS BEFORE WE GOT HERE. THEY KNEW ALL ALONG.
I MESSED UP, IRIS. I DIDN'T WANT HIM TO STILL BE OUT THERE. I HOPED HE WAS LOST IN HYPERTIME...

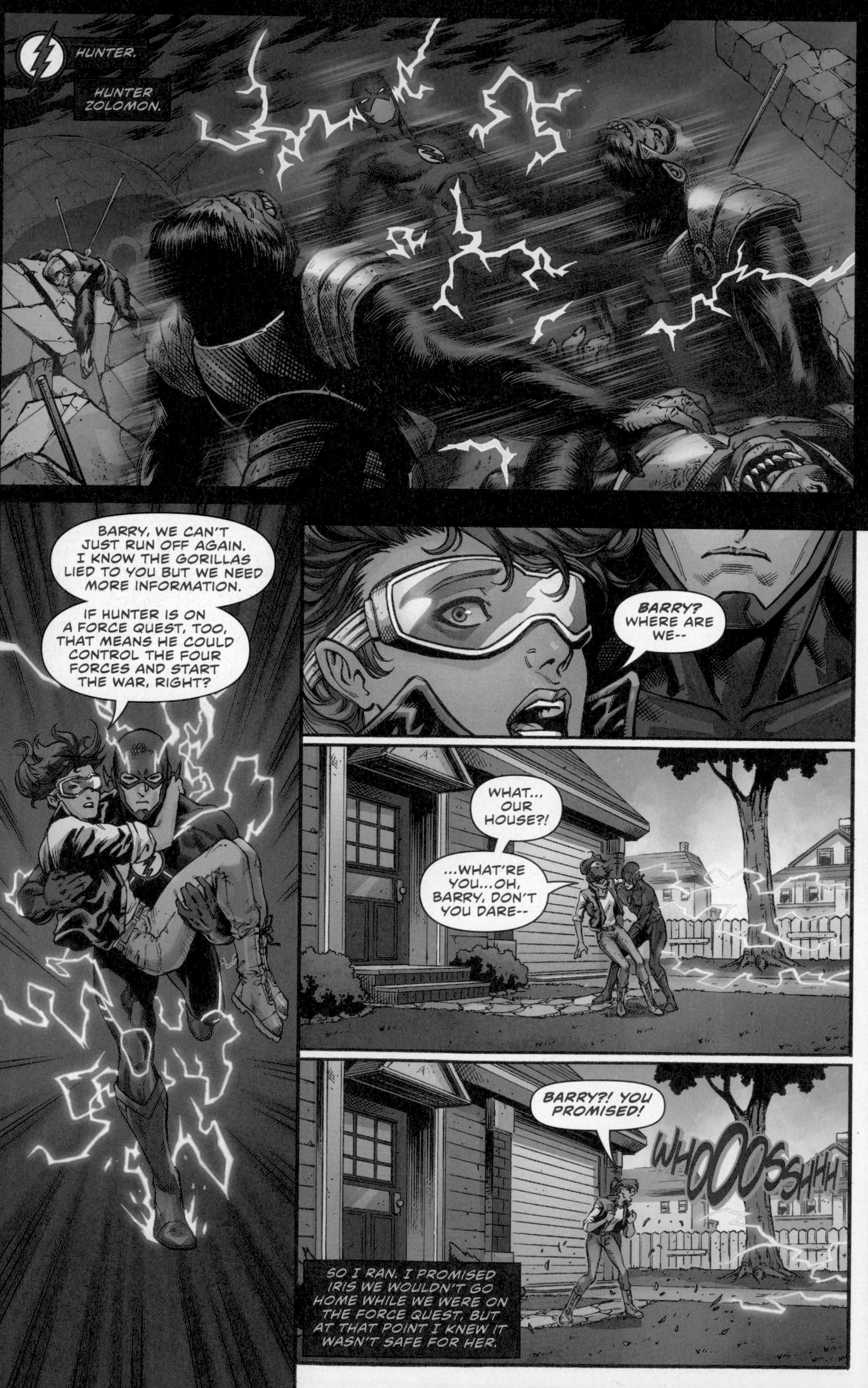
HUNTER.
HUNTER ZOLOMON.
BARRY, WE CAN'T JUST RUN OFF AGAIN. I KNOW THE GORILLAS LIED TO YOU BUT WE NEED MORE INFORMATION.
IF HUNTER IS ON A FORCE QUEST, TOO, THAT MEANS HE COULD CONTROL THE FOUR FORCES AND START THE WAR, RIGHT?
BARRY? WHERE ARE WE--
WHAT... OUR HOUSE?!
...WHAT'RE YOU...OH, BARRY, DON'T YOU DARE--
BARRY?! YOU PROMISED!
WHOOOOSSHHH
SO I RAN. I PROMISED IRIS WE WOULDN'T GO HOME WHILE WE WERE ON THE FORCE QUEST, BUT AT THAT POINT I KNEW IT WASN'T SAFE FOR HER.

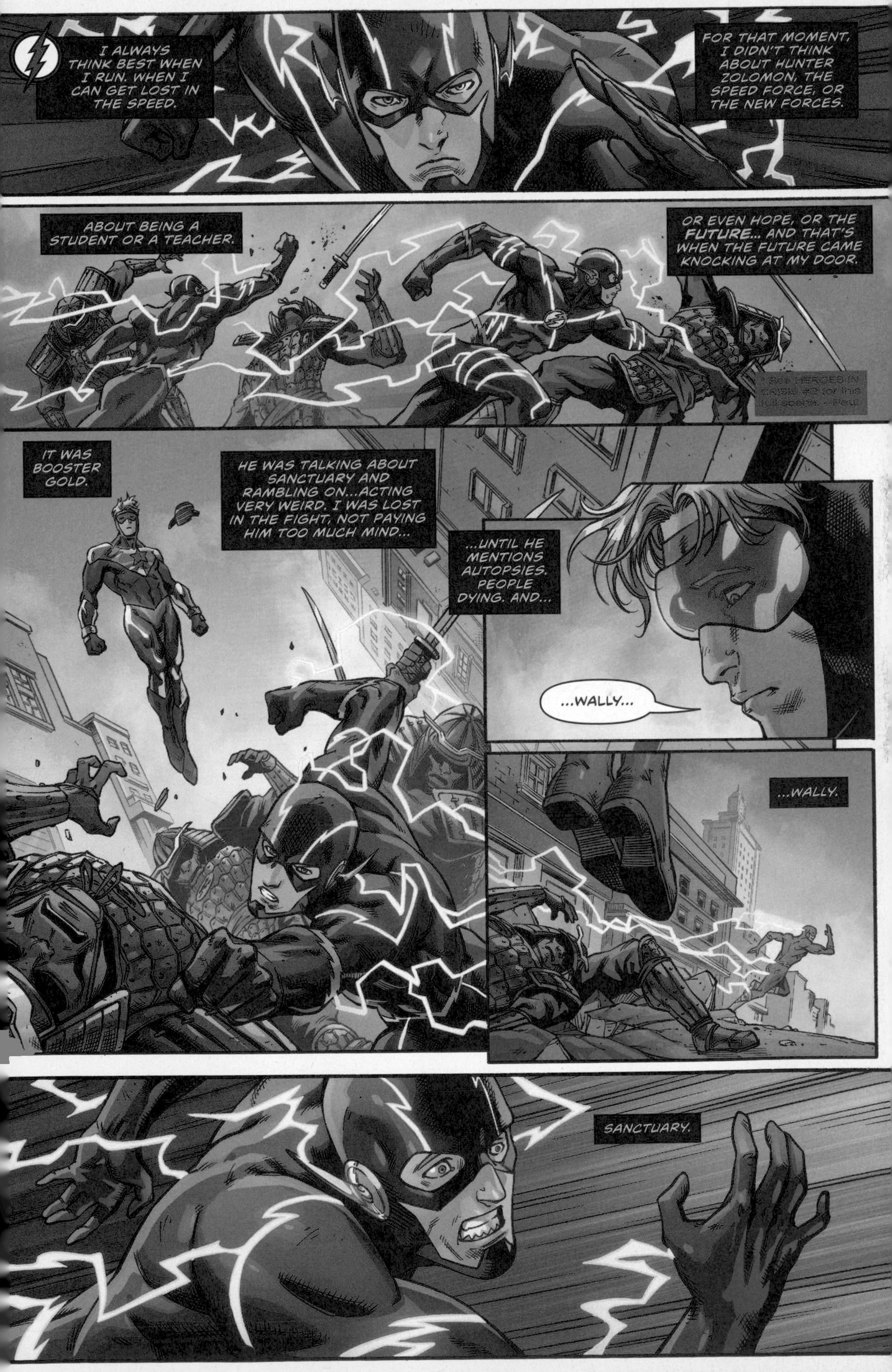
I ALWAYS THINK BEST WHEN I RUN. WHEN I CAN GET LOST IN THE SPEED.
FOR THAT MOMENT, I DIDN'T THINK ABOUT HUNTER ZOLOMON, THE SPEED FORCE, OR THE NEW FORCES.
ABOUT BEING A STUDENT OR A TEACHER.
OR EVEN HOPE, OR THE FUTURE... AND THAT'S WHEN THE FUTURE CAME KNOCKING AT MY DOOR.
*See HEROES IN CRISIS #2 for this full scene. --Paul
IT WAS BOOSTER GOLD.
HE WAS TALKING ABOUT SANCTUARY AND RAMBLING ON...ACTING VERY WEIRD. I WAS LOST IN THE FIGHT, NOT PAYING HIM TOO MUCH MIND...
...UNTIL HE MENTIONS AUTOPSIES. PEOPLE DYING. AND...
...WALLY...
...WALLY.
SANCTUARY.

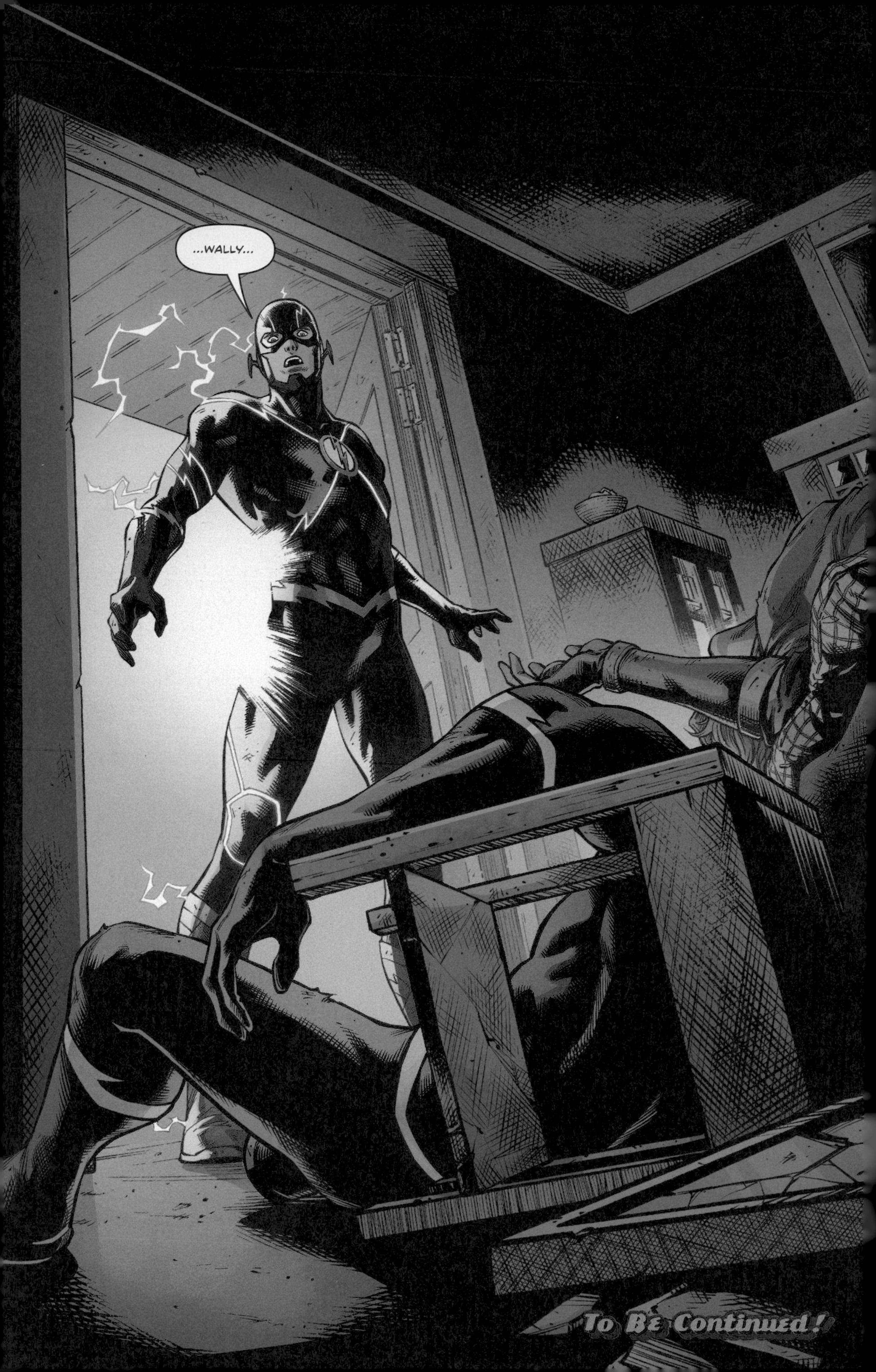
...WALLY...
To Be Continued!

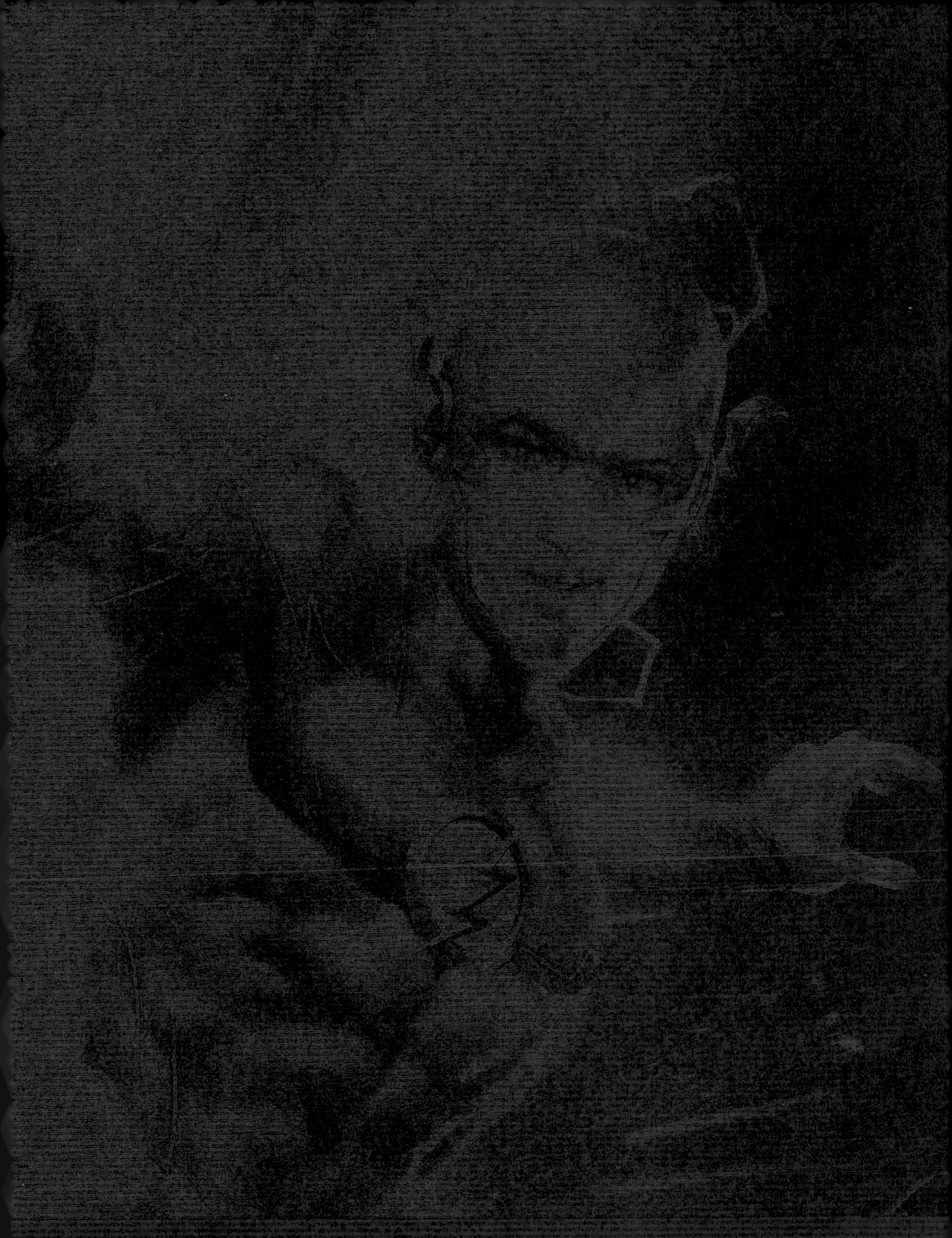

VARIANT COVER GALLERY

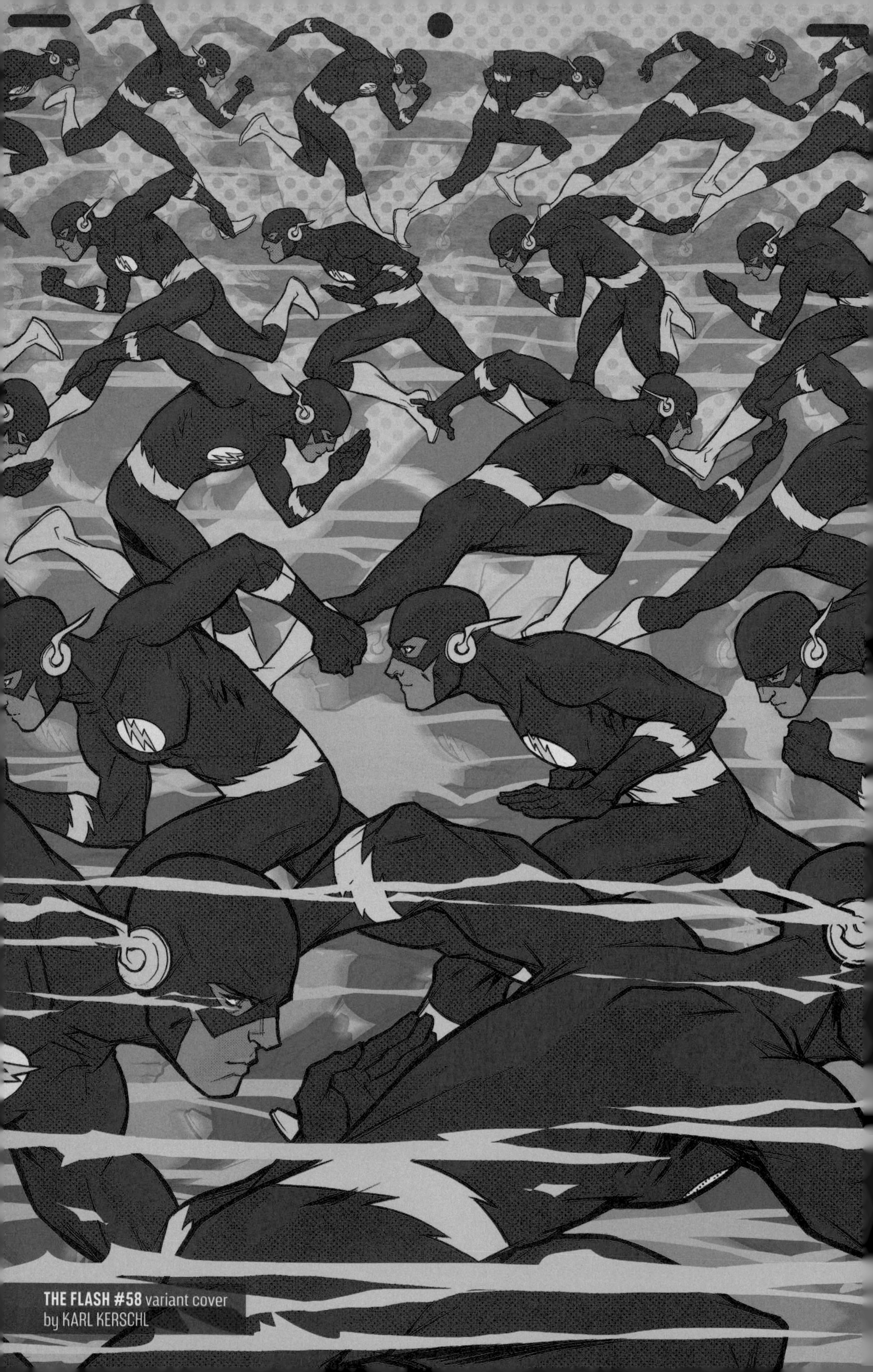

THE FLASH #58 variant cover
by KARL KERSCHL

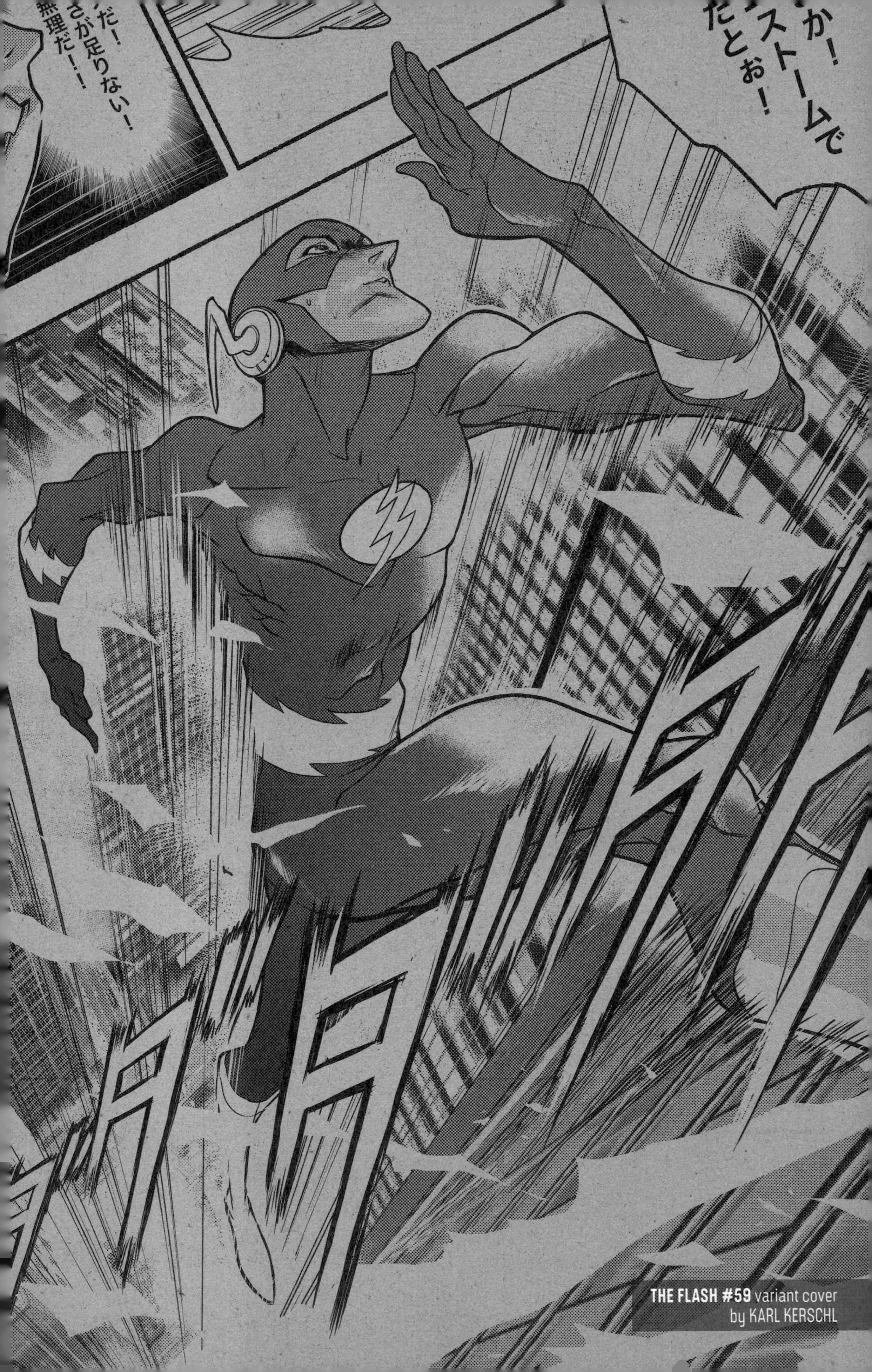
か！
ストームで
たとぉ！
だ！
さが足りない！
無理だ！！！

THE FLASH #59 variant cover
by KARL KERSCHL

THE FLASH #60
variant cover
by DERRICK CHEW

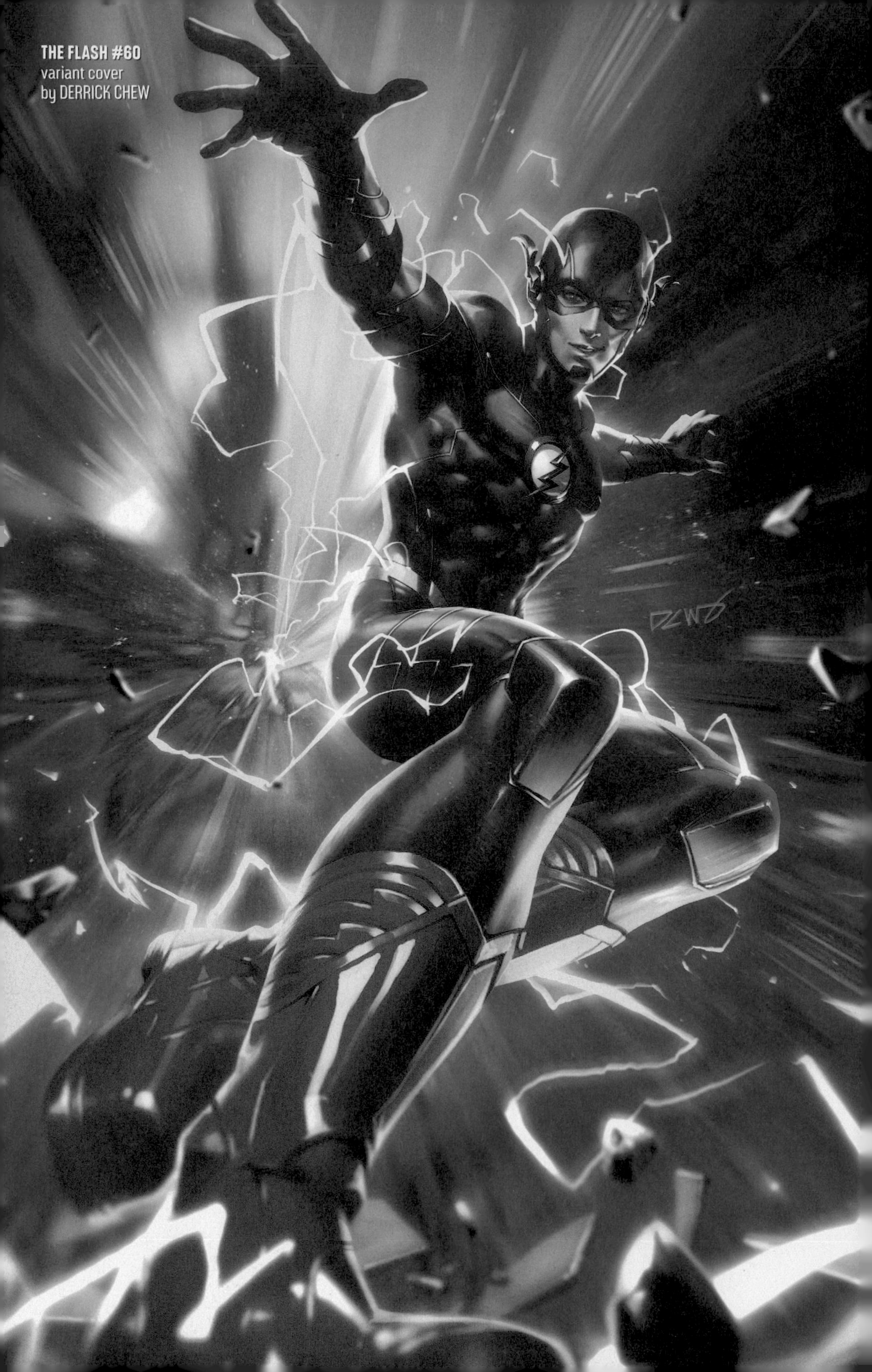

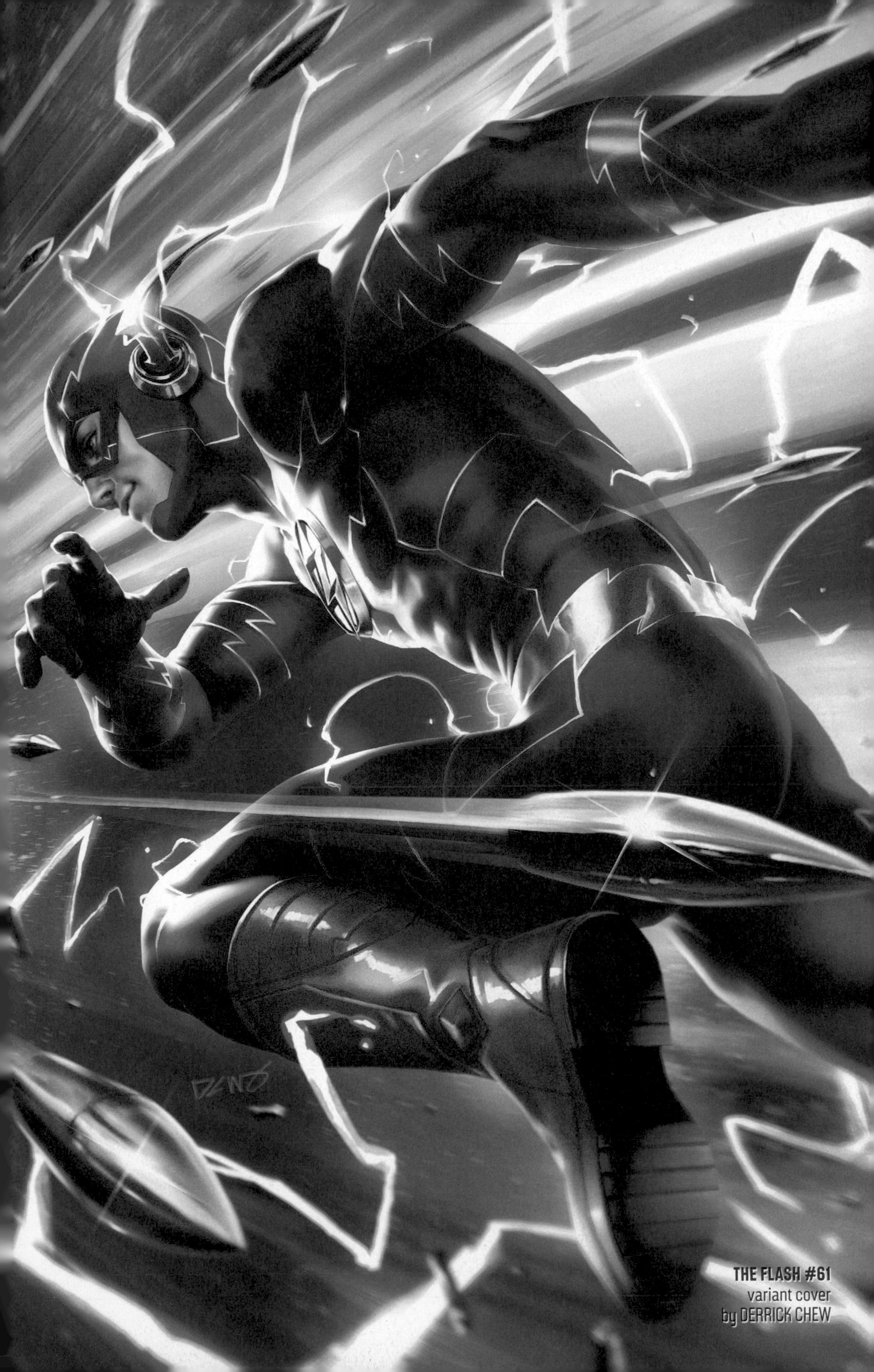

THE FLASH #61
variant cover
by DERRICK CHEW

THE FLASH #62 variant cover
by JAE LEE and JUNE CHUNG

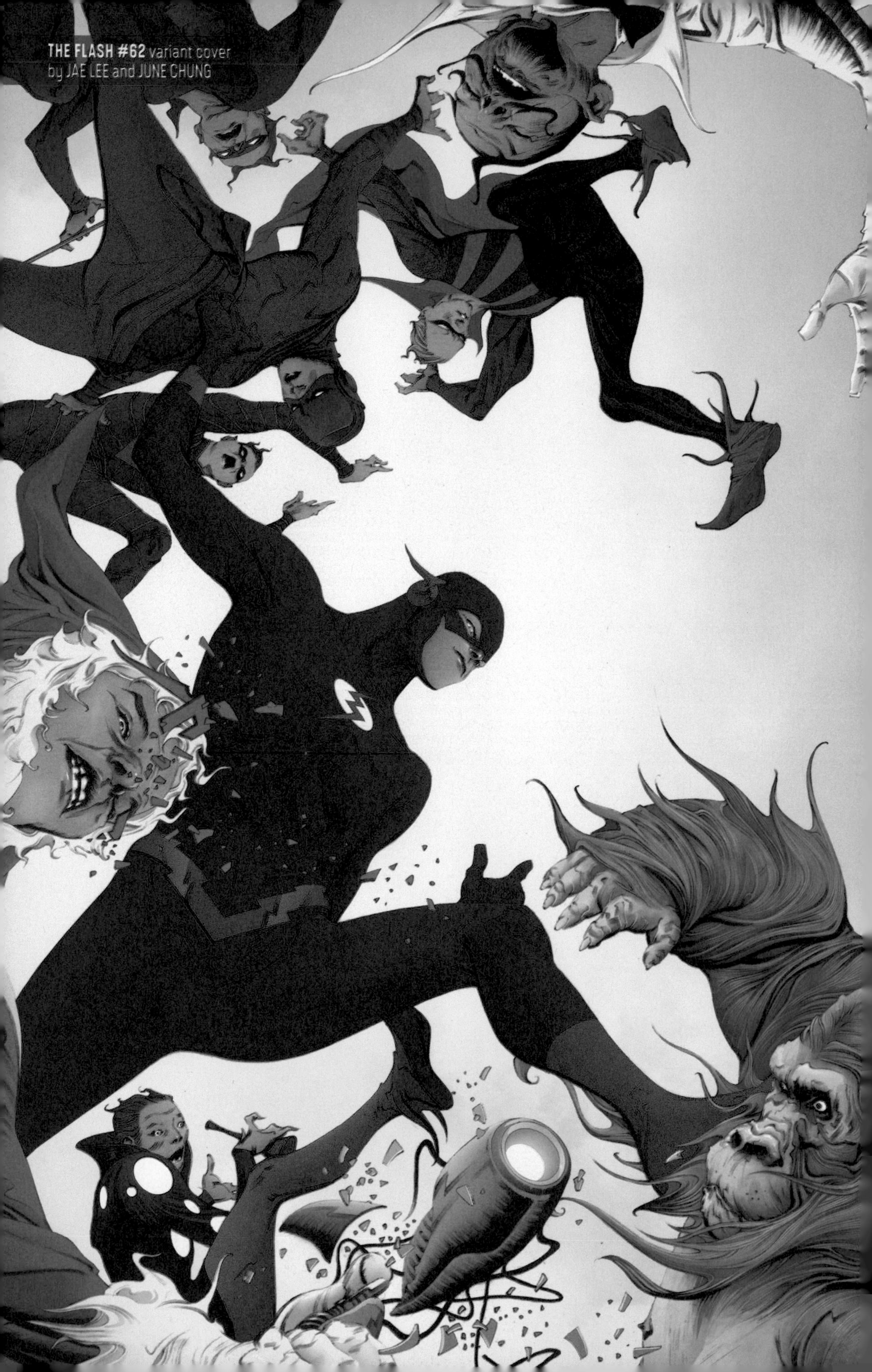

THE FLASH #63 variant cover
by HOWARD CHAYKIN

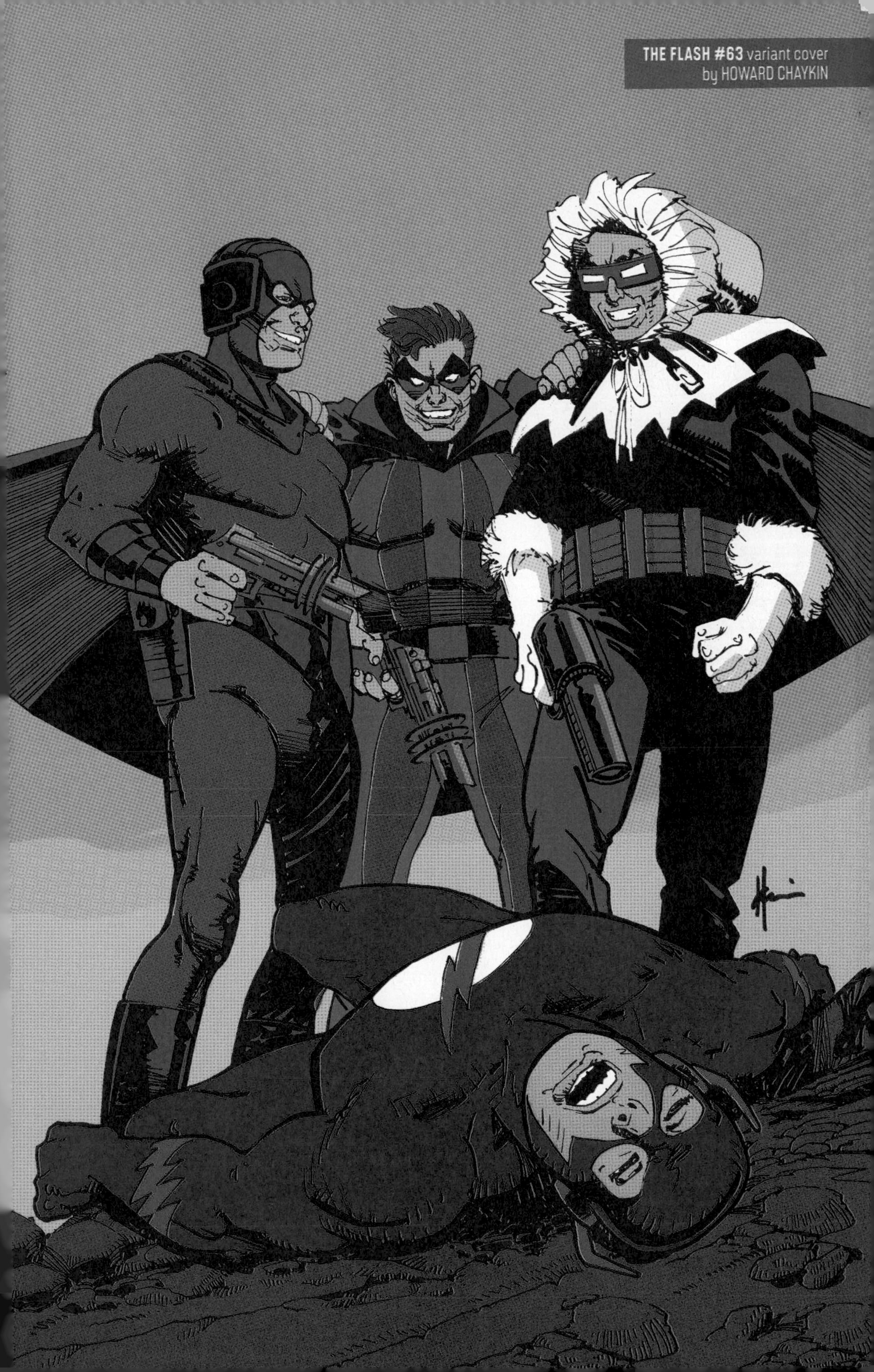

"Joshua Williamson's writing is on point."
– **NERDIST**

"Williamson makes [The Flash] as accessible as possible to new readers."
– **COMIC BOOK RESOURCES**

DC UNIVERSE REBIRTH
THE FLASH
VOL. 1: LIGHTNING STRIKES TWICE
JOSHUA WILLIAMSON
with CARMINE DI GIANDOMENICO and IVAN PLASCENCIA

VOL.1 LIGHTNING STRIKES TWICE
JOSHUA WILLIAMSON ★ CARMINE DI GIANDOMENICO ★ IVAN PLASCENCIA

JUSTICE LEAGUE VOL. 1:
THE EXTINCTION MACHINES

TITANS VOL. 1:
THE RETURN OF WALLY WEST

HAL JORDAN AND
THE GREEN LANTERN CORPS VOL. 1:
SINESTRO'S LAW

Get more DC graphic novels wherever comics and books are sold!